GW01372462

The Changing Law

Fiona Patfield and Robin White

Leicester University Press
Leicester, London and New York

© Editors and Contributors, 1990

First published in Great Britain in 1990 by Leicester University Press
(a division of Pinter Publishers Ltd)

All rights reserved. No part of this publication may be
reproduced, stored in a retrieval system, or transmitted, in any
form or by any means, electronic, mechanical, photocopying,
recording or otherwise, without the prior permission of the
Leicester University Press.

Editorial offices
Fielding Johnson Building, University of Leicester,
University Road, Leicester, LE1 7RH

Trade and other enquiries
25 Floral Street, London, WC2E 9DS and PO Box 197, Irvington, NY 10533

British Library Cataloguing in Publication Data
A CIP cataloguing record for this book is available
from the British Library
ISBN 0–7185–1331–2

Library of Congress Cataloging-in-Publication Data
Patfield, Fiona.
   The changing law / by Fiona Patfield and Robin White.
    p.   cm.
   Includes index.
   ISBN 0–7185–1331–2
   1. Law reform – Great Britain. I. White, Robin, C.A. II. Title.
KD654.P37   1990
340.3′0941 – dc20

90-37107
CIP

Filmset by Mayhew Typesetting, Bristol, UK
Printed and bound in Great Britain by Biddles Ltd

The publication of this volume has been generously supported by:

Bray & Bray Solicitors, Leicester
The Chambers of David Barker QC, King Street, Leicester
The Chambers of Paul Spencer, New Street, Leicester
Cole & Cole, Solicitors, Oxford
Harvey Ingram Stone & Simpson Solicitors, Leicester
Howes Percival, Solicitors, Northampton
The Leicestershire Law Society
The Northamptonshire Law Society
Shoosmiths & Harrison, Solicitors, Northampton

Contents

Preface		ix
Tables of Statutes		xi
Table of Statutory Instruments		xvii
Table of other documents		xix
Table of Cases		xx
1	Influences, pressures and agents for change Robin C.A. White	1
2	The rise and fall of negligence Jon Holyoak	20
3	The protection of informal interests in land Mark Thompson	40
4	Family law, the Law Commission and socio-legal research Judith Masson	57
5	Regulating the City Fiona Patfield and Ian Snaith	72
6	The changing rules of evidence Marquita Inman	94
7	National security versus civil liberty Richard Stone	119
8	Changing attitudes: the case of racial discrimination David Bonner	138
9	Making social security law simpler David Pollard	157
10	Jurisdiction agreements: time for a change Jan Grodecki	177

11	United Kingdom barriers to a common market in legal development *Malcolm Ross*	196
12	The reform of the legal profession *Fiona C. Cownie*	213
13	'And that man dying' *Tony Bradney*	235
14	Codification and criminal law reform *Edward Griew*	256

Index 270

Preface

The publication of this volume marks the Silver Jubilee of the law school at Leicester University. When we were planning our Jubilee activities, we decided, like many law schools before us, to produce a permanent record of the scholarship of the law school. We also decided that the publication should not be too self-indulgent and that we would hope to publish a volume of essays which contributed both individually and collectively to the advancement of the discipline of law.

Like the law school itself, the result is overtly pluralist. The reader will find between these covers a range of styles of legal scholarship. This law school is committed to supporting the full range of such styles of scholarship. The change referred to in the title reflects not only the themes of case and statute law development and of law reform, but also the developments that have come about in the past quarter of a century in our approach to legal scholarship. Learning the law and advancing the discipline are no longer achieved simply by studying cases and statutes; policy, theory and sound empirical research all have increasingly important roles.

All the contributors bar two – Jan Grodecki and Edward Griew – are current members of the Faculty of Law. Jan Grodecki was the foundation professor of law and the success of the law school owes much to his leadership until his retirement. As Emeritus Professor of Law at the University, he retains a welcome interest in the continuing evolution of the law school. Edward Griew has also played a formative role in the life of the law school; he is currently professor of law at the University of Nottingham. We are grateful to both of them for agreeing to contribute to this Jubilee volume.

We are also very grateful to those members of the legal profession listed at the front of this book whose sponsorship has enabled us to produce so handsome a work to mark our Silver Jubilee.

The essays were delivered at varying times between October 1989 and March 1990. Since the publication process involved going straight to page proofs, there has been very little opportunity to add new material at proof stage.

Finally, our thanks go to the Faculty Office who typed the essays of those not yet hooked on word processors, and to Leicester University Press for their assistance in the preparation and production of this book.

Fiona Patfield
Robin White
University of Leicester
July 16 1990

Table of Statutes

Administration of Justice Act 1985
    Part II   40, 214

Adoption Act 1976
    s.14(3)   69

Animals Act 1971   16

Atomic Energy Authority Act 1971
    s.9   124

Carriage by Air Act 1961   188

Carriage of Goods by Sea Act 1971   187

Child Benefit Act 1975   159
    s.2   165

Children and Young Persons Act 1939
    s.38   101

Children Act 1975
    s.10(3)   68
    s.105   67

Children Act 1989
    Part I   68
    s.4   69
    s.96   101, 105

Civil Evidence Act 1968   106

Civil Evidence Act 1972
    s.3   113

Civil Evidence (Scotland) Act 1988
    s.2   106

TABLE OF STATUTES

Civil Jurisdiction and Judgments Act 1982	193
s.32	193
Companies Act 1989	89, 93
s.192	78, 82
Consolidation of Enactments (Procedure) Act 1949	16
Consumer Credit Act 1974	
s.140	187
Contempt of Court Act 1981	
s.10	129, 131
Criminal Attempts Act 1981	
s.6	265
Criminal Evidence Act 1898	
s.1	112
Criminal Evidence Act 1965	9
Criminal Evidence (Northern Ireland) Order 1988	99
Criminal Justice Act 1972	11
Criminal Justice Act 1982	
s.72	99
Criminal Justice Act 1987	
ss.4–5	106
Criminal Justice Act 1988	10
s.24	106
s.32	105
s.34	100
Criminal Law Act 1967	
s.1	265
s.13	167
Criminal Law Act 1977	
s.2	257
s.5	265
s.13	265
Data Protection Act 1984	
s.27	120, 121
Domestic Violence and Matrimonial Proceedings Act 1976	59
Employment Protection Act 1975	160
Employment Protection (Consolidation) Act 1978	
s.140	187
Employment Subsidies Act 1978	160

European Communities Act 1972	13
Fair Employment (Northern Ireland) Act 1989	
ss.2–6	154
s.12	154
s.13	154
s.33	154
s.49	155
Fair Trading Act 1973	90
Family Income Supplements Act 1970	159
Family Law Reform Act 1987	
s.4	69
Financial Services Act 1986	73, 81, 82, 86, 92, 93
s.62	89
Forgery and Counterfeiting Act 1981	
s.13	265
Housing Finance Act 1972	159
Housing and Planning Act 1986	
s.55	155
Housing Act 1988	
s.137	155
Human Organs Transplants Act 1989	10
Inheritance (Provision for Family and Dependants) Act 1975	64
Insolvency Act 1986	
s.336	55
Interception of Communications Act 1985	120, 134
s.2	122
Iron and Steel Act 1982	
s.3	122
s.6	122
s.7	122
s.9	122
Land Charges Act 1925	42
Land Charges Act 1972	42
s.4(6)	43
Land Registration Act 1925	
s.20	43, 50
ss.48–56	43
s.58	43
s.70	46, 50
s.86	48

Law Commissions Act 1965	15
s.3	259
Law of Property Act 1925	
s.1	41
s.2	42, 53
s.14	54
s.26	53
s.27	53
s.36	53
s.198	42
s.199	41, 42
Law of Property (Miscellaneous Provisions) Act 1989	40
Law Reform (Miscellaneous Provisions) (Scotland) Act 1985	
s.36	104
Matrimonial Causes Act 1973	
s.42	69
Matrimonial Homes Act 1967	9
Matrimonial Homes Act 1983	45
s.2	48
Ministry of Social Security Act 1966	159
Misuse of Drugs Act 1971	
s.52	9
National Insurance Act 1966	160
National Insurance Act 1970	159
National Insurance Act 1971	159
Offences against the Person Act 1861	258
Official Secrets Act 1911	
s.1	127
s.2	119, 135
Official Secrets Act 1989	119, 135, 136
s.1	136
s.2	136
Planning Enquiries (Attendance of Public) Act 1982	124
s.1	124
Police and Criminal Evidence Act 1984	16
s.78	117
Prevention of Terrorism (Temporary Provisions) Act 1984	
Sched. 3, para, 4	123

TABLE OF STATUTES

Prosecution of Offences Act 1985	16
Public Order Act 1986	
s.9	265
Race Relations Act 1965	138, 139, 141
s.1	142, 147
s.3	152
s.5	147
Race Relations Act 1968	139, 140, 141
s.1	142
s.7	149
s.8	145, 146, 149
s.17	152
s.19	152
ss.21–3	152
s.27	150
Race Relations Act 1976	139, 140, 141
s.1	142, 143, 144
s.3	142
s.4	149
s.5	146
s.8	149
s.9	149
s.12	148
ss.17–19	148
s.19A	151, 155
s.20	150
s.21	149
s.22	149
s.25	148, 150
s.26	150
s.28	144
ss.29–31	153
s.35	146
s.38	147
s.41	150
s.42	121, 150
s.51	153
ss.54–6	153
s.57	153
ss.58–61	153
s.62	153
s.63	153
s.65	142
s.66	153
s.69	121
s.71	151

s.75	150
s.78	142

Restriction of Offensive Weapons Act 1959
s.1	9

Restriction of Offensive Weapons Act 1961	9
Safety of Sports Grounds Act 1975	10
Sex Discrimination Act 1975	139

Sexual Offences (Amendment) Act 1976
s.2	103

Social Security Act 1975
s.59A	167
Sched.4	170
Sched.20	170

Social Security Act 1980	159
Social Security Act 1986	159, 160
Social Security Benefits Act 1975	159
Social Security and Housing Benefits Act 1982	159, 160
Social Security Pensions Act 1975	159
s.6	170

Solicitors Act 1974
s.2	40

Telecommunications Act 1984
s.106	124

Theft Act 1968
s.32	265

Unfair Contract Terms Act 1977	24
War Damage Act 1965	9

Table of Statutory Instruments

Child Benefit (General) Regulations 1976, SI 1976: No. 965
  reg. 5(a) — 165
  reg. 7C — 166
  reg. 15 — 166

Child Benefit and Social Security (Fixing and Adjustment of Rates) Regulations 1976, SI 1976: No. 1267
  reg. 2 — 168

Crown Court (Amendment) (No. 5) Rules 1988 SI: No. 2160

Income Support (General) Regulations 1987, SI 1987: No. 1967 — 165
  reg. 10A — 172
  reg. 29 — 172
  Sched. 2 — 173

Industrial Tribunals (Rules of Procedure) Regulations 1985 SI 1985: No. 16
  r.7 — 123

Land Registration Rules 1925, R & O 1925: No. 1093
  r.8 — 50
  r.83 — 50

Social Security (Adjudication) Regulations 1986, SI 1986: No. 2218 — 161

Social Security (Claims and Payments) Regulations 1987, SI 1987: No. 1968 — 161
  reg. 27 — 169

Social Security (Overlapping Benefits) Regulations 1989, SI 1979: No. 597
  reg 8 — 169

Social Security (Payments on Account, Overpayments and
 Recovery) Regulations 1987, SI 1987: No. 491
 reg. 17   172

Statutory Maternity Pay (General) Regulations 1986, SI 1986:
 No. 1960 reg. 17   174

Supplementary Benefit (Duplication and Overpayments)
 Regulations 1980, SI 1980: No. 1580
 reg. 2   172
 reg. 7   170

Supplementary Benefit (Single Payments) Regulations
 1981, SI 1981: No. 1528
 reg. 6   172

Table of other documents

EEC Treaty

Article 5	209
Article 30	203, 204, 210, 211
Article 36	204
Article 48	200, 211
Article 85	202
Article 86	202, 205, 208
Article 90	205
Article 177	15, 196, 197 et seq

European Convention of Human Rights

Article 6	105
Article 8	119
Article 10	119
Article 11	119

Table of Cases

United Kingdom

The Abidin Daver, [1984] AC 398	193
Abbey National Building Society v. *Cann*, (1989) 57 P & CR 381, [1990] 1 All ER	51, 52
Abse v. *Smith*, [1986] 1 All ER 350	215
The Adolf Warski, [1976] 2 Lloyd's Rep. 241	190, 191, 192
Alexander v. *Home Office*, [1988] 1 WLR 968	153
Amanuel v. *Alexandros Shipping Co*, [1968] QB 464	188
Amin v. *Entry Clearance Officer, Bombay*, [1983] 2 AC 818	151
Anns v. *London Borough of Merton*, [1978] AC 728	12, 21, 22, 23, 24, 25, 27, 29, 33, 36, 38
Applin v. *Race Relations Board*, [1973] QB 815	142
Argy Trading Development Co. Ltd v. *Lapid Developments Ltd*, [1977] 1 WLR 444	34
Ashton v. *Turner*, [1981] 1 QB 137	23, 31
Aswan Engineering Establishment Co. v. *Lupdine Ltd*, [1987] 1 WLR 1	26
The Atlantic Song, [1983] 2 Lloyd's Rep. 394	190, 192
The Atlantic Star, [1974] AC 436	193
Attock Cement Co. Ltd v. *Romanian Bank for Foreign Trade*, [1989] 1 Lloyd's Rep. 572	185

TABLE OF CASES

Attorney-General's Reference (No. 1 of 1977), [1977] 1 WLR 473	9
Attorney-General v. *Guardian Newspapers (No. 2)*, [1988] 3 All ER 545	129, 130, 133
Attorney-General v. *Jonathan Cape*, [1975] 3 All ER 484	129, 133
Austrian Lloyd SS Co. v. *Gresham Life Assurance Society Ltd*, [1903] 1 KB 249	182, 183
Bagot v. *Stevens Scanlon & Co*, [1966] 1 QB 197	23
Baker v. *Rabbetts*, (1954) 118 JPN 303	101
Bank of Nova Scotia v. *Hellenic Mutual War Risks Association (Bermuda) Ltd*, [1989] 3 All ER 628	30
Banque Financière de la Cité SA v. *Westgate Insurance Co. Ltd*, [1989] 2 All ER 952	30
Barkworth v. *Customs and Excise Commissioners*, [1988] 3 CMLR 759	198
Barnhart v. *Greenshields*, (1853) 9 Moo PC 18	42
Bater v. *Bater*, [1951] P 35	98
Batty v. *Metropolitan Realisations*, [1978] QB 554	23
Ben Stansfield v. *Carlisle City Council*, (1982) EG 475	26
The Benarty, [1985] QB 325	188
Bendall v. *McWhirter*, [1952] 2 All ER 333	44
Bottomley v. *Bannister*, [1932] 1 KB 458	23
Bourgoin v. *Minister of Agriculture, Fisheries and Food*, [1986] QB 716	203, 208
Bradford City MC v. *K (minors)*, The Times, 18 August 1989	105
Brikom Investments Ltd v. *Carr*, [1979] QB 467	47
Bristol and West Building Society v. *Henning*, [1985] 1 WLR 778	51, 52
Bulmer v. *Bollinger*, [1974] Ch. 401	198, 199
Burmah Oil v. *Lord Advocate*, [1965] AC 75	9
Calder v. *McKay*, (1860) 22 D 741	183
Calveley v. *Chief Constable of the Merseyside Police*, [1989] QB 136	33

TABLE OF CASES

Case	Page
Candlewood Navigation Co. Ltd v. *Mitsui OSK Lines*, [1986] AC 1	26
Caparo Industries PLC v. *Dickman*, [1990] 2 WLR 358	12, 32, 36, 39
Carvalho v. *Hull, Blyth (Angola) Ltd*, [1979] 3 All ER 280	182
Caunce v. *Caunce*, [1969] 1 WLR 286	45, 46, 47
Chandler v. *DPP*, [1964] AC 763	123, 127, 131, 132, 136
Chattopadhay v. *Headmaster of Holloway School*, [1982] ICR 132	143
Chief Adjudication Officer v. *Brunt*, [1988] AC 711	15
Church of England Building Society v. *Piskor*, [1954] CH. 553	51
City of London Building Society v. *Flegg*, [1986] Ch. 605	53, 54, 55, 56
Clarke v. *Bruce Lance & Co*, [1988] 1 WLR 881	28
Commission for Racial Equality v. *Amari Plastics*, [1982] 1 QB 1194	154
Commission for Racial Equality v. *Dutton*, [1989] 1 All ER 306	144
Compagnie Tunisienne de Navigation SA v. *Compagnie d'Armement Matitime SA*, [1971] AC 572	180
Council of Civil Service Unions v. *Minister for the Civil Service*, [1985] 1 AC 374	119, 126, 130, 133
Re Cox and Neve's Contract, [1891] 2 Ch. 109	41
Clarke v. *Eley (IMI) Kynoch Ltd*, [1982] IRLR 482	145
Crabb v. *Arun District Council*, [1976] Ch. 169	56
Curran v. *Northern Ireland Co-ownership Association Ltd*, [1987] AC 718	27, 32
Customs & Excise Commissioners v. *ApS Samex*, [1983] 3 CMLR 194	198, 201
D & F Estates Ltd v. *Church Commissioners for England*, [1988] 3 WLR 368	26, 27
DPP v. *Blastland*, [1985] 2 All ER 1095	99, 100

DPP v. *Boardman*, [1985] AC 427	111
DPP v. *Kilbourne*, [1973] AC 729	97
De Lusignan v. *Johnson*, (1973) 240 EG 499	43
Donoghue v. *Stevenson*, [1932] AC 562	12, 20, 21, 22, 24, 28, 29, 36, 38
Dorset Yacht Co. Ltd v. *Home Office*, [1970] AC 1004	21
Duke v. *GEC Reliance Ltd*, [1988] 1 All ER 626	200, 207, 208
Ealing LBC v. *Race Relations Board*, [1972] AC 342	142
The El Amria, [1981] 2 Lloyd's Rep. 119	189, 191, 192
The Eleftheria, [1970] P 94	189, 190
Ellinger v. *Guinness Mahon and Co.*, [1939] 4 All ER 16	190, 192, 195
Elliot Steam Tug Co. v. *The Shipping Controller*, [1922] 1 KB 127	26
Esso Petroleum Co. Ltd v. *Mardon*, [1976] QB 801	29
Evans Marshall & Co. Ltd v. *Bertola*, [1973] 1 WLR 349	180, 181, 190, 191
Factortame Ltd v. *Secretary of State for Transport*, [1989] 2 All ER 692	206, 207, 208, 211
The Fehmarn, [1958] 1 WLR 159	178, 190, 191, 194
Ferris v. *Weaven*, [1952] 2 All ER 333	44
Fisher v. *Bell* [1961] 1 QB 394	9
Forsikringsaktieselskapet Vesta v. *Butcher*, [1986] 2 All ER 488	30
The Forum Craftsman, [1985] 1 Lloyd's Rep. 291	184
Fothergill v. *Monarch Airlines*, [1981] AC 251	188
The Frank Pais, [1986] 1 Lloyd's Rep. 529	180, 181, 182, 184, 190, 192
Re G (a minor), [1987] 1 WLR 1461	98
Garden Cottage v. *Milk Marketing Board*, [1984] AC 130	203

TABLE OF CASES

Garland v. British Rail Engineering Ltd, [1982] 2 All ER 402	208
Gautret v. Egerton, (1867) LR 2 CP 371	26
Gienar v. Meyer, (1796) 2 HBI 603	178
Gissing v. Gissing, [1971] AC 886	51
Greater Nottingham Co-operative Society Ltd. v. Cementation Piling and Foundations Ltd and others, [1989] QB 71	30
H v. H (a minor), [1989] 3 WLR 933	98
Hampson v. Dept of Education and Science, [1989] IRLR 69, CA, (1990) 140 New LJ 853, HL	145, 150
Hanlon v. The Law Society, [1981] AC 124	15
Harris v. DPP, [1952] AC 694	111
The Hilda Maru, [1981] 2 Lloyd's Rep. 510	186
Hill v. Chief Constable of West Yorkshire, [1989] AC 53	32, 34
Hillingdon LBC v. Commission for Racial Equality, [1982] AC 779	154
Hodgson v. Marks, [1971] Ch. 892	46, 50, 55
Hoerter v. Hanover etc. Works, (18893) 10 TLR 103	180, 181, 182
Holcombe v. Hewson, (1810) 2 Camp 391	97
Holden v. White [1982] QB 679	26
The Hollandia, [1983] 1 AC 565	182, 187, 188
Hollington Bros v. Rhodes, [1951] 2 All ER 578	43
Hornal v. Neiberger Products, [1957] 1 QB 247	98
Hunt v. Luck, [1901] 1 Ch. 45, affmd [1902] 1 Ch. 428	42
Investors in Industry Ltd v. South Bedfordshire District Council, [1986] QB 1034	32
Inwards v. Baker, [1965] 2 QB 29	56
The Iran Vojdan, [1984] 2 Lloyd's Rep. 380	180, 181, 184
Re JS (a minor), [1980] 1 All ER 1061	98
Jess B Woodcock & Sons Ltd v. Hobbs, [1955] 1 WLR 152	44
Johnson v. Machielsne, (1811) 3 Camp 44	178, 180, 181

TABLE OF CASES xxv

Jones v. *National Coal Board*, [1957] 2 QB 55	95
Jones v. *Department of Employment*, [1989] QB 1	33
Junior Brooks v. *Veitchi*, [1983] 1 AC 520	22, 23
Khanna v. *Ministry of Defence*, [1981] IRLR 333	143
Kling v. *Keston Properties Ltd*, (1985) 49 P & CR 212	50
Kingsnorth Finance Co. Ltd v. *Tizard*, [1986] 1 WLR 783	47, 52
The Kislovodsk, [1980] 1 Lloyd's Rep. 183	191
Kuruma v. *R*, [1955] AC 197	117
Langbrook Properties Ltd v. *Surrey County Council*, [1970] 1 WLR 161	26
Law v. *Garrett*, (1878) 8 Ch. D 26	178, 189
Leigh and Sillavan v. *Aliakmon Shipping Co. Ltd*, [1986] AC 785	25, 26, 38
Lloyds Bank v. *Rosset*, [1988] 3 All ER 915, CA: [1990] 1 All ER 111, HL	50, 52
London Borough of Waltham Forest v. *Scott Markets*, [1988] 3 CMLR 773	197
Lonrho PLC v. *Fayed*, [1989] 2 All ER 65	203
Lonrho PLC v. *Shell*, [1981] 2 All ER 456	203
Lord Advocate v. *Scotsman Publications Ltd*, [1989] 2 All ER 852	129
Lyus v. *Prowsa Developments Ltd*, [1982] 1 WLR 1044	43
M v. *Cain, The Times*, 15 December 1989	98
McConnel and Reid v. *Smith*, (1911) 1 SLT 333	183
McLoughlin v. *O'Brien*, [1983] AC 410	22
McMahon v. *DES*, [1982] 3 CMLR 91	200
Mackender v. *Feldia*, [1967] 2 QB 590	184, 185, 190
The Makefjell, [1976] 2 Lloyds Rep. 29	182, 183, 190, 191, 192, 194
Majfrid, [1942] P 45, [1942] P 145	34
Makin v. *AG for New South Wales*, [1894] AC 57	110

Mandla v. *Dowell Lee,* [1983] 2 AC 548	142, 143
Meer v. *Tower Hamlets LBC, The Times,* 3 June 1988	145
Midland Bank Ltd v. *Hett, Stubbs and Kemp,* [1979] Ch. 384	29, 44
Midland Bank Ltd v. *Farmpride Hatecheries Ltd,* (1981) 260 EG 493	47
Midland Bank Trust Co. Ltd v. *Green,* [1981] AC 513	43, 48
Mills v. *Winchester Diocesan Board of Finance,* [1989] 2 All ER 317	33
Minories Finance Ltd v. *Arthur Young (a firm),* [1989] 2 All ER 105	35
Mitchil v. *Alestree,* (1676) 1 Vent 295	20
Myers v. *DPP,* [1965] AC 1001	9, 95
National Bank of Greece v. *Pinios,* [1989] 3 WLR 185	30, 31
National Provincial Bank Ltd v. *Ainsworth,* [1965] AC 1175	9, 44, 45, 46, 47, 55
Newstead v. *Department of Transport,* [1986] 2 CMLR 196	201
Noone v. *North-West Thames RHA,* [1988] IRLR 195	153
Noor Mohammed v. *R,* [1949] AC 182	111
Norwich City Council v. *Harvey,* [1989] 1 All ER 1180	35
O'Hare v. *HM Advocate,* [1948] JC 90	112
Ojutiku v. *Manpower Services Commission,* [1982] ICR 661	145
Owen and Briggs v. *James,* [1982] ICR 618	143
Paddington Building Society v. *Mendelsohn,* (1985) P & CR 244	52
Peabody Donation Fund (Governors of) v. *Sir Lindsay Parkinson & Co. Ltd,* [1985] AC 210	32, 36
Peffer v. *Rigg,* [1977] 1 WLR 285	43
Perera v. *Civil Service Commission,* [1983] IRLR 166	145

In Re A Petition of Right, [1915] 3 KB 649	125, 126
Poster v. *Slough Estates*, [1968] 1 WLR 1515	45
Potato Marketing Board v. *Drysdale*, [1968] 3 CMLR 331	200
Potato Marketing Board v. *Robertsons*, [1983] 1 CMLR 93	200
Practice Direction, [1986] 2 All ER 226	215
In Re Prestige Group PLC, [1984] 1 WLR 337	154
R(SB)2/82	175
R v. *Abadom*, (1983) 76 Cr App R 48	114
R v. *Bibi*, [1980] 1 WLR 1193	14
R v. *Bond*, [1906] 2 KB 389	111
R v. *Braithwaite*, 24 November 1983, unrepoted	113
R v. *City Panel on Takeovers and Mergers, ex parte Guinness PLC*, [1989] 2 WLR 863	79, 81, 90
R v. *Curr*, [1968] 2 QB 944	257
R v. *Curry and Keeble*, [1983] Crim. LR 737	110
R v. *Fulling*, [1987] 2 All ER 65	108
R v. *Goodchild*, [1977] 1 WLR 473	9
R v. *Harz and Power*, [1967] 1 AC 760	97
R v. *Hayes*, (1977) Cr App R 194	101
R v. *Henn and Derby*, [1978] 1 WLR 1031, CA, [1981] AC 850, HL	201
R v. *Home Secretary, ex parte Hosenball*, [1977] 1 WLR 766	120, 134
R v. *Hunt*, [1987] 1 All ER 1	95
R v. *ILEA, ex parte Hinde*, [1985] 1 CMLR 716	200
R v. *Inhabitants of Eriswell*, (1790) 100 ER 815	94
R v. *Khan*, (1981) 73 Cr App R 190	101
R v. *Lawrence*, [1977] Crim. LR 492	103
R v. *Licensing Authority, ex parte Smith Kline & French Laboratories Ltd*, [1989] 2 All ER 113	207
R v. *MacKenny*, (1980) 72 Cr App R 78	114, 115
R v. *Masih*, [1986] Crim. LR 395	115
R v. *Mason*, [1987] 3 All ER 481	117

R v. *Mills*, (1976) Cr App R 327	103
R v. *Monopolies and Mergers Commission, ex parte Argyll Group PLC*, [1986] 1 WLR 763	79
R v. *Monopolies and Mergers Commission, ex parte Elders IXL Ltd*, [1987] 1 WLR 1221	80
R v. *Monopolies and Mergers Commission, ex parte Matthew Brown PLC*, [1987] 1 WLR 1235	80
R v. *O'Loughlin*, [1988] 3 All ER 431	99
R v. *Oakwell*, [1978] 1 All ER 1223	110
R v. *Panel on Takeovers and Mergers, ex parte Datafin PLC*, [1987] 2 WLR 699	79
R v. *Powell*, [1986] 1 All ER 193	113
R v. *Quinn*, [1983] Crim. LR 475	98
R v. *Rance*, (1976) 62 Cr App R 118	111
R v. *Samuel*, [1988] 2 WLR 920	108
R v. *Secchi*, [1975] CMLR 383	200
R v. *Secretary of State for the Home Department, ex parte Herbage*, [1986] 3 All ER 209	207
R v. *Secretary of State for Home Department, ex parte Ruddock*, [1987] 2 All ER 518	131, 132, 137
R v. *Secretary of State for Social Security, ex parte Bomore Medical Supplies*, [1986] 1 CMLR 34	200
R v. *Secretary of State for Social Services, ex parte Schering Chemicals Ltd*, [1987] 1 CMLR 277	199
R v. *Sims*, [1946] KB 531	111
R v. *Smellie*, (1919) 14 Cr App R 128	105
R v. *Straffen*, [1952] 2 QB 911	111
R v. *Turnbull*, [1977] QB 224	109, 110
R v. *Turner*, (1974) 60 Cr App R 80	114, 115
R v. *Wallwork*, (1958) 42 Cr App R 152	101
R v. *Watts*, [1983] Crim. LR 541	113
R v. *Wright and Ormerod*, (1987) (unreported)	101
R v. *X, The Times*, 3 November 1989	105
Racecourse Betting Control Board v. *Secretary of State for Air*, [1944] Ch. 114	178

Reid v. *R*, [1989] 3 WLR 771	110
Reid v. *Rush & Tompkins Group*, [1989] 3 All ER 228	35
Roberts Petroleum Ltd v. *Bernard Kenny Ltd*, [1983] AC 192	5
Rochdale BC v. *Stewart John Anders*, [1988] 3 CMLR 431	197
Ross v. *Caunters*, [1980] Ch. 297	23
Rowling v. *Takaro Properties*, [1988] AC 473	33
Rustenburg Platinum Mines Ltd v. *South African Airways*, [1979] 1 Lloyd's Rep. 19	188
Re St Piran Ltd, [0000] 1 WLR 1300	79, 88
Saif Ali v. *Sidney Mitchell & Co*, [1980] AC 198	25
Science Research Council v. *Nasse*, [1979] QB 144	138, 142
Scotmotors (Plant Hire) Ltd v. *Dundee Petrosea Ltd*, [1982] SLT 181	179, 183
Scott v. *R*, [1989] 2 WLR 924	110, 112
Secretary of State for Defence v. *Guardian Newspapers*, [1984] 3 All ER 601	119, 125, 128, 131, 132
Selvey v. *DPP*, [1970] AC 304	112
The Sennar (No. 2), [1985] 1 WLR 490	182, 183, 189
Shiloh Spinners Ltd v. *Harding*, [1973] AC 691	45
Showboat Entertainment Centre v. *Owen*, [1984] 1 All ER 836	142
The Sindh, [1975] 1 Lloyd's Rep. 372	183
Sirros v. *Moore*, [1975] QB 118	25
Smith v. *Littlewoods Organization Ltd*, [1987] AC 241	27, 34
Southern Water Authority v. *Carey*, [1985] 1 All ER 1077	35
Steel v. *Union of Post Office Workers*, [1988] 1 WLR 64	145
Stephens v. *Anglia Water Authority*, [1986] AC 785	25
Street v. *Denham*, [1954] 1 WLR 624	44

TABLE OF CASES

Tai Hing Cotton Mill Ltd v. *Lui Chong Hing Bank Ltd,* [1986] AC 80   29, 30, 31, 38

Taylor v. *Stibbert,* (1794) 2 Ves Jr 438   42

Taylor Fashions Ltd v. *Liverpool Victoria Trustees Co. Ltd,* [1982] QB 133   56

Thake v. *Maurice,* [1986] QB 844   30

Thompson v. *R,* [1918] AC 221   111

Tilling v. *Whiteman,* [1980] AC 1   6

Tracomin SA v. *Sudan Oil Seeds Co. Ltd (No. 1),* [1983] 1 WLR 1026   186, 193

Trendtex Trading Corporation v. *Crédit Suisse,* [1982] AC 679   180, 181, 184, 185, 189, 191, 194

Van Oppen v. *Clerk to the Bedford Charity Trustees,* [1989] 1 All ER 273 confirmed (1989) 139 NLJ 900   35, 38

The Visha Prabha, [1979] 2 Lloyd's Rep. 286   190, 192

Weller & Co. v. *Foot & Mouth Disease Research Institute,* [1966] 1 QB 569   22

William and Glyns Bank Ltd v. *Boland,* (1978) 36 P & CR 448   46

William and Glyns Bank Ltd v. *Boland,* [1981] AC 487   10, 45, 46, 47, 51, 52, 54, 55, 56

Wilson v. *TB Steelwork Co. Ltd, The Times* 21 January 1978   142

Winkworth v. *Edward Baron Development Co. Ltd,* [1986] 1 WLR 1512   46

WMPTE v. *Singh,* [1987] ICR 837   143

Wroth v. *Tyler,* [1974] CH. 30   45

YTC Universal Ltd v. *Trans Europa SA,* (1968) 112 SJ 842   190

Yuen Kun Yeu v. *Attorney-General of Hong Kong,* [1988] AC 175   27, 28, 29 31, 36

The Zamora, [1916] 2 AC 77   125, 126, 130, 132

Zarcynska v. *Levy,* [1979] 1 All ER 836   142

Australia

Barnes v. *Sharpe*, (1910) 11 CLR 462	97
Bunning v. *Cross*, (1978) 141 CLR 54	116
Caltex Oil (Australia) Pty Ltd v. *Dredge Willemstad*, (1976) 136 CLR 529	22
Contractors Ltd v. *MTE Control Gear Ltd*, [1964] SASR 47	182
Hanessian v. *Lloyd Triestine SA di Narigazione*, (1951) 68 WN (NSW) 98	184
Martin v. *Osborne*, (1936) 25 CLR 367	96
Milirrpum v. *Nabalco Pty Ltd*, (1971) 17 FLR 141	114
Perry v. *R*, (1983) 57 ALJR 110	110, 111
R v. *Pfitzner*, (1976) 15 SASR 171	97
R v. *Reynolds*, (1975) CRNS 141	115
Sutherland Shire Council v. *Heyman*, (1985) 60 ALR 1	27, 36
Wilson v. *R*, (1970) 123 CLR 334	97

Canada

G and E Auto Brokers Ltd v. *Toyota Canada Inc*, (1981) 117 DLR (3rd) 707	183
Khalij Commercial Bank Ltd v. *Woods*, (1985) 17 DLR (4th) 358	179, 183
R v. *Dietrich*, [1971] 1 CCC (2d) 49	114
Vetrovec v. *R*, (1982) 136 DLR 89	100
Westcott v. *Alsco Products of Canada Ltd*, (1960) 26 DLR (2d) 281	182

Ireland

Limerick Corporation v. *Crompton and Co*, (1910) 2 Ir R 416	190

United States

Addington v. *Texas*, (1979) 441 US 418	97
Carbon Black Export v. *The SS Monrosa*, (1958) 254 F 2d 297	179
Coy v. *Iowa*, (1988) 487 US 1012	105
Griggs v. *Duke Poer Co.*, (1971) 401 US 422	143
Gulf Oil Corp. v. *Gilbert*, (1947) 330 US 501	179
Hochheiser v. *Superior Court*, (1984) 161 Cal App 3d 777	105
Krulewitch v. *US*, (1949) 336 US 440	113
Lewis v. *Southmore*, (1972) 480 SW (2d) 180	114
M/s Bremen v. *Zapata Off-Shore Company (The Chaparral)*, (1972) 407 US 1	179, 186, 190, 194, 195
Wm Muller & Co. Inc v. *Swedish American Line Ltd*, (1955) 224 F 2d 806	179
Neil v. *Biggers*, (1972) 409 US 188	109, 110
Nute v. *Hamilton Mut. Ins. Co*, (1856) 72 Mass. (6 Gray) 174	179
Olmstead v. *US*, (1928) 277 US 438	116
People v. *McDonald*, (1984) 37 Cal (3d) 351	109
State v. *Chapple*, (1983) 135 Ariz 281	109
University of California Regents v. *Bakke*, (1978) 438 US 265	146
US v. *Amaral*, (1973) 488 F (2d) 1148	99, 109
US v. *Edwards*, (1987) F (2d) 262	114
US v. *Dotson*, (1987) 817 F (2d) 1127	114
US v. *Downing*, (1985) 753 F (2d) 1224	115

Court of Justice of the European Communities (by case number)

Case 26/62, *Van Gend en Loos,* [1963] ECR 1	205
Case 10/71, *Hein,* [1971] ECR 723	205
Case 167/73, *Rheinmuhlen,* [1974] ECR 139	198
Case 51/75, *EMI* v. *CBS,* [1976] ECR 811	204

Case 13/77, *GB Inno* v. *ATAB*, [1977] ECR 2115	210
Case 175/78, *Saunders,* [1979] ECR 1129	197
Case 34/79, *R* v. *Henn and Derby,* [1979] ECR 3795	205
Case 96/80, *Jenkins* v. *Kingsgate (Clothing Products) Ltd*, [1981] ECR 911	204
Case 158/80, *Rewe* v. *Hauptzollamt Kiel,* [1981] ECR 1841	209
Case 14/83, *Von Colson,* [1984] ECR 1921	200, 207
Case 192/85, *Newstead,* [1988] 1 All ER 129	201
Case 197/86, *Brown,* [1988] 3 CMLR 403	197
Case 222/86, *Heylens,* [1987] ECR 4097	211
Joined Cases 266 & 7/87, *R* v. *Pharmaceutical Society of Great Britain,* [1989] 2 All ER 758	197, 198

1 Influences, pressures and agents for change

Robin C.A. White

Introduction

In a book, written in 1953,[1] with the same title as this volume, Denning LJ (as he then was) described the law as 'often uncertain' and 'continually being changed ... by the judges'.[2] He praised the processes of evolutionary change that characterize the development of the common law. Denning identified three instincts which are at the core of the spirit of the British constitution and remain constant in the march of progress. These are the instincts for justice and for liberty, and a practical instinct which results in the balancing of 'rights with duties, and powers with safeguards so that neither rights nor powers shall be exceeded or abused'.[3] Despite many of his forward-looking views on the law-making role of judges, much of this little book harks back to the values of an earlier era, as is patently clear in his final two essays on the rights of women and the influence of religion. Nevertheless the essays represent one of the early contributions of a judge to the debate on what causes the law to change and how change is accomplished in a system which places so great a value on certainty and predictability.

What is it that causes the law constantly to be changing? Is it simply the march of time? Does the state of the law in 1990 bear any resemblance to the law of 1965 when Leicester University law school was established? Has Denning's identification of a practical instinct for workable change survived the passage of years? The chapters in this volume discuss a diversity of subject-matter and offer a range of solutions to the topics they address. Are these chapters capable of producing any coherent statement about influences, pressures and agents for change? The task of this introductory chapter is to look at some of the things that cause our law to change and to place the contributions of the substantive chapters in this volume in any framework that is suggested.

---

1. A. Denning, *The Changing Law*, London, Stevens (1953).
2. Ibid., Preface, at vii.
3. Ibid., at 3.

Terminology

The title of this chapter suggests a division of causes of change into influences, pressures and agents. This is really a division into processes and agents of change.[4] Processes are a series of events or activities which operate to produce change. Agents can be divided into law-creating agents and law-determining agents; both include the individuals or institutions whose activities result in change in the law, but only the law-creating agents exert a direct influence on the content of the law.

Processes could obviously cover more than influences and pressures, but this chapter is not the place to suggest an overly elaborate analysis. Influences refer to those things or events which have the power of producing an effect; the causal link is often unobtrusive or indirect. By contrast, pressures are much more direct in impact; they are those things or events which make a strong and direct demand for change. They may not necessarily be more likely to actually result in change.

Adopting this terminology and typology enables the substance of this chapter to be reduced to tabular form as shown in Tables 1.1 and 1.2.

Table 1.1 Breakdown of influences and pressures

Influences	Legislation	inputs
		outputs
	Cases	inputs
		outputs
	Proposals for change	domestic
		European
		international
	Public opinion	proactive
		reactive
	Analysis and research	
	Scholarship	
	Custom	
Pressures	Legislation	outputs
	Cases	outputs
	Public opinion	proactice
		reactive
	Events	domestic
		European
		international

---

4. A division suggested by Schwarzenberger in G. Schwarzenberger and E. Brown, *A Manual of International Law*, Professional Books (6th edn, 1976), Ch. 4.

Table 1.2 Breakdown of law-creating and law-determining agents

Law-creating agents	Parliament	primary legislation secondary legislation
	Judges	appellate decisions first instance decisions
	Community institutions	Council/Commission European courts
	International organizations	Binding resolutions
Law-determining agents	Judges	appellate decisions first instance decisions
	Reform institutions	Law Commission Royal Commissions Other bodies
	Politicians	ministers back benchers opposition overseas
	Lobbyists	
	Solicitors and barristers	
	Academics	
	Individuals and corporations	

Influences

Legislation

Francis Bennion identifies the key features of the statute law of a modern legislature on the British model.[5] He argues that legislation:

is largely promoted and wholly administered by the government (or executive), enacted by a parliament broadly supporting the government (senatorial quirks of an upper house being set aside), and interpreted by, and enforced on the orders of, an independent judiciary ... Statute law, piecemeal rather than systematic, is produced over the years in response to needs as they arise in society. It is inert, tending to remain stranded after the needs have passed or changed. Parliament, too congested with business to keep its legislation updated, is forced to rely on

---

5. F. Bennion, *Bennion on Statute Law*, London, Longman (3rd edn, 1990), at 9.

law reform agencies. These however are not organised and financed on a scale sufficient for the task.[6]

It is possible to analyse the influence of legislation into inputs and outputs. It is trite to say that a new statute exercises an influence for change; change is at the very heart of the legislative process. It is the use of the statute which actually results in change and sometimes the application of the legislation produces unexpected results. Bennion argues that statute users are not primarily the ordinary citizen, but rather the 'practising lawyer (on the bench, at the bar or in a solicitor's office), the public official, or the non-legal professional adviser (such as the accountant, planner or estate agent)' and 'company lawyers'.[7] The raw text, which is the input, is only effective once it has been processed[8] by a statute user and applied to a particular situation. This is the output of legislation. How statute users process legislative texts[9] is, of course, coloured by judicial attitudes to statutory interpretation, which is in turn affected by the arcane techniques of legislative drafting adopted in the United Kingdom.[10]

Outputs of legislation include the decisions of courts and tribunals on the application of the legislative provisions. The loose form of monitoring the effects of legislation which exists in the United Kingdom can also exercise an influence. This is especially true in the case of taxation where there is an annual statute implementing the government's tax policy. It is also increasingly true in the social security field.[11]

Often the purpose of legislation is to change behaviour. One of the best examples is the legislation on race discrimination;[12] yet David Bonner concludes that the legislation's 'effects in terms of reducing racial inequality appear minimal'.[13] In this case, it seems that the changing law is not reflected in changing attitudes.

Cases

A large part of the law of England and Wales is the common law, which grows through recorded judicial decisions. The influence of the reporting

---

6. Ibid.
7. Ibid., at 210.
8. Ibid., Parts III and IV.
9. See Pollard, *infra*, Ch. 9 for a plea for a simple approach to statutory drafting in the field of social security law.
10. See generally F. Bennion, *supra* n.5, Part I; J. Bell and G. Engle, *Statutory Interpretation*, London, Sweet & Maxwell (2nd edn, 1987), Ch. 8; W. Dale, *Legislative Drafting — a new approach*, London, Butterworths (1977); and *The Preparation of Legislation*, (Report of the Renton Committee), Cmnd 6053 (1975).
11. There has been significant primary social security legislation every year since 1979 with the exception of 1987.
12. See Bonner, *infra*, Ch. 8.
13. Ibid., at 155.

of cases in the development of the common law should not be underestimated.[14] One modern problem is the sheer volume of reported material, which now includes the full texts of many formerly unreported decisions stored on the LEXIS database. The increasing availability of unreported cases led to an upsurge in the citing of unreported decisions before the courts. The House of Lords responded with the controversial dictum of Lord Diplock in *Roberts Petroleum Ltd* v. *Bernard Kenny Ltd*:[15]

My Lords, in my opinion, the time has come when your Lordships should adopt the practice of declining to allow transcripts of unreported judgments of the civil division of the Court of Appeal to be cited upon the hearing of appeals to this House unless leave is given to do so; and that such leave should only be granted upon counsel's giving an assurance that the transcript contains a statement of some principle of law, relevant to an issue in the appeal to this House, that is binding upon the Court of Appeal and of which the substance, as distinct from the mere choice of phraseology, is not to be found in any judgment of that court that has appeared in one of the generalised or specialised series of reports.

The response to this dictum has been highly critical.[16] The critical comment reflects the character of the common law. Bartholomew comments:

The somewhat amoeboid principles of the common law grow or are restrained by their application, re-application or non-application to varying fact situations. They are re-phrased, re-stated and re-iterated over and over again, and what eventually emerges is often startlingly different from that from which one started. The great principle of the common law in this context is that 'great oaks from little acorns grow' — this is the *leitmotif* of the judicial process. It is of the essence of the common law system that freedom, and all the other principles of law, broaden down from precedent to precedent.[17]

This reflects the inputs and outputs of cases. The inputs are the facts and arguments of litigants and their lawyers, which present the judges with the opportunity to develop the law, while the outputs are the judgments of the courts on those facts and arguments. This dependency of the common law on real facts is a central feature of judge-made law. The judges have consistently expressed a distaste for hypothetical points

---

14. See *Report of the Law Reporting Committee*, HMSO (1940).
15. [1983] 2 AC 192 at 200.
16. Goodhart, Letter in New LJ, 1 April 1983, at 296; Munday, 'The Limits of Citation Determined', *Law Society's Gazette*, 25 May 1983, at 1337; Tapper, Letter in *Law Society's Gazette*, 29 June 1983, at 1636; Bartholomew, 'Unreported Judgments in the House of Lords' New LJ, 2 September 1983, at 781; Bennion, Letter in New LJ, 30 September 1983, at 874; Harrison, 'Unreported Cases: Myth and Reality', *Law Society's Gazette*, 1 February 1984, at 257; see also Andrews, 'Reporting Case Law: Unreported Cases, the Definition of a *Ratio* and the Criteria for Reporting Cases' (1985) 2 *Legal Studies* 205.
17. Bartholomew, 'Unreported Judgments in the House of Lords' New LJ, 2 September 1983, 781, at 782.

of law.[18] This means that one of the prime movers for the development of the common law are litigants, who fund cases before the courts. There has been very little study of what influences litigants to bring cases. Indeed many litigants immortalized in the law reports will have had no idea on embarking on the litigation of the significance of their instructing lawyers to take or defend the case.

Some agencies have made use of test case strategies,[19] but generally the effectiveness of such action has been limited because of the practice of individualizing disputes adopted by the courts. Roger Smith concludes that any judgment on the value of a test case strategy must 'remain tentative and perhaps ambiguous' and that such cases are 'clearly not a particularly effective way of improving the lot of large numbers of claimants'.[20]

Proposals for change

Again it is trite to say that proposals for change are influences for change. The modern law is a constantly changing body of rules. Proposals for change will come from a variety of sources, both official and unofficial. The character of the body or individuals proposing change will be considered below under the heading of law-determining agents. The inclusion of the item here is to note the impact of calls for change not only on the wholly domestic level, but also resulting from our membership of the European Communities and from our participation in international organizations. Some of these proposals operate on the official level: that is, they are part of the machinery of law-creating accepted by the state. So bills before Parliament are at their initial stages proposals for change, which will be refined and finalized during the parliamentary consideration of them. There are parallels in the European Community, where proposals for legislation can only emanate from the Commission and are then subject to careful scrutiny and comment under the Community's legislative processes.[21] Analogous processes accompany proposals for change on the international level. Since such changes usually[22] require

---

18. See, for example, *Tilling* v. *Whiteman*, [1980] AC 1, per Lord Wilberforce at 17–18, and per Lord Scarman at 25.
19. See T. Prosser, *Test Cases for the Poor*, CPAG, 1983, and J. Cooper and R. Dhavan (eds), *Public Interest Law*, Oxford, Blackwell, 1986, *passim*, but especially at 143–5, 207–8 and 244–5.
20. Smith, 'How Good Are Test Cases?' in J. Cooper and R. Dhavan (eds), *Public Interest Law*, Oxford, Blackwell, 1986, 271, at 284.
21. See generally D. Freestone and J. Davidson, *The International Framework of the European Communities*, London, Croom Helm, 1988, Ch. 4; D. Coombes, *Politics and Bureaucracy in the EEC*, London, Allen and Unwin, 1970, Ch. 4; and Philip, 'Pressure Groups and Policy-Making in the European Community' in J. Lodge (ed.), *Institutions and Policies of the European Community*, London, Frances Pinter, 1983, at 21.
22. Exceptions include binding resolutions of international organizations taken by majority decision, such as the fixing of the budget of the United Nations Organization under Article 17 of the United Nations Charter.

the express consent of the state bound, they are closer to general influences than the processes of change on the domestic and European level. Apart from these formal law-making processes, there are a myriad of proposals for the alteration of the law of England and Wales put forward by interest groups and individuals. Many of these have little direct impact, but may fertilize the acorns from which the principles of the common law grow or may develop into pressures for change to which government chooses to respond.

Public opinion[23]

Public opinion is both reactive and proactive. The division is a fine one which may not always be easy to make. Proactive public opinion suggests change and lobbies for it, while reactive public opinion tends to oppose change already proposed. Proactive public opinion is, therefore, likely to be positive in intent, whereas reactive public opinion is likely to be negative in intent. Many who are lobbying for change pray in aid public opinion, which is, in truth, a difficult concept. This is because public opinion is not a single notion but a *mélange* of many views reduced to some sort of common denominator.[24]

Analysis and research

Those engaged in analysis and research like to think that change is always informed by an understanding of the operation of the existing order of things. Much analysis and research is designed to identify the causes rather than merely the symptoms of some condition which is under consideration. The extent to which analysis and research informs and influences change has varied. The Report of the Royal Commission on Criminal Procedure[25] was notable for its sound research base and for the series of studies it commissioned to inform its thinking and recommendations. By contrast, the Lord Chancellor's Civil Justice Review[26] attracted considerable criticism for the hasty and restricted

---

23. See J. Farrar, *Law Reform and the Law Commission*, London, Sweet & Maxwell, 1974, Ch. 6; C.K. Allen, *Law in the Making*, Oxford, Oxford University Press (7th edn, 1964), at 428–35; and W. Friedmann, *Law in a Changing Society*, Harmondsworth, Penguin (2nd edn, 1972), at 21–2.
24. Public opinion is frequently cited in favour of proposals for change, but as Judith Masson points out in Ch. 4 *infra*, very little research on what people want informs new legislation.
25. Report of the Royal Commission on Criminal Procedure (Philips Commission), 1981, Cmnd 8092; for comments on the Report and its 'constellation of research studies' see Leigh, 'The Royal Commission on Criminal Procedure' (1982) 44 MLR 296.
26. Cm 394 (1988). On the machinery for reforming civil procedure, see Wilson, 'Reviewing Civil Procedure: The Machinery of Review — Problems and Proposals', (1985) 4 Civil JQ 213.

nature of the research which it commissioned and for failing to have regard to a considerable body of research available on the issues under consideration. The charge was that the outcome of the Review was determined more by predetermined policy considerations than rational argument.[27] Nevertheless, the very existence of the sort of comments made about the Philips Commission and the Civil Justice Review indicate that analysis and research can justify their label as influences for change.

Scholarship[28]

Scholarship is categorized separately not because analysis and research do not merit the label scholarship, but in order to distinguish academic work whose primary objective is to find out the current state of affairs rather than to form part of a corpus of knowledge on which formal proposals for change are to be based.[29] In considering change, scholarship plays a lesser role, though, paradoxically, in some cases it can be a more potent influence because it lacks a direct link with contemplated change.

Despite this distinction between analysis, research and scholarship, it may perhaps be argued that taking the wider view is too alien to our traditions of legislative reform and the development of the common law. The courts of England and Wales have shown considerable reluctance to consider wider issues than those strictly necessary for the determination of the issue before them. The 'Brandeis brief' containing detailed economic, social and other data pertinent to the issue before the court has never found favour with British judges.[30] In his contribution[31] Richard Stone argues that the multiplicity of references in statutory texts to an ill-defined concept of national security suggests a need for a common legislative definition of the concept, but he remains deeply pessimistic about the likelihood of statutory intervention in this area. Clearly no court in an individual case could purport to define the concept across a wide range of applications.

---

27. Some analogous issues are touched on by Masson in Ch. 4 *infra*.
28. For a detailed discussion of, and challenge to, English legal scholarship, see Wilson, 'English Legal Scholarship' (1987) 50 MLR 818.
29. J.B. Ames, the second Dean of Harvard Law School, referred in an essay entitled 'The Vocation of the Law Professor' to the law professor's position giving 'an excellent opportunity to exert a wholesome influence upon the development of the law by his writing'. See J.B. Ames, *Lecture on Legal History*, 1913 at 354.
30. See briefly M. Zander, *The Law-Making Process*, Weidenfeld & Nicolson (3rd edn, 1989), at 263–5, but note that even in the United States where such briefs are a common feature of litigation, it is argued by some commentators that justices of the Supreme Court do not always fully appreciate the significance and social consequences of their decisions: see D. Horowitz, *The Courts and Social Policy*, The Brookings Institution, 1977.
31. *Infra*, Ch. 7.

Custom

In shaping the content of the common law, judges have often suggested that the source of their declaration of the law is custom. Zander states that these claims are 'likely to be more poetic than historically accurate'.[32] He goes on to argue that many customs were no more than the invention of judges. There is nevertheless a place for custom among the influences for change. Research in recent years has increasingly shown a gap between the 'law in the books' and the 'law in action',[33] and it is surely wrong to suggest that how the law is used has no influence on its future development.

Pressures

Legislation

It will be the outputs of legislation which constitute pressures for change. This will occur where the effect of the change is not what Parliament had intended. The anomalous result must be corrected. As is well known, the decision of the Divisional Court in *Fisher* v. *Bell*[34] on the interpretation of s.1(1) of the Restriction of Offensive Weapons Act 1959 necessitated the passing of the Restriction of Offensive Weapons Act 1961. Indeed, it will often be a decision of the courts which highlights the anomaly.[35] Despite a tight parliamentary schedule, the unexpected interpretation is such that it cannot be ignored and must be corrected.

Cases

Similar pressure can arise from judicial decisions clarifying the content of common law rules. Two statutes enacted in 1965[36] were responses to 'unacceptable' statements of the content of the common law in cases decided that year.[37]

---

32. M. Zander, *The Law-Making Process*, Weidenfeld & Nicolson (3rd edn, 1989), at 375.
33. See, for example, Beale and Dugdale, 'Contracts between Businessmen: Planning and the Use of Contractual Remedies' (1975) 2 Brit. J of Law and Soc. 45; and M. McConville and J. Baldwin, *Courts, Prosecution and Conviction*, Oxford, Clarendon Press, 1981.
34. [1961] 1 QB 394.
35. Another example is the amendment of the Misuse of Drugs Act 1971 by s.52 of the Criminal Law Act 1977 as a result of the decisions in *Goodchild*, [1977] 1 WLR 473 and *Attorney-General's Reference (No. 1 of 1977)*, [1977] 1 WLR 1213.
36. The Criminal Evidence Act 1965 and the War Damage Act 1965.
37. *Myers* v. *DPP*, [1965] AC 1001 and *Burmah Oil* v. *The Lord Advocate*, [1965] AC 75 respectively. The decision in *National Provincial Bank* v. *Ainsworth*, [1965] AC 1175 had to wait until the enactment of the Matrimonial Homes Act 1967 for its reversal. See comments by Thompson at pp.44–7 below.

Public opinion

Reactive public opinion is more likely to impose pressure for change than proactive public opinion. This may be reaction to incidents or to decisions of the courts. Reactive public opinion undoubtedly contributed to Parliament's about-turn in the introduction of appeals against lenient sentencing contained in the Criminal Justice Act 1988.[38] Another example is provided by the Safety of Sports Grounds Act 1975, which was prompted by the tragedy at the Ibrox Park football ground in Glasgow in January 1971 when 66 people were crushed to death and over 140 injured in a staircase leading from one of the terraces. The subsequent report[39] showed that existing controls over safety were inadequate.

The reaction of academics and practitioners to the case of *William and Glyns Bank Ltd* v. *Boland*[40] excited so much attention that the matter was referred to the Law Commission, but as Thompson notes in Chapter 3, the issue proved too contentious for any consensus to emerge and the matter still rests on case law. Public reaction and even consideration by the institutions charged with law reform does not guarantee change; sometimes the inherent uncertainty of the common law is preferred.

Events

It is not necessary to labour comment on this heading, since it echoes the previous section where public opinion responding to events adds to the compelling nature of calls for change. In 1989 the government added what is now the Human Organs Transplants Act 1989 to its legislative programme in response to allegations that kidneys from paid donors from outside the United Kingdom had been transplanted at a London hospital and to combat the threat of a foreign national setting up an agency in the United Kingdom to recruit live donors for payment.[41]

Again the events may be wholly domestic, European or international in dimension. It is probably true that domestic events have the greatest impact. It is not difficult to understand why responses to the loss of the *Herald of Free Enterprise* were more dramatic than to greater loss of life from other ferry disasters elsewhere.

---

38. C. Emmins and G. Scanlan, *Blackstone's Guide to the Criminal Justice Act 1988*, Blackstone Press (1988), at 162-4.
39. *Report of the Inquiry into Crowd Safety at Sports Grounds* by the Rt Hon. Lord Wheatley, Cmnd 4952 (1972).
40. [1981] AC 487, and see Thompson pp.45-7 and 51-6 below.
41. Lord Henley, HL Vol. 510, col. 842, 19 July 1989.

Law-creating agents

Parliament

Parliament is the paramount law-creating agent. Each year there is a programme of primary and secondary legislation, which creates new areas of law and fine-tunes existing areas. Most of the changes are evolutionary rather than revolutionary. The selection of legislation is a matter for the government of the day which controls legislative time in the Houses of Parliament. However, although it is the main law-creating agent, the parliamentary process is not the forum in which new law is formed and developed. The parliamentary stage in the creation of a new rule is merely the ritual by which the rule gains its status as a rule of primary or secondary legislation. It can certainly be argued that the preparatory work outside Parliament is at least as important as the parliamentary process. Since most bills are government bills, the processes by which government policy is formed and the processes of consultation inherent in the preparation of the text of a bill are of considerable significance.[42] Who is consulted will depend on the complexion of the government of the day and on recognition of the relevant interest groups. For example, it is inconceivable that a bill affecting the structure and organization of the legal profession would not involve consultation with the Bar and The Law Society. Where broad interests are affected, the devices of Green Papers and White Papers[43] are used to report the proposals and to gauge responses to them. Consultation is not, of course, the same as having one's views taken into consideration.

Much change is enacted by delegated legislation, which is subjected to even less parliamentary scrutiny than primary legislation. Often there is a formal requirement for consultation[44] but real control by Parliament is slight.[45]

Judges

It is no longer controversial to say that judges make law. The debate has moved on to consider how they make law and what limits there are on

---

42. For a discussion of the sources of the Criminal Justice Act 1972 which illustrate the central role of consultation, see Moriarty, 'The Policy-Making Process: How It is Seen from the Home Office' in N. Walker (ed.) *Penal Policy-Making in England*, Cambridge, Institute of Criminology (1977) extracted in M. Zander, *The Law-Making Process*, London, Weidenfeld & Nicolson, (3rd edn, 1989), at 3–6.
43. This process was adopted in relation to the Courts and Legal Services Bill and is the subject of Fiona Cownie's contribution at Ch. 12 *infra*.
44. For example, the requirement of consultation with the Social Security Advisory Committee in certain social security matters.
45. See Hayhurst and Wallington, 'The Parliamentary Scrutiny of Delegated Legislation' [1988] PL 547.

judicial creativity in this area. Lord Devlin finds the mandate for creativity in a notion of consensus. In a key passage in his book *The Judge*, he says:

I have now made it plain that I am firmly opposed to judicial creativity or dynamism as I have defined it, that is, of judicial operations in advance of the consensus. The limit of consensus is not a line that is clearly marked, but I can make certain what would otherwise be uncertain by saying that a judge who is in any doubts about the support of the consensus should not advance at all. This however leaves open quite a large field for judicial activity. In determining its extent it is, I think, necessary to distinguish between common law and statute law. This is because the requirement of consensus affects differently the two types of law. The public is not interested in the common law as a whole. When it becomes interested in any particular section of it, it calls for a statute; the rest it leaves to judges.[46]

The large question mark over this approach is how judges determine whether there is the consensus which provides the mandate for creativity. Much of the focus of the literature is on the law-making role of the appellate courts, especially the Court of Appeal and the House of Lords. This is understandable since the formal doctrine of precedent operated in this country restrains lower-level judges from digressing into frolics of legal innovation, but every case must start with a trial judge and with the presentation of issues and argument by lawyers at first instance. The impact of the early stages of the great cases should not be ignored. Making decisions involves choice. Nevertheless the overwhelming majority of trials do not involve novel points of law, but are more concerned with the establishment of facts and the application of well-settled principles of law to them. Perhaps more than anything else, it is the narrow background of those from whom the judiciary are selected which has resulted in a cautious approach which is illustrated by the process of 'dissimulation' exposed by Paterson.[47]

Jon Holyoak's contribution[48] on the case law on the duty of care in negligence illustrates the ebb and flow of judicial prescriptions on the outer limits of what may now properly be regarded as the leading tort. However there is no suggestion in this chapter of where the judges find the consensus referred to by Lord Devlin as the basis for judicial creativity. Perhaps the retreats from the advances made in *Anns* v. *London Borough of Merton*[49] and the retreat even from certain aspects of *Donoghue* v. *Stevenson*[50] suggested by *Caparo*[51] are reflections of consensus. But in the sound common law tradition, Holyoak examines

---

46. P. Devlin, *The Judge*, Oxford, Oxford University Press (1979) at 9.
47. A. Paterson, *The Law Lords*, London, Macmillan (1982), at 130.
48. Ch. 2 *infra*.
49. [1978] AC 728.
50. [1932] AC 562.
51. [1990] 2 WLR 358.

what the judges say rather than what motivates them to say it.[52] Ultimately the chapter illustrates the problems of case law development building precedent upon precedent. The final design — if design is not too planned a term to use and if completion of the design can be determined! — displays the influence of many architects using material brought haphazardly to the site by a miscellany of litigants. Nevertheless in the classic tradition of common law commentary, Holyoak is able to discern trends and patterns in the labyrinthine building and clearly enjoys wandering these corridors.

Community institutions

The Council of the European Communities, and in some areas also the Commission, have considerable powers to pass legislation affecting the United Kingdom and perhaps the most sweeping delegated legislative power is that arising under the European Communities Act 1972 in order to implement Community law which is not self-executing, notably directives. Once again there is literature showing that the formal parts of the legislative process within the Community are only a small part of the overall process by which rules come into being.[53]

The Court of Justice of the European Communities, in particular, as the interpreter of Treaty provisions, has developed the law of the European Communities, adopting an overtly integrationist role. Generally this has been welcomed, but there are those who take a more critical view of the matter.[54]

International organizations

The role of international organizations is included for completeness. Their law-creating capacity is limited in the United Kingdom, since international obligations are clearly separated from domestic laws in this country. In the absence of implementation, the international rule cannot be pleaded at the domestic level.[55] Nevertheless, there are occasions when international organizations can pass binding resolutions which have a domestic impact, though these will seldom be in areas which change the

---

52. Contrast Bradney, Ch. 13 *infra*.
53. See, for example, materials cited *supra* n.21.
54. See H. Rasmussen, *On Law and Policy in the European Court of Justice*, Martinus Nijhoff, (1986); and responses to the work: Weiler, 'Review Essay' (1987) 24 CML Rev. 555 and Cappelletti, 'Is the European Court of Justice "Running Wild"?' (1987) 12 EL Rev. 2.
55. I. Brownlie, *Principles of Public International Law*, Oxford, Oxford University Press (3rd edn, 1979), at 45-51.

law of the United Kingdom. More often, they will constrain the action of government.[56]

Law-determining agents

The limited role of parliamentary legitimation of legislation and the constraints on the role of judges in the development of the law produce a situation in which those institutions labelled law-determining agents take on a more significant role in changing the law. Some of the same institutions appear under this heading as under the previous heading. How this occurs can most easily be illustrated in the case of judges. If the decision of an appellate court states a new or modified rule of law applicable to the facts of that case, that is traditionally regarded as the *ratio* of that case and is a proposition of law binding on those courts obliged to follow that decision under the doctrine of precedent. But if it is merely an illustration of what the judges would conclude in another situation than that before the court, then it will not be *ratio*, it will be only persuasive authority, and will not change the law. To argue that such statements do not shape or determine the law in some way is to take too rigid and formal a view of the nature of legal rules. Law-determining agents then are those bodies whose contributions help to shape the law and whose views and writings mould material which may come before a law-creating agency at some stage.

Judges

Judges are important law-determining agents because of their influence. This reflects their institutional significance and gives them a *political* power which invests their pronouncements with worth beyond their inherent reasoning. So Lord Lane's unreasoned pronouncement that the proposals of the Lord Chancellor for the restructuring of the legal profession were 'sinister'[57] carried far greater weight than such a comment by a practising solicitor or barrister, academic or lay person. Such a statement is not, of course, law-determining, but statements on sentencing made by the Lord Chief Justice, though not in any way binding, are determinative of the law and have a direct effect on the lives of those appearing before the Crown Court.[58]

Judges determine the law by applying it to cases before them. They do

---

56. For example, decisions of the Security Council under Article 25 of the United Nations Charter are binding on the members of the United Nations. The United Kingdom, as a permanent member of the Security Council, is, of course, in a position to veto any such resolutions of which it disapproves.
57. Reported in *The Guardian*, 17 February 1989.
58. See, for example, *Bibi*, [1980] 1 WLR 1193.

not often create the rule, but, even when they do not, they give an existing rule new life by their application of it to specific circumstances. Where the rule is legislative in origin and so binding upon them, they sometimes apply the rule with reluctance and call for legislative action to change what is seen by them to be an unsatisfactory rule.[59]

Causes and effects cannot always be readily identified. Jan Grodecki's contribution[60] notes a paradox in the development of certain rules of the conflict of laws. On the one hand, the judges are displaying a less chauvinistic view of foreign law, but on the other seem reluctant to accept the will of the parties expressed in their contract for the choice of forum. Malcolm Ross argues in his contribution[61] that the response of English judges to the influence of Community law has been 'largely unambitious and, more importantly, lacking in *communautaire* spirit'.[62] For him the reference procedure under Article 177 EEC offers an opportunity for clarification that should appeal to the traditions of inventiveness and flexibility that characterize the common law. He regrets the absence of a free movement of legal traditions into the courts of this country.

Reform institutions

Reform institutions can be divided into the permanent and the *ad hoc*. The most important modern reform institutions are the Law Commissions established by the Law Commissions Act 1965. The Law Commissions for Scotland and for England and Wales build on the traditions of the Law Revision Committee established by Lord Sankey in 1934 and its successor the Law Reform Committee established by Lord Simmonds in 1952.[63] The Law Reform Committee was concerned exclusively with civil matters and was joined by the Criminal Law Revision Committee as the equivalent in criminal matters established by the Home Secretary in 1959. The major permanent institutions today are the Law Commissions and the Criminal Law Revision Committee.

The Law Commission for England and Wales[64] consists of a judge seconded from his judicial business to act as chairman together with four

---

59. For example, in *Hanlon v. The Law Society*, [1981] AC 124 and *Chief Adjudication Officer v. Brunt*, [1988] AC 711.
60. Ch. 10, *infra*.
61. Ch. 11, *infra*.
62. At 212 *infra*.
63. See Blair, 'The Law Reform Committee: The First Thirty Years' (1982) 1 Civil JQ 64.
64. See generally J. Farrar, *Law Reform and the Law Commission*, London, Sweet & Maxwell, 1974; and Chorley and Dworkin, 'The Law Commissions Act 1965' (1965) 28 MLR 675. For the background of the idea, see Gardiner and Martin, *Law Reform Now*, London, Gollancz, 1963. For a largely anecdotal and self-indulgent account of the Law Commission by a disillusioned civil servant, see R. Oerton, *A Lament for the Law Commission*, Countrywise Press, 1987.

Law Commissioners. Practice has resulted in two of these being academic appointments and two practitioner appointments. The term of office is five years. The Law Commission has a modest supporting staff of around fifty, which includes research staff and parliamentary counsel. The work of the Law Commission can be divided into four main areas: statute law revision, consolidation, codification, and proposals for reform. The most mundane task is statute law revision, which is the task of clearing the statute book of redundant statutory material. Consolidation is the important task of drawing together existing statutory provisions into a single coherent statute. This seemingly simple task involves the identification of the relevant statutory provisions, the development of a coherent plan for the presentation of the rules in a single statute, and possibly the drafting of new clauses to provide common definitions and to join the various parts into a single whole. A new parliamentary procedure had been adopted to smooth the parliamentary passage of such legislation.[65] In essence this procedure enables corrections and minor improvements to be included without the necessity for the full parliamentary consideration of the legislation. Where more than minor amendments are needed, the Law Commission has adopted a practice of publishing its proposals and indicating the significant new material.[66]

The task of codification involves the reduction of case law and statute into a single coherent text. It is a restatement of the law. Difficulties can arise where the drawing together of the rules of statute and the common law reveal lacunae or a need for amendment of the existing rule. Codifying statutes, like the Animals Act 1971, must pass the normal legislative processes and so there is much greater likelihood that the carefully constructed package produced by the authors of the code will be tinkered with by Parliament.[67] Edward Griew's contribution[68] examines the background to the proposed codification of the criminal law. It describes the code as essentially a restatement of the law with elements of reform, and tackles the distinction between restatement and reform. The chapter modestly argues that enactment of the code might have a modest reforming tendency going beyond the familiar advantages claimed for codification in the Law Commission's report.

This leaves the final task, that of reforming the existing law. The Law Commission has adopted the task of producing working papers upon which wide consultation is sought both within and without government

---

65. Consolidation of Enactments (Procedure) Act 1949.
66. J. Spencer, *Jackson's Machinery of Justice*, Cambridge, Cambridge University Press (1989), at 503.
67. Codification has proved to be an emotive topic among commentators. See Hahlo, 'Here Lies the Common Law' (1967) 30 MLR 241; Diamond, 'Codification of the Law of Contract' (1968) 31 MLR 361; Cretney, 'The Codification of Family Law' (1981) 44 MLR 1; Beldam, 'Prospects for Codification' and Leigh, 'Approaches to Codification', both in I. Dennis (ed.), *Criminal Law and Justice*, London, Sweet & Maxwell, 1987; Wells, 'Restatement or Reform', [1986] Crim. LR 314.
68. *Infra*, Ch. 14.

circles.[69] In the light of responses to the working papers, the Law Commission produces a final proposal for the Lord Chancellor. The Law Commission has enjoyed some success in reforming the law and certainly provides support for those who argue that a coherent approach to changing the law is needed in addition to the haphazard development of the law through judicial decisions, which depends on the existence of litigants with the 'right' case prepared to pursue the matter to appellate level, or through the normal crowded legislative programme of government. It has been suggested that the success rate of the Law Commission has slowed in recent years.[70] This seems to be the result of the Law Commission being the servant of the Lord Chancellor's Department. It appears that Lord Hailsham, as Lord Chancellor, has much less regard for the work of the Law Commission than had his predecessors. It is also undoubtedly true that many important reforms affect the interests of a number of government departments, and interdepartmental sensitivities inhibit progress. The lukewarm response to the Law Commission's criminal code may reflect, in part, its enormous impact on the work of the Home Office.

Judith Masson's contribution[71] surveys the significant contribution of the Law Commission to the development of family law, but is critical of its lack of emphasis on empirical research and its focus on 'black letter' research. She goes on to survey the empirical work carried out in family law in the 1970s and 1980s, though again not uncritically. Like the judges dealing with the case law development of the common law, Masson seems to be hankering for the holy grail of consensus. She concludes: 'Law reform without [empirical] research may produce clearer sets of rules but it will not provide workable, efficient and just reformed law'.[72]

Ad hoc bodies also play an important part in changing the law. The most significant *ad hoc* bodies are Royal Commissions. Perhaps the most important in recent years has been the Royal Commission on Criminal Procedure, whose work led to the enactment of the Police and Criminal Evidence Act 1984 and the Prosecution of Offences Act 1985.[73] The use of bodies like Royal Commissions institutionalizes the processes of consultation that can give legitimacy to major changes of direction in the operation of the law. It allows a degree of insulation

---

69. See North, 'Law Reform: Processes and Problems' (1985) 105 LQR 338.
70. Stephen Cretney, a former Law Commissioner, notes that, of the reports produced between 1965 and 1976, only six out of a total of forty-one reports of the Law Commission remained unimplemented, whereas of the eighteen reports produced between 1977 and 1982, over half remained substantially unimplemented. See Cretney, 'The Politics of Law Reform — A View from the Inside' (1985) 48 MLR 493, at 498-9.
71. *Infra*, Ch. 4.
72. At 71 *infra*.
73. See J. Benyon and C. Bourn, *The Police: Powers, Procedures and Proprieties*, Oxford, Pergamon Press (1986).

from party politics, even in such sensitive areas as policing the community. Spencer comments:

A Royal Commission is the best way of getting a high-level overhaul of a substantial field of law and its administration. But it is slow because the members are busy people who can meet only at intervals; there is no permanent secretariat, and the machinery has to be built up for each inquiry. This is only worth the effort where there is a major problem to deal with, and in the past this sometimes meant that lesser problems were never addressed at all.[74]

In recent years, the government has chosen to take a more interventionist role in reform through the use of carefully delimited commissioned research followed by consultation papers and White Papers setting out its proposals for change. This has occurred with legal aid,[75] civil justice,[76] and the legal profession.[77]

The rest

The remaining agents in Tables 1.1 and 1.2 on pages 2–3 (politicians, lobbyists, solicitors and barristers, academics, individuals and corporations) can be summed up as 'the rest', because their role as law-determining agents is exceedingly small. They undoubtedly have a role, but because they have no institutional status, they lack influence. In almost every case where an individual, organization or corporation has had a significant effect in determining the shape of the law, it is the adoption of their views by an agent with influence which has resulted in the success of their proposals. Agents categorized as 'the rest' are much more likely to be involved in the processes of changing the law through their activities within the headings of influences and pressures.

However, in another sense, what these agents do determines the law in action and therefore collectively and unconsciously they may have a much greater impact on the operation of the law than is often assumed. But it remains a hidden contribution which only emerges when some large-scale socio-legal research project identifies the totality of actions which produce the operation of a complex modern system of legal regulation. This group therefore clearly justifies its inclusion in the category of law-determining agents.

---

74. J. Spencer, *supra* n.66, at 500.
75. See Lord Chancellor's Department, *Legal Aid Efficiency Scrutiny*, June 1986, followed by *Legal Aid in England and Wales: A New Framework*, Cm 118 (1987), noted by Baldwin, 'Legal Aid in England and Wales: A New Framework' (1987) 6 Civil JQ 205.
76. See Civil Justice Review consultation papers and Cm 394 (1988).
77. See Cownie, Ch. 12, *infra*.

Concluding comments

This volume is more about the changing law than about law reform. From the interests of some members of a large law school, a selection of contributions on the theme of change has emerged. Eclectic in coverage and style, they range from the traditional expositions of case law to the newly emerging areas of legal scholarship that challenge us to look at the language of the law more critically.[78] There are tantalising hints at new ideas and approaches to the study of a changing law rather than the topic of law reform or the need for change. The contribution on the City Code[79] suggests that self-regulation by major institutions may develop into a new sort of common law outside the system of state regulation. Like the contribution on evidence[80] it points to the need for greater recognition of the roles of other disciplines, such as economics and psychology in the operation of the law.

This leads to an age-old dichotomy: that between those who believe that the law should follow slowly the 'prevailing climate of the times' and those who believe that the law should create new norms for social behaviour. The British tradition is the former.[81] Judges, like Lord Devlin seeking consensus as the justification judge-made law, prefer to root their choices in responsiveness to current social conditions. Evolution is preferred to revolution.

---

78. See Bradney, Ch. 13, *infra*.
79. *Infra*, Ch. 5.
80. *Infra*, Ch. 6.
81. See, for example, Zander, 'Promoting Change in the Legal System' (1979) 42 MLR 489; and Smith, 'An Academic Lawyer and Law Reform' (1981) 1 *Legal Studies* 119.

2 The rise and fall of negligence

Jon Holyoak

Introduction

The tort of negligence has always seemed to be one of the more disorderly beasts in the legal stable. From its creation in its modern form in 1932, innumerable precedents have been established, showing the outer limits of the tort. For five decades, these precedents tended to point in a consistent direction with the scope of the tort steadily expanding, especially in relation to the key concept of duty of care, the first essential to establish in proving liability. However, recent years have seen a considerable reverse in this trend, with decision after decision restricting the scope of the duty of care and thus of the tort of negligence.

This chapter seeks to examine both the rise and the fall, to consider the policy reasons which may lie behind both phases in the story of the duty of care and thus of negligence, and to establish the current position of the tort.

The rise of negligence

This is a well-charted story which can be described relatively briefly. Claims based on the careless conduct of the defendant had been allowed for well over two centuries,[1] but it was not obvious to most[2] that the various precedents for claiming against negligent defendants had anything in common. Much-needed unity was of course introduced into the subject by the decision in *Donoghue* v. *Stevenson*.[3] A bare majority of the House of Lords clearly accepted the existence of a general principle to govern all cases of negligence[4] and that accordingly it was not

---

1. For example, *Mitchil* v. *Alestree* (1676) 1 Vent 295.
2. Cf. Winfield (1926) 42 LQR 184, 195–9.
3. [1932] AC 562.
4. [1932] AC 562 at 580, 603–4 and 619.

necessary to fit a negligence claim into any pre-existing category of cause of action. Equally, it was directly accepted by Lord MacMillan that the principles of the tort would adapt and develop in accordance with developing social attitudes,[5] and Lord Atkin implicitly accepted this in suggesting that an obvious social wrong such as the poisoning of an innocent drinker by a dead snail, must be accompanied by a legal remedy.[6] At the heart of the new approach lay a clear moral and legal view of responsibility arising from proximity between the parties with the moral obligation naturally arising between neighbours now being translated into a legal one.

The *Donoghue* principle gained instant widespread and soon universal acceptance, but the true significance of the simple yet logical approach adopted in the case took longer to become clear. It was not until relatively recent times, in *Dorset Yacht Co. Ltd* v. *Home Office*,[7] that the primacy of the *Donoghue* formula was reasserted; it was to be regarded as a statement of principle which ought normally to be applied and as such ought to be applicable irrespective of past precedent. The flexibility of the duty of care was also enhanced by the *Dorset Yacht* decision, with an acceptance by the House of Lords that considerations of public policy were always relevant in considering the duty question and, in the instant case, such factors militated in favour of the imposition of a duty. Thus, from 1970 onwards we can see that principle and policy, rather than precedent, were to be the guiding elements in litigation concerning duty of care.

From here it was but a short step to the logical development represented by the decision of the House of Lords in *Anns* v. *London Borough of Merton*.[8] *Donoghue* had created the general approach to duty of care, based on neighbourhood or proximity. *Dorset Yacht* had created a presumption that the *Donoghue* approach should be the one adopted. In *Anns*, Lord Wilberforce was able to fuse these two aspects together, so that in any case where there was sufficient proximity or neighbourhood between the parties such that the defendant ought to have had the plaintiff in mind, there would be a legal presumption in favour of a duty of care. Clearly, in most accidents there would be often literally close proximity between the parties and thus in most cases argument about duty would cease, given the presumption. Equally however, Lord Wilberforce made clear that the presumption in favour of a duty could be rebutted, if there were countervailing policy or other considerations. Rapidly, the approach outlined by Lord Wilberforce in *Anns* came to be adopted in preference to Lord Atkin's much-quoted comments in *Donoghue*.

---

5. [1932] AC 562 at 619.
6. [1932] AC 562 at 588.
7. [1970] AC 1004. See especially at 1026–7, per Lord Reid.
8. [1978] AC 728.

Why should *Anns* have had such impact? The simplicity of the approach, particularly the ease of operating the pro-duty presumption, must have been a relevant factor. So too must the very simple logic at the heart of the fusing of the *Donoghue* and *Dorset Yacht* approaches, namely that a presumption in favour of using the *Donoghue* proximity-based approach neatly leads to a presumption in favour of a duty whenever sufficient proximity is to be found. Finally, it may be suggested that the *Anns* approach had the nebulous concept of 'fairness' on its side. Given that negligence is composed of the elements of duty, breach and consequent damage, it should perhaps be that the courts ought to be reluctant to eliminate plaintiffs at the first legal hurdle, duty of care, when this has the effect of preventing any discussion at the breach stage of whether or not there was any actual negligence.

Overall, the progression from *Donoghue* to *Anns* represented a continuous and internally cogent strand of legal development, and few clouds appeared to be on the horizon. Ironically, the ease and logic of the expansion of duty of care was, however, to prove its undoing, as it expanded into new areas subsequent to the *Anns* decision.

Negligence after Anns

The simple approach laid down by Lord Wilberforce remorselessly swept all before it. The old restrictive approach to nervous shock was an early casualty[9] but of far greater significance was the parallel decision to open the way to easier claims in negligence in respect of pure economic loss. Previously courts had always been keen to restrict such liability, sometimes through holding that no duty was owed in respect of it,[10] and sometimes arguing on the basis of the unforeseeability of such losses.[11] However, this uncertainty and equivocation appeared to be removed when the House of Lords directly applied the *Anns* test to the economic loss issue in *Junior Books* v. *Veitchi*.[12]

It was accepted that, prima facie, a duty of care should still be capable of arising even though the loss in question was purely economic in character. However, note was also taken of the possible hazards of overgenerous compensation for economic loss, so use was made of Lord Wilberforce's invitation, in *Anns*, to limit the scope of the duty by restricting the duty to persons in an especially close relationship of proximity, far closer than that needed in an ordinary claim. The fact that the parties in *Junior Books* (the owner of a new building and his nominated subcontractor) were in a relationship almost akin to one of contract was

---

9. *McLoughlin* v. *O'Brien*, [1983] 1 AC 410.
10. Cf. *Weller & Co.* v. *Foot & Mouth Disease Research Institute*, [1966] 1 QB 569.
11. Cf. *Caltex Oil (Australia) Pty Ltd* v. *Dredge Willemstad* (1976) 136 CLR 529.
12. [1983] 1 AC 520.

regarded as significant, as was the fact of their extensive prior dealings.

Junior Books may have seemed at the time to be an exciting shift in the role of negligence, pushing it into protection of expectation interest, hitherto the sole province of the law of contract. It has become clearer subsequently, not least from the fact that no successful claim based on the *Junior Books* decision has yet been reported, that the case is of little practical impact. That said, the principle that duties of care are owed in respect of pure economic loss, though under fire, just remains, if only in relation to economic loss caused by careless statements. This area may properly be regarded as the high-water mark in the expansion of negligence through the generous approach to duty issues.

In another way, too, litigation after *Anns* brought the tort of negligence into closer contact with the world of contractual relations. The old 'red herring' that the mere presence of a contract was enough to deny the parties any tortious remedy, as expressed most recently in *Bagot* v. *Stevens Scanlan & Co.*,[13] and the even older and 'redder herring' that the absence of a contract could prevent third parties suing in tort,[14] clearly could not survive the post-*Anns* presumption of a duty of care, particularly when in *Anns* itself no reference had been made to the presence of a contract being a factor which may rebut that presumption. Quickly, and with direct adoption of the *Anns* formula, both anomalies of the past were rectified[15] and the tort of negligence could exist alongside contractual relationships, subject, of course, to the operation of any valid exclusion clauses.

If the frame is frozen in 1983 it is possible to view the tort of negligence and its approach to the duty question as being in a healthy position. Use of a clear concept — proximity — meant that imposition of a duty of care occurred clearly in most cases. The policy problems of compensation for economic loss had led to a more restrictive approach being taken there, and there was always the overriding policy discretion for the exceptionally difficult case. Its use is well-illustrated by reference to *Ashton* v. *Turner*;[16] normally an injured car passenger would expect to be owed a duty by the car driver but, normally, the two parties are not engaged in a high-speed getaway from a burglary conceived and executed while extremely drunk. To uphold a duty in such a case would be repugnant to ordinary people, and to their insurers; no duty was found to exist in such circumstances.

However, this surface appearance of health in the condition of the tort of negligence was misleading. The tort was fully extended over a wide range of situations. Just as an army is best attacked when its lines of supply are fully extended, so likewise did negligence come under fire in subsequent years.

---

13. [1966] 1 QB 197.
14. *Bottomley* v. *Bannister*, [1932] 1 KB 458.
15. *Batty* v. *Metropolitan Realisations*, [1978] QB 554; *Ross* v. *Cannters* [1980] Ch. 297.
16. [1981] 1 QB 137.

The retreat from Anns

Why was it necessary?

It is salutary to pause now that, as we shall see, the retreat from *Anns* has developed into a consistent approach, and to ask why the broad sweep of negligence liability through the generous imposition of duties of care should so quickly have come under attack. First, it seems that the role of the duty question had altered very substantially. After *Anns*, the presumption was in favour of the presence of a duty and most claims rushed through this stage on to the meatier issues of breach and damage, but this was far removed from the view of the original authors of the duty concept, whose intention was to use the duty of care as a device to restrict rather than to encourage the imposition of a duty of care. Lord Atkin was unequivocal on the point when he said that 'acts or omissions which any moral code would censure cannot in a practical world be treated so as to give a right to every person inured by them to demand relief. In this way rules of law arise which limit the range of complainants and the extent of their remedy.'[17] He then went on to offer the classic formulation restricting the duty of care to neighbours, that is, those in proximity. At the very least, this was designed to restrict the numbers of possible plaintiffs, and thus of actions, whereas after *Anns* only the most unlucky complainants would find that no duty of care was owed to them.

Second, it is suggested that the *Anns* formulation, although it may be rightly praised for its simple approach, may also be equally criticized for its oversimplicity. Comment has already been made on the wide range of situations which the tort could cover, but it must be questionable whether the same principle is appropriate for use in simple running-down cases or day-to-day factory accidents as in complex disputes about defective office blocks or inaccurate investment advice.

This point may be developed into a somewhat distinct variant with reference to the earlier remarks about the arrival of negligence after *Anns* into areas that were formerly the preserve of contract. There would inevitably be a clash between the broad principles of negligence liability and the often closely argued and carefully formulated precise words of the contractual agreement. This tension would inevitably be exacerbated by another simple fact, namely the unexpected nature of tort's intrusion into the contractual domain. It is true to say that, subject only to the Unfair Contract Terms Act 1977, parties to a contract are always able to exclude or control any tortious liabilities, but this will not happen if the parties have no inkling of the possible creation of a new tortious duty when they are establishing the basis of their contractual relationship. Likewise the financial consequences of a contract and

---

17. *Donoghue* v. *Stevenson*, [1932] AC 562 at 580.

relevant insurance arrangements may need to be altered if different and additional legal liabilities are unexpectedly added. Naturally, the further and faster the tort of negligence was expanding, the more uncertainty was created and the more frequent and significant disruption to pre-existing contractual arrangements was likely to occur.

So there were good reasons for the attack on the widest notions of duty of care. So also there were ample opportunities for such an attack to be made. Since negligence was a unique blend of legal rules and policy, either could be altered so as to restrict the ambit of the tort. In fact the attack took place on both fronts.

Restricting duty as a matter of law

There are four distinct methods whereby, as a matter of law, no duty of care may be found, notwithstanding the presence of proximity between the parties. These 'no-duty' situations arise, first, in cases of long-standing immunities and exceptions where negligence has no role to play. Second, there are restrictions placed on the role to be played by the proximity test. Third, and most important, the definition of proximity can be varied so as to make it harder to find a duty of care. Fourth, the presence of a contract may affect the tortious duty.

Long-standing immunities and exceptions need not be covered at length, since they have not changed at all during the recent convulsions in the tort of negligence. An extensive immunity still attaches to various aspects of the legal process[18] and the lack of any duty in relation to percolating underground waters has recently been confirmed.[19]

Of greater importance are the cases where the proximity test cannot be used due to precedent. At one stage it might have been thought that any such restrictive approach might not survive the simple logic of *Anns*. However, any such argument was stopped by the decision of the House of Lords in *Leigh and Sillavan* v. *Aliakmon Shipping Co. Ltd.*[20] This litigation was between the buyers of goods that were being shipped from Korea to England and the shipping line carrying the goods. Bad stowage of the goods during the voyage caused them to be damaged. Due to a variation of the normal international carriage contract procedures which had occurred, the buyers were unable to sue in contract and instead sought to claim for the damage and consequent economic loss suffered as a result of being obliged to accept the defective cargo. Crucially, at the time of the damage, property in the goods had not passed to the buyer.

Lord Brandon of Oakbrook considered whether the *Anns* principle was

---

18. See *Saif Ali* v. *Sydney Mitchell & Co.*, [1980] AC 198; *Sirros* v. *Moore*, [1975] QB 118.
19. *Stephens* v. *Anglia Water Authority*, [1987] 1 WLR 1381.
20. [1986] AC 785.

applicable. Clearly the owner of a ship and the consignee of goods on board are in a relationship of proximity, but Lord Brandon explained that the *Anns* approach was intended for use in situations, as in the case itself, which were completely novel and not analogous to any previous case where the duty issue was considered. On the facts of the *Aliakmon*, *Anns* was inappropriate since there was a clear precedent denying the existence of a duty of care towards a person whose interests are affected by damage to a chattel in relation to which they have contractual rights, but not ownership rights. Such a rule was laid down in *Elliot Steam Tug Co.* v. *The Shipping Controller*[21] and had recently been confirmed in *Candlewood Navigation Co. Ltd* v. *Mitsui OSK Lines*.[22]

An obvious comment to make about this decision is that it was not the most sensible way of limiting the scope of negligence to allow the far-reaching *Anns* test to continue to be used in novel cases, thus ensuring that the very uncertainty which Lord Brandon appeared to wish to eliminate could easily recur. It may be presumed that further restrictions imposed subsequently on duty reflect a realization of this. It is also the case that the number of past precedents likely to prevent the use of the tort of negligence appears, for the most part, small. Apart from the immunities already outlined, it also appears to be the case that no duty in negligence will arise if there is no liability for a similar but intentional act; indeed this lies at the root of the cases on percolating underground waters.[23] Users of rights of way also seem unable to use negligence actions.[24]

Two far more significant exceptions also exist, however, and their existence has been confirmed by recent authority. First, it is clear at present that duty, and thus liability, can only arise in cases where defective property damages something other than itself. If, however, the defective property harms itself only, by becoming damaged without outside interference, this now clearly falls outside the mainstream of negligence after several recent decisions, notably *Aswan Engineering Establishment Co.* v. *Lupdine Ltd*,[25] and the House of Lords case of *D&F Estates Ltd* v. *Church Commissioners for England*.[26] It does seem that any plaintiff in this position may still be able to characterize his losses as purely economic in character and try his luck with a *Junior Books* claim, in the narrow range of situations where this may still be possible. It is ironic that this recent burst of case law has confirmed the law's approach on this matter when in fact there was nothing more than

---

21. [1922] 1 KB 127.
22. [1986] AC 1.
23. *Langbrook Properties Ltd* v. *Surrey County Council*, [1970] 1 WLR 161 esp. at 178; cf. *Ben Stansfield* v. *Carlisle City Council* (1982) 265 EG 475, on which see Murdoch (1983) 99 LQR 178.
24. *Gautret* v. *Egerton*, (1867) LR 2 CP 371; *Holden* v. *White*, [1982] QB 679.
25. [1987] 1 WLR 1.
26. [1988] 3 WLR 368.

a general assumption, rather than clear precedent, in favour of this view in the past,[27] and when other common law jurisdictions have been happy to allow such claims.[28] It is also clear that the exception to this rule created by *D&F* in the case of 'complex structures' is an area where more litigation will be necessary to establish the precise scope of the exception.

The other traditional 'no-duty' situation that has been given added force in recent years is the rule that mere nonfeasance — an omission to act, as opposed to a positive but negligent act — does not give rise to a duty of care. Again, authority in this jurisdiction has been difficult to find though the view is generally accepted,[29] and this misfeasance/nonfeasance dichotomy lies at the heart of the recent 'no-duty' decisions in *Smith* v. *Littlewoods Organization Ltd*[30] and *Curran* v. *Northern Ireland Co-ownership Association Ltd*.[31]

It is a clear indication of contemporary trends in the tort of negligence that these assumptions of the past, far from being questioned, are now readily turned into high-level judicial authority. It is now clear that we are left with a substantial and clear set of exceptions where the duty test, whatever it may be, cannot be applied.

The alternative approach to all this, and one also used by the courts in recent years, is to redefine the content of the duty test, so as to make findings that a duty of care exists less frequent. This trend first became clear in the *Curran* case, which concerned the liability of a public authority for building inspection. Far from accepting and extending the *Anns* principle, Lord Bridge of Harwich launched an attack on *Anns*. He pointed to judicial criticism of the case, to academic questioning of its basis and to the refusal of the High Court of Australia to accept its approach.[32] He then, ominously, declined to suggest that it should be overruled, but merely not in any way extended. He proceeded to limit the role of *Anns* with reference to the particular statutory powers in question.[33]

These threats came to fruition in what is a keynote case in the retreat from *Anns*, that is, the decision of the Privy Council in *Yuen Kun Yeu* v. *Attorney-General of Hong Kong*.[34] The plaintiffs fell victim to a fraud perpetrated by the promoters of a deposit-taking company who took that description literally and fled with the proceeds. The plaintiffs

---

27. C. Miller and Lovell, *Product Liability* p.328.
28. B. Feldthusen, *Economic Negligence: the Recovery of Pure Economic Loss*, Carswell, (1984) p.185.
29. For example, W. Rogers (ed.) *Winfield & Jolowicz on Tort*, Sweet & Maxwell (12th edn, 1984) p.80.
30. [1987] AC 241.
31. [1987] AC 718. See Smith & Burns (1983) 46 MLR 147; Hepple [1987] All ER Rev. 284–5.
32. *Sutherland Shire Council* v. *Heyman*, [1985] 60 ALR 1.
33. See below.
34. [1988] AC 175.

turned to the Hong Kong government, whose officials had statutory powers to investigate suspect companies and to revoke their registration, and claimed that the government's negligence had caused them substantial loss. Giving the judgment of the Judicial Committee, Lord Keith of Kinkel commented on the increasingly adverse reaction that the *Anns* duty test was receiving and stated that 'the two stage test formulated by Lord Wilberforce for determining the existence of a duty of care in negligence had been elevated to a degree of importance greater than its merits, and greater perhaps than its author intended.'[35]

However, if the *Anns* test had been misinterpreted, had it also been misconceived? Lord Keith gave an affirmative answer: 'foreseeability does not of itself, automatically, lead to a duty of care.'[36] Further, said Lord Keith, foreseeability of harm was a necessary ingredient of the duty relationship, but not an exclusive one. A stricter test was needed, and Lord Keith found it by direct reference to *Donoghue* v. *Stevenson*[37] itself and the assertion by Lord Atkin[38] that neighbours are people 'closely and directly' affected by one's act and that the duty of care is owed to neighbours. So, from this point onwards a duty of care would not depend merely on foreseeability but would only arise when, within that, the parties were in a suitably close and direct relationship of proximity. In *Yuen* itself it was clear that no such relationship accepted, in view of the wide range of citizens to whom the relevant government officials might owe a duty in the execution of their tasks, and the basic fact that it was after all the fraudulent promoters, not the Hong Kong government who had made off with the plaintiff's deposits. Likewise, application of the *Yuen* test in subsequent cases has meant that solicitors are not in a sufficiently close and direct relationship towards third parties when advising their clients that they owe a duty to a potential beneficiary under clients' wills whose inheritances are reduced by allegedly negligent advice to clients.[39]

The new 'close and direct' formula appears to have two distinct effects. The 'close' element is designed simply to reduce the number of potential plaintiffs, and it has this effect particularly in cases such as *Yuen* which are actions against regulatory or supervisory bodies with a wide range of powers and duties designed to be exercised in favour of a wide range of parties. The 'direct' element has a distinct, if slightly overlapping role. It is designed to highlight the true defendant, the person actually responsible for the plaintiff's losses (in *Yuen* the fraudulent promoters), rather than anyone less obviously and only indirectly to blame. The overlap of course arises in so far as the

---

35. Ibid. at 191.
36. Ibid.
37. [1932] AC 562.
38. Ibid. at 580, 581.
39. *Clarke* v. *Bruce Lance & Co.* [1988] 1 WLR 881.

indirectly responsible party may well, as in *Yuen*, be a regulatory or supervisory public body.

After *Yuen*, the test in duty of care cases remains one of proximity, albeit a more restricted one. By no means all the cases in the retreat from *Anns* can escape criticism of their reasoning, but *Yuen* at least has the support of negligence's founding fathers in *Donoghue*. Even so, Lord Keith's judgment does not have the full courage of its convictions since the conclusion reached is that the *Anns* test 'is not to be regarded as in all the circumstances a suitable guide to the existence of a duty of care';[40] this would seem to leave open the resurrection of the *Anns* test in an unspecified future situation, but it is the *Yuen* test which is now normally used in judgments.

The fourth and final legal restriction on duty is also the most complex. The question is a simple one — can a tortious duty of care exist alongside a contractual one between the same parties? The answer is less simple. It seemed that the courts were moving happily towards an acceptance of concurrent liability in tort and contract in such cases as *Esso Petroleum Co. Ltd* v. *Mardon*[41] and *Midland Bank* v. *Hett, Stubbs and Kemp*,[42] but the picture has been clouded by dicta of Lord Scarman in *Tai Hing Cotton Mill Ltd* v. *Lui Chong Hing Bank Ltd*.[43] This case was one in which a spectacular fraud was perpetrated by an accounts clerk employed by a client of the bank. It was held as a matter of banking contract law that the customer owed only the most minimal duties to their bank and would not be liable for the substantial losses. It was then argued that the customer owed a tortious duty of care to the bank, but this was rejected by Lord Scarman in clear terms: 'Their Lordships do not believe that there is anything to the advantage of the law's development in searching for a liability in tort where the parties are in a contractual relationship. This is particularly so in a commercial relationship.' He went on to say that it was 'correct in principle and necessary for the avoidance of confusion in the law to adhere to the contractual analysis on principle because it is a relationship in which the parties have, subject to a few exceptions, the right to determine their obligations to each other, and for the avoidance of confusion because difference consequences do follow according to whether liability arises from contract or tort, e.g. in the limitation of action'.

The impact of these trenchant remarks has been variable. They were easy to criticize as being contrary to the developing trend of the growing interaction of tort and contract[44] and as being *per incuriam* through completely ignoring cases such as *Esso Petroleum* and *Midland Bank*.

---

40. [1988] AC 175 at 194.
41. [1976] QB 801.
42. [1979] Ch. 384.
43. [1986] AC 80.
44. Holyoak 'Tort and Contract after *Junior Books*', (1983) 99 LQR 591.

The courts at times have completely ignored the decision[45] and in other cases circumvented it, for example by regarding it as a rule of construction, not one of law.[46] However, there seems to be a gradual increase in the use of the *Tai Hing* and the mere presence or the actual contents of the contract have been cited to justify a 'no-duty' finding in several recent cases. These include *Banque Financière de la Cité SA* v. *Westgate Insurance Co. Ltd*[47] and *National Bank of Greece* v. *Pinios*.[48] In *Banque Financière*, *Tai Hing* was regarded as a general, though not necessarily universal rule; however, there were good reasons for a 'no-duty' finding too — the complaint was of an omission, not an act, and policy considerations also pointed in the same direction. In the *National Bank* case, Lloyd LJ also regarded *Tai Hing* as the normal rule, unless the tortious act was in a different field from that subject to the contractual agreement.

Another important case which relies on *Tai Hing* is *Greater Nottingham Co-operative Society Ltd* v. *Cementation Piling and Foundations Ltd and others*.[49] Here the defendants were subcontractors carrying out piling who negligently damaged an adjacent property, thus adding to the cost and expense of the work on the plaintiff's property and causing them economic loss. To complicate matters further, the defendants also had a collateral contract with the plaintiff under which they incurred various obligations concerning design and materials but not the performance of the work. It was held by the Court of Appeal that this contractual relationship prevented the use of a tortious duty of care. This was not, however, on the basis of a blanket rule to this effect, but rather because the silence in the contractual relationship acted so as to negate the specially close relationship of proximity and reliance needed to found a post-*Junior Books* action for pure economic loss; the whole case turns on this aspect.

Faced with this range of different approaches, it is necessary to attempt to assess the true position of *Tai Hing* today. It is suggested that the case has a restricted application. It should be remembered that the level of contractual duty owed by customer to banker is very low, far lower than the ordinary level of care expected by the tort of negligence — this was why the banks were seeking to use a tort action. This, however, is very different from the routine contractual situation where the parties are often seeking to establish a definite obligation (e.g. to arrive in London by 4 p.m.), rather than a mere duty to take reasonable care (i.e. by driving safely on the way to London). In the latter case, it

---

45. Cf. *Thake* v. *Maurice*, [1986] QB 844.
46. Per Hobhouse J in *Forsikringsaktieselskapet Vesta* v. *Butcher* [1986] 2 All ER 488 at 510–1.
47. [1989] 2 All ER 952.
48. [1989] 3 WLR 185. See also *Bank of Nova Scotia* v. *Hellenic Mutual War Risks Association (Bermuda) Ltd* [1989] 3 All ER 628.
49. [1989] QB 71.

is easy to see that the greater duty in contract must logically incorporate the lesser duty in tort and indeed the presence of a tortious duty helps to fulfil the contractual obligation. Thus in most cases the contract and tort actions should coexist; this appears to be behind the comments of Lloyd LJ noted in the *National Bank of Greece* case above. However, in the rarer situation where the contractual duty is lower than the tortious standard of care, it is concomitantly difficult to see how the greater can logically be included within the lesser. The parties may well be taken as having excluded tort by their formulation of a contract with a low standard of care, especially where there is a background of long-standing trade practice, as in the *Tai Hing* itself. This reasoning also seems compatible with the approach in the *Banque Financière* case which, like *Tai Hing* and the *National Bank of Greece* cases, is rooted in the commercial/financial sector, to which, it will be recalled, Lord Scarman's observations were particularly directed. It is therefore anticipated that *Tai Hing* will have a role to play where closely negotiated agreements or well-established custom mean that the contract will, implicitly, exclude a tortious duty, but that in many other cases, the two forms of action will continue to coexist.

In conclusion to this section, it may in summary be suggested that rules of law have restricted the concept of the duty of care in various ways. The *Yuen* decision is the most important way in which the wings of duty have been clipped, redefining proximity back to what it was fifty or more years ago. Not content with this, the courts have sought to add to or develop the instances where no duty arises, with the *Tai Hing* and subsequent cases seeking to add another major exception to the list in the form of parallel contractual obligations leading to a 'no-duty' conclusion in at least some tort cases.

As a whole these decisions clearly succeed in the aim of restricting the use of the tort of negligence. Whether, however, the piecemeal attack on the tort along several different routes was the most sensible method of proceeding is less clear; simplicity is not now a feature of the duty issue. The actual decisions are also very easy to criticize for their frequent failure to work through all the consequences of such a change; both *Tai Hing* and *Yuen*, among others, can be criticized on this ground. It is also ironic that the restrictions on duty again have created uncertainty, and even if there are no unexpectedly surprised defendants accompanying the retreat from *Anns*, there must at the very least be many wasted insurance premiums.

Restricting the duty as a matter of policy

As has been seen with reference to *Ashton* v. *Turner*,[50] policy questions

---

50. [1981] 1 QB 137. n.16, *supra*.

have always been capable of limiting or obviating the duty of care. However, the role of policy has been greatly enhanced following the decision of the House of Lords in *Peabody Donation Fund (Governors of) v. Sir Lindsay Parkinson & Co. Ltd*,[51] perhaps the decision most clearly representing the turn of the tide of successful negligence actions.

In *Peabody*, developers employed architects to draw up plans for a housing development incorporating a flexible drainage system, due to difficult local soil conditions. Local authority approval of these plans was granted. Later the architects changed the plans to ordinary drainage; the local authority discovered this, but did nothing. The drains were unsuccessful and had to be replaced at vast cost. The plaintiffs sued, *inter alia*, the local authority for failing to use their powers to enforce compliance with the original plan. The House of Lords held that no duty was owed by the local authority. Lord Keith of Kinkel stated that 'in determining whether or not a duty of care of a particular scope was incumbent upon a defendant it is material to take into consideration whether it is just and reasonable so to do'.[52] In applying this discretion, it was noted that the local authority's duty of care is confined within its own narrow statutory context of the health and safety of occupiers, and did not extend to protect the wallets of developers. On the other hand, the developers had far broader responsibilities over the whole building operation. It was with the developers and their professional advisers that responsibility clearly lay.

Within this enhanced policy discretion, several themes common to several cases have emerged which, it is hoped, will give structure to future consideration of policy. In *Curran* v. *Northern Ireland Co-ownership Association Ltd*,[53] the *Peabody* test was applied and particular emphasis was given to the statutory context in which the respondents were operating. Their powers of inspection were for financial control purposes in the context of improvement grants; therefore they owed no duty in respect of the quality of the building work. The purpose of the legislation was also important in denying the existence of a duty owed by local authorities to commercial developers in *Investors in Industry Ltd* v. *South Bedfordshire District Council*.[54]

A second emergent theme is that there will be a 'no-duty' finding where the imposition of a duty would have adverse consequences, when negligence would create rather than solve problems. A good example is *Hill* v. *Chief Constable of West Yorkshire*,[55] where the issue was whether the police owed a duty towards future victims and their relatives

---

51. [1985] AC 210.
52. Ibid. at 241.
53. [1987] AC 718.
54. [1986] QB 1034 esp. at 1062. See also *Caparo* v. *Dickman, The Times* 12 February 1990.
55. [1989] AC 53.

when investigating, unsuccessfully, previous crimes. Again Lord Keith spoke on the policy question. He conceded that imposition of duties was often in the public interest, but in such cases as this, 'the imposition of liability may lead to the exercise of a function being carried on in a detrimentally defensive frame of mind . . . the result would be a significant diversion of police manpower and attention from their most important function, that of the suppression of crime.'[56] This issue was also addressed in *Rowling* v. *Takaro Properties*,[57] an action alleging negligence by a New Zealand government minister in dealing with the finances of a resort development. Lord Keith gave the judgment of the Judicial Committee and denied the existence of a duty on various policy grounds. In particular, he referred to the danger of overkill, with the result that defendants will become ultra-cautious in their work with equally adverse consequences to the interest of their clients as a whole. Lord Keith claimed that there were reasons for believing that *Anns* itself had had this effect on local building inspectors who responded to the threat of liability by unnecessarily increasing foundation depths, imposing a heavy financial burden on the community. (Lord Keith failed to reveal the source of this belief.)

A third theme is that the courts will be reluctant to permit a duty of care to be created when there are other appropriate remedies. In *Rowling*, the existence of a possible judicial review of the minister's action was mentioned. In *Jones* v. *Department of Employment*,[58] a claim of negligence by a claimant against the DSS adjudication officer was rejected on the grounds that both judicial review and a full system of statutory appeals were available to rectify any errors. Similarly, in *Calveley* v. *Chief Constable of the Merseyside Police*,[59] an action by police officers claiming negligent conduct of an internal police investigation was rejected, with reference to statutory appellate rights and the possibility of a judicial review.[60]

A fourth theme emerging from *Rowling* is perhaps more dubious. Lord Keith[61] referred to the notion that it is rare for government ministers to be negligent, as opposed to merely mistaken, in their interpretation of legislation, and that the supposed rarity of a breach of duty should be relevant in deciding whether a duty should be imposed in the first. This seems something of a *non sequitur*, and a cynic might suggest that the judges are becoming more executive-minded than the executive itself.

---

56. Ibid. at 63.
57. [1988] AC 473.
58. [1989] QB 1.
59. [1989] QB 136.
60. In *Mills* v. *Winchester Diocesan Board of Finance*, [1989] 2 All ER 317, it was held that the existence of a statutory right of appeal in respect of erroneous advice given by the Charity Commissioners was a key element in denying the availability of a negligence action.
61. [1988] AC 473 at 502.

These themes clearly emerge from recent decisions of high authority. However, it is suggested that there is another, deeper, strand running through these and other cases. It is becoming clear that what lies at the heart of many of these 'no-duty' cases is a decision by the courts to pin down more precisely where true responsibility for the events complained of really lies. At its simplest, it can be pointed out that it was the murderer, not the police, who killed the plaintiff's daughter in *Hill* or that it was the builders, not the Northern Ireland Housing Executive, who negligently rebuilt the plaintiff's property in *Curran*. This assertion of true responsibility of course also lies at the heart of the curtailment of indirect duties of care in *Yuen*,[62] and also in the rejection of a duty in most third-party situations, as decided in *Smith* v. *Littlewoods Organization Ltd*.[63]

However, it is suggested that this quest for true responsibility is also at the heart of cases where the proximity between the two parties arises only in a specific context, such as a contract *inter se*, or other joint activity. In these cases, the courts have also shown a willingness to confine any tortious duty to within that specific context. An early example of this is the *Majfrid*.[64] The plaintiffs left their two barges moored at the second defendants' wharf. Later, the first defendants arrived with their ship and unlawfully moved the barges, so as to berth their own vessel, onto ground unsuitable at low water. This was discovered but ignored by the second defendants. It was held that no liability arose; in the context of their activities, the wharfingers' sole obligation was to ensure the safe initial berthing of vessels and there was no continuing duty. A more recent and perhaps clearer example is *Argy Trading Development Co. Ltd* v. *Lapid Developments Ltd*,[65] where a lease of warehouses was granted by the defendants to the plaintiffs. The lease obliged the plaintiffs to insure against fire but in fact the defendants continued to do this, asking the plaintiffs for a contribution. In due course the defendants ceased to insure without notifying the plaintiffs who suffered loss when subsequently the inevitable fire broke out. Croom-Johnson J found that the parties were in a suitably close relationship for a negligent misstatement claim but went on to limit the duty to one to give accurate information at the time of the contract. In the context of this action, both parties had overlapping responsibilities; 'after all, a reasonable man checks his insurances from time to time, at least annually', opined the judge. In other words, the plaintiffs' own responsibility to look after their own affairs overwhelmed any such obligation on the part of the defendants.

A specific example of contractual rights affecting the duty question

---

62. See text following n.34.
63. [1987] AC 241.
64. [1942] P. 45, upheld [1942] P. 145.
65. [1977] 1 WLR 444.

arose from *Southern Water Authority* v. *Carey*.⁶⁶ Main contractors were liable for any defects in the plaintiff's new sewage works, and subcontractors excluded by the contract from liability. Subsequently the plaintiffs endeavoured to sue some of the subcontractors in negligence, but this claim was rejected on the basis that the duty of care on the part of the subcontractors was restricted by the context of the various contractual clauses (though not contractually binding on them). The contractual setting, though not overriding, was highly relevant in establishing the respective responsibilities of the parties and thus the scope of the duty intended, and likewise in delineating the area of risk accepted (and insured against) by the plaintiff. A similar decision, allowing a subcontractor to shelter behind an exclusion clause to which he was not privy, was reached by the Court of Appeal in *Norwich City Council* v. *Harvey*.⁶⁷

This theme of proper responsibility has been further echoed in two recent cases, showing how it is emerging as a dominant theme in negligence litigation. In *Van Oppen* v. *Clerk to the Bedford Charity Trustees*,⁶⁸ the plaintiff was a schoolboy injured while playing rugby. He was not insured, and claimed that the school had been negligent in not advising him to obtain appropriate insurance. The claim was unsuccessful, and Boreham J referred to insurance as a matter over which the school had no effective control; their responsibilities existed, but in other, well-defined areas, and the ultimate discretion regarding insurance lay with the parents, rather than with the school. The whole relationship between school, pupil and parent was examined and it was concluded that the school had never assumed any legal responsibility over the insurance of pupils. Similarly, 'responsibility' lies at the heart of *Minories Finance Ltd* v. *Arthur Young (a firm)*.⁶⁹ Here the question was whether the Bank of England owed a duty in its supervisory role to the auditors of another bank which had become insolvent and had exposed the auditors to the risk of legal action. No such responsibilities were found to affect the Bank of England and the claim against them was struck out.

These assertions of individual responsibility — it is for the Van Oppen family to insure or for the Currans to employ their own surveyor — and their accompanying denials of, in many cases, public authority liability represent a consistent strand in many cases. They also happen to accord with the dominant domestic political ethos of the 1980s and may be seen as the legal equivalent of the political rejection of the more paternalist values of the previous decade, suggesting that the policy base of the law of negligence will always mean that its role will fluctuate in accordance

---

66. [1985] 1 All ER 1077.
67. [1989] 1 All ER 1180.
68. [1989] 1 All ER 273, confirmed by the Court of Appeal (1989) 139 NLJ 900.
69. [1989] 2 All ER 105. See also *Reid* v. *Rush & Tompkins Group* [1989] 3 All ER 228.

with the dominant mood, as Lord Macmillan suggested it would in *Donoghue* itself.

Negligence today

In assessing the place of negligence today, after all these dramatic changes in recent years, two questions arise. First, has negligence found a coherent posture to adopt on the all-important duty of care question? Second, are further changes in prospect in future years? However, it is first necessary to consider whether the courts have abandoned attempts to formulate an overall approach to duty cases.

A retreat from Donoghue?

The first problem in considering whether a coherent approach to the duty of care issue has emerged is the recent decision of the House of Lords in *Caparo Industries PLC* v. *Dickman*,[70] a case concerning the potential liability of an auditor of a company to present and future shareholders. The Law Lords went out of their way to emphasize that coherence was impossible to achieve. Cases since *Anns* had 'emphasized the inability of any single general principle to provide a practical test which could be applied to every situation'.[71] As we have seen, it was indicated that the key elements in duty were not just foreseeability alone but also proximity and fairness. These latter concepts, in the view of Lord Bridge, were inherently imprecise and were merely 'convenient labels to attach to the features of different specific situations which, on a detailed examination of all the circumstances, the law recognized pragmatically as giving rise to a duty of care'. In view of this, he felt, the law had now moved away from consideration of general principles common to all negligence cases and now 'attached greater significance to the more traditional categorization of distinct and recognizable situations as guides to the existence, the scope and the limits of the varied duties of care which the law imposed'.

This speech indicates, at the very least, the burial of the broad and flexible approach to duty of care stemming from *Anns*, though, as will be argued shortly, echoes of *Anns* remain with us. The speech, however, also seems to represent a retreat not just past *Anns*, but past *Donoghue* v. *Stevenson* itself, in its apparent rejection of almost six decades of a general approach to duty and the judicial quest for broadly applicable guidelines.

The impact of the speech will clearly be at the forefront of the future development of the duty of care issue. Several possibilities emerge. One

---

70. [1990] 2 WLR 358.
71. Per Lord Bridge, ibid., at 364.

is that the general comments about duty will be seen as more extreme than the context of the case made necessary, and will come to be marginalized. Another possibility is that the speech will be seen as no more than a confirmation of the long-standing trend to treat claims for economic loss caused by negligent misstatements in a different, and more restrictive, way. Certainly, examples of where different rules apply to the duty question, given by Lord Oliver, include areas such as misstatement and duties in respect of third parties, long-regarded as outside the mainstream.

However, it is argued that the impact of the speech will not be as great as it may seem at first sight. It will be far from easy to jettison the accumulated ideas and attitudes that have gone to make up the general approach to duty of care. In addition, the general approach to duty cannot be entirely discarded. Lord Bridge goes on to cite with approval the views of Brennan J, in the High Court of Australia in *Sutherland Shire Council* v. *Heyman*[72] that 'the law should develop novel categories of negligence incrementally and by analogy with established categories.' It is clear that evolution of negligence by increment and analogy with the pre-existing law can only occur if the pre-existing law and its basis are properly understood, and this, in turn, can only happen if the fundamentals that lie at the heart of past duty cases are used as the basis of that evolution. Thus the concepts of foreseeability, proximity and fairness will still lie close to any future developments in negligence.

A coherent approach to duty

Far from the picture of chaos espoused by Lord Bridge in *Caparo*, it is clear that the courts have come close to success in formulating a cogent and consistent approach to duty of care in the aftermath of the change in judicial attitude in the mid-1980s. The fact that fewer claims in negligence are now succeeding should not conceal the fact that the law of negligence now pursues its goals more efficiently and effectively in a reasonably logical way.

In terms of the legal redefinition of proximity in *Yuen*, it is true that claims based on indirect proximity will no longer be tenable, but this simply has the effect of focusing legal liability on the true perpetrators of the tort in question, albeit that in the case itself they were untraceable. Likewise in policy cases, one of the clearest justifications for holding that it is unreasonable to impose a duty on one party is that someone else bears the true responsibility. *Peabody* is just such a case; the fact that the local authority owed no duty did not affect the question of the liability of the developer's professional advisers, other than to leave them responsible for 100 per cent of the plaintiff's losses, rather than the 75 per cent they may have expected to bear had the local authority carried their share of the blame. Thus what seems at first sight to be a negative

---

72. (1985) 60 ALR 1.

'no-duty' decision actually has the effect of making the chief culprits of the negligence in question more to blame, rather than less. Indeed, the tenor of many of the cases assigning responsibility in recent years has been to focus the spotlight of liability more accurately in this way, though admittedly sometimes it does reveal that no one (or no effective defendant) can be found; *Van Oppen* is perhaps such a case. What we are therefore seeing is a tort of negligence that now ignores peripheral or minor duties of care but with the result that in the usual case, where there is a more important duty present, the focus on that is made all the sharper.

There are some clear exceptions to this. The great reluctance of the courts to allow claims for economic loss, outside negligent misrepresentation cases, stands out as one, as does the refusal of the courts to allow parallel claims in both tort and contract in certain post-*Tai Hing* cases. However, even in these cases, the result of the lack of a tortious duty is not always to deprive the plaintiff of a remedy, but rather simply to route them into another field of law, usually the law of contract. To a considerable extent, cases in these two areas could easily be cited alongside the cases in the policy category where a tortious remedy is denied on the grounds of the availability of an alternative remedy and a cogent exception to the usual duty approach may be emerging in this area.

If the position now is compared with that of ten years ago, it may be suggested that the essence of the *Anns* test in fact remains in place. 'Is there enough proximity?' and 'Are there any countervailing policy considerations?' remain the two questions that must be asked though each now receives a more cautious answer. Broad concepts of foreseeability are replaced by the more restrictive rules of 'close and direct proximity'. This is a different answer but not a fundamentally different approach; still the courts are seeking to restrict the number of claimants now, as then in *Donoghue*. Likewise, the increased range of countervailing policy considerations does not change the consistent place that policy has always had in duty of care cases. This reduction in the number of duties is however well-balanced by the increased force of the many duties that remain, and also perhaps by the continuing ability of the tort to develop and extend to new situations, as permitted by the *Aliakmon* decision, though this element seems incompatible with Lord Bridge's speech in *Caparo*.

Future prospects

At the end of a period of such turmoil, it would be bold to make too many definite projections. However, it has just been argued that the *Anns* test has to a substantial degree survived all the heat and noise of recent battles, and this alone suggests a certain durability to this approach of duty of care. Likewise, it has been found possible to delimit clearly most of the recent restrictions on duty created both by law and policy, which suggests that a certain coherence is at least in the process of emerging in relation to these exceptions, once some of the as yet unanswered questions have been worked out through further litigation. Recognition of that coherence is believed to be essential in ensuring that future negligence developments remain compatible with the present law.

It may therefore be suggested that the approach to duty of care questions is reasonably consistent and predictable. If this is so, it then follows that such an internally cogent body of law is less likely to be substantially upset by anything other than the strongest of external forces, and it is difficult to see any such force imminent. The major objection to the rise of negligence at times seemed to be its sheer uncertainty and this ground of attack is of course lost once stability is reasserted. Indeed, *Caparo* can be criticized just because of its inherently unsettling effect, if Lord Bridge's invitation to abandon general principles is accepted. The adaptation of the tort to contemporary opinions is always going to be possible, given its inherent flexibility and this too militates against the likelihood of fundamental objections arising, at least to the duty element.

The tort of negligence, as evidenced by its duty of care element, therefore seems in fair shape, with a coherent and consistent approach discernible, notwithstanding recent changes which have affected duty issues, generally in peripheral cases. No one doubts, after all, that a driver owes a duty to the pedestrian with whom he collides, or that the doctor owes a duty to his patient, or that of the employer to the employee.

There is ground for cautious optimism that the tort will now enter into one of the more settled phases in its exciting life, and that duty of care will retreat from the legal headlines once more and return to the relative obscurity that has characterized much of its history. This view is based on the underlying strengths and consistency of the court's approach to the duty of care issue, and assumes that *Caparo*'s effect will be limited, as suggested above. It is hoped that the accuracy of this tentative prediction will not be found to be wanting in a Golden Jubilee essay on negligence.

3 The protection of informal interests in land

Mark Thompson

Introduction

In recent years, there has been a marked increase of interest in the law and practice of conveyancing. Not unsurprisingly, much of the public concern has centred on the issue of cost, and in particular, the fees charged by solicitors for undertaking this work. Matters came to a head in 1983 when Mr Austin Mitchell, MP introduced, as a Private Member's Bill, the House Buyers Bill 1983, the principal intention of which was to break the solicitors' monopoly of conveyancing.[1] This Bill attracted wide parliamentary support, but was withdrawn in response to a government undertaking to introduce legislative proposals. Prior to introducing legislation, the Conveyancing Committee was established and its First Report led to the introduction of licensed conveyancers.[2]

In addition to considering what tests of competence should be required of non-solicitor conveyancers, the Committee was also asked to consider the scope for simplifying conveyancing practice and procedure. This task was performed in 1985 with the publication of the Second Report which contained numerous recommendations for improving the system. Coupled with this Report, there have been other initiatives in this area directed towards the reform of conveyancing law. In recent years the Law Commission has been particularly active in the area of real property, publishing a number of proposals to modernize and improve land law and conveyancing.[3] This, together with the work done by the Commission's Standing Committee on Conveyancing, has done much to

---
1. Established by the Solicitors Act 1974, s.2.
2. Administration of Justice Act 1985, Part II.
3. Reports of Working Papers include Law Commission No. 181, *Trusts of Land* (1989); Law Commission No. 158, *Third Report on Land Registration* (1987); Law Commission WP No. 109, *Passing of Risk* (1988); Law Commission WP No. 99, *Mortgages* (1987). For recent implementation of three recommendations, see Law of Property (Miscellaneous Provisions) Act 1989.

ensure that the issues relating to land transfer remain prominent on the agenda, with the result that quite far-reaching changes, both to land law and conveyancing are in the process of being made.

It is obviously desirable, from the point of view of the consumer, that the process of conveyancing should be as quick and inexpensive as is reasonably possible. In promoting such a goal, however, care must be taken that others who may be interested in the land are not unfairly prejudiced. This difficulty lies at the heart of one of the greatest tensions in land law: the desire to facilitate land transactions, on the one hand, as opposed to the desire of others to maintain and secure the use of the land itself, on the other. Recent developments in the law have highlighted this tension quite starkly. The aim of this chapter is to show how the law has developed to give rather more weight to people's expectations of maintaining residential security in the home than was once the case,[4] and to suggest how the law may develop in the future.

The structure of ownership of rights in land

In order to assess the changes that have occurred in land law, it is necessary to sketch the structure within which they have operated.[5] The 1925 legislation wrought substantial changes in English land law, a principal effect of which was to facilitate conveyancing by the twin methods of simplifying the traditional land law and by stimulating the spread of registration of title.

In so far as unregistered land is concerned, the essential strategy of the legislation is well known. The number of estates in land that could exist at law were reduced to the fee simple absolute in possession and the term of years absolute, all other estates existing only in equity. Similarly, the number of third party rights affecting land, which would bind a purchaser regardless of notice, was also substantially reduced.[6]

Traditionally, equitable interests were binding upon a purchaser of the land on the basis of notice: the only person who would take free from an equitable interest was the bona fide purchaser of the legal estate for value without notice. For a purchaser to achieve this prized status, however, was no easy task. He was required to show that he had made reasonable inquiries to ascertain the existence of such interests.[7] This included conducting a full investigation of title, he being bound by any rights which could have been discovered by undertaking such inquiries.[8] He

---

4. See K.J. Gray, *Elements of Land Law*, Butterworths (1987), at 13.
5. For a fuller account, see R.E. Megarry and H.W.R. Wade, *The Law of Real Property*, Stevens (5th edn, 1984), at 123–40.
6. Law of Property Act 1925, s.1(1),(2),(3).
7. See Law of Property Act 1925, s.199.
8. See *Re Cox and Neve's Contract* [1891] 2 Ch.109.

would also be bound by the beneficial interests of people in actual occupation,[9] although at the time when this rule developed, almost certainly not if the legal owner was also in occupation of the land.[10]

The nature of these inquiries that a purchaser was required to make necessarily resulted in making land transfer more complex and time-consuming. Accordingly the reforms consolidated in the 1925 legislation sought to address these issues. A fundamental change was to ensure in time that the traditional, repetitive system of investigation of title would be replaced by a system of registered title. Until that objective was achieved, and it is still some considerable distance from attainment, the position of the purchaser was also radically improved with regard to unregistered land. In particular, the burden imposed upon him in respect of inquiries to be made concerning equitable interests was eased substantially.

The basic scheme of the legislation with regard to these matters was to make an essential distinction between interests of a commercial type and interests of a family type. The former class of interests are of a kind which are normally granted only in return for payment and can only sensibly be enforced against the actual land in question, a good example being a restrictive covenant. The latter category of interest was of a type that traditionally arose under some sort of family arrangement. A paradigm of this was an interest under a strict settlement, whereby a life interest would be created with remainders elsewhere.

The strategy which was then adopted was to make the former category of interest registrable under the Land Charges Act 1925.[11] The holder of such an interest should then protect it by registration. If he did so, this would constitute actual notice to all persons for all purposes,[12] with the result that no purchaser could take free from it. If he failed to register, then the interest would become void against specified types of purchaser who would consequently not be bound by it.[13] With regard to family interests, a different approach was taken. For this type of interest, machinery was devised which, if complied with, ensured that the existing beneficial interests were overreached, that is transferred from the land to the purchase money.[14] The beneficial interests would not affect a purchaser and were kept off the title.

The essential divide in unregistered land between registrable interests and overreachable interests is, to a considerable extent, also seen in registered conveyancing. In that system, the register is said to act like a

---

9. *Taylor* v. *Stibbert* (1794) 2 Ves Jr 438, at 440; *Barnhart* v. *Greenshields* (1853) 9 Moo PC 18, at 32–3; *Hunt* v. *Luck* [1901] 1 Ch. 45, at 52, affmd [1902] 1 Ch. 428.
10. Maudsley, 'Bona Fide Purchasers of Registered Land' (1973) 36 MLR 25, 33; Thompson, 'Prospective Decisions in Conveyancing', [1984] Conv 362, 366–70.
11. Now the Land Charges Act 1972.
12. Law of Property Act 1925, s.198.
13. Land Charges Act 1972, s.4; Law of Property Act 1925, s.199(1).
14. See Law of Property Act 1925, s.2.

mirror reflecting perfectly the state of a proprietor's title. Interests which are not to be overreached are protected on the register, either by way of notice or by caution.[15] The details of the interests which are overreachable are not entered upon the register but are protected by a restriction[16] which requires a purchaser to operate the relevant machinery in order to effect registration. Unless these interests can also qualify as overriding interests, to be considered below, a purchaser will not be concerned with any interest which has not been protected on the register.[17]

Registrable interests

In both systems of land ownership, a considerable premium is placed upon the registration of interests. Looking first at the unregistered system, a purchaser of land is concerned with any legal rights which might affect the property. Other than that, he can satisfy himself regarding the existence of equitable interests by the simple expedient of searching in the Land Charges Registry.[18] Beyond matters revealed by this search, a purchaser would be unaffected by other equitable interests from which he would take free. The strategy adopted by the legislation, therefore, reduced considerably the need to make inquiries when purchasing land, thereby facilitating conveyancing.

The simplification of conveyancing by making the enforcement of equitable interests dependent upon registration is achieved at a price. That is that people who fail to register have their interests defeated with the result that their expectations are sacrificed on the altar of conveyancing efficiency. A good example of this occurred in *Midland Bank Trust Co. Ltd* v. *Green*.[19] A father granted his son an option to purchase valuable farming land. On discovering that the option had not been registered, the father conveyed the land to his wife, who knew of the option, for £500, which was a considerable undervalue. It was nevertheless held by the House of Lords that she was a purchaser for money or money's worth with the result that the option was void against her for non-registration.[20] It is easy to see why some commentators found the

---

15. Land Registration Act 1925, ss.48–56.
16. Land Registration Act 1925, s.58.
17. Land Registration Act 1925, s.20; *De Lusignan* v. *Johnson* (1973) 240 EG 499. But see the much criticized decisions in *Peffer* v. *Rigg* [1977] 1 WLR 285 and *Lyus* v. *Prowsa Developments Ltd* [1982] 1 WLR 1044 and the discussion by Thompson, 'Registration Fraud and Notice' [1985] CLJ 280.
18. The difficulties caused by the defective scheme adopted by the Land Charges legislation are beyond the scope of this chapter. See *Report of the Committee on Land Charges*, Cmnd 9825 (1956); and Wade, 'Land Charge Registration Reviewed' [1956] CLJ 216.
19. [1981] AC 513. See also *Hollington Bros* v. *Rhodes* [1951] 2 All ER 578.
20. Land Charges Act 1972, s.4(6).

justice of this result, to say the least, questionable,[21] in that the conveyancing statutes seemed to have been manipulated for personal gain. As against that, it may be pointed out that the son's loss was entirely financial and arose out of a transaction where legal advice is highly likely to have been taken. This indeed was the case with the result that the son's solicitors were liable to him for a very large sum in negligence.[22] Where, perhaps, the insistence upon registration may be more open to question is with regard to rights and expectations that derive from less formal arrangements. It is with such interests that this chapter is mainly concerned and, in particular, rights deriving from co-ownership. It is hoped to show that the law has changed in its attitude to the problems that arise in that it displays rather more sympathy for people claiming occupancy rights of an informal nature than was previously the case.

The deserted wife's equity

In a series of cases in the 1950s there developed a right which became known as the deserted wife's equity.[23] Put briefly, the gist of this right derived from a wife's right, as against her husband, not to be evicted from the matrimonial home. If deserted, her right acquired the status of an equity which could bind a purchaser. In *National Provincial Bank Ltd* v. *Ainsworth*[24] a husband owed a bank £6,000. Having deserted his wife, he then conveyed the matrimonial home to a company which he owned and the company then mortgaged the house to the bank. The issue in the case was whether the wife had an overriding interest in the home binding upon the bank. The House of Lords held that she did not. She had merely personal rights which were not capable of binding a genuine purchaser,[25] and the so-called 'deserted wife's equity' was held not to be an interest in property.

It is clear that in reaching this conclusion, the House of Lords were mindful of the conveyancing implications of the issue. Lord Upjohn said:

> It had been the policy of the law for over a hundred years to simplify and facilitate transactions in real property. It is of great importance that persons should be able freely and easily to raise money on the security of their property.[26]

---

21. Green, 'Void Land Charges — Literalism Triumphs in The House of Lords' (1981) 97 QR 518.
22. *Midland Bank Trust Co. Ltd* v. *Hett, Stubbs & Kemp* [1979] Ch. 384.
23. *Bendall* v. *McWhirter* [1952] 2 QB 466; *Street* v. *Denham* [1954] 1 WLR 624; *Jess B.Woodcock & Sons Ltd* v. *Hobbs* [1955] 1 WLR 152.
24. [1965] AC 1175.
25. Cf. *Ferris* v. *Weaven* [1952] 2 All ER 333.
26. [1965] AC 1175, at 1233–4.

It would hinder such a policy to require a mortgagee to make inquiries of a spouse in occupation of the property, particularly regarding the nature of this supposed right, and accordingly the need for such an inquiry was precluded by the decision and the reliability of the register was reinforced.

Legislative reaction to the *Ainsworth* decision was swift. Under the Matrimonial Homes Act 1967,[27] a spouse is given a statutory right to occupy the matrimonial home. This right is capable of binding a purchaser of the land but, crucially, only if it is protected by the registration of a Class F land charge or by way of a notice as appropriate. Unless it is so protected, the rights of a spouse *qua* spouse cannot prejudicially affect a purchaser.

From the conveyancing perspective, this statutory solution poses few problems[28] in that the new right is made to fit the general pattern of equitable rights being either overreachable or registrable.[29] From the point of view of the spouse, however, the position is less than ideal and certainly inferior to that which pertained prior to *Ainsworth*. This is precisely because the protection of the right is dependent upon registration. As Lord Denning MR put it:

[It] enables a wife ... to register a Class F charge. But that ... [is] of precious little use to her, at any rate when she [is] still living at home in peace with her husband. She would never have heard of a Class F charge; and she would not have understood it if she had.[30]

Herein, of course, lies the principal problem. It is all very well, in the interests of simplifying conveyancing, to insist upon the registration of equitable interests in land. The difficulty is that unless the holder of an interest has taken legal advice he or she is extremely unlikely to know of such a requirement. When such rights arise in a domestic situation, where a lack of formality is quite common, this is likely to be the case. When the consequences of favouring the conveyancing interest is that a person may lose his/her home as a result of an unauthorized transaction effected by the legal owner, then the argument in favour of security of transaction becomes less compelling.

This problem has arisen on several recent occasions. Initially, the approach taken was to favour the conveyancing interest. In *Caunce* v. *Caunce*[31] a matrimonial home was conveyed into the sole name of the

---

27. See now Matrimonial Homes Act 1983.
28. But see *Wroth* v. *Tyler* [1974] Ch. 30 and the discussion by Barnsley, 'Conveying The Matrimonial Home — Some Problems Facing Solicitors And Their Clients' [1974] CLP 76.
29. For limited exceptions, see *Poster* v. *Slough Estates* [1968] 1 WLR 1515 (tenant's right to remove fixtures); and *Shiloh Spinners Ltd* v. *Harding* [1973] AC 691 (equitable right of re-entry).
30. *Williams & Glyn's Bank Ltd* v. *Boland* [1979] Ch. 312, at 328.
31. [1969] 1 WLR 286.

husband but the wife was a beneficial tenant in common. He, unbeknown to her, created three mortgages and the issue in the case was whether the bank was bound by her rights in the property. As it was conceded, unlike the position in *Ainsworth*, that she had a proprietary interest in the house, this depended on whether the bank had notice of her interest, she being in occupation of it all the material times. Stamp J decided in favour of the bank. Having cited Lord Upjohn's remarks on the policy of the law being to simplify conveyancing, he held that when the legal owner is in possession of land, a purchaser is not fixed with constructive notice of the rights of other occupiers. The contrary view would, in his opinion, introduce unworkable and undesirable burdens on mortgagees.[32]

Change to favour the occupier

Stamp J's approach to this type of problem found a ready echo in the judgment of Templeman J, at first instance, in *Williams & Glyn's Bank Ltd* v. *Boland*.[33] In this case, to secure an overdraft, Mr Boland mortgaged the house to a bank. He was the sole proprietor of the house but it was conceded that his wife was a beneficial co-owner. The bank had, prior to taking the mortgage, made no inquiries of Mrs Boland, who was in actual occupation of the property. The only difference between *Boland* and *Caunce* was that on this occasion title to the land was registered, so that the issue was whether Mrs Boland had an overriding interest within s.70(1)(g) of the Land Registration Act 1925, rather than whether the bank had constructive notice of her rights. This turned largely on whether or not she could be said to be in actual occupation of the land, within the meaning of the paragraph.

At first instance, Templeman J asserted that to hold in favour of the wife would necessitate a mortgagee inquiring both whether a wife was in occupation and whether she had an interest in the land. He was of the view that it was 'neither necessary nor desirable to construe the words "actual occupation" to have such wide and almost catastrophic results'.[34] The conveyancing consequences of deciding against the bank did not, however, trouble the appellate courts unduly, where rather greater consideration was given to the plight of the wife, who faced homelessness owing to the action of her husband. This different attitude is clearly seen in the judgment of Lord Denning MR who said:

---

32. Ibid., at 294, but cf. *Hodgson* v. *Marks* [1971] Ch. 892.
33. (1978) 36 P&CR 448.
34. Ibid., at 454. For Lord Templeman's hostility to the subsequent House of Lords' decision in *Boland*, see *Winkworth* v. *Edward Baron Development Co. Ltd* [1986] 1 WLR 1512, at 1515.

If a bank is to do its duty, in the society in which we live, it should recognise the integrity of the matrimonial home. It should not destroy it by disregarding the wife's interest in it — simply to ensure that it is paid the husband's debt in full — with the high interest rates prevailing. We should not give monied might priority over social justice.[35]

These sentiments struck a chord in the House of Lords. For Lord Scarman, the importance of the decision was not to be judged solely by its impact on conveyancing practice. Regard should properly be had to the fact that if Mrs Boland succeeded then the protection of married women in the home would be strengthened, whereas, if she lost, this interest could be weakened or destroyed by an unscrupulous husband.[36] Lord Scarman took the view that the interests of social justice favoured the increased protection of married women and that, if the result of that was to cause difficulties to the conveyancers, then this was an acceptable price to pay. Similarly Lord Wilberforce, who had sat in *National Westminster Bank Ltd* v. *Ainsworth*, and who gave the leading speech in the instant case, was unimpressed by the alleged chaos that would be wrought in conveyancing by deciding in favour of the wife. Referring specifically to the anxieties expressed by Templeman J, he said:

What is involved is a departure from an easy-going practice of dispensing with enquiries as to occupation beyond that of the vendor and accepting the risks of doing so. To substitute for this practice of more careful enquiry as to the fact of occupation, and if necessary, as to the rights of occupiers cannot, in my view of the matter, be considered as unacceptable except at the price of overlooking the widespread development of shared interests of co-ownership.[37]

The decision in *Boland* is, of course, inconsistent with the ethos underlying *Caunce* v. *Caunce*. That decision was related to what was meant by constructive notice in unregistered land and was not actually overruled in *Boland*. Nevertheless, it was apparent that, in the light of *Boland*, it would be unwise to rely on *Caunce*, and it has since become clear that if the facts were to recur, *Caunce* would not be followed and that the mortgagee would be held to have constructive notice of the woman's rights.[38] It is clearly sensible that the two systems of land ownership should have a consistent approach to this important problem.

To digress slightly, it is unfortunate that the two systems are not in harmony on other related points. It was decided in *Boland* that the effect of actual occupation is to upgrade any minor interest into an overriding

---

35. [1979] Ch. 312, 322–3. See also *Brikom Investments Ltd* v. *Carr* [1979] QB 467, at 484, per Lord Denning MR.
36. [1981] AC 487, at 509–10.
37. Ibid., at 508–9.
38. *Midland Bank Ltd* v. *Farmpride Hatcheries Ltd* (1981) 260 EG 493; *Kingsnorth Finance Co. Ltd* v. *Tizard* [1986] 1 WLR 783.

interest.[39] Actual occupation of the land is, therefore, an alternative means of protecting an interest to making an entry on the register. This seems appropriate, as it is probably the case that people who actually live in property feel that their rights are protected by that fact alone without feeling the need to consult a lawyer, which in reality is what would be necessary if registration were to be insisted upon. In unregistered conveyancing, on the other hand, actual occupation of the land is not a safety net. If, as in *Midland Bank Co. Ltd* v. *Green*,[40] a person holds a registrable interest but has not registered it, then the fact that he is in actual occupation of the land is irrelevant. The interest becomes void against a purchaser for non-registration. This is unfortunate and probably unintentional, in that it seems to have occurred as a result of an accidental legislative mishap.[41] It would be a desirable reform if, in the unregistered land system, actual occupation could be an alternative method of protecting all equitable interests, be they registrable or not.

The reaction to Boland

Returning to the main theme, the decision in *Boland* excited enormous academic interest.[42] It also generated great concern on the part of conveyancers and lending institutions, the latter, in particular, fearing that the efficacy of their mortgages would be seriously undermined by the potential existence of numerous claims of the type asserted by Mrs Boland. So intense was this concern that the matter was referred to the Law Commission, who reported in 1982.[43]

The Law Commission, while sensitive to the problems faced by co-owners, and spouses in particular, nevertheless favoured what might be termed the conveyancing interest. The view was taken that to allow this type of interest to affect a purchaser, who in practice is most likely to be a mortgagee, despite it not being protected in any way either in the Land Charges Register[44] or on the register of title, represented an

---

39. Except, of course, for those rights where it is specifically provided that they cannot exist as overriding interests, such as a spouse's statutory right of occupation or interests existing behind a strict settlement: see Matrimonial Homes Act 1983, s.2(8))(b); Land Registration Act 1925, s.86(2).
40. [1981] AC 513.
41. See Wade, 'Land Charge Registration Reviewed' [1956] CLJ 216, at 228; Moriarty (1984) 100 LQR 376, at 407; Thompson 'Registration Fraud and Notice' [1985] CLJ 280, at 298.
42. See e.g., Forrest, 'Trusts For Sale and Co-ownership' (1978) 42 Conv (NS) 194; Freeman, 'Monied Might and The Matrimonial Home' (1981) 11 Fam. Law 37; Martin, 'Section 70(1)(g) and the vendor's spouse' [1980] Conv 361; Murphy, 'Monied Might and Social Justice' (1979) 42 MLR 567; Thompson 'Overreaching After Boland' (1986) 6 LS 140.
43. Law Commission No. 115 (1982). This view is no longer held: Law Commission No. 158 (1987), para. 2.67.
44. There is no available land charge which would include within its definition an interest behind a trust for sale.

undesirable state of affairs. The enforceability of such rights, as a result of *Boland*, necessitated extensive inquiries being made of all occupants of the house with a corresponding increase in expense and delay in effecting conveyancing transactions. To overcome this difficulty, which ran counter to the general trend of simplifying conveyancing, it was proposed that for the future such interests should only be enforceable if protected in the appropriate manner by registration.[45]

The obvious flaw in this proposal is the difficulty adverted to earlier, that the insistence upon registration of an interest especially one deriving from beneficial co-ownership where the arrangements between parties, who are usually a married couple or an unmarried couple who are cohabiting, is that such arrangements are commonly informal and entered into without legal advice. In the absence of such advice, it is hardly realistic to expect a beneficial co-owner, who is not also a legal co-owner, to protect his or her interest by registration. The practical effect of implementing such a proposal would have been to simplify the conveyancing process, but at the expense of those possessing rights in the property.

The only legislative response to the issues at the centre of *Boland* and the Law Commission Report was the introduction in 1985 of the Land Registration and the Law of Property Bill. Under the provisions of this Bill, a distinction was drawn between married and unmarried occupants of the home. In the case of the former category of people, if they had a beneficial interest in the home and were in occupation then their interests would be protected, either as an overriding interest or through the doctrine of notice. For the latter category, no such protection would exist; they would have to register their beneficial interest if it was to bind a purchaser for value. Leaving aside the ethical aspects of this distinction, from a purely conveyancing point of view the Bill was flawed. If a house was in dual occupation, the purchaser would need to know the marital status of the occupant who was not the legal owner. Rather than being spared the need to make inquiries of occupiers, a purchaser would instead have to address distasteful questions to people in occupation. Not surprisingly, the Bill proved controversial[46] and was ultimately withdrawn, and the matter left to case law.

Unauthorized mortgages

A good deal of the concern that was generated by the *Boland* decision arose from the assumption that it would affect all mortgagees alike. This was of particular concern to building societies. The feared scenario was

---

45. This scheme was intended to be coupled with a regime of statutory co-ownership of the matrimonial home.
46. HL, Vol. 462, col. 604, 16 April 1985.

that of a man buying a house in his name alone but with a contribution to the purchase price by his spouse or intended cohabitee, who would thereby acquire a beneficial interest in it. She would then take up occupation of the property before the mortgage was completed, thereby establishing priority over the mortgagee. This fear was particularly keenly felt where title was registered, in that, owing to section 20 of the Land Registration Act 1925, the crucial date for assessment of priorities seemed not to be the date when the transaction takes place but when it was registered.[47] There will almost always be a delay between the two events, this registration gap allowing sufficient time for the woman to take up occupation and establish her overriding interest. The mortgagee would subsequently be unable to gain possession of the property against her in the event of a subsequent default on the mortgage. Yet not only would the mortgagee not know of her existence, there would have been no sure way in which he could have found out about her.

Such an outcome would have tilted the balance too far in favour of occupiers and placed the institutional lenders in an invidious position. Making inquiries of the borrower as to whether anyone would be living with him is not sufficient because any inquiries, to be effective, must be addressed to the holder of the adverse right.[48] True, in most cases where this was to be so, the borrower would reveal that a person was to live with him and then inquiries could be made of her or she could be made a party to the mortgage. If, however, he did not reply honestly, then there was no ready means available for the mortgagee to ensure that there would be no prior interests. It seems unacceptable that a purchaser should be at risk of taking subject to interests of which he has no reasonable prospect of discovering, particularly if the interest is of a common type.[49]

This particular problem has since been defused by the judiciary, adopting two lines of reasoning. The first is to close the registration gap. In *Lloyds Bank* v. *Rosset*[50] a house was transferred to Mr Rosset, who was registered as sole proprietor but his wife had a beneficial interest in it. The property was acquired with the help of a mortgage. It was clear that she was in actual occupation at the time when the mortgage was registered but it was far less clear whether she was in actual occupation when the mortgage was created. Although it was accepted that section 20 of the Land Registration Act pointed to the former date being the crucial time, it was held that, for the purpose of s.70(1)(g), the date when the mortgage was created must be the time at which the person must be in

---

47. Registration takes effect retrospectively as of the date when the application for registration was received at the Land Registry: Land Registration Rules 1925, r.83(2) as substituted by Land Registration Rules 1978, r.8(2).
48. Land Registration Act 1925, s.70(1)(g); *Hodgson* v. *Marks* [1971] Ch. 892, at 932, per Russell LJ.
49. See also *Kling* v. *Keston Properties Ltd* (1985) 49 P&CR 212, at 222, per Vinelott J.
50. [1988] 3 All ER 915. See Thompson, 'Priorities in Registered Land' [1988] Conv 453. The decision itself was reversed on the facts: [1990] 1 all ER 1111.

actual occupation.[51] This reasoning, while convenient, is, as the Court of Appeal itself recognized, contrary to the scheme of the Act.[52] It was nevertheless extended in *Abbey National Building Society* v. *Cann*.[53] In this case, it was argued that a beneficial co-owner had gone into occupation prior to completion, which took place later the same day when the mortgage was also created. The majority of the Court of Appeal, however, refused to divide the day up into parts and held that even had she gone into occupation, that event and the mortgage occurred simultaneously and that, therefore, she did not have an overriding interest binding upon the building society. This, however, is highly suspect in that it conflicts directly with previous Court of Appeal authority,[54] and it must be regarded as dubious whether this decision will ultimately be sustained on this point.[54a]

The second line of reasoning is also directed at this problem. In *Bristol and West Building Society* v. *Henning*[55] a house was conveyed into the sole name of Mr Henning in consideration of £12,900, of which £11,000 was provided by the building society who took a legal charge over the house. The balance was derived from a sale of an earlier home in which Mr Henning, who was not actually married to the mortgagor, had an interest. She argued that this interest transferred to the new property and was binding upon the building society who had made no inquiries of her. The Court of Appeal, without citing *Boland*, decided in favour of the mortgagee.

In reaching what appears to be a strange result, Browne-Wilkinson LJ adopted the following reasoning. To establish an interest in the property at all, she must show an intention on the part of the Hennings that she have an interest in it. This is inferred from her contribution to the purchase price and a resulting trust arises in her favour.[56] Having established that she obtained an interest through this inferred intention, the Lord Justice went on to hold that because she knew that a mortgage was being obtained to finance the purchase of the house, the further intention should be imputed to her that the interest of the building society was to have priority over her interest.

This reasoning has been criticized in detail elsewhere.[57] The gist of

---

51. The majority held that she was in actual occupation at that date and therefore held an overriding interest.
52. See D.G. Barnsley, *Conveyancing Law and Practice* (3rd edn, 1988), at 53. Cf. Sparkes, 'Occupiers: When Do They Bite?' [1986] Conv 309. The Court of Appeal approach was approved by the House of Lords in *Abbey National Building Society* v. *Cann* [1990] 1 All ER 1085.
53. (1989) 57 P&CR 381. See Beaumont, 'Mortgage Fraud, Equitable Priorities and Overriding Interests' [1989] Conv 158.
54. *Church of England Building Society* v. *Piskor* [1954] Ch. 553. See Beaumont, *supra*, n.53, at 163.
54a. The decision was nevertheless upheld by the House of Lords overruling *Church of England Building Society* v. *Piskor* [1990] 1 All ER 1085.
55. [1985] 1 WLR 778.
56. *Gissing* v. *Gissing* [1971] AC 886. See generally, M.P. Thompson, *Co-ownership*, at 35–46.
57. Thompson, 'Relief For First Mortgagees' (1989) 49 MLR 245.

that criticism is that in *Gissing* v. *Gissing*,[58] which the Court purported to apply, it was categorically stated that in determining how a beneficial interest in land was to be held, regard must be had to the intention of the parties at the time when it was acquired. If they had not considered the matter, the court cannot impute to them an intention which it was satisfied they would, as reasonable persons, have formed if they had considered it. Yet in *Henning*, Browne-Wilkinson LJ expressly found that she had given no thought to the question of priority, but nevertheless imputed an intention to her.[59] Despite this, however, the decision has been followed[60] and must be taken to represent the law.

Notwithstanding criticism of the reasoning, the result of the case can be defended. Unlike the position in *Boland*, the co-owner in *Henning* knew both that a mortgage was being taken out and why it was being taken out. Her position was in no way prejudiced by her partner's action; rather it was improved in that they could not have had a house at all without the mortgage. With the exception of *Lloyds Bank* v. *Rosset*,[61] in all cases where a mortgagee has been adversely affected by the rights of a beneficial co-owner, the legal owner has been dealing with the property to effect a business deal of some kind for his own benefit. In practice this means that the mortgage was created some time after the property was acquired. This was not true on the highly unusual facts of *Lloyds Bank* v. *Rosset* where, quite unknown to his wife, who thought quite reasonably that there were sufficient funds available to buy the property outright, the legal owner borrowed by way of mortgage to assist in the purchase of the house and the bank was bound by her interest.[61a] Such facts are extremely unlikely to recur with any regularity.

The position which has now been reached in dealings where there is one legal owner of the property is this. If the legal owner enters into unauthorized dealings, using the home as security, then the mortgagee must be beware. He should check to see if there are any other people living in the property and, if there are, ensure either that they do not have an interest in it or that they consent to the mortgagee's interest having priority. This, it must be accepted, may be a difficult task, particularly if the borrower seeks to disguise the fact that there are others interested in the property.[62] Nevertheless, in modern society when it is quite common for both partners in a relationship to be in employment, it is quite likely that, despite the house being in one person's name, others may be interested in it and have the expectation of continuing to

---

58. [1971] AC 886, at 904 per Lord Diplock.
59. [1985] 1 WLR 778, at 882.
60. *Paddington Building Society* v. *Mendelsohn* (1985) P&CR 244. A similar principle underlies *Abbey National Building Society* v. *Cann* (1989) 57 P&CR 381 where, it is submitted, it should not have been applied. See also House of Lords approach: [1990] 1 All ER 1805.
61. [1988] 3 All ER 915.
61a. The finding that Mrs Rosset had an interest in the home was reversed by the House of Lords who, therefore, allowed the bank's appeal: [1990] 1 All ER 111.
62. See *Kingsnorth Finance Co. Ltd* v. *Tizard* [1986] 1 WLR 783.

live there. In a situation where the house is being used as security for a loan, perhaps for business purposes, but in any case for the purposes of the legal owner, it seems quite reasonable for duties to be imposed upon the lender and protection afforded to the occupier. On the other hand, when the mortgage is created for the purpose of financing the acquisition of the house itself, the position of the mortgagee is relatively secure and it is clear that the early anxieties have largely been assuaged. It would seem that a reasonable compromise has been struck in this area between protecting the security of occupiers and protecting the security of transactions.

Dispositions by two trustees[63]

Thus far the discussion has centred on the situation where there is sole ownership at law but co-ownership in equity and on how the law has developed to protect the rights of the beneficial co-owner. For many years the position when a transaction was effected by two co-owners was not thought to be worth serious discussion. The reason for this lack of attention was that when there is co-ownership the land is held upon a trust for sale.[64] Section 2 of the Law of Property Act 1925 provides that a conveyance to a purchaser of a legal estate in land shall overreach any equitable interest in the land if the conveyance is made by two trustees for sale. Section 26(3) provides that a purchaser shall not be concerned to see that the requirement that the beneficiaries entitled in possession consent to the transaction has been complied with and section 27 appears to clinch the matter, in favour of a purchaser, by providing that he is not to be concerned with the trusts affecting the proceeds of sale subject to a trust for sale provided that he takes a conveyance from the trustees for sale. Taken together, it seemed plain that the key to the overreaching machinery was the presence of two trustees for sale. Provided that the money was paid to them, the interests of the beneficiaries took effect only against the money and not against the land.

It was generally agreed, therefore, that if the transaction in *Boland* had been effected by two trustees instead of one, the result would have been different. Then, to almost universal consternation, the Court of Appeal decided to the contrary in *City of London Building Society* v. *Flegg*.[65] A house, named Bleak House, was purchased and Mr and Mrs Maxwell-Brown were registered as proprietors. A substantial part of the purchase price was provided by the Fleggs who became beneficial tenants in common and who shared the house with the Maxwell-Browns, their daughter and son-in-law. To provide finance for the purchase, a mortgage was created in favour of the Hastings and Thanet Building

---

63. See generally Thompson, 'Dispositions By Trustees For Sale' [1988] Conv 108.
64. Law of Property Act 1925, s.36.
65. [1986] Ch. 605. For cogent criticism, see Hayton, 'Are Occupiers' Overreachable Interests Really Overriding?' (1986) 130 NLJ 208.

Society. Subsequently, without informing the Fleggs, the Maxwell-Browns created two further mortgages until, finally, in 1982 £37,500 was borrowed to pay off all three existing mortgages and a mortgage created in favour of the plaintiff, who later sought possession. This issue was whether the Fleggs had an overriding interest binding upon the mortgagee.

The Court of Appeal held, reversing Judge Thomas at first instance, that the Fleggs did have an overriding interest despite the mortgage having been created by two trustees for sale. It is unnecessary, for present purposes, to analyse the reasoning of the Court of Appeal, which was based principally on a novel argument concerning section 14 of the Law of Property Act 1925,[66] in that the House of Lords restored the orthodox position by emphatically holding that a disposition by two trustees for sale would overreach the interests of beneficiaries with interests behind the trust, irrespective of whether or not they were in actual occupation or consented to the transaction.[67]

For reasons which are easy to understand, the decision was met with general relief.[68] It had been felt that the Court of Appeal decision had seriously affected the integrity of conveyancing transactions by undermining the overreaching machinery, long seen as central to land law. As against this trend, however, and in marked contrast to its reaction to the *Boland* decision, the Law Commission has provisionally recommended that the *Flegg* decision be reversed by legislation. In a thought-provoking Working Paper,[69] the Commission canvasses various options as to what the law should be and provisionally concludes that there should be no overreaching of the beneficiaries' interest unless they consent to the transaction, regardless of whether there are two trustees for sale.

There is much merit in this proposal. The ability of two trustees for sale to overreach beneficial interests has always left open the possibility of someone in the position of Mr Boland simply appointing another trustee to effect the transaction with him, thereby defeating his wife's interest: a prospect which has never seemed appealing. More importantly, from the point of view of the beneficiaries in occupation, it will not be obvious to them that the justice of the case has altered significantly because two people hold the legal title rather than one. Again it is quite likely, although admittedly this was not the case in *Flegg* itself, that a person in occupation may well not have been legally advised as to how best to safeguard his or her position.

If one looks at the matter from the perspective of a mortgagee, while it would of course be simpler if the *Flegg* rule was maintained, its

---

66. See Thompson, 'Overreaching After Boland' (1986) 6 LS 140.
67. *City of London Building Society* v. *Flegg* [1988] AC 54.
68. See Clarke, 'Land Law and Trusts' [1987] All ER, Review 144, at 149–52 and casenotes cited therein.
69. Law Commission WP No. 106, *Overreaching* (1988).

reversal should not be seen as too drastic a blow. First, as was pointed out by the Law Commission, the overreaching machinery is only effective in overreaching interests that exist behind a trust for sale. An occupier may have a different type of right: for example, the person may be solely beneficially entitled,[70] in which case the overreaching machinery would not operate. The mortgagee should, therefore, in any event make inquiries of all occupiers even if there are two trustees for sale. Second, the point can also be made that the decision in *Boland* operates almost exclusively when a home is being used as a security for a loan sometime after the house has been acquired. In this type of transaction, there is much to be said for the argument that the lender should have to determine whether other people have prior interests in the property before obtaining the prized position of a secured creditor[71] with priority over most other interests. If this argument is valid when there is only one holder of the legal title, it should surely remain so if there are two legal owners of the property, a matter which, from the point of view of the intending lender, may well be a matter of pure chance.

Conclusions

At the outset of this chapter, it was stated that land law and conveyancing have been undergoing a considerable review. Many changes to both law and practice have emerged from this and will continue to do so. This chapter has concentrated on one aspect of how the law has changed, to focus in particular on the different attitude that has been taken towards the rights of occupiers. While *National Provincial Bank* v. *Ainsworth* and *Williams & Glyn's Bank* v. *Boland* are readily distinguishable, in that in the former case the wife had no recognizable property right whereas in the latter case she did, the two decisions do nevertheless provide an interesting contrast in attitudes. The emphasis in *Ainsworth* is strongly in favour of the simplification of conveyancing with the attendant desire to reduce the onus of inquiry placed upon a purchaser. In *Boland*, on the other hand, much greater concern is shown for the position of the wife with the view clearly expressed that conveyancers must adapt their practices to come to terms with the increased protection being afforded to occupiers.

The decision in *Boland* is not an isolated example of this attitude. Together with the increased protection given to rights arising under trusts, there has been an increased flexibility shown to the question of how rights are acquired. This has led to the quite dramatic rise in

---

70. Ibid., paras 3.2, 6.6. See *Hodgson* v. *Marks* [1971] Ch. 892.
71. Cf. the protection given to the members of a family with regard to the home on bankruptcy: Insolvency Act 1986, s.336.

reported decisions involving proprietary estoppel,[72] a doctrine which is characterized by a lack of formality in arrangements between people. This developing doctrine could easily be the subject of a chapter in itself and is mentioned merely in passing as further evidence of the law's increasingly sympathetic reaction to recognizing and enforcing informal rights affecting land.

The decision in *City of London Building Society* v. *Flegg*, although probably inevitable on the basis of the framework of the law as it was established in 1925, does represent a check to this trend and it is hoped that the Law Commission's provisional proposals ultimately become law. Then, in view of the restrictions placed upon the scope of *Boland*, it is thought a reasonable compromise will have been achieved between the competing tensions of protecting occupiers and facilitating conveyancing referred to earlier. This one issue does show, however, that reforming land law and conveyancing involves more than clearing away technicalities and that when pursuing the laudable goals of making conveyancing less expensive and more speedy, sight should not be lost of the need to consider what rights may be affected as a consequence.

---

72. For prominent examples, see *Inwards* v. *Baker* [1965] 2 QB 29; *Crabb* v. *Arun District Council* [1976] Ch. 169; *Taylors Fashions Ltd* v. *Liverpool Victoria Trustees Co. Ltd* [1982] QB 133 n. See Gray, *supra* n.4, Chapter 13.

4 Family law, the Law Commission and socio-legal research*

Judith Masson

Introduction

This chapter does not seek to review the debate of the early 1970s about the proper function of socio-legal studies,[1] rather it starts from the standpoint that empirical research has a contribution to make to both the understanding of current law and the development of new law. This position cannot be taken as an answer in itself because issues remain of what that contribution is and how it can be made.

Research which has a function other than adding to the stock of knowledge may be viewed by some as being used in the negative sense of that word. Researchers too may be used. They may cease to have control over the subject-matter of the research; their work may be controlled by those who wish to extend or, more frequently, to limit the scope of the inquiry and they may find others constructing arguments around their findings which are not thoroughly based on the research. Funding mechanisms already make researchers vulnerable because the emphasis on useful research demands that researchers explain the need for their research in particular ways. Also the growing practice of the funding organization determining the subject, budget and time-scale further limits the possibility of large-scale studies directed by researchers. Those conducting empirical socio-legal research have not escaped these constraints but neither have they seen use of their research in the more positive sense. Neither the findings nor the wider implications of the research which has been undertaken seem to have been taken on board by those reforming the law. Thus Lord McGregor and others who thought that empirical research could make a positive contribution to

---

* This chapter is based on a paper given at the socio-legal group's annual conference in Oxford in March 1988. I should like to thank Mavis Maclean and Stephen Cretney for their helpful comments; the views expressed remain my own.
1. See Campbell and Wiles, 'The Study of Law & Society in Britain' (1976) 10 Law & Society Review 547.

improving and reforming the law have been disappointed.[2] Moreover, it does not appear that the case for empirical research into law has been substantially furthered over the last twenty-five years. In consequence, much of the reformed law is defective and funding for empirical research remains precarious.

It is not possible here to review the development of law and research during a quarter of a century across a broad range of subjects, although it would be interesting to see whether the explanations below would hold good in other subject areas. Instead, family law, a topic included in the Law Commission's programmes of law reform which has also been the subject of a comparatively large number of empirical research projects, is examined.

The work of the Law Commission

The Law Commission chose family law as one of the first areas for consideration and has continued to make proposals throughout the period.[3] It is clear that the Law Commission would regard their work in family law as successful law reform,[4] although Kerr LJ, a former Chairman of the Law Commission used the more neutral term 'achievement' and also noted that there had been some failings.[5] Success in the Law Commission's terms seems to be measured by the enactment of proposals or bills contained in final reports.[6] The Law Commission's Twenty-third Annual Report lists twenty-six final reports in the area of family law, of these only three have not led to legislation.[7] Moreover, it is only in the area of family law that the Law Commission has accomplished so much reordering of the statute book for codification, one of the Commission's original aims, to be a real possibility.[8]

---

2. O.R. McGregor, *Social History and Law Reform*, London, Stevens (1981).
3. *Law Commission First Annual Report 1965-66* (1966) item X, para. 77; Law Commission No. 14, *Second Programme of Law Reform*; Law Commission No. 54, *Third Programme of Law Reform*.
4. See Cretney, 'The Politics of Law Reform' (1985) 48 MLR 493, at 498; success may be only a comparative term.
5. Kerr, 'Law Reform in Changing Times' (1980) 96 LQR 505, at 533. The failings were to codify the law; to convince government of the value of law reform; and to obtain different consideration from Parliament for its measures.
6. Concern with the number of unimplemented reports is clear from Kerr, *supra*, n.5, but Cretney has questioned whether this is a problem for the Law Commission in *supra*, n.4, at 499ff. Any other measures of success would require clearer definition of the aims of reforming legislation and research to monitor its effect.
7. Law Commission No. 176, *Twenty-third Annual Report 1987-88* (1988). Those which did not lead to legislation were No. 53, *Solemnisation of Marriage*; No. 86, *Matrimonial Property*; and No. 175, *Matrimonial Property*.
8. Lord Scarman, 'Law Reform — the British Experience', The Jawaharlal Nehru Memorial Lecture (1979) quoted in Law Commission, *Twentieth Annual Report 1984-5*, para. 1.25, but the Children Act 1989 may make codification unnecessary — see Gibson 'The Law Commission' [1986] CLP 57, 65.

The importance of the Law Commission's work in family law should not be underestimated.[9] In the area of husband and wife there has been only one Act, the Domestic Violence and Matrimonial Proceedings Act 1976, which has not been the result of Law Commission recommendations.[10] This short Act was proposed by a private member and succeeded, in the face of considerable opposition, largely because of feminist campaigners who exposed the plight of battered women for whom the legal system provided inadequate remedies. During this period there was also legislation relating to children but much of this concerned the public care of children which is not within the Law Commission's work. The Law Commission's recent work on custody and guardianship, together with proposals on child care arising out of the DHSS Review of Child Care Law,[11] will produce the most fundamental reform of child law this century.[12]

Measuring success in law reform solely by reference to the structure of the statute book ignores fundamental issues. Does the law provide what people want? Is it provided in acceptable ways so that it will be used by those who need it? Will it produce the desired results? Of course, law that has merely been changed or consolidated has been reformed but one might expect a body such as the Law Commission to raise its sights higher.

The Law Commission's virtual monopoly over work on family law reform during the past twenty-five years means that its approach to law reform and to empirical research has predominated. Ensuring that empirical research is able to make a greater contribution may be more about educating the Law Commission than changing what researchers do.

From its inception the Law Commission emphasized the importance of research to the process of law reform: 'Clearly each project involves a certain amount of research and a certain amount of consultation. But while in the majority of cases research must come before consultation in some instances it is useful to reverse the order.'[13] The research envisaged in the beginning was not empirical research. This may not be surprising: in 1965 there was little work in law of this type in this country. Although the Second Annual Report of the Commission first made mention of an empirical study — John Hall's study of divorce court satisfaction certificates[14] — it was not until the Fifth Report that

---

9. See Deech, 'The work of the Law Commission in Family Law' in M. Freeman (ed.), *Essays in Family Law 1985*, Stevens (1986) 57, at 63.
10. Deech also notes the effect of the Law Commission on judicial decision-making in *supra*, n.9, at 75.
11. Brenda Hoggett, QC Law Commissioner, was a member of the inter departmental group which produced the *Review of Child Care Law* (1985).
12. Per Lord Mackay of Clashfern, Lord Chancellor, HL, Vol. 502, col. 487, 6 December 1988, Children Bill (2nd Reading).
13. Law Commission No. 4, *First Annual Report 1965-6*, para. 16.
14. Law Commission No. 12, *Second Annual Report 1966-7*, para. 78. This research was published as WP 15 (1968).

the Law Commission appeared to be involved in the promotion of studying the operation of law. There the Law Commission noted that it had participated in a decision of 'paramount importance' to set up the Oxford Centre for Socio-legal Research which 'would be invaluable to us in our work'.[15] The report for the following year merely noted that the Office of Population, Censuses and Surveys (OPCS) had done a survey for the Commission on Matrimonial Property.[16] However, the Seventh Report was most fulsome on the topic of empirical research:

> Our experience has caused us to give careful thought to ways and means of making greater use of the social sciences both in determining law reform priorities and in the preparation of proposals. It would be in our opinion dangerous to assume that the working paper technique because it is indispensible is therefore itself sufficient.[17]

This was extended the following year in a seminar entitled 'The Future of Law Reform' where '[t]he principal positive conclusion was that some improvement might be made in the use of social sciences in the service of law.'[18] It does not seem that the Law Commission acted on this. The Ninth and Tenth Annual Reports make no mention of empirical research. The Law Commission did not sponsor empirical research in family law and made only limited use of work that had been done in relation to its proposals for reform of family provision law[19] and the matrimonial jurisdiction of magistrates.[20]

The Eleventh Report returned to the subject of law reform and the social sciences. This time the Law Commission had had exploratory talks with the Social Sciences Research Council (SSRC) (now the ESRC) 'with the object of informing ourselves better about the nature of the contribution that social scientists can make to the processes of law reform'.[21] Again there is little in the annual reports to show that these discussions produced a more positive approach within the Commission, rather things seemed to continue as they had done before. Towards the end of the period there is perhaps some indication that the Law Commission was really beginning to act on its statements about social science research. However, in his Hamlyn Lecture in 1979 Lord McGregor noted that the Law Commission's resolve to 'evolve a standard procedure for harnessing social sciences to law reform . . . has remained an aspiration'.[22]

---

15. Law Commission No. 36, *Fifth Annual Report 1969–70*, para. 96.
16. Law Commission No. 47, *Sixth Annual Report 1970–71*, para. 45.
17. Law Commission No. 50 (1972), para. 2.
18. Law Commission No. 58, *Eight Annual Report 1972–3*, para. 76.
19. J.E. Todd and L.M. Jones, *Matrimonial Property*, HMSO (1972). See Law Commission No. 52, *First Report on Family Property: A new approach* and Law Commission No. 61, *Second Report on Family Property: Family Provision on Death*, para. 13.
20. See Law Commission WP 53 and Law Commission No. 77, *Report on Matrimonial Proceedings in Magistrates Courts* (1976) and O.R. McGregor, L. Blom-Cooper and C. Gibson, *Separated Spouses*, Duckworth (1970).
21. Law Commission No. 78, para. 6.
22. *Supra*, n.2, at 9.

It would be difficult to argue that the areas of family law chosen by the Law Commission were not those requiring reform or that the order in which they were tackled was perverse. However, there has been some debate about whether reform of the court system should precede reform of the substantial law relating to child custody.[23] The Law Commission's own working party on a Family Court was shelved first while the establishment of the courts to replace Assizes was pending and then when the Finer Committee on One Parent Families was set up.[24] Later the Law Commission worked on reforming the matrimonial jurisdiction of magistrates almost as if it had never heard of the case for a Family Court.[25] In addition, the decision by the Law Commission to look at the financial consequences of divorce in 1980 might be questioned on the basis that this was an area only recently legislated and one which would have been affected by proposals from the Commission which had failed to reach the statute book.[26] It seems from the introduction to Report No. 103 that the Law Commission was reluctant to consider this topic but felt pressured to do so under the weight of correspondence to Members of Parliament and the Lord Chancellor's Department.[27]

Originally the Law Commission had stressed that it wanted to consult on law reform not only with lawyers but also with laymen.[28] In the first few years of its operation it received a substantial number of proposals for reform in all areas, including family law, from the general public.[29] These do not seem directly to have shaped the law reform programmes which were largely selected by the Law Commission. Although in both the Seventh and the Sixteenth Reports the Commission had referred to using the social sciences to determine law reform priorities,[30] no work in family law was done to establish what changes the public saw as desirable. Rather, the Law Commission obtained its understanding of current public concerns from correspondents. Since as an organization it wanted to appear responsive to public opinion, it could not ignore a mass of letters when it had no other way of knowing what the public wanted.

---

23. Ibid., at 63; A. Morris, H. Giller, E. Szwed and H. Geach, *Justice for Children* (1980) 125, at 140. Hoggett, 'Family Courts or family law reform – which should come first?' (1986) 6 LS 1. The government has given priority to substantive reform — see *The Law on Child Care and Family Services*, Cm 62 (1987), para. 12.
24. Cmnd 5629 (1974); Law Commission No. 64, *Ninth Annual Report*, para. 31.
25. See Law Commission No. 77, *Report on Matrimonial Proceedings in Magistrates Courts*.
26. Law Commission No. 86. A Private Member's Bill was introduced by Lord Simon but was unsuccessful.
27. Law Commission No. 103, paras 2-5 .
28. First report, *supra*, n.13, para. 137.
29. For example, in its first year it received eighty-three proposals for reform of family law of which 24 per cent came from members of the public — *supra*, n.13, para. 129 and appendix II; see also *supra*, n.14, appendix III.
30. *Supra*, n.17; Law Commission No. 113 (1981), para. 1.15.

A similar point can be made in respect of the proposals in the working papers. The Law Commission had stated that 'consultation' was an important part of the process of law reform. They described the process of consultation as 'working in the open',[31] although this is perhaps an overstatement. The working papers set out provisional proposals for law reform which to a large extent determined its scope, its form and certainly the processes by which legal decisions would be made.[32] The choices and thus the potential input of those replying to working papers were quite limited. Moreover, by 1978 the Law Commission itself was wondering whether its consultation processes were effective.[33] Few responses were received from 'ordinary people'. A glance at any of the reports shows that respondents were mostly academics, professional groups of lawyers and voluntary organizations. In addition, the periods allowed for consultation meant that membership organizations which did reply, such as the Mothers' Union, the National Housewives' Register, the National Townswomens' Guild, etc., would not usually have been able to consult their members. Rather than seek an alternative to this type of consultation which would provide information about ordinary people's views, the Law Commission decided to draft short forms of the working papers which might receive more press coverage and attract a response, and also 'issues papers' to canvass views before provisional proposals were formulated.

Lord McGregor, writing about reform of debt enforcement and the magistrates' matrimonial jurisdiction, attributes the failure of reform to the lack of public knowledge and public opinion:

The lack both of historical knowledge and of official statistical information about the actual working and social results of the two jurisdictions meant that there was no public awareness of the issues involved, no public assessment of the quality of justice with which citizens were being served and no general public opinion upon which the committees' recommendations could bite. The truth is that nobody knew what was happening and nobody cared.[34]

The same could be said about a number of the areas with which the Law Commission was concerned in its family law programme.

In some areas, notably financial provision in divorce (and perhaps illegitimacy), there was public opinion but it was not the product of a considered view of the facts but reaction to hard-luck stories and the work of the Campaign for Justice in Divorce which had been very successful in portraying its view of the consequences of marriage

---

31. *Supra*, n.15, para. 3. Consultation was largely with those who were sent copies of Working Papers although these might be sent to the legal and national press (Second Annual Report, *supra*, n.14, para. 12); see Cretney, *supra*, n.4, at 505.
32. See R. Oerton, *Lament for the Law Commission*, Countrywise Press (1987), at 64ff. For a rather jaundiced view of the consultation and the development from Working Paper to Final Report.
33. Law Commission No. 97, *Fourteenth Annual Report 1978-9*, para. 14.
34. *Supra*, n.2, at 64.

breakdown in the media. The failure to inform and educate public opinion and thus provide a platform for law reform may not only have undermined the quality of work done by the Law Commission but also restricted the quantity and the subject-matter. In its Fifteenth Report, 1979-80, the Law Commission noted its concern about the non-implementation of a considerable number of its recommendations, a phenomenon which had not occurred in the first few years of its operation.[35] This was also referred to by Kerr LJ in his lecture 'Law Reform in Changing Times', where he noted that law reform was 'like politics no more than the art of the possible'.[36] When the Law Commission could not show that there was public pressure for its proposals it was unlikely to obtain government parliamentary time for them nor would Private Members be eager to take them up. Conversely, they were constrained to follow the opinions of a tiny minority and consider finance after divorce at a time when they did not view this as appropriate.

During their first twenty-five years there was only one instance when the Law Commission attempted to establish public opinion on a family law topic through empirical research. This was in relation to the ownership of property, particularly the family home, by married couples. A study was undertaken by OPCS,[37] which was used in the first, second and third reports on family property.[38] That study attempted to find out what couples did with their property, how they considered the property to be owned and what they wanted the law to provide. The difference between how the property was owned in law and how the couples viewed the ownership of property was an example of the rules not according with the parties' intentions, and provided good grounds for law reform. The third element, what the parties wanted from the law, posed more problems since questions were formulated on the basis of hypothetical rules. The difficulties of this strategy became only too clear from the questions on inheritance rights on death. At the time (1971), spouses had rights on intestacy to the first £8,750 of the deceased's estate (£30,000 if there were no children).[39] In cases where the deceased's intestacy or will failed to make reasonable provision for the surviving spouse he or she could seek a discretionary award in proceedings against the estate.[40] Testamentary freedom existed in theory but was tempered by Family Provision legislation. Having established that less than a quarter of spouses made wills and thus that there was potentially heavy reliance on the rules of intestacy, the OPCS canvassed views on fixed rights of inheritance. If introduced, these would restrict the testamentary

---

35. Law Commission No. 107, *Fifteenth Annual Report 1979-80*, para. 1.6.
36. *Supra*, n.5, at 526.
37. Todd and Jones, *supra*, n.19.
38. Law Commission No. 52; Law Commission No. 61; Law Commission No. 86.
39. Family Provision Act 1966, s.1; see Todd and Jones, *supra*, n.19, at 35ff.
40. Inheritance (Family Provision) Act 1938 (as amended).

freedom which the majority did not seek to exercise because they thought, apparently, that their property would be appropriately distributed without a will.

Opinions were divided but the majority expressed dislike of the need to apply to the court for a share of the estate where this was not provided.[41] However, there was little support for the proposal that the wife should have a right to one-third of assets on the death of the husband.[42] Thus the research provided opinions and facts but these were inconsistent. Consequently, the Law Commission felt justified in ignoring the research findings. The legislation which followed, the Inheritance (Provision for Family and Dependants) Act 1975, substantially changed the law on Family Provision but the outcome of the widow's/widower's claim rested on judicial discretion and would thus probably require court action. The current review of intestacy law did not re-examine this issue.[43]

Although the Law Commission obtained information about the ownership of the matrimonial home and the wishes of married couples, it was not able to use this information to achieve the desired co-ownership. The reasons for this must be a matter of conjecture, but it is clear that the Law Commission made very little of the findings of the survey in Report No. 86 and became absorbed in the intricacies of the highly complex scheme they had chosen to provide statutory co-ownership. In the face of opposition from lawyers (who objected to the scheme's complexity) and with the very real fear that co-ownership in the form chosen would not protect a spouse whose name was not on the title deeds, the proposal was shelved. It is ironic that one of the few failures of the Law Commission's terms was in an area where their proposals had some basis in public opinion.

The Law Commission's emphasis in preparing working papers has always been on 'black letter' research. The Law Commission has had no 'in-house' facilities for undertaking empirical research and has only commissioned the OPCS survey and a few small-scale studies in family law. Only two studies undertaken by the Law Commission have been published by them — John Hall's study of certificates of satisfaction,[44] and Priest and Whybrow's study of custody decisions.[45] Two small studies of judicial separation were also commissioned.[46] Over the same

---

41. Todd and Jones, *supra*, n.19, at 47.
42. Ibid., at 54. This was the figure proposed by the Law Commission in WP 42, *Family Property Law*, para. 4.19.
43. WP No. 108; para. 4.9. A 'survey of options' on the topic of intestacy was proposed, para. 1.1 and was carried out see Law Commission No. 187, para 1.
44. *Supra*, n.14.
45. Law Commission, *Custody Law in Practice in the Divorce and Domestic Courts*, supplement to WP 96 (1986).
46. See Law Commission No. 107, *Fifteenth Annual Report*, para. 2.24. These were subsequently published in Garlick, 'Judicial Separation — a Research Study' (1983) 46 MLR 719; S. Maidment, *Judicial Separation*, SSRC, (1982).

period a number of black letter law studies were commissioned,[47] in addition, substantial work was undertaken by the Commission's staff. It seems that the Commission was not seeking material on the working of law although they did make some use of it when it happened to be available.

Despite the repeated statements in the annual reports about the value of the social sciences, there does not appear to have been any effective commitment to obtaining empirical research. One reason for this may have been the effect such research would have had on the time taken to reform a given area of law. Interest in empirical research seemed to be greatest at a time when there was considerable concern about non-implementation. The Law Commission's concern with implementation may indicate that the time added by empirical research would have slowed the execution of reforms unacceptably.[47]

Where research material was available the Law Commission did not ignore it, but there is little in the working papers or reports to suggest that the Commission had gained anything from it other than a mere description of what happened in practice. Indeed, apart from the OPCS survey, the studies which were commissioned were descriptive ones. Moreover, in the case of Priest and Whybrow's study[48] the practice in custody had already been described in a large-scale study by Eekelaar[49] and a more limited one by Maidment.[50] That there was a wide range of outcomes from the exercise of judicial discretion in cases concerning children was well known. A further study could update the existing work but analyses would be more important both for understanding the current practice and reforming the law. These could seek to establish the reasons for judicial divergence or the long-term effect of different outcomes on parent–child relationships. The first would require access to a sample of the judiciary and magistrates; the second access to those involved in proceedings and their children. In the past, the Lord Chancellor's Department has been extremely reluctant to allow either of these types of data collection,[51] and consequently there has been no substantial work on judges handling family law cases and only limited work on outcomes. Researchers have had to obtain samples of ordinary people by taking their names from public documents[52] or finding them

---

47. Deech, *supra*, n.9, at 65. Cretney *supra*, n.4, at 503 suggests that knowing the circumstances of most people does not help to solve specific problems. However, this objection only applies to descriptive research.
48. *Supra*, n.45.
49. J. Eekelaar, E. Clive et al., *Custody after Divorce*, SSRC (1977).
50. Maidment, 'A Study of Child Custody' (1976) 6 Fam. L 200.
51. Zander, 'Promoting Change in the Legal System' (1979) 42 MLR 489, at 502; Wilson, 'English Legal Scholarship' (1987) 50 MLR 818, at 850; Feldman, 'The nature of legal scholarship' (1989) 52 MLR 498, at 510.
52. This technique was used by Murch in his study of the circumstances of families in divorce proceedings; see Murch, 'The Role of Solicitors in Divorce Proceedings' (1977) 40 MLR 625, at 626.

through other services like doctors or social workers. These methods are time-consuming and expensive and are not always successful.[53]

The Law Commission might be expected to be better placed than individual researchers at universities to obtain permission for these types of data collection. The reasons given for not permitting such studies — pressures on judicial time and interference with the litigant's free access to the courts — are not so overriding as to preclude research or make it unethical. Other public service professionals frequently participate in research,[54] although studies may be vetted to ensure that time will not be wasted. The Association of Directors of Social Services, for example, must approve studies involving social work staff. It is good practice to give interviewees a choice whether to participate in research. Priest and Whybrow were able to speak to some judges and magistrates, but no attempt appears to have been made to obtain a random sample or use a standardized interview technique.[55] Consequently only anecdotal material was obtained.

Empirical work in family law

During the 1970s and 1980s there were a considerable number of empirical studies relating to family law. John Eekelaar examined the matrimonial jurisdiction of registrars,[56] decisions in custody cases,[57] and more recently, with Mavis Maclean, the outcome and effects of financial settlements on divorce.[58] At Bristol University there have been a number of studies directed by Gwyn Davis and Mervyn Murch on the divorce process,[59] and recently Murch has published a study commissioned by the Lord Chancellor's Department on Overlapping Jurisdictions,[60] which contains valuable information from consumers about the court process.

---

53. They are also open to criticism — see David Napley's comments on J. Baldwin and M. McConville, 'Negotiated Justice' (1977), 74 Law Soc. Gaz. 830.
54. The dearth of research into private law and the work of the courts can be contrasted with the active research programmes commissioned by the Home Office and the Department of Health.
55. *Supra*, n.54, paras 1.3, 1.6, 6.6.
56. W. Barrington Baker, J. Eekelaar, C. Gibson and S. Raikes, *The Matrimonial Jurisdiction of Registrars*, SSRC (1977).
57. *Supra*, n.49.
58. J. Eekelaar, M. Maclean, *Maintenance after Divorce*, Clarendon Press (1986); M. Maclean and J. Eekelaar, *Children & Divorce: Economic Factors*, Centre for Socio-legal Studies (1984).
59. Murch, *supra*, n.52; and *Justice and Welfare in Divorce*, London, Sweet & Maxwell (1980); Davies, Macleod and Murch, 'Undefended divorce: should s.41 of MCA 1973 be repealed?' (1983) 46 MLR 121; Elston, Fuller and Murch, 'Judicial hearings of undefended divorce petitions' (1975) 38 MLR 609.
60. M. Murch, *The Overlapping Family Jurisdiction of the Magistrates, Court and County Court*, Socio Legal Centre for Family Studies, University of Bristol (1987).

Susan Maidment carried out two small-scale studies on custody decisions and judicial separation.[61] Carol Smart studied solicitors advising and acting in maintenance cases.[62] There has also been some work on the victims of domestic violence and their experience of the legal process.[63] The Lord Chancellor's Department also commissioned a major study into conciliation from Newcastle University.[64] If a broader view of family law is taken, studies of adoption and step-parent adoption[65] may be included as well as numerous studies on the working of the care system.[66] These latter studies are interesting because it appears that many of their findings will lead to law reform.[67] Studies were commissioned for the Child Care Law Review;[68] research by the Dartington Research Unit,[69] by Jean Packman[70] and Jane Rowe,[71] has shaped proposals for the reform of the law on place of safety orders, access to children in care and the powers of care authorities.

Although existing empirical research in family law tends to be descriptive, studies can be divided into three categories: those which provide information about the court process; those which provide information about solicitors; and those which provide information about litigants. Grouping studies together helps to draw out general impressions of the operation of the system, identify potential problems across different areas like custody and maintenance and also to develop further research proposals. The available research permits some general conclusions about the difficulties associated with the type of family law that has been developed over the last twenty-five years.

Modern family law is largely a collection of discretionary remedies rather than a statement of rights and a system for enforcing them.

---

61. Maidment, *supra*, nn.46 and 50.
62. C. Smart, *The ties that bind*, RKP (1984).
63. J. Pahl, *A refuge for battered women*, HMSO (1978); S. Edwards, *Police response to domestic violence in London*, Polytechnic of Central London (1986); M. Borkowski, M. Murch and V. Walker, *Matrimonial Violence*, Tavistock (1983).
64. University of Newcastle upon Tyne, *Report to the Lord Chancellor's Department on the costs and effectiveness of conciliation in England and Wales* (1989).
65. J. Masson, D. Norbury and S. Chatterton, *Mine, Yours and Ours?* HMSO (1983); O. Gill and B. Jackson, *Adoption and Race*, London, Batsford (1983).
66. Children Act 1975, s.105 provided for research into its provisions and a number of studies were commissioned — see *Children Act 1975, Second Report to Parliament* (HCP 1984–5 20); and the numerous studies noted in M. Shaw, *Family Placement for Children in Care*, BAAF (1987), at 15–20.
67. Through their influence on the *DHSS Review of Child Care Law*, (1985). They have also been disseminated amongst social workers and their managers in order to improve practice — see DHSS, *Social Work Decisions in Child Care* (1985).
68. See DHSS, *Review of Child Care Law* (1985), Annex C, HMSO.
69. S. Millham, R. Bullock, K. Hosie and M. Haak, *Lost in Care*, Aldershot, Gower (1986); S. Millham, R. Bullock, K. Hosie and M. Little, *Access Disputes in Child-care*, Gower (1989).
70. J. Packman, J. Randall and N. Jacques, *Who Needs Care?*, Oxford, Blackwell, (1986).
71. J. Rowe and L. Lambert, *Children Who Wait*, ABAA (1973).

Discretionary remedies impose a heavy burden on the judiciary[72] to ensure formal justice, that is, that like cases end with like orders. Evidence indicates that this burden is not being discharged very satisfactorily. Perhaps the most stunning example of this is in the DHSS Stepparent Adoption Study which found that the success rate for uncontested applications was 90 per cent in one county and 10 per cent in another county in the same year.[73] Discretionary remedies also impose a heavy burden on legal advisers, both when explaining what the law is[74] and when advising whether a proposed settlement should be accepted. The operation of family law is based in practice on out of court negotiation. The cost of litigation is high and the effect of the Legal Aid Charge means that both legally aided and non-legally aided clients pay the cost of the dispute if matrimonial property is involved. Where the parties agree it is not clear that the court does more than merely rubber-stamp the agreement. Little consideration had been given to these elements of the operation of family law when reforms were being devised.[75] This is an area where substantial research needs to be done, particularly if more emphasis is placed on the legal system as a service.

When research concentrates on what the courts do in individual cases, the expectations of potential litigants and the symbolic effect of law may be overlooked. The symbolic importance of law can be seen from Carol Smart's work on solicitors in Sheffield.[76] The advice women clients received depended not only on what the law appeared from the texts to state, but also on the solicitors' and the women's perceptions about what they had the right to expect.[77] Solicitors often found it difficult to convince a male client that he would be expected to support his wife after divorce.[78] This may be understandable considering that there was not then (nor is there now) any clear statement about this in the legislation. The role of the solicitor in conveying (and changing) the meaning of the law to clients also comes out clearly from Priest and Whybrow's study of joint custody.[79] Solicitors appeared to minimize the importance of the

---

72. The Law Commission considered that complete discretion in reallocation of property following divorce would be an 'abdication of responsibility by Parliament in favour of the judiciary' — Law Commission No. 103, *The Financial Consequences of Divorce: the basic policy*, Cmnd 8041, para. 69.
73. Masson et al., *supra*, n.65, at 84.
74. *Supra*, n.62, Chapter 8.
75. '[L]aw reform must concern itself as much with the form, arrangement and procedures of the law as with its substance' — Law Commission No. 4, *First Annual Report*, para. 135.
76. *Supra*, n.62. The proposals for child law are made with this directly in mind. The term parental rights is replaced by parental responsibility which is shared by married parents and retained by both of them after divorce — see Law Commission No. 178, paras 2.4, 2.11. See also Children Act 1989, Part I.
77. *Supra*, n.62, Chapter 8.
78. Ibid., at 166.
79. *Supra*, n.45. Judges also interpreted the effect of custody orders to make them more acceptable to the parents — see para. 5.22.

differing types of custody order so as to make their clients more willing to accept what the court had ordered.[80] Although there is evidence that clients' ideas about the law are confused and inaccurate, this should not be interpreted as showing that the law does not have a symbolic effect. Perhaps the emphasis on discretionary remedies has produced views that rights no longer exist in the context of family law. A person who believes that he or she has no rights is unlikely to seek remedies or adopt a strong negotiating position. The limited research available does not justify the conclusion that the emphasis on discretion deters claims for maintenance, property adjustment or custody. However, taken with the earlier finding that widows and widowers would prefer a system of protected inheritance which did not require court proceedings, this is a matter for further investigation.

Studies of litigants show that most of them dislike court proceedings, are irked by the time wasted and the unpleasant surroundings where they wait for their case to be called, and some at least find judges or magistrates arrogant and unpleasant.[81] Court proceedings, even in cases where there is no dispute, produce high levels of anxiety in clients. Consequently, they may feel that they need a representative even though their solicitor and the Legal Aid system would not agree.[82] Thus it would seem unlikely that the public would use the courts where this was not strictly necessary. Moreover, there is some evidence from studies of the DSS and Housing Departments that applications for maintenance and for injunctions are not made because the applicant (usually the wife) wants a court order, but so that she can prove to some official that her marriage has broken down. Again, further research on the reasons for litigation in family law disputes (and non-disputes) is necessary. The current state of knowledge might suggest that 'reforms' such as joint custody for parents and step-parents[83] and court orders allowing unmarried parents legally to share parental rights,[84] might be used by only a tiny minority of those who effectively share such rights outside the law. Thus despite reform, the law still fails to secure that people's legal status accords with their actions.

The descriptive nature of most of the empirical studies in family law means that these ideas drawn from an overview of the research cannot be clearly established from the available analyses. Only a minority of

---

80. *Supra*, n.45, paras 5.11, 5.22, 5.23.
81. *Supra*, n.60, Chapter 13.
82. *Supra*, n.60, at 75–7. Legal Aid has not been available for undefended divorce proceedings since the introduction of Special Procedure.
83. Adoption Act 1976, s.14(3) (Children Act 1975, s.10(3)) required the court to dismiss adoption applications if a custody order made under the Matrimonial Causes Act 1973, s.42 in favour of the parent and step-parent would better safeguard the child's welfare.
84. Family Law Reform Act 1987, s.4. Under the Children Act 1989, s.4 unmarried parents will be able to register a formal agreement instead of seeking a court order but this too may be too bureaucratic for those who have chosen not to marry.

studies in family law have attempted to go beyond a fairly basic description of their subject-matter. In some cases the data would not have warranted or withstood complex analysis. However, there have been some other failings by researchers. It is not unknown for counts and comparisons to be made and conclusions drawn which are not statistically valid;[85] more frequently the published material does not indicate this and the reader must turn to his or her own calculator. It is obviously essential that conclusions are firmly based on the data. The restricted scope of many inquiries is relevant here as well. It is unsatisfactory, for example, to try to determine people's reasons for taking proceedings purely from looking at their characteristics from court papers or interviewing their legal advisers. In many cases researchers have had no alternative because of their inability to gain access to the people. Conclusions drawn from such research are less credible (rightly so) and thus less likely to be taken seriously as a basis for law reform.

The same holds true for the proposals for reform which some researchers have made. In most cases only part of the proposal can be seen as based on the research findings, part may be based on other findings but much is usually owed to the researchers' unresearched views on the role of the legal system and what people want from it. Such proposals have not apparently been taken seriously as a basis for legislation. If research were given a higher profile, proposals made by those with detailed and intimate knowledge of the subject would be seen as the basis for law reform, possibly after further research and informed debate.

Conclusion

The first requirement of research which could form the basis of legislation is that it should help to establish what people want. This, as the OPCS study showed, is not a simple matter. Public opinion must be informed before it can be formed. Knowledge of specific likes and dislikes is only valuable where it relates to what is on offer, preferably that which has been experienced by the respondents. Also, there is little point in establishing (even in research commissioned by the Lord Chancellor's Department) that litigants want comfortable and spacious waiting-areas in courts if the costings for court buildings are never going to allow the creation of such facilities. Where research is commissioned by those who have the power to use it, they must be prepared to let the findings influence their priorities. This approach requires a general acceptance of the principle that the legal system provides a service for taxpayers and, as such, should attempt to serve those who pay for it. It is

---

85. It would be unfair to single out examples but readers should note how far research reports include chi-square statistics or other significance tests.

difficult to imagine any public or private company being allowed to treat its customers as the legal system does.

A programme of law reform could start not as the Law Commission did but by establishing views on the system, both from those who have been involved in family law litigation and those who have not. It would aim to establish a set of rules which were thought to be appropriate to govern marriage and a series of processes for dealing with different types of dispute and for consensual ending of a union. Clearly this would require more than empirical research; the Law Commission could provide a useful service in examining the legal basis for the proposed developments and attempting to ensure that a coherent body of law was produced.

Even if such a radical approach is rejected, the case has been made for more and better research which goes beyond a mere description of what occurs in the courts. The second generation of research should attempt to establish more about the views of litigants, the effect and effectiveness of their advisers and the judicial process. This will require access to litigants, co-operation from the profession and the involvement of the judiciary. Law reform without research may produce clearer sets of rules but it will not provide workable, efficient and just reformed law.

5 Regulating the City

Fiona Patfield and Ian Snaith

Introduction

Deregulation, Regulation and Self-Regulation

The debate between the proponents of deregulation, essentially free marketeers fuelled by the writings of the Chicago economists, and the proponents of regulation has been applied to many different areas of economic activity. Systems of self-regulation have emerged as an alternative to deregulation or legal regulation. Clearly, there are those who would assert that self-regulation is closely allied to (or indeed a form of) deregulation.[1] It is not the intention of this chapter to pursue the argument of a dichotomy between deregulation and self-regulation, but rather that of a dichotomy between self-regulation and legal regulation. This argument will be pursued as a means of considering the effectiveness and desirability of the City Panel on Takeovers and Mergers which operates under the City Code.

It is necessary at this point, for the sake of clarity, to allude to the suggestion that self-regulation should be distinguished from non-statutory regulation. Some proponents of this argument have asserted that the type of regulation to be found in the City Code is better described as non-statutory regulation than as self-regulation.[2] While not wanting to take issue with this view, it does nevertheless seem that the distinction made in this case is largely semantic or symbolic when one considers the composition of the Panel.[3] The flaws, which this chapter will argue lie in the present system of regulating takeovers and mergers in the interests of

---

1. See, e.g., Cranston, 'Regulation and Deregulation: General Issues' in R. Tomasic (ed.), *Business Regulation in Australia* CCH Australia Limited (1984), at 13–41; and Tomasic, 'Business Regulation and the Administrative State' in Tomasic, op cit., at 43–67.
2. E.g., A. Beevor, Speech delivered to Institute of Economic Affairs Conference on *Law and Economics*, 17 May 1989, at 3.
3. See *infra*, text at p.74.

shareholders, apply whether the system is described as self-regulation or non-statutory regulation. Accordingly, it is not proposed to draw any distinction between the two. (It would seem, however, that the concept of non-statutory regulation may serve the function of distinguishing the Panel, which is without any statutory basis, from the Self Regulatory Organisations under the Financial Services Act 1986, which fit into the statutory pattern of regulation but are described as 'self-regulatory'.)

In this essay an attempt is made to consider the arguments for and against self-regulation by analysing the working of the Code and the Panel from 1986 to 1989 on the basis of some of the Panel's published statements. Space does not permit the analysis of all statements but some indication of the functioning of the Panel system is provided by those selected.

The characteristics of the City Code

This section describes how, in general terms, the City Code works and why it is to be classified as a system of self-regulation.

The Code applies to takeover bids for all public companies (listed and unlisted) and for certain private companies which have formerly had shares listed or otherwise subject to certain public dealings.[4] The Code 'represents the collective opinion of those professionally involved in the field of takeovers as to good business standards and as to how fairness to shareholders can be achieved'.[5] This 'opinion' is expressed in the form of ten General Principles and thirty-eight Rules (excluding the 'SARs' or Rules Governing Substantial Acquisitions of Shares). Both General Principles and Rules are 'to be interpreted to achieve their underlying purpose'[6] and both may be relaxed or modified by the Panel in a particular case. This is seen by the defenders of self-regulation in this field as a key virtue of the system.

The Panel compiles and interprets the Code and deals with disputes over its application. The Panel consists of a Chairman, Deputy Chairman and a non-representative member (all appointed by the Bank of England), together with the representatives of twelve organizations made up of associations of market professionals or users and Self Regulatory Organisations (SROs) (operating within the system of regulation established by the Financial Services Act 1986). The day-to-day work of the Panel is carried out by its executive, which monitors and investigates bids and which can be consulted and asked for a ruling before or during a bid. Such consultation is advocated by the Code in its Introduction as a means of avoiding and resolving doubts about whether a proposed

---

4. See *City Code on Takeovers and Mergers* (hereafter the 'Code'), 'Introduction', at A7.
5. Ibid., at A1.
6. Ibid., at A3.

course of action will be a breach of the Code. This is intended to mitigate the uncertainty that flows from the flexible application and interpretation of the Code and the use of a teleological approach to its contents.

The Panel hears appeals against executive rulings and first instance disciplinary cases brought by the executive against those alleged to have violated the Code. A right of appeal exists against a Panel decision to an Appeal Committee in the following circumstances: if the Panel proposes disciplinary action after finding a breach; if it is alleged that the Panel has acted outside its jurisdiction; or, if a Panel decision does not recognize a market-maker or fund manager as exempt for the purposes of the Code. In other cases, appeal is only available with the leave of the Panel. The Appeal Committee is composed of two Panel members who were not involved in the original decision and the Chairman of the Appeal Committee, who is a former holder of high judicial office.

Both the composition and the *modus operandi* of the Panel underlie its status as a system of self-regulation. It will be argued below that the proponents of the system overstate the problems of setting up a statutory system which could operate flexibly. However, the composition of the Panel — even after the changes announced as a result of the review of its operations in the light of the Guinness Affair[7] — represents self-regulation by financial (rather than industrial) interests. Only the appointee of the CBI and the three appointees of the Bank of England represent industrial or public sector organizations. The other eleven members represent the private financial sector; although three of them sit for SROs, which are organizations professionally concerned with the regulation of the financial services industry.

Arguments for the self-regulatory system embodied in the City Code

Flexibility

The strongest argument in favour of the present system is its flexibility.[8] Flexibility is allowed for in the purposive approach provided for in the General Principles. However, it has been suggested that this flexibility is not always fully utilized.[9] The extent to which this is so may be partly due to the fact that the Panel fears 'unacceptable inconsistency',[10] which is unfair[11] and may dilute industry support. The

---

7. Panel Statement, 11 May 1987.
8. See generally, Beevor, *supra*, n.2; Hurst, 'Self Regulation versus Legal Regulation' 5 The Co. Lawyer 161; and J. Gower, *Review of Investor Protection: A Discussion Document*, HMSO (1982).
9. Hurst, *supra*, n.8, at 167.
10. Beevor, *supra*, n.2, at 11.
11. Hurst, *supra*, n.8, at 167.

corollary of this is that, were the Panel to use its discretion more fully, it may well lose the industry approval which appears essential to the maintenance of a self-regulatory system. Also, it may be open to an attack of arbitrariness. Arguably, 'arbitrariness' is particularly serious as it cannot sufficiently be controlled by recourse to the courts because judicial review will be 'historical' in most cases.[12] On the other hand, the role of the Appeal Committee mitigates the criticism that excessive exercise of flexibility may lead to uncontrolled arbitrariness.

The flexibility of the Panel's operation can be divided into two elements. First, the application and interpretation of the Code by the use of the General Principles as well as the Rules, and the application of the spirit as well as the letter of its provisions to novel situations represent one form of flexibility. Second, amendments to the text of the Code can be announced and given immediate effect without the need for the government or legislative action that would be necessary for primary or secondary legislation.

Recent Panel decisions illustrate the benefits of the flexible interpretation and application which the Code allows. In a number of decisions the Code was applied to a wholly novel situation. Thus in *Statutory Water Companies*[13] a formula was devised to deal with the problem of companies with different share classes having different voting rights, which rights also varied with the size of shareholdings. The general principle of equal treatment for shareholders was applied, for the purpose of the rules relating to limits on holdings and mandatory bids, by reference to the maximum possible voting rights obtainable by the arrangement of shareholdings. Similarly, in *BP Britoil*[14] the problem of the government 'golden share' in a target company was resolved by allowing the bidder to bid for more than 50 per cent of the ordinary shares without reference to the single golden share which gave its holder majority voting rights in the event of a bid. This was despite the wording of Rules 9 and 10 which, interpreted literally, would prevent any bid in such a case by requiring that the bid be conditional on obtaining a majority of votes. This gave the shareholders an opportunity to consider the bid, but left the final outcome in the hands of the government as golden shareholder. The alternative approach would have prevented a bid from being launched until the government had decided to relinquish the rights conferred by the golden share.

A particularly striking example of the use of flexible interpretation of the Code is provided by the *Hogg Robinson* case,[15] which was described

---

12. See, for example, *R* v. *Panel on Takeovers and Mergers, ex parte Datafin PLC* [1987] 2 WLR 699 and *R* v. *City Panel on Takeovers and Mergers, ex parte Guinness PLC* [1989] 2 WLR 863.
13. Panel Statement on Statutory Water Companies, 6 June 1988, [1988] JBL 415.
14. Panel Statement, 23 December 1987, [1988] JBL 165.
15. Panel Statement, 4 August 1987, [1987] JBL 481.

by Morse as illustrating flexibility as part of the case for self-regulation.[16] In that case the rule against further bids for the same offeree company by the same bidder within one year of an earlier unsuccessful bid was applied to a different company created from the demerger of parts of the original target company. On a literal interpretation of Rule 35 a new bid would have been possible as a different company was involved, but the Panel ruled that the interest of the company in being protected from a continuing state of siege justified the application of the rule to a bid which would have the same practical effect. In a further application of flexibility, a dispensation was then given to the bidder under Rule 35 by limiting the period of restriction to nine months.

Some of the most dramatic examples of flexibility and innovation in the application of the Code have concerned the treatment by the Panel of conflicts with overseas regulatory procedures in situations where those procedures were, arguably, being used as defensive measures by a target company. Having established its approach to references to the UK Monopolies and Mergers Commission by the Office of Fair Trading,[17] the Panel had to deal with the issue of overseas anti-trust litigation in *Minorco/Consolidated Goldfields PLC*.[18] It decided that, despite the absence of any reference in Rule 21 to litigation as a frustrating measure by the offeree board requiring the approval of the shareholders, General Principle 9 extended to litigation in the United Kingdom or overseas. On the facts of the case this finding was to little avail as the continuation of an action by a company in which the offeree had a 49 per cent holding was not the subject of any order by the Panel requiring shareholder approval because of the absence of 'legal control' and the particular arrangements which governed the running of that US company. However the extension of the General Principle to a novel situation is significant as an example of flexibility.

In *BAT Industries PLC*[19] it was decided that political lobbying would not fall within Rule 21 and that assistance to and intervention in litigation on the side of the regulators of the insurance industry in certain US state jurisdictions did not, on the facts, amount to frustrating action. However, in a decision upheld by the Appeal Committee, the Panel allowed the offer to lapse with a new bid, permitted by way of dispensation from the operation of Rule 35, so long as it was made within twenty-one days of the final decision of the US regulatory authorities about the suitability of the offeror's arrangements in relation to the target's insurance subsidiaries. An overall ceiling of one year from the

---

16. [1987] JBL 481.
17. See the Code, Rules 12 and 9.4; *Emess Lighting/Rotaflex PLC*, Panel Statement, 11 June 1986, [1986] JBL 410; and *Hanson Trust PLC/Imperial Group PLC*, Panel Statement, 11 February 1986, [1986] JBL 315.
18. Panel Statement, 9 May 1989.
19. Panel Statement, 15 September 1989.

date of the Appeal Committee decision was imposed on the timing of a new bid. In a statement on the uses of flexibility, the Appeal Committee referred to the need for the orderly and consistent development of the application of the Code but accepted that the absence of a precedent did not justify a refusal to grant a dispensation to deal with overseas regulatory issues.

It must be noted, however, that the flexibility exhibited by the Panel in the interpretation and application of the Code may be used in favour of those who are subject to regulation as well as for the purpose of more effective regulation. Thus the Code may be applied so as to take no action against a party found to be in breach,[20] or even to refuse to take action to rectify an acknowledged wrong against shareholders 'bounced' into accepting an offer over one weekend in breach of the Code.[21] Also, the Panel's flexibility has limits. It is not seen as being available to fill gaps if neither a General Principle nor a Rule is involved — in such a case the Panel may express a view without making a formal ruling.[22] The problems of uncertainty that can flow from flexibility in the interpretation and application of the Code are perhaps obvious.[23] They are the price which is paid for the benefits of flexibility.

The flexibility of the Code in providing for its own speedy amendment to deal with problems and rapid market change has not been demonstrated unambiguously. Thus, in the case of the technical amendments required to prevent a recurrence of the problem of the double counting of acceptances which occurred in *Blue Circle Industries*,[24] a period of seven months elapsed between the bid and the announcement of the amendments. Such a timespan would be sufficient to allow for the amendment of a statutory instrument or code applied by a statutory body, although the Panel did announce certain immediate measures to ameliorate the problem in the interim.[25] Similarly, the amendments necessitated by the 'Big Bang'[26] could have been introduced by statutory instrument as the changes in the markets with which they dealt were announced long before their implementation. On the other hand, the Panel acted within two months to announce an amendment in relation to fixed price offers which clarified a rather vague provision of the Code.[27] It also dealt speedily and effectively with perceived difficulties

---

20. See *Rexnord Holdings UK PLC/Avdel PLC*, Panel Statement, 23 December 1988.
21. See *Irish Distillers PLC*, Panel Statement, 17 November 1988, [1989] JBL 150.
22. *Tozer, Kemsley & Milbourn (Holdings) PLC/Molins PLC*, Panel Statement, 30 June 1987, [1987] JBL 483.
23. See, e.g. Panel Statement on Offer Announcements, 10 September 1987, [1988] JBL 70; *Scottish and Newcastle PLC/Matthew Brown PLC*, Panel Statement, 12 December 1985, [1986] JBL 312; and Panel Statement, 17 December 1987, [1988] JBL 164.
24. Panel Statement, 4 March 1988, [1988] JBL 323.
25. Panel Statement, 27 October 1988.
26. See Panel Statement on Multi-Service financial organizations and the Takeover Code, 6 October 1986, [1987] JBL 42.
27. Panel Statement, 17 December 1987, [1988] JBL 164.

with the advertising techniques of parties to bids, with short selling and with the role of the boards of predators and targets in the light of the Guinness Affair.[28]

If it is assumed that a statutory system for the regulation of takeovers must take the form of a set of rules contained in a statute or in delegated legislation, flexibility of interpretation and application or flexibility in amendment would not be available. However, a statute could be used to establish a body with effective sanctions and investigative powers to operate a code of practice — based on principles as well as rules — devised by that body. Such a system could operate with the same degree of flexibility in interpretation and amendment, and on the basis of the same approach to judicial reviews as the present Panel and Code. It could also overcome the difficulties of liaison with other systems and of enforcement and investigation.[29] It would also be indirectly answerable to Parliament and, thus, reflect the public interest more clearly than a self-regulatory body.[30]

Speed and low cost

The benefits of speed and low cost are said to derive from the informality of proceedings before the Panel[31] and the speed with which advance advice can be given by the Panel executive (stopping serious damage from occurring).[32] However, there is no obvious reason why an adequately funded statutory body could not conduct informal proceedings and provide advance advice speedily. It is possible that the advance advice facility would not work as well without the level of industry support which is currently given to the self-regulatory system,[33] but the need for certainty and a willingness to deal more sympathetically with those who used the facility might compensate for that.

Small amount of litigation

The argument that the present system generates little litigation is based on comparisons with jurisdictions, such as the United States and

---

28. See Panel Statement, 26 March 1986, [1986] JBL 318; Panel Statement, 30 July 1987 (now Code, Appendix 3), [1987] JBL 480.
29. The difficulties in enforcement and investigation are discussed *infra*, text at pp.82 and 85, respectively.
30. The amendments to the Financial Services Act 1986, in s.192 of the Companies Act 1989 and the changes to SRO and Security and Investment Board (SIB) rules that have flowed from them are a clear indication of the feasibility of such an approach. They permit the use of 'statements of principle' by the SIB and the SROs under that legislation and make disciplinary measures (but not an action for breach of statutory duty) available to enforce such 'principles'.
31. Hurst, *supra*, n.8.
32. Beevor, *supra*, n.2.
33. The importance of industry support is discussed *infra*, text at p.80ff.

Australia, which operate on the basis of statutory regulation.[34] In a sense this argument is an aspect of the low-cost argument, but because it is so frequently claimed as an advantage[35] it deserves separate attention. Clearly, reducing litigation is not necessarily always a good thing in itself thus it is important to consider why the Code tends to reduce litigation. The reduction in litigation may be due partly to the advance advice facility of the Panel executive mentioned above. It may also represent satisfaction with the Code. More likely, however, it is a reflection of the fact that a non-statutory code does not create a cause of action in an aggrieved person.[36] In any case, the people who may be aggrieved may not be the companies or their respective managements, but rather the investors whose dealing with the Panel are significantly less.[37]

The attitude of the courts to the judicial review of the decisions of the Panel is the major factor in reducing their involvement in its operation. As is well known, the Court of Appeal in *R* v. *Panel on Takeovers and Mergers, ex parte Datafin PLC*,[38] which established the availability of judicial review of the Panel's decisions, made clear the limited circumstances in which a remedy would actually be given. Sir John Donaldson followed the approach to the proceedings of the Monopolies and Mergers Commission in *R* v. *Monopolies and Mergers Commission, ex parte Argyll Group PLC*[39] in emphasizing 'the awareness of the court of the special needs of the financial markets for speed on the part of decision makers and for being able to rely on those decisions as a sure basis for dealing on the market'.[40] Consequently the Master of the Rolls made it clear that:

[I]n the light of the special nature of the panel, its functions, the market in which it is operating, the time scales which are inherent in that market and the need to safeguard the position of third parties, who may be numbered in thousands, all of whom are entitled to continue to trade upon an assumption of the validity of the panel's rules and decisions, unless and until they are quashed by the court, I should expect the relationship between the panel and the court to be historic rather than contemporaneous.[41]

This decision and the decision of the Court of Appeal in *R* v. *City Panel on Takeovers and Mergers, ex parte Guinness PLC*[42] make it clear that the Panel's proceedings will continue to be free from frequent litigation.

---

34. See, e.g., Beevor, *supra*, n.2; Hurst, *supra*, n.8; and Gower, *supra*, n.8.
35. E.g., Beevor, *supra*, n.2 and Gower, *supra*, n.8.
36. Hurst, *supra*, n.8. Cf. *Re St Piran Ltd* 1 WLR 1300, where the Code was recognized as indicating an appropriate standard of conduct: Hurst, *supra*, n.8, at 167n.
37. An extra-legal compensation order may be available: see *infra*, see text at p.83.
38. [1987] 2 WLR 699.
39. [1986] 1 WLR 763.
40. [1987] 2 WLR 699, at 716.
41. Ibid., at 718.
42. [1989] 2 WLR 863.

However, as a former chairman of the Panel has pointed out,[43] this approach of the courts is not limited to non-statutory bodies. *Argyll* is not the only case on the operation of the Monopolies and Mergers Commission in which the courts have made it clear that in considering judicial review applications they will have regard to the nature of the process with which the Commission is involved and the fact that the financial market acts on its decisions.[44] This suggests that a statutory basis for a body performing the role of the Panel need not result in excessive judicial intervention or intervention that is inappropriate in the context of the financial markets.

Any disadvantages that might arise from the absence of access to the courts is mitigated by the availability of recourse to the Appeal Committee. In the *BAT*[45] ruling, the Appeal Committee stated that its role was to consider appeals and was not to be limited to reviewing the decisions of the Panel on the grounds of procedural fairness and rationality. However, by analogy with the role of an appeal court, the Committee stressed that it would not substitute its own exercise of discretion for that of the Panel. Thus, under the present system, appeal on the merits against the Panel's decisions is available in many cases — albeit leave is required in cases not involving disciplinary matters, questions of jurisdiction or the exempt status of market-makers or fund managers. Such an appellate system could, however, readily be achieved under a statutory system by the use of a Tribunal.

Industry support

Another advantage of the present system is said to be its level of industry support, but even Beevor has described this as 'less obvious'.[46] This support is said to be based on a belief that the present system is preferable to the alternative.[47] It is said to be important, in the interests of fairness, to have this support when administering a code with such wide discretionary powers.[48] Industry support is thus seen to be necessary to allow the sacrifice of the short-term gain of an individual party in order to further the industry interest in avoiding greater restriction on all.

A starting point in evaluating this benefit may be to ask why the Code enjoys industry support. It has been suggested[49] that this is

---

43. Alexander, 'Judicial Review and City Regulators' (1989) 52 MLR 640.
44. See also *R* v. *Monopolies and Mergers Commission, ex parte Elders IXL Ltd* [1987] 1 WLR 1221 and *R* v. *Monopolies Commission, ex parte Matthew Brown PLC* [1987] 1 WLR 1235.
45. Panel Statement, 15 September 1989.
46. *Supra*, n.2, at 6.
47. Ibid.
48. Ibid.
49. Beevor, *supra*, n.2, at 7.

because of the advance advice facility. Other possible reasons, which might occur to a more cynical observer, are the absence of serious sanctions and the desire for the industry not to become subject to scrutiny from a public statutory body. If this is so, then the sacrifice, in fact, being made here may be the sacrifice of a wider public interest to the interests of the industry. This is taken up below. On the other hand, two arguments that can be made about the benefits of industry support are as follows. First, a statutory body with serious powers of enforcement and a rigorous attitude may lose industry support and that this may lead to a crisis of confidence with serious economic consequences. Second, industry support leads to a better supply of expert personnel on the regulatory body thus increasing its efficiency, speed and ability to exercise discretion.

A problem which persists is that if industry support is necessary in order to make a system, like the current system, with no effective sanctions work, then this may mean a certain amount of 'playing to the gallery'.[50] This may mean that the discretion (which, it is argued, can only be allowed because of industry support) will not be exercised fully. Thus, the advantage which industry support gives in this respect is illusory and we are left with the likelihood that industry supports self-regulation because it gains from it.

It is difficult to assess those instances in which the Panel might have been influenced by the need to retain industry support or in which the absence of such support might have resulted in a different decision. In its approach to the *Guinness* decision, the Panel exhibited caution in suspending its hearing and awaiting the outcome of the judicial review proceedings despite the observations of the Master of the Rolls in the *Datafin* case.[51] This, however, may have owed more to a concern to behave properly in relation to the courts than to a perceived need to maintain industry support.[52] The decision to amend the Code in relation to the need for a fixed price for offers[53] at a minimum figure determined by reference to the price paid in recent purchases by the bidder or its concert party had the effect of relieving predators from the difficulties likely to be experienced in making bids in the immediate aftermath of the crash of October 1987 when shares had been bought at high pre-crash prices. The Panel amended Rule 6.1 to fix the period at three months in place of the vaguer rule applying to purchases when an offer was 'reasonably in contemplation'. Could this have been intended to preserve 'industry' support by predator clients and their advisers?

The Panel's decision[54] to amend Rule 19, note 1 to place greater

---

50. Ibid.
51. [1987] 2 WLR 699.
52. See *R* v. *City Panel on Takeovers and Mergers, ex parte Guinness PLC* [1989] 2 WLR 863; *Guinness PLC/The Distillers Company PLC*, Panel Statement, 14 July 1989 and the comment by Morse, [1988] JBL, at 163 and 329.
53. Panel Statement, 17 December 1987.
54. Panel Statement, 6 February 1989, [1988] JBL 149.

reliance on the advisers of the parties to police meetings at which information is provided or views are expressed when those meetings are held during a bid but involve only selected shareholders (and thus run the risk of breaking the rule requiring equality of information to all shareholders) is an example of increased reliance on the support of the financial services industry. Similarly, the post-Guinness changes to the Code to ensure that all board members are kept informed of the progress of a bid[55] rely in part, according to the statement announcing the new approach, on the parties' advisers to ensure that directors are aware of their responsibilities.

Could those rulings in which an apology satisfies the Panel, or only a reminder is given about a breach because an act was done in 'good faith' (albeit without consulting the executive), or actions are allowed that are contrary to a statement recently issued because they are perceived to be in the interests of shareholders[56] be intended to maintain industry support? If they are, then they illustrate the weakening of the regulatory process by the need to maintain such support.

Arguments against the self-regulatory system embodied in the City Code

Lack of effective sanctions

The absence of effective sanctions is a problem which is endemic to self or non-statutory regulation. Although the Panel can pass matters on to another body for enforcement, the penalty then becomes a matter for that other body, albeit after the Panel has ruled on the Code issues.[57]

It is asserted that this self-regulatory system enjoys industry support which leads to compliance without the need for sanctions. However the problem will always be those in the industry who see greater potential short-term benefits in not complying with the Code. Those benefits are well illustrated by the fact that fees, payable to Hambros, the advisers to Hoylake in its £13 billion bid in 1989 for BAT, were to vary from £5 million to £30 million depending on the predator client's success.[58]

---

55. Panel Statement, 30 July 1987 (now appendix 3 to the Code), [1987] JBL 480.
56. See, e.g., *Demerger Corporation/Extel Group PLC*, Panel Statement, 23 April 1986, [1986] JBL 407; *The Gateway Corporation PLC*, Panel Statement, 15 June 1989; and *Gateway PLC*, Panel Statement, 18 August 1989.
57. See, e.g., *Wm Low & Co PLC/Budgens PLC*, Panel Statement, 1 August 1989. In addition, s.47A(2) and (5), inserted in the Financial Services Act 1986 by s.192 of the Companies Act 1989, acknowledges that a breach of a code, such as the City Code, can be used as a basis for disciplinary proceedings by the SIB or the SROs under that Act but only on the basis of a complaint by the body whose Code was breached. In the case of the City Code that would be after a Panel finding that there was a breach with possible appeal to the Appeal Committee.
58. *The Independent*, 29 November 1989.

While such arrangements do not necessarily lead to a breach of the Code (and there was no breach involved in that case), it is unrealistic to assume that the size of the amount at stake for adviser and client alike will not place a strain on voluntary compliance. This is, after all, an industry with a vested interest in the freedom of the takeover market. As mentioned above, the need to court industry support may lead to a lack of rigorousness in enforcing the Code, especially with respect to activity outside the letter of the Code.

The effects of the absence of legally enforceable sanctions at the disposal of the Panel itself vary. Because of the existence of the Financial Services Act 1986 and the regime it establishes to regulate the investment industry, sanctions are available to the SIB and the SROs under that legislation. Since the review of the Panel's operation in the aftermath of the Guinness affair, it has been clear that those bodies may withdraw authorization to carry on investment business from violators of the Code and may use their power over those in the investment business to require them to 'cold-shoulder' others who have broken the Code by not acting for them in takeovers. The latter action could apply to the predator or target company while the withdrawal of authorization under the Financial Services Act 1986 is more likely to apply to advisers. Against a target or predator it is also possible for the Stock Exchange to withdraw the facilities of the securities markets.[59] The Panel itself has built, on the basis of these sanctions, an order that a successful predator company which acted in breach of the Code should pay compensation to shareholders in a target company who took a lower price than would have been offered had the Code been adhered to.[60] However, such compensation orders will only be available when the loss of specific shareholders can be estimated and obedience to such an order is not directly enforceable by legal process. In the *Guinness* case itself a significant proportion of the amount payable to shareholders was paid to Argyll, the rival bidder, in return for a release from at least part of the legal liability that might be found to exist in litigation between Argyll and Guinness. Such additional pressure on a company to obey a compensation order will not always be available.

The absence of sanctions is an ultimate issue in the operation of the Code. In so far as parties and their advisers are willing to 'play the game', sanctions can take the form of a decision to delay a bid, to prohibit a new bid within a certain period or to order the disposal of a shareholding.[61] However, such decisions rest on the willingness of parties to comply. Their use does not answer the fundamental criticism

---

59. See the Code, 'Introduction', Part 1(c).
60. See *Guinness PLC/Distillers PLC*, Panel Statement, 14 July 1989, in which an award was estimated to cost Guinness £85 million was made.
61. See, e.g., *Woolworth Holdings PLC/Dixons PLC*, Panel Statement, 10 June 1986 and *Inoco PLC/Petranol PLC*, Panel Statement, 30 May 1986, [1986] JBL 409.

that sanctions are not available at the end of the day if a party defies the Panel. It should be noted that the Panel's ability to withdraw the status of an exempt market-maker or an exempt fund manager is an acute example of a penalty which, while only operating within the Code system, is a major sanction because of its direct economic effects.[62]

The nature of the sanctions which are available to the Panel is such that it is not possible for a penalty such as a fine to be imposed. Consequently, the Panel has never attempted to make such an order — as opposed to the compensation order made in the *Guinness* case. The disciplinary sanctions available against advisers are administered by the relevant agency under the Financial Services Act 1986 and not by the Panel directly.[63] The sanctions of withdrawing the facilities of the securities markets or 'cold-shouldering' which are available against the bidder or the target are similarly imposed by others and are draconian. The absence of more modest sanctions for lesser but significant breaches by the parties, rather than their advisers, results in the imposition of responsibility on advisers for breaches by parties to the bid as well as for breaches by the advisers themselves.[64] It can also result in the absence of any action whatsoever if a party had no advisers.[65] Conversely, where criticism is directed at an adviser and delay is imposed on the bid process to correct its error the client suffers.[66] This may recruit market forces against the adviser for the future and may be necessary to serve the overriding purpose of protecting shareholders in the target.[67]

One way of addressing this problem without a complete statutory system of regulation is a non-statutory code with statutory powers of enforcement. Beevor argues that this would be unacceptable given the wide discretion of the Panel.[68] However, as has been argued above, this discretion is not widely used. Also, the argument is circular because the discretion may become meaningless without effective sanctions. The system to be operated under the Financial Services Act 1986, after its amendment by the Companies Act 1989, shows that a combination of a Code operating by principles and rules, with enforceable penalties, is possible. This makes the position of the Panel outside such legislation

---

62. See, e.g., *Raine Industries PLC/Tarmac PLC/Ruberoid PLC*, Panel Statement, 19 October 1988 where this power was used to police the improvements required by the Panel in a firm's procedures.
63. The Panel decides on the question of a breach of the Code but the sanction is decided by the other body.
64. See, e.g., the Code, 'Introduction', General Principles 3 and 5, Rules 3.1, 3.2, Rule 19 note 1, and Panel Statement, 30 July 1987 (in a passage omitted from Appendix 3 of the Code) regarding the involvement of advisers.
65. *Manchester Football Club*, Panel Statement, 13 October 1989.
66. *Meat Trade Supplies PLC*, Panel Statement, 6 October 1989.
67. This view was expressed in *Tozer Kemsley & Milbourn (Holdings) PLC/Molins PLC*, Panel Statement, 30 June 1986, [1987] JBL 483 where a disruption to a bid was avoided for this reason.
68. *Supra*, n.2.

singularly anomalous. Applied to the Panel, such a system could facilitate effective financial penalties for relatively minor infractions and overcome the deficiencies of the present system — particularly with parties as opposed to advisers. This could also ensure that decisions, both on whether a breach of the Code has occurred and on the appropriate disciplinary action or other penalty, would be made by the same body. This would avoid duplication of effort and could ensure that the penalty was appropriate to the seriousness of the breach.

Lack of investigative powers

The Panel lacks rigorous investigative powers. This problem is closely linked to the absence of direct sanctions available to the Panel. The very absence of such sanctions prevents the use by the Panel, as an investigatory body, of 'plea bargaining' of the kind which gave rise to the information supplied by Ivan Boesky in the United States insider-dealing scandal of the late 1980s. The reliance on financial advisers to police the activities of their corporate clients is attributable to the Panel's lack of investigatory powers as well as to the easier availability of sanctions against operators in the financial services industry.

The Panel's approach to the Guinness affair illustrated the problem. It depended on access to the interim report of the DTI inspector and evidence available to him to decide on breaches of the Code during the Distillers bid.[69] While information can be passed from the Panel to the DTI with a view to the appointment of an inspector, this is of limited use in cases of a routine nature. The Panel does not claim to have the ability to check on the accuracy of the information used by the parties in circulars despite the centrality of such documents in the scheme of the Code and in the provision of accurate information to shareholders.[70] As a result of the Guinness affair, Appendix 3 of the Code exhorts directors to consult the Code and emphasizes the importance of the participation of the full board in a bid. However, it is hard to see how the Panel can be sure that it receives information about abuses, especially if financial advisers are not privy to all deliberations.

In some cases the Panel relies on 'assurances' of the procedures used,[71] thus highlighting the limited resources available for investigation. In other cases the Panel does gather information.[72] It liaises with the Stock Exchange Surveillance Department for information on share-dealing and

---

69. *R v. City Panel on Takeovers and Mergers, ex parte Guinness PLC* [1989] 2 WLR 863 and *Guinness PLC/The Distillers Company PLC*, Panel Statement, 14 July 1989.
70. See *Imperial Group PLC*, Panel Statement, 11 March 1986, [1986] JBL 315.
71. *United Newspapers PLC/Extel Group PLC*, Panel Statement, 18 May 1987, [1987] JBL 303.
72. *Turner & Newall PLC/AE PLC*, Panel Statement, 17 October 1986 and 27 October 1986, [1987] JBL 140 illustrates a successful investigation of a party's adviser.

one party in a bid may point out possible breaches of the Code by the other or its advisers. However, the Panel's inability to demand documents or to insist on replies to questions, either under oath or informally, clearly hampers it. Also, particular problems arise in cases in which the existence of 'chinese walls' inside multi-service financial organizations are central to compliance with the Code.[73] Fuller investigative powers would assist in detecting breaches in such internal barriers.

A statutory body could be furnished with appropriate powers of investigation to supplement its liaison with other authorities such as the Stock Exchange and the DTI. In order to ensure that the speed and flexibility of the present decision-making process at the level of the Panel executive was maintained under such a statutory body, such powers would be used only when grounds for suspicion existed.

'Capture'

The theory of 'capture' of regulatory agencies is well known.[74] It should be acknowledged that the phenomenon of capture is common to both statutory and non-statutory forms of regulation. In either context one of the reasons for it is likely to be 'the revolving door', which is connected to the need for expert personnel and results in constant association with (and possibly reliance on) the regulated, leading to a desire to minimize confrontation. The phenomenon is exacerbated in a self-regulatory situation:

> A problem which all voluntary schemes share is the suspicion that self-regulation is a facade for self-protection. This suspicion is derived partly from the motivation for such schemes and partly from the personnel of the administration. In schemes in which the industry supplies the regulators the suggestion that the poacher is performing the office of game-keeper is not inapposite.[75]

The problem of the bodies represented on the Panel was implicitly acknowledged by the review of its operations carried out as a result of the Guinness affair.[76] As a result of that process, The Securities Association and the Investment Managers Regulatory Organization — two of the SROs created under the Financial Services Act 1986 — became member organizations, an additional lay member to be appointed

---

73. See, for example, the Code, Appendix 3.2.
74. See, e.g., Cranston, *supra*, n.1; Tomasic, *supra*, n.1; Blakeney and Barnes, 'Industry Self-Regulation: An Alternative to Deregulation? Advertising — A Case Study' (1982) 5 UNSWLJ 133; Fels, 'The Political Economy of Regulation' (1982) 5 UNSWLJ 29; and Rowe, 'Economic Theories of the Nature of Regulatory Activity' in Tomasic (ed.), *supra*, n.1, at 147.
75. Blakeney and Barnes, *supra*, n.74, at 146.
76. Panel Statement, 11 May 1987.

by the Bank of England was added and the practice of cross-membership with the Securities and Investment Board was commended and continued. A new Chairman and two deputies completed the new structure. This increased the number of members who might be expected to have an orientation towards regulation and implicitly acknowledged the particular risks of capture by the financial services industry. However, the dominance of the financial sector *vis-à-vis* the industrial sector, noted above, remains.

Furthermore, because self-regulatory systems have no effective sanctions they rely, as has been mentioned above, on industry support in order to function. This tends to constrain their rigour. Capture would be indicated, in the case of the Panel, in decisions which tend to preserve the freedom of action in takeovers, especially by refusing to exercise discretions. Possible examples of such decisions have been discussed above.[77]

One of the difficulties with the application of the theory of capture in this case is that its proponents see it as a corruption of regulation intended originally to be in the public or consumer interest.[78] The function of the Panel, unlike the Monopolies and Mergers Commission for example, is not to protect the consumer or the public interest, but only to achieve fair treatment for company shareholders,[79] who are insiders in the security regulation system. Thus, the argument would go, the theory of capture has no application here. However, this theoretical objection to the application of the capture theory is probably not well-founded for two reasons. First, company shareholders can be seen as consumers within the securities regulation system; and, second, in ensuring 'allocation of industrial resources on as fair and well-informed a basis as possible',[80] the Panel is surely supposedly aiming to act in the public interest. On the other hand, if it is true that there is no public or consumer interest being protected here, then that raises more fundamental questions about the whole scheme of regulation. These are alluded to below.

Capture should not be seen as endemic to all regulation but merely a problem which those who create regulatory systems need to anticipate by safeguards in the regulatory structure.[81] Thus, while statutory regulation would not necessarily 'cure' the problem of capture, it has the potential to ameliorate it significantly. Much of that effect would be achieved by giving meaningful sanctions which would decrease the need to court industry support. The inclusion of a larger proportion of panel members who were independent of the financial services industry and of major corporations might also be more likely under a statutory system.

---

77. See text accompanying nn.51–6.
78. See, especially, Rowe, *supra*, n.74 and Fels, *supra*, n.74.
79. Beevor, *supra*, n.2, at 1–2.
80. Beevor, *supra*, n.2, at 2. See also *The British Petroleum Company PLC/Britoil PLC*, Panel Statement, 23 December 1987, [1987] JBL 165.
81. Cranston, *supra*, n.1.

Lack of sufficient court monitoring

The arguable lack of sufficient court monitoring has already been discussed.[82] This arises from the fact that the courts have indicated a largely historical role, which is not always adequate. However, there are arguments against allowing court review of regulatory decisions.[83] One argument is that common lawyers' techniques may not be suitable 'to evaluate the kinds of decisions made by many regulatory bodies'.[84] Another is that 'the courts are not equipped to evaluate the desirability of a particular policy'.[85] These objections to court review, if they stand at all, stand whether the body is statutory or non-statutory. However, the willingness of the courts to take into account the importance of decisions in the context of markets when reviewing the acts of the Monopolies and Mergers Commission indicate that giving a body a statutory basis does not mean that judicial review of an intrusive and disruptive kind necessarily follows.[86]

A statutory body could, therefore, be treated similarly to the present Panel in terms of judicial review. It could also operate a system of appeals from the statutory panel to an appeal committee similar to the existing structure. The rejection in the *BAT* case[87] by the Appeal Committee of the executive's attempt to limit the role of that body to review indicates that an appeal to a tribunal should not be seen as an obstacle to effective regulation by those who run the present system. It would present no greater obstacle under a statutory structure.

Creation of causes of action

Non-statutory codes cannot create a cause of action in the aggrieved. This has already been mentioned and ties in with the next point about who might be aggrieved or interested. However, even under the present Code system, judicial notice can be taken of behaviour contrary to the Code when discretion is exercised by a court — for example in the context of a winding-up petition based on the just and equitable ground.[88]

It is also possible for a person who suffers loss as a result of a breach

---

82. See the text accompanying nn.12, 38–41.
83. See Wettenhall and Bayne, 'Administrative Aspects of Regulation' in Tomasic (ed.), *supra*, n.1, at 69.
84. Wettenhall and Bayne, *supra*, n.83, at 97.
85. Wettenhall and Bayne, *supra*, n.83, at 98.
86. See, e.g., *R v. Monopolies and Mergers Commission, ex parte Argyll Group PLC* [1986] 1 WLR 763 and discussion above, text accompanying nn.38–44.
87. *Bat Industries PLC*, Panel Statement, 15 September 1989; see discussion above, text accompanying n.19.
88. E.g., *Re St Piran Ltd*, [1981] 1 WLR 1300, at 1307, per Dillon J.

of the Code which also amounts to a breach of the rules of a self-regulatory organization or of SIB rules to use an action for breach of statutory duty under section 62 of the Financial Services Act 1986. However, under the Companies Act 1989 such actions are to be limited to 'private investors' — a term to be defined in regulation.[89] This weakens the force of such proceedings as a means of policing the behaviour of those being regulated since such investors are less likely than institutional investors to have the resources of time and money to pursue litigation. Any such litigation will also require a plaintiff to establish loss flowing from a breach of the rules applicable under the Financial Services Act 1986. It will often be difficult to quantify the loss to any particular person caused by a breach of the Code. A statutory system could follow the US model whereby the agency may impose a penalty and recover compensation for distribution among individuals who have suffered loss.

A wider interest

As long as the system is self-regulatory and only investor protection is recognized as an aim, then the competing demands of others (for example, employees and the general public) to have an interest recognized are excluded. Statutory regulation, on the other hand, amounts to accommodation of competing interest groups.[90] It is arguable that matters such as the competition, regional policy and employment implications of takeovers are better handled by the use of the Office of Fair Trading and the Monopolies and Mergers Commission. However, even the protection of shareholders and the process of balancing that interest against the public interest in, for example, avoiding 'short-termism' in corporate investment decisions by making takeovers more difficult, involves wider concerns. For that reason parliamentary accountability represented by a statutory system is necessary. Even if the policy implemented by a new system were unchanged, that decision would be a legitimate matter for public debate within the legislature. It should not be left to a private decision-making body. The present system allows a degree of public interest-oriented input through, for example, the nominees of the Bank of England and the SROs on the Panel and liaison with the Stock Exchange and the DTI. However, it is submitted that this does not allow sufficient scope for public political decision-making on the system to be set up. Once established, a new system could be left to operate without day-to-day political interference in the operation of the commission or panel entrusted with statutory powers.

---

89. Companies Act 1989, s. 193 inserting a new s.62A into the Financial Services Act 1986.
90. Stigler, 'The Theory of Economic Regulation' (1971) 2 *Bell Journal of Economics and Management Science* 3; Fels, *supra*, n.74; Rowe, *supra*, n.74.

What has been the approach of the Panel on the question of competing interests? A large part of the answer to this question may be found in the fact that the primacy of shareholder concerns is often acknowledged by the Panel. This approach has been endorsed by the Court of Appeal in the *Guinness* judicial review case.[91] The Panel has also acknowledged the contrast between its own function and that of public authorities.[92] The competition law system operated under the Fair Trading Act 1973 is seen as providing protection to the public interest, while the Code deals with the protection of the interests of shareholders. The latter may be threatened by the possible manipulation of the market in corporate control by predators who, for example, gradually acquire shares up to a controlling shareholding or pay a premium to only some shareholders to make an offer which gives inadequate information or time for consideration and so 'bounces' shareholders into acceptance. Equally the system is concerned with potential abuses by management who may deprive shareholders of their opportunity to bid by the use of frustrating action such as the creation of 'poison pills'.

Such a provision of responsibility may be an effective means of reconciling interests. However, it is in fact impossible wholly to segregate different interests in this way. The Panel's own statements sometimes acknowledge the relevance of concerns other than the interests of shareholders. In its response to the CBI's fears about the vulnerability of companies to bids, the Panel, after setting out the limits of its role, acknowledged that it would 'nevertheless, have serious concerns if representatives of industry and commerce, who are the customers of the financial markets, felt that the practices accepted as normal in those markets were unfair and that some correction could be achieved through the medium of the Code'.[93] No changes were accepted by that report on the basis of such hypothetical 'serious concerns' but the relevance of other interests was acknowledged.

In rulings of the Panel two examples of concerns which may conflict with the immediate interests of the shareholders can be seen. One is the concept of protecting a company from constant siege by bidders. This might be seen as an interest of management which, if upheld, would deprive shareholders of the possibility of considering a bid — an interest the Panel is concerned to protect. In such cases the Panel sometimes characterizes the need of the company for such protection as a long-term shareholder interest in the profitability of the company's business, although the ill effects of protracted uncertainty on management and employees are also acknowledged.[94] Where a wider public interest —

---

91. *R* v. *City Panel on Takeovers and Mergers, ex parte Guinness PLC* [1989] 2 WLR 863.
92. See, e.g., *The British Petroleum Company PLC/Britoil PLC*, Panel Statement, 23 December 1987, [1987] JBL 165.
93. Panel Statement on the Report of the Panel Working Party on Takeover Rules and Practices, 26 July 1989.
94. See, e.g., *Hogg Robinson*, Panel Statement, 4 August 1987, [1987] JBL 481 and *Storehouse PLC*, Panel Statement, 23 June 1989.

such as that in orderly markets and adherence to legal rules — conflicts with the immediate shareholder concern to be able to consider a bid, the Panel may be less ready to give the longer-term concern priority. Thus in *Minorco/Consolidated Goldfields PLC*[95] the Panel used affidavit evidence to decide whether insider-dealing had taken place or concert parties had existed in breach of the Code when that very matter was already subject to a DTI inquiry. The decision that the bid should not lapse was justified in part on the basis that shareholders should be able to decide on the offer, thus arguably putting shareholder interests above the general interest in orderly markets. This contrasts with the frequent practice seen, for example, in the *Argyll/Distillers* ruling[96] of prohibiting a bid within a certain time after an earlier statement of intent not to bid (usually subject to significant changes of circumstances in the meantime), despite the consequences of denying shareholders in the target the opportunity to consider the offer.

The inability or unwillingness of the Panel to take account of regional interests led to particular difficulties in the *Irish Distillers* case[97] — partly because of the application of the Code in the Irish Republic. The fact that Irish national sensitivities played no part in the ruling caused considerable anger in Dublin. The absence of any provision for Irish or Scots representatives on the Panel highlights the issue. At the minimum this omission will cause problems with the acceptability of Panel rulings in some cases, although it is not a matter within the area subject to the Panel system. The Fair Trading Act 1973 allows such matters to be considered as part of the operation of competition law.

Mismatch between statutory and self-regulation

Perhaps the clearest argument to emerge from this survey of the Panel's operation is the difficulty of liaison between the Panel and other agencies — all of which have a statutory basis. The fact that disciplinary measures have to be applied by SROs, the SIB or the Stock Exchange after a Panel ruling giving rise to sanctions operated by those bodies has already been noted. In addition, while the direct relationship of the Panel with the courts by way of judicial review has been worked out, the relationships of rulings on for instance, the binding nature of an acceptance in respect of shares has not. In the *Irish Distillers* case[98] that problem was exacerbated by the fact that the courts of another state were involved. However, the question of whether the Panel might insist that a person held in litigation to have had its offer accepted should not enforce its

---

95. Panel Statement, 24 October 1988, [1989] JBL 68.
96. Panel Statement, 10 September 1985, [1986] JBL 233.
97. Panel Statement, 17 November 1988, [1989] JBL 150.
98. Panel Statement, 17 November 1988, [1989] JBL 150.

contractual rights due to a breach of the Code is unresolved. If the Panel had statutory backing it could be given such power unequivocally, and the imposition of direct sanctions as a result of exercising legal rights in contravention of the Code might be expressly permitted.

Similarly, there is a mismatch between investigations by the DTI and the Panel's decision in the same case.[99] The need of the Panel to use evidence supplied by the DTI in the *Guinness* case has already been noted. *A fortiori* greater difficulties will be experienced *vis-à-vis* overseas regulators or courts.[100] The relationship between the Panel and the Office of Fair Trading and the Monopolies and Mergers Commission is well worked out, but that with the SROs and the SIB is in its infancy.

While better co-ordination between the various regulatory bodies is required, the provision of a statutory basis for the Panel's work would remove one anomaly and could only assist in streamlining the regulatory process applicable to takeovers and mergers.

Conclusions

A leading proponent of the present system has stated that '[t]hose who currently want to replace the panel with a more statutory based system seem to want to do so as a matter of principle rather than because of any identified inadequacies in the present system.'[101] This chapter has attempted not only to raise points of principle but also to demonstrate inadequacies.

The foregoing material suggests that particular difficulties exist in relation to investigation and enforcement. The Panel lacks statutory power to order the production of documents, which hampers its investigative capacity. Its inability to impose effective, legally binding sanctions also undermines its role as a 'watchdog' of the City. These problems with investigations and enforcement, which arise from the non-statutory nature of the Code, are exacerbated by problems of capture or a perception that it operates on the basis of a 'City Club'. Some investigations have been less than rigorous or have occurred too late. Even where the investigations are rigorous and timely, the penalties imposed may not adequately punish the infringer or deter others from similar behaviour. The draconian nature of certain penalties which may be imposed under the Financial Services Act 1986 may discourage their use; and the absence of power, for example, to impose fines results in the absence of a rationally graduated system of penalties. Thus, the risk of detection

---

99. See *Minorco/Consolidated Goldfields PLC*, Panel Statement, 9 May 1989.
100. See *Minorco/Consolidated Goldfields PLC*, Panel Statement, 9 May 1989 and discussion above, text accompanying nn.17 and 18.
101. Beevor, *supra*, n.2, at 9.

and the likely penalty are inadequate in a situation where significant financial gains may be made from infringing behaviour.

The present degree of flexibility enjoyed by the Panel is desirable. There appears to be no reason why regulators under a statutory system could not be given a similar degree of flexibility coupled with a duty to investigate and, where appropriate, to impose significant statutorily enforceable sanctions. A precedent already exists in the new system of principles and rules introduced to the Financial Services Act 1986 by the Companies Act 1989. The exclusion of the Panel from that statutory system and the consequent mismatch between its role and that of the SROs, the SIB and the DTI is evident.

The development of such a co-ordinated statutory system which included the Panel's role would be the culmination of an evolutionary process which began in 1968. Concern with, and rules to implement, investor protection in the context of takeovers and mergers have evolved from the minimal self-regulatory rules of the early Panel to a sophisticated system heavily dependent on statutory provisions (for example, the structure set up under the Financial Services Act 1986). The inclusion of the Panel in the statutory system would conclude a process of change in which the self-regulatory period may be seen to represent a useful but ultimately inadequate phase. It remains to be seen whether the adoption of the proposed European Community Takeover Directive will result in the development of such a system.[102]

---

102. See *European Community Proposal for a Thirteenth Company Law Directive Concerning Takeovers: A Consultative Document*, DTI (1989), 22–42; *Barriers to Takeovers in the European Community* (a study commissioned by the Department of Trade & Industry from Coopers and Lybrand), HMSO (1989); and *Barriers to Takeovers in the European Community: A Consultative Document*, DTI (1990).

6 The changing rules of evidence

Marquita Inman

Introduction

Most evidence rules are of comparatively recent origin and the product of fragmentary development. The unstructured character of the subject reflects its evolution as 'a series of largely isolated responses to particular problems at different times'.[1] Leading scholars have differed over the extent to which rules were influenced by fear of perjury,[2] jury trial and the adversary system.[3] The 'best evidence' rule accorded pre-eminence by Baron Gilbert[4] owed more to philosophical than to legal precepts, but remained dominant until displaced in significance by the 'relevance' principle.[5]

Although 'proof' should constitute the primary concern of such a subject, judges have had remarkably little to say about it. Principles of exclusion have instead been the major preoccupation, the stated rationales of which often being inconsistent and the scope of which often uncertain.

Eulogistic appraisals of the subject[6] stand in contrast to more recent stringent criticisms. The latter point to lingering anachronisms of a subject fashioned in the context of procedural and social structures long since vanished,[7] and paucity of principle in comparison to a lush

---

1. W. Twining, *Theories of Evidence* (1985), at 1.
2. I. Wigmore, *Evidence in Trials at Common Law*, (3rd edn, 1940), para. 8.
3. Compare views in E. Morgan, Foreword to *Model Code of Evidence* (1942), at 36–7; J. Thayer, *Preliminary Treatise on Evidence* (1898), at 180; I. Wigmore, *supra*, n.2, para. 8; 9 Holdsworth, *History of English Law* (1926), at 127–8.
4. *Law of Evidence* (1754).
5. *Infra*, p.96.
6. E.g., Lord Kenyon CJ in *R* v. *Inhabitants of Eriswell* (1790) 100 ER 815, at 823; S. Greanleaf, *Treatise on the Law of Evidence* (16th edn, J.H. Wigmore, 1899), at 730.
7. Australian Law Reform Commission Report No. 38, *Evidence* (1987) (hereinafter ALRC 38), para. 6; Miller, 'Beyond the Law of Evidence' (1967) S Calif. LR 1, at 7.

exuberance of detail.[8] Evolution by *stare decisis* has induced formalism as a substitute for fundamental analysis of how rules interrelate[9] or the uncertainties caused by intrinsic malleability of some key conceptual constructs. Issue has been taken with the soundness of propounded distinctions,[10] conventional processes of reasoning, and assumptions shaping many rules.[11] Sporadic and inconsistent infusion of policy elements extrinsic to questions of reliability or relevance provides further ground for criticism.

Judges have formally renounced responsibility for radical reform,[12] which is thus a legislative responsibility. Hitherto, statutory reforms have been largely piecemeal and have failed in some areas to prevent reemergence of outmoded judicial approaches. In contrast to some jurisdictions, major codification has thus far met with resistance in England. A factor doubtless contributing to the incoherence of this part of the law is absence of consensus concerning its fundamental objective. According to one view, trials are conducted to 'find out the truth'.[13] This view doubtless accords with expectations of litigants who, as Frank noted, 'do want the courts to discover the true facts of their case'.[14] To Lord Scarman, however, trial is primarily a cathartic substitute for vengeful self-help wherein truth is 'an abstraction with which lawyers are only marginally concerned'.[15] To the Australian Law Reform Commission (ALRC), a trial is not a search for objective truth,[16] but the credibility of the litigation system depends, the Commission argues, on the appearance of attempting to find facts.[17] What emerges from litigation, the Commission contends, is a 'new kind of truth'.[18]

The last analyses are unsatisfactory. The credibility of the litigation process depends not merely on the *appearance* of attempting to find facts but upon a genuine commitment towards accomplishing that objective, albeit that some facts are intrinsically elusive. Formulated standards of proof acknowledge that dispute resolution does not aspire to absolute certainty. Temporal, practical and policy constraints may place obstacles in the path of the truth quest. Where this is so, however, such impediments should be recognized for what they are and modified as far as possible

---

8. McCormick 'Tomorrow's Law of Evidence' (1938) 24 ABAJ 507, at 508.
9. E. Morgan, *Some problems of Proof* (1956), at 170.
10. E.g., Loevinger, 'Facts, Evidence and Legal Proof' (1958) West. Res. LR, 154 *passim*.
11. Ibid. See also Brooks 'The Law Reform Commission of Canada's Evidence Code' (1978) Osgoode HLJ 241 *passim*.
12. See, e.g., *Myers* v. *DPP* [1965] AC 1001, at 1021; *R* v. *Hunt* [1987] 1 All ER 1, at 12.
13. *Jones* v. *NCB* [1957] 2 QB 55, at 63, per Denning LJ.
14. *Courts on Trial* (1949), at 396.
15. *Truth and the Legal Process* (E.H. Young Memorial Lecture, 1976), at 1.
16. ALRC 38, para. 34; Report No. 26 *Evidence (Interim)* (1985) (hereinafter ALRC 26), Vol. 1, para. 58.
17. ALRC 26, Vol. 1, para. 571.
18. ALRC 38, para. 31; ALRC 26, para. 54.

within the operative framework. To equate such shortcomings with 'justice' and to use that term in contradistinction to 'truth'[19] introduces a conceptualisation which removes incentive to improvement and leaves scope for legitimatization of an order of system priorities in which truth ascertainment is relegated to an inappropriately low position.

Much of the present law of evidence (including aspects examined in the ensuing discussion), is defective not merely because the rules fail as instruments of truth ascertainment, but because they amount to positive 'obstructions to intelligent observation'.[20] A number of rules fail the test of empirical psychological assessment and there is much need for reform on this basis alone. Meaningful reform also requires development of new vocabularies and concepts. As Loevinger observes, it is probably impossible to rationalize rules of evidence so long as they continue to be discussed and formulated in language itself containing errors and fallacies we seek to correct.[21] Moreover, it is necessary to come to recognize that the type of reasoning required in processing human and social data is not that which has often been adopted by the courts hitherto. Progress ultimately requires a jettisoning of the principal intellectual tools of the common law — the creation and conceptualisation of arbitrary categories and the syllogistic reasoning of which such categories are an indispensable part.[22]

It is proposed in the remainder of this chapter to explore some areas which cause particular concern and which have been the subject of recent reform debates. This discussion will be followed by some general comments pertinent to future reforms.

Relevance

Although relevance is nominally the threshold principle of evidence admissibility, considerable uncertainty abounds as to its precise legal meaning. The requisite connection between tendered evidence and issues is unclear. Whereas Stephen suggested that the *factum probans* should render another fact probable,[23] Wills considered to be relevant all constituent parts and details of a transaction in issue,[24] to which some judges have added subordinate incidents and further facts necessary to identify or explain them.[25] Some judges consider that evidence increasing the probability of existence of a fact, however marginally, passes the

---

19. Scarman, *supra*, n.15, at 7.
20. E. Morgan, *Significant Developments In the Law* (1946), at 1.
21. *Supra*, n.10, at 163
22. Loevinger, *supra*, n.10, at 174.
23. *Digest of the Law of Evidence* (8th edn, 1907), art. 1.
24. *The Law of Evidence* (3rd edn, 1938), at 3-5.
25. *Martin* v. *Osborne* (1936) 55 CLR 367, at 375, per Dixon J.

relevance test,[26] whereas others consider sufficient relevance to be a matter of 'degree and opinion'.[27] Views also conflict over whether direct[28] or indirect[29] connection to the ultimate issue suffices or whether the judge must consider that tendered evidence actually meets the specified standard.[30]

Failure of the common law to yield an approach satisfactory to logicians is perhaps unsurprising in view of the degree to which the notion of relevance often serves more as a vehicle for policy discretion than a means of signifying a logical relationship between evidence and subject-matter. In some jurisdictions attempts have been made to pin-point discretionary relevance criteria deemed to be legitimate. Customarily included are such considerations as danger of unfair prejudice, confusion, undue waste of time and the possibility of misleading fact-finders.[31] Whilst in England such criteria have constituted latent components in judicial decisions,[32] they have not always been articulated. Distillation in codified form would assist in establishing a degree of analytical clarity absent hitherto.

Quantum of proof

Consideration of the burden of proof by English reform bodies[33] has so far been perfunctory and it is a subject meriting more systematic empirical attention. Given that there are differential standards of proof, it would seem crucial that judges and fact-finders appreciate their purport, particularly in criminal cases where the standard is ostensibly designed to ensure that errors work against the prosecution. Misgivings of some judges[34] concerning juror capacity to distinguish appropriately between civil and criminal standards are justified by empirical findings indicating a juror tendency towards underestimation of the latter and overestimation of the former.[35]

There remains a preoccupation at appellate level with lexical exactitude

---

26. E.g., *Wilson v. R* (1970) 123 CLR 334, at 344, per Menzies J.
27. *R v. Harz and Power* [1967] 1 AC 760, at 785, per Thesiger J.
28. *DPP v. Kilbourne* [1973] AC 729, at 756 per Lord Simon.
29. E.g., *Barnes v. Sharpe* (1910) 11 CLR 462, at 472, per Griffith CJ. For further variations, see ALRC Research Paper No. 7, *Relevance* (1982), Chs 1, 2.
30. E.g., *R v. Pfitzner* (1976) 15 SASR 171, at 196.
31. E.g., US Federal Rules of Evidence, Rule 403; ALRC 38, Draft Evidence Bill, Cl. 117; Law Reform Commission of Canada Draft Evidence Code (1975), s.5. Compare Canadian Federal/Provincial Task Force *Report on Evidence* (1981), at 77-9.
32. E.g., *Holcombe v. Hewson* (1810) 2 Camp 391.
33. Criminal Law Revision Committee, *11th Report (Evidence: General)* (1972) (hereinafter CLRC 11th Report), paras 137-42; Law Commission Report No. 143, *Codification of the Criminal Law*, para. 6.8.
34. E.g., Burger CJ in *Addington v. Texas* 441 US 418 (1979), at 424-5.
35. Simon and Mahan, 'Quantifying Burdens of Proof' (1971) 5 Law and Soc. Rev., 319.

in jury directions on the standard of proof.[36] This has failed to counteract the obscurity of the operative formulae and the form of direction given may have little effect.[37] Suggestions that the requisite inductive inferences might be assisted by statistical techniques or numerically precise jury instructions[38] have thus far been rebuffed.[39] Some commentators regard such approaches as presenting the danger in criminal cases of convictions more readily obtained than under the standard of subjective certainty supposedly conveyed by the legal formula.[40] The prevalent judicial view appears to be that the matter is inherently qualitative rather than quantitative.

The undoubted uncertainty surrounding the meanings (if any) to be ascribed to probative standards has yet to be systematically addressed. In civil cases involving serious allegations there has been some blurring of distinctions between civil and criminal standards.[41] Moreover, the extent to which applicable standards in civil cases can or should be objectively applied is unclear.[42] It may be that appropriate conclusions are reached by fact-finders intuitively. It may rather be the case, however, that there is simply a need to maintain an appearance of accuracy in order to preserve the credibility of the justice system. Obscurity may also be viewed as possessing the functional utility of facilitating authoritative dispute resolution.[43] This may ultimately preclude too detailed a consideration of the legalistic incantations devised by the courts.

Demeanour in assessment of witness evidence

Witness demeanour continues to be imbued with evidential significance and juries are directed to have regard thereto in assessing witness

---

36. E.g., *R* v. *Quinn* [1983] Crim. LR 475.
37. See, e.g., S. Wishman, *Anatomy of a Jury* (1986), at 249. Sealy and Cornish, 'Juries and the Rules of Evidence' [1973] Crim. LR 208. Cp. Kerr et al., 'Guilt Beyond Reasonable Doubt' (1976) 34 Jnl Pers. and Soc. Psychol., 282; Australian Institute of Criminology Seminar Proceedings, *infra*, n.206, at 53.
38. See W. Loh, *Social Research in the Judicial Process* (1984), at 523–37 for a review of such approaches.
39. See, e.g., ALRC 26, Vol. 1, para. 474 and Vol. 2, App. C, paras 290–2; *Re J.S. (a minor)* [1980] 1 All ER 1061, at 1066.
40. Tribe, 'Trial by Mathematics' (1971) 84 Harv. LR, 1329.
41. E.g., *Bater* v. *Bater* [1951] P 35, at 36–7; *M* v. *Cain The Times*, 15 December 1989. Compare *Hornal* v. *Neuberger Products* [1957] 1 QB 247, at 266. See also *Re G (a minor)* [1987] 1 WLR 1461, at 1466, 1469; The Hon. Mr Justice Waterhouse, 'Allegations of Child Abuse' in A. Levy (ed.), *Focus on Child Abuse* (1989), at 9; *H* v. *H (a minor)* [1989] 3 WLR 933, at 937–40, 944–6.
42. ALRC 26, Vol. 1, App. C, Ch. 16
43. Nesson, 'Reasonable Doubt and Permissive Inferences' (1979) 92 Harv. LR, 1187, at 1194.

reliability. Some judges have already questioned this,[44] and such scepticism is shared by the ALRC.[45] Psychological studies, some of which are cited by the ALRC,[46] indicate an average skill in detecting mendacity from non-verbal communication as not exceeding chance level. Moreover, forensic fact-finders and investigators may misapprehend indicators such as confidence, which may have a null or negative correlation with reliability.[47]

This calls into question one of the rationales for exclusion of hearsay evidence as well as the view that preservation of orality in criminal proceedings is an important priority.[48] The psychological research also provides an empirical basis for opposing reforms tending to inhibit invocation of an accused's right not to testify at trial since demeanour of innocent defendants under cross-examination may create false impressions.[49] Such factors led the ALRC to propose preservation of the right of an accused to make an unsworn statement at trial.[50] In England that right has regrettably undergone precipitous abolition.[51]

Cross-examination

A central tenet of evidence jurisprudence is the perceived efficacy of cross-examination in testing accuracy and veracity of evidence. It is an assumption underlying many exclusionary rules including the rule against hearsay. Although regarded by Wigmore as the 'greatest legal engine ever invented for the discovery of truth',[52] it is regarded as dispensable in Continental systems. Even in common law jurisdictions, opinions have

---

44. E.g., Lord Devlin, *The Judge* (1979), at 63; Sir Brian MacKenna, 'Discretion' (1973) IX *Irish Jurist* 1, at 1.
45. ALRC 26, Vol. 1, para. 586.
46. Ibid. See also P. Ekman, *Telling Lies* (1985), at 162; Kohnken, 'Behavioural Correlates of Statement Credibility' in H. Wegener et al. (eds), *Criminal Behaviour and the Justice System* (1989), at 280.
47. See, e.g., E. Loftus, *Eyewitness Testimony* (1979), at 100-1; A. Yarmey, *The Psychology of Eyewitness Testimony* (1979), at 150-1, 155.
48. See views cited in *infra*, n.197 and *DPP v. Blastland* [1985] 2 All ER 1095, at 1099, per Lord Bridge.
49. See recommendations in CLRC 11th Report, paras 108-13 and op. cit. Cl. 5 Draft Bill; Criminal Evidence (Northern Ireland) Order 1988 No. 1987 (NI 20), s.4. Note also Home Office, *Report of the Working Group on the Right of Silence* (1989), paras 113-5.
50. ALRC 26, Vol. 1, para. 592; ALRC 38, para. 94.
51. Criminal Justice Act 1982, s.72.
52. *Supra*, n.2, para. 1367. See also Scottish Law Commission Report No. 100, *Evidence* (1986), para. 3.21; *Report of Working Group on Identification Procedure Under Scottish Criminal Law*, Cmnd 7096 (1978), para. 2.07; *US v. Amaral* 488 F (2d) 1148 (1973), at 1152; *R v. O'Loughlin* [1988] 3 All ER 431, at 436; *DPP v. Blastland* [1985] 2 All ER 1095, at 1099.

been sharply divided on the efficacy of the technique, with a growing recognition of its capacity to obfuscate rather than elucidate.[53]

Weight is lent to scepticism by increasingly sophisticated psychological analyses of potentially distorting effects of questioning modes and leading questions.[54] Such factors may arise in any interrogation, but particular dangers may arise in the courtroom where a witness is under stress.[55] Time lapses following event perception as well as pre-trial interviews and influences may in any event distort memory to a degree which precludes accurate retrieval however vigorously cross-examination is applied. Such factors carry significant implications for law reform since rules or proposals based on the technique's assumed efficacy demand reappraisal in the light of modern studies.[56]

Corroboration warnings

The common law developed mandatory requirements that judges in criminal trials should warn juries of a need for caution before convicting on uncorroborated evidence of accomplices or complainants in sexual cases.[57] There is still doubt over the precise meaning of corroboration in this context, which creates difficulties in administering the warnings and many unmeritorious appeals have been based on merely technical defects in summing up.

A further defect of the present approach is the treatment of all witnesses of the specified types as presumptive liars. Such an assessment lacks any empirical support. Moreover, the assumption that the rules conduce to the protection of defendants has been called into question by research indicating that they appear to have the opposite effect.[58] It also

---

53. E.g., ALRC 38, para. 9; ALRC 26, Vol. 1, paras 587, 618, 663; Select Committee of Legislative Council of South Australia, *Final Report, Unsworn Statements* (1981), at 15; Justice R.W. Fox, 'Expediency and Truth Finding in the Modern Law of Evidence' in E. Campbell and L. Waller (eds), *Well and Truly Tried* (1982), at 151; Damaska, 'Presentation of Evidence and Factfinding Precision' (1975) 123 U Pa. LR 1083, at 1094.
54. See, e.g., L. Taylor *Eyewitness Testimony* (1982), at 53–6; ALRC 26, para. 618 and materials there cited; Inman, 'Police Interrogation and Confessions' in S. Lloyd-Bostock (ed.), *Psychology in Legal Contexts* (1981), at 52–8; Cahill and Mingay, 'Leading Questions and the Police Interview' (1986) 2 *Policing* 212.
55. Note ALRC 26, Vol. 1, para. 586 and views there cited.
56. See McCormick, *Evidence* (3rd edn, 1984), para. 31; ALRC 26, Vol. 1, paras 587, 663. Compare *DPP* v. *Blastland* [1985] 2 All ER 1095, at 1099.
57. Corroboration requirements formerly applicable to children were abolished by the Criminal Justice Act 1988, s.34; see also Home Office Research and Planning Unit Paper 41 (1987).
    Child witnesses falling into the categories referred to in the text will remain subject to the rules there considered.
58. Sealy and Cornish, *supra*, n.37; Hans and Brooks, 'Effects of Corroboration Instructions in a Rape Case on Experimental Juries' (1977) 15 Osgoode Hall LJ, 701; Sealy, 'Instructional Sets in Trials of Rape' in P. van Koppen et al. (eds), *Lawyers on Psychology and Psychologists on Law* (1989).

seems that such warnings have a tendency to distract and confuse juries in a way that diverts deliberations from the crucial task of organizing evidence.[59]

There is a trend in other jurisdictions towards abolition of mandatory warnings in favour of individuation of witness assessment.[60] In England, although the Criminal Law Revision Committee (CLRC) disapproved the accomplice rule,[61] it has twice recommended retention of the sexual case requirement.[62] It is to be hoped that a different view will be taken by the Law Commission which is currently reviewing this area of the law.

Competence of child witnesses

Children's evidence remains subject to competence tests based on unjustified generalized assumptions of untruthfulness[63] and arbitrary *de facto* distinctions.[64] Although children may fail the legal competence test merely due to incapacity during the *voir dire* to grasp abstractions such as 'truth' and 'lying', no residual category of eligible child witness has been created in England.[65]

The important question of psychological competence is not addressed by present tests. Wide individual differences occur in all age groups in respect of memory, inferential abilities, propensity to suggestibility and ability to convey information informatively and relevantly.[66] Research

---

59. Sealy, 'Decision Processes in the Jury Room' in H. Wegener et al. (eds), *supra*, n.46, at 169; S. McCabe and R. Purves, *The Shadow Jury at Work* (1974), at 45.
60. The sexual case warning has become optional in a number of jurisdictions including California, Vermont, New Zealand and New South Wales. The warning has been outlawed in some jurisdictions including Pennsylvania and Minnesota; see also Canadian Criminal Code 1970 (as amended), s.264.4 and Victorian Law Reform Commission Report No. 13, *Rape and Allied Offences* (1988). The ALRC favours a 'request' warning in relation (*inter alia*) to sexual cases and accomplice evidence — see ALRC 38, para. 238. See also *Vetrovec* v. *R* (1982) 136 DLR 89.
61. 11th Report, para. 185.
62. Op. cit., para. 186; Working Paper on *Sexual Offences* (1980), para. 49. Compare the recommendations in Home Office, *Report of the Advisory Group on Video Evidence* (1989), paras 5.17–5.31.
63. See comments in Scottish Law Commission Discussion Paper 75, *Evidence of Children and Other Potentially Vulnerable Witnesses* (1988), para. 4.62.
64. Note observations in *Baker* v. *Rabbetts* (1954) 118 JPN 303; *R* v. *Wallwork* (1958) 42 Cr. App. R. 152; *R* v. *Hayes* (1977) 64 Cr. App. 194; *R* v. *Wright and Ormerod* (1987) (unrep.); *R* v. *Khan* (1981) 73 Cr. App. R 190; CLRC 11th Report, paras 204–6.
65. Cp. Evidence Amendment Act 1988 (SA), ss.4, 5. Note also general remarks in Flinn et al., 'Children's Knowledge of Court Proceedings' (1989) 80 Brit. Jnl Psychol. 285, at 295–6.
    In England an understanding of a 'duty to speak the truth' is a prerequisite of reception of unsworn evidence of children in criminal and civil cases — see Children and Young Persons Act 1939, s.38 and Children Act 1989, s.96(2).
66. ALRC 26, Vol. 1, para. 243.

findings point to the impossibility of identifying an age above which all children can be regarded as psychologically competent.[67]

Any scheme of reform in this area requires incorporation of principles regulating all stages of the legal process. Faulty interview techniques[68] and repeat interviews[69] render children's evidence particularly susceptible to contamination and preclude effective application of expert techniques such as context reinstatement[70] and statement validity analysis.[71]

With younger children, the manner of courtroom questioning is the key to elicitation of reliable evidence. The New Zealand Department of Justice recently noted the absence of provision for such children to give evidence in an age-appropriate manner[72] and commended increased use of assistance of expert child specialists in sexual abuse proceedings.

The ALRC has proposed a revised competence test requiring capacity to understand and respond rationally to questions as well as truth-telling obligations.[73] Discretion would be conferred on trial judges to conduct inquiries and rule young children competent to answer simple factual questions but incompetent regarding abstract inferential questions.[74] This recommendation affords improved prospects of appropriate treatment of child witnesses, but is less radical than some suggested approaches.[75]

---

67. See, e.g., reviews in op. cit, para. 242; G. Davies and R. Flinn, 'The Accuracy and Suggestibility of Child Witnesses' in G. Davies and J. Drinkwater (eds), *The Child Witness* (1988); Dunning 'Research On Children's Eyewitness Testimony' in S.J. Ceci et al. (eds), *Perspectives on Children's Testimony* (1989).
68. See, e.g., remarks in *Report of the Inquiry into Child Abuse in Cleveland* Cm 412 (1988), paras 12.8–12.64; *State* v. *McKellar* (1983) (Haw. Circ. Ct. No. 85-0553); H. Wakefield and R. Underwager *Accusations of Child Sexual Abuse* (1988), Chs 1, 3, 8; Westcott et al., 'The Use of Anatomical Dolls in Child Witness Interviews', *Adoption and Fostering* (forthcoming); Scottish Law Commission Discussion Paper 75, *supra*, n.63, paras 4.44–4.49 and para. 3.13; *Re M. (a minor)* [1987] FLR 293; *C* v. *C* [1987] 1 FLR 321; Enright, 'Dolls As An Aid to Interviewing Children' in A. Levy (ed.), *supra*, n.41.
69. Note Cleveland Report, *supra*, n.68, para. 12.50.
70. See Wilkinson, 'Context Effects in Children's Event Memory' in M. Gruneberg et al. (eds), *Practical Aspects of Memory* (1988).
71. See Raskin and Yuille, 'Problems in Evaluating Interviews of Children in Sexual Abuse Cases' in S.J. Ceci et al. (eds), *supra*, n.67.
72. *The Child Sexual Abuse Study; Role of Expert Witnesses in Criminal Trials* (1989).
73. ALRC 38, paras 64, 65.
74. ALRC 26, Vol. 1, para. 522. Note the less sophisticated approach advocated in Home Office Advisory Committee Report, *supra*, n.62, paras 5.2–5.16. Note also NSPCC, *Protecting Children Into The 1990's* (1989).
75. E.g., Wakefield and Underwager, *supra*, n.68, at 147. Compare approach in US Federal Rule 601.

Vulnerable witnesses

Introduction

Whilst some degree of special consideration might be appropriate for other categories of vulnerable witnesses,[76] recent reform debate has focused on rape complainants and children.

Complainants in rape cases

At common law, sexual history evidence relating to the complainant was admitted if deemed relevant to consent or credibility and evidence of unchaste reputation was admitted for impeachment purposes. Vociferous criticisms in all jurisdictions have induced a varied array of modifications. Radical approaches included total exclusion of evidence of acts with third parties,[77] reputation evidence[78] or matters outside the ambit of a closed list of exceptions.[79] Further approaches place precise limits on introduction of evidence of acts involving the accused[80] or confine admissibility to material specifically rebutting prosecution evidence.[81]

Statutory reform in England has introduced a discretion exercisable with regard to 'fairness to the accused'.[82] The legislation followed neither recommendations for fixed rules contained in the Heilbron Report,[83] nor the thrust of some views expressed in parliamentary debate.[84] Full interpretative elucidation is still awaited, but the Court of Appeal has indicated that probing merely with a view to blackening a complainant's character is unjustifiable.[85] Research indicates, however, that this edict has not been uniformly applied.[86]

Pressure continues for more fundamental reform in England. Evaluation of such proposals requires attention to factors additional to the sensitivities of complainants. The primary focus must remain the protection of

---

76. See Scottish Law Commission *supra*, n.63, Part 6; and Home Office Advisory Committee Report, *supra*, n.62, Ch. 3.
77. E.g., Michigan, New Hampshire Oklahoma state codes. Compare the qualified exclusionary approach in Canadian Criminal Code 1970 (as amended), s.246.6.
78. E.g., Kentucky, Oregon, Massachusetts state codes; US Federal Rule 412; Rape Offences (Proceedings) Act 1958 (Vict.), s.37 A (1).
79. E.g., New Jersey and Montana state codes; Canadian Criminal Code 1970 (as amended), s.246.6. Note discussion in J. Temkin, *Rape and the Legal Process* (1987), at 119-33 and ALRC 26, Vol. 2, App. C, paras 178-9.
80. E.g., Michigan; Crimes Act 1900 (NSW) s.409 B (3).
81. E.g., North Dakota and West Virginia state codes.
82. Sexual Offences (Amendment) Act 1976, s.2.
83. Advisory Group Report on the *Law of Rape*, Cmnd 6352 (1975), paras 131-8.
84. E.g., HC Deb, Vol. 905, cols 811-12, 13 February 1976.
85. *R* v. *Mills* (1978) 68 Cr. App. R 327 (approving *R* v. *Lawrence* (1977) Crim. LR 492.
86. Z. Adler, *Rape on Trial* (1987).

innocent defendants. However, the interests of justice also demand that verdicts are based on facts rather than mere prejudice. Rape trial jurors have been found in all jurisdictions to be influenced to such a degree by victims' sexual history that its reception as evidence risks conversion of the proceedings into a trial of the complainant's morals rather than of the accused's guilt.[87]

A reasonable reform goal would thus seem to be confinement of such evidence to the maximum extent compatible with preservation of the accused's right to present all relevant evidence in support of his defence. The Scottish solution has been the introduction of a discretion exercisable in the 'interests of justice',[88] which, it is contended, protects in equal measure the interests of the accused, the complainant and the public at large.[89] So interpreted, such a formula fails to prioritize the protection of accused persons.

An efficacious means of accommodating all salient considerations may be fashioned by combining several elements of schemes found or proposed in other jurisdictions. This would involve creation of a rebuttable presumption of irrelevance of evidence of the complainant's sexual history coupled with procedural reforms. Included in the latter would be a requirement of advance notice of proposed questions or evidence, coupled with an *in camera* hearing to determine relevance,[90] provision at that hearing of legal representation for the complainant,[91] and a requirement that written reasons for admissibility are filed and available for public scrutiny.[92] Such a combination of measures would curb some of the more flagrant shortcomings highlighted in research whilst ensuring that specific decisions are unhindered by formalistic restraints disadvantaging innocent defendants.

Child witnesses

A climate of concern over child witnesses, particularly in cases of alleged sexual abuse, has prompted numerous procedural and evidential reforms in recent years.[93] In England and Scotland, further reports on aspects of the problem are awaited.

---

87. See, e.g., ALRC 26, Vol. 1, para. 403; V. Hans and N. Vidmar, *Judging the Jury* (1986), Ch. 13; H. Feild and L. Bienen, *Jurors and Rape* (1980), Ch. 4.
88. Law Reform (Miscellaneous Provisions) (Scotland) Act 1985, s.36.
89. P Fraser, cit. 1985 SLT (News), at 186.
90. This procedure is adopted in some American jurisdictions including North Carolina and Vermont. In Wyoming a written motion is required ten days prior to trial. Compare procedure set out in Canadian Criminal Code 1970 (as amended), s.246.6(3).
91. Provided in Ohio state trials.
92. Cf. Crimes Act 1900 (NSW) s.409 B (7); Law Reform Commission of Victoria Report No. 13, *Rape and Allied Offences* (1988), Summary, para. 22(b).
93. Papers presented at the International Conference on Children's Evidence, University of Cambridge, 1989, provide recent reviews of major jurisdictions (conference volume forthcoming).

Some recent modifications have been directed towards the creation of child-friendly environments and support provision.[94] Whilst such initiatives are generally unobjectionable, the same cannot be said of any contemplated routine use of screens[95] or video-link evidence[96] in criminal cases in view of their tendency to create a premature inference of guilt of the accused. A presumption that trauma will follow participation in conventional court processes is unjustified[97] and the converse is the case in some instances.[98]

Although there is some limited scope under present law for admissibility of children's out of court statements in substitution for testimony,[99] it has been argued that such evidence, particularly in the form of videotaped statements,[100] should be more widely admissible. Any such reform must incorporate adequate precautions. In particular, recordings originating in therapeutic settings should be inadmissible,[101] except where usage is adjudged by the court to further the interests of

---

94. See reviews in Scottish Law Commission, *supra*, n.63 and Scottish Law Commission Research Paper, *Evidence from Children* (1988).
95. For consideration of European Convention on Human Rights, Art. 6.3(d) in this context, see Scottish Law Commission, *supra*, n.63, paras 4.14–4.15. Compare *R* v. *X* [1989] *The Times*, 3 November and *R* v. *Smellie* (1919) 14 Cr. App. R 128 and note constitutional issues considered in *Coy* v. *Iowa infra*, n.97 *passim*.
96. Introduced by Criminal Justice Act 1988, s.32; Crown Court (Amendment) (No. 5) Rules 1988 (SI 1988: 2160). Usage commenced in January 1989.
97. See observations in *Coy* v. *Iowa* 487 US 1012 (1988), Lexis at *14 and *20; compare dissenting view of Justice Blackmun at *31–*33, resting on a misleading use of a research report by G. Goodman et al, 'The Emotional Effects of Criminal Court Testimony on Child Sexual Assault Victims' in Davies and Drinkwater (eds), *supra*, n.67. See also *Hochheiser* v. *Superior Court* 161 Cal. App. 3d 777 (1984,) at 792–3; *Brief for American Psychological Association as Amicus Curiae in Kentucky* v. *Stincer* (1987); Australian Law Reform Commission Discussion Paper No. 40, *Children's Evidence By Video Link* (1989); Law Reform Commission of Victoria Report No. 18, *Sexual Offences Against Children* (1988).
98. See views cited in Scottish Law Commission, *supra*, n.63, para. 4.22. See also *Report of Committee on Criminal Procedure in Scotland, Second Report* (Thomson Report), Cmnd 6218 (1975), para. 43.31; Wakefield and Underwager, *supra*, n.68, at 148–50; Berliner, 'The Child Witness' (1985) 40 U Miami LR 167, at 174–5; *Brief for American Psychological Association*, *supra*, n.97 and items there cited.
99. Medically certified unfitness will normally be a precondition of admissibility — see review in McEwan, 'Documentary Hearsay Evidence — Refuge for the Vulnerable Witness?' [1989] Crim. LR 629. Note, in relation to committal proceedings, Criminal Justice Act 1988, s.33. On applicability of the Civil Evidence Act 1968 to children's statements, see *Bradford City MC* v. *K (minors)* [1989] *The Times*, 18 August; cp. Children Act 1989, s.96(3).
100. E.g., Williams, 'Child Witnesses' in P. Smith (ed.), *Criminal Law* (1987); NSPCC, *Submission to the Home Office Advisory Group on the Admissibility of Video Recorded Interviews* (1988). See also Scottish Law Commission, *supra*, n.63, paras 5.37–5.51; P. Hill and S. Hill, 'Note - Videotaping Children's Testimony' (1987) 85 Mich. LR 809; V. Nield, Address to Police Federation Annual Conference, 1987; Home Office Advisory Committee Report, *supra*, n.62, Ch. 2.
101. Note Cleveland Report, *supra*, n.68, para. 12.42.

justice. Significant delay in bringing a case to trial[102] would be a relevant consideration in this regard, although accelerated processing procedures would constitute a preferable solution to this problem.[103]

It is unlikely that purely evidential adjustments will satisfactorily resolve all the difficulties arising in cases involving vulnerable child witnesses. Successful reform requires integration of evidential and procedural elements, an approach too often precluded by the limited terms of reference of committees and reform agencies charged with the review of such issues.

Hearsay evidence

Hearsay reform is a continuous preoccupation in all jurisdictions, some of which have undertaken codification ranging in form from virtual reproduction of the common law[104] to incorporation of so wide a range of exceptions as to detract from the generality of the exclusionary rule.[105] Some piecemeal reforms have reflected topical concerns[106] or a wish to utilize reliable documentary evidence,[107] whilst others have involved declassification of some species of hearsay. Some jurisdictions have seen an increasing divergence between civil and criminal cases, most dramatically in Scotland where legislation has effected unqualified abolition of the hearsay rule in civil cases.[108]

In England, the Civil Justice Review Body[109] concluded that the procedural scheme introduced for civil cases in 1968,[110] and broadly favoured for implementation in criminal cases by the CLRC,[111] is so elaborate as to be ineffective. Judicial opposition[112] to a provisional proposal[113] for total abolition of the exclusionary rule in civil cases led

---

102. Note remarks in New Zealand Department of Justice Report, *supra*, n.72.
103. In criminal cases, the procedure set out in Criminal Justice Act 1987, ss.4, 5 might be suitably adapted in this context.
104. E.g., Ontario Law Reform Commission Draft Evidence Act (1976); US Uniform Rules of Evidence (1953).
105. E.g., ALI Model Code of Evidence (1942); US Federal Rules of Evidence (1975).
106. See, e.g., US state laws on use of videotaped children's evidence summarized in Scottish Law Commission, *supra*, n.63, Appendix, and *Brief for American Bar Association as Amicus Curiae in Coy* v. *Iowa* (1988), Appendix.
107. E.g., Criminal Justice Act 1988, s.24. In England such provisions have usually received restrictive interpretation — see McEwan, *supra*, n.99, at 638.
108. Civil Evidence (Scotland) Act 1988, s.2. Compare the recommendation in Scottish Law Commission, *supra*, n.52, Part III. The Commission does not recommend abolition in criminal cases — see Discussion Paper 77, *Criminal Evidence* (1988).
109. Consultation Paper No. 6, *General Issues* (1987) para. 211.
110. Civil Evidence Act 1968.
111. 11th Report, paras 235-65.
112. See *Report of Review Body on Civil Justice*, Cm 394 (1988), para. 268.
113. Consultation Paper, *supra*, n.109, para. 212.

to a modified recommendation for a 'wide ranging enquiry'.[114] English criminal cases remain subject to the common law regime of exclusionary rule, subject to discrete exceptional categories supplemented by statutory provisions. An integrated review encompassing both civil and criminal hearsay is not presently in contemplation.

Such a review, when undertaken in Australia, resulted in a proposal for a complex differentiated scheme drawing distinctions between degrees of hearsay and, in criminal cases, between evidence adducible by defence and prosecution respectively.[115] Kirby J, in a dissenting view, adjudged this scheme to be too complicated and proposed instead the admissibility of all hearsay, subject to discretionary criteria of reliability, convenience, justice and public policy.[116]

The traditional pattern of hearsay law, still operative in England in criminal cases, and carried over into many reform schemes, is based on unjustified *a priori* assumptions underlying both the exclusionary rule and exceptions thereto. The former relate to perceived efficacy of demeanour and cross-examination in indicating and testing accuracy of evidence as well as assumed incapacity of fact-finders to evaluate evidence in other ways. The latter reflect unjustified expectations of reliability of evidence which passes arbitrary tests of admissibility. Issue may also be taken with the very notion that there is always a firm dichotomy between evidence legally classified as 'hearsay' and 'firsthand' knowledge. Such thinking overlooks the extent to which much evidence regarded as legally unobjectionable in fact consists of matter classifiable as 'hearsay'. In many areas, reformulation of the conceptual construct is more appropriate than a 'liberalising of rules based on illogical and archaic classifications'.[117] Whilst reliability of certain types of hearsay is undoubtedly questionable,[118] it is more appropriate in most instances to individualize consideration of tendered evidence from the perspective of cogency and justice than to perpetuate outmoded formalism.

Aspects of criminal evidence

Confessions

The assumption underlying the confession exception to the hearsay rule is presumed reliability. Although revised grounds of exclusion have

---

114. Op. cit., para. 270.
115. ALRC 26, Vol. 1, Ch. 32; ALRC 38, Ch. 10.
116. ALRC 26, Vol. 1, paras 723-9.
117. Loevinger, *supra*, n.10, at 165.
118. Note the psychological analysis set out in ALRC 26, Vol. 1, paras 664-71.

recently been provided,[119] the manner of their application continues to put innocent confessors at risk of conviction.

The effects of overt coercion and failure to comply with currently operative legal procedures have traditionally formed the focus of concern in determining confession admissibility. False confessions may, however, arise spontaneously or in consequence of the subtle psychological questioning methods which increasingly form the modern context of interrogation of suspects.[120] It will normally be the personal characteristics of the accused which determine capacity to resist such techniques and vulnerability towards false self-incrimination is not confined to persons suffering from permanent states of mental abnormality.

Despite recent statutory reforms[121] which provide a framework of concepts capable of accommodating such considerations, English courts have continued to perpetuate approaches developed at common law. In the absence of evidence of mental impairment or abnormality, prospects of confession exclusion continue to depend on external factors such as impropriety[122] or breach of legal standards[123] by police investigators. The judicially created lacunae in exclusionary criteria present a disturbing prospect for innocent confessors, since confession evidence, once admitted, is highly damaging and has a measurable impact on jurors' decisions.[124]

Psychological studies[125] and authenticated miscarriages of justice[126] urge the conclusion that confessions constitute a category of inherently unreliable evidence. Admissibility criteria must facilitate consideration of 'internalized' as well as 'externalized' factors affecting reliability in specific cases. Such an approach has recently been recommended by the ALRC[127] and the New Zealand Evidence Law Reform Committee.[128]

Since the *voir dire* procedure may provide an ineffective screen for all false confessions, it is undesirable to permit conviction on the basis of

---

119. Police and Criminal Evidence Act 1984, ss.76, 78. Relevant aspects of the former common law rules are reviewed in M. Inman, *Memorandum of Evidence presented to Royal Commission on Criminal Procedure* (1979). For a review of the reform proposals of the Royal Commission (1981) see Inman, 'The Admissibility of Confessions' [1981] Crim. LR 469.
120. See, e.g., Inman, *supra*, nn.54, 119; and S. Kassin and L. Wrightsman (eds), *The Psychology of Evidence and Trial Procedure* (1985), Ch. 3; J. Walkley, *Police Interrogation* (1987) *passim*.
121. *Supra*, n.119.
122. *R* v. *Fulling* [1987] 2 All ER 65.
123. E.g., *R* v. *Samuel* [1988] 2 WLR 920.
124. See empirical studies described by Kassin and Wrightsman, *supra*, n.120.
125. See, e.g., Inman, *supra*, n.54 and Gudjonsson and MacKeith 'Retracted Confessions' (1988) 28 *Med. Sci. Law* 187.
126. E.g., cases considered in 'Justice', *Miscarriages of Justice* (1989), Ch. 3 and HC, Standing Committee H col. 804 (1987–8).
127. ALRC 38, para. 154(d); Draft Bill Cl. 73(2).
128. *Report on Confessions* (1987), para. 122.

an uncorroborated confession, whatever the circumstances of its elicitation.[129] An attempt to amend the law by requiring adduction of evidence independently corroborative of a confession recently met with defeat in Parliament.[130] It is to be hoped that this will not discourage future attempts to introduce this much needed reform.

Identification evidence

Miscarriages of justice in all jurisdictions have drawn the attention of inquiries and reform bodies[131] to visual identification evidence. Such evidence, as the Devlin Committee noted, has latent defects which the usual courtroom tests may not detect.[132] Witness confidence may be negatively correlated to accuracy[133] and cross-examination may only strengthen the confidence of a mistaken witness.[134] Accuracy may be affected by numerous 'estimator variable' combinations as well as 'system variables' which may not be known to the cross-examiner or apprehended by the witness.[135]

The Devlin Committee concluded that since a reasonable doubt will always be present in relation to identification evidence, it should not be possible, (save in exceptional circumstances), to convict upon it in the absence of supporting evidence.[136] Judicial opposition[137] to this proposal led to pre-emptive action to avoid legislation. In *R* v. *Turnbull*,[138] the Court of Appeal created a dichotomy between 'poor quality' evidence which would require supporting evidence and 'good quality' evidence

---

129. Compare comments in 'Justice' *supra*, n.126 and *Report of an Inquiry By the Hon. Sir Henry Fisher* (1977), Ch. 23.
130. Drafts amendments to Criminal Justice Bill (1988) debated in HC, Standing Committee H cols 801-30, (1987-8). This debate is considered in Inman 'Psychological Theory and Forensic Use of Confession Evidence', Paper presented at First European Conference On Law and Psychology, University of Limburg, 1988.
131. E.g., CLRC 11th Report, paras 196-203; *Report on Evidence of Identification in Criminal Cases* (Devlin Report) (1976); *Report of Working Group on Identification Procedure Under Scottish Criminal Law* Cmnd 7096 (1978); Thomson Report, *supra*, n.98, Chs 12, 46; ALRC 26, Vol. 1, Chs 18, 37; ALRC 38, Ch. 15.
132. Devlin Report, *supra*, n.131, paras 1.24, 4.25.
133. See *supra*, n.47. See also references to expert opinions referred to in *State* v. *Chapple* 135 Ariz 281 (1983), at 291 and *People* v. *McDonald* 37 Cal (3d) 351 (1984), at 364. Compare views expressed in *Neil* v. *Biggers* 409 US 188 (1972).
134. Devlin Report, *supra*, n.131, paras 1.24, 2.5. Compare views in *US* v. *Amaral* 488 F (2d) 1148 (1973), at 1152 and Report of Working Group, *supra*, n.131, para. 2.07.
135. G. Wells, *Eyewitness Identification* (1988), Ch. 2.
136. *Supra*, n.131, para. 8.4.
137. See Lord Devlin, *supra*, n.44, Ch. 6.
138. [1977] QB 224.

which, although necessitating a cautionary warning, would be capable of founding a conviction.[139]

It has been contended[140] that the *Turnbull* guidelines have not been assiduously applied. Even if it were otherwise, however, their effectiveness is doubtful. As Lord Devlin observed,[141] the dubious notion of 'quality' is a novelty in the law of evidence, conceptually narrower than 'reliability'. The approach is, moreover, even more closely confined by the two specific instances of 'poor quality' cited by the court,[142] which have come to form the main focus of judicial attention.[143] Furthermore, the only 'quality' indicator may be the identifying witness's own estimate of the period of observation and such periods are commonly overestimated.[144]

The Devlin proposals have, with minor modification, formed the basis for recent reform proposals in Australia[145] and England.[146] The ineffectiveness of the present law in avoiding miscarriages of justice[147] renders such implementation an urgent priority.

Similar fact evidence

Ever since Lord Herschell declared (in effect) that evidence merely showing propensity towards misconduct is generally inadmissible for the purpose of proving guilt,[148] confusion has abounded. As Murphy J observed, courts have regularly admitted evidence for the ostensibly prohibited purpose 'despite protestations to the contrary'.[149]

Paucity of fundamental analysis has been the consequence of undue preoccupation with the impossible task of attempting to rend coherence from the inconsistent convolutions of the courts. Admissibility justifications couched in terms of 'relevance' fail to bear close scrutiny, since Lord Herschell's specification of relevance to an 'issue'[150] still causes

---

139. Loc. cit., at 228–30. Compare the formulation in *Scott* v. *R* [1989] 2 WLR 924, at 934, per Lord Griffiths — 'reasonable quality'.
140. T. Sargant and P. Hill, *Criminal Trials* (1986) at 4; 'Justice', *supra*, n.126, para. 3.11.
141. *Supra*, n.44, at 192.
142. Fleeting glimpses and identification in difficult circumstances.
143. See, e.g., *R* v. *Oakwell* [1978] 1 All ER 1223; *R* v. *Curry and Keeble* [1983] Crim. LR 737; *Reid* v. *R* [1989] 3 WLR 771; 'Justice', *supra*, n.126, para. 3.11.
144. See, e.g., Wells and Murray, 'What Can Psychology Say About The *Neil* v. *Biggers* Criteria . . .' (1983) 68 Jnl Applied Psychol. 347; Shiffman and Bobko, 'Effects of Stimulus Complexity on the Perceived Duration of Brief Temporal Events' (1974) 103 Jnl of Experimental Psychology 156.
145. ALRC 38, paras 191, 192.
146. 'Justice', *supra*, n.126, para. 3.12. Compare *Scott* v. *R* [1989] 2 WLR 924, at 934.
147. 'Justice', *supra*, n.126, para. 3.11.
148. *Makin* v. *AG for NSW* [1894] AC 57, at 65.
149. *Perry* v. *R* (1983) 57 ALJR 110, at 115–16.
150. *Makin* v. *AG for NSW* [1894] AC 57, at 65.

doubt. One end of the spectrum of interpretations views a guilty plea as putting in issue every defence theoretically open,[151] whereas the other confines admissibility to matters relevant to live issues.[152]

Assuming identification of a 'relevance' target, admissibility based on probability arguments is difficult to justify. Involvement in misconduct, (albeit similar), on other occasions, is not of itself probative of the present charge.[153] In the final analysis such evidence remains merely circumstantial. Prejudice, however, is likely to lead to sidestepping of the process of inferential reasoning, leading to conviction on the basis of character alone.[154] Even where a genuine attempt is made to employ appropriate reasoning, such evidence can distract attention from weaknesses of other prosecution evidence. Fact-finders may more readily incline to feeling satisfied of guilt by the tendency of such material to 'carry evidence over the onus barrier'.[155] Erroneous evaluation may also stem from inappropriate attribution of stable character traits.[156] Stipulation of admissibility tests in terms of 'striking similarity'[157] compounds such problems, since conviction rates increase discernibly on the basis of this characteristic alone.[158] Reform efforts have so far been directed towards devising new categories or examples of 'relevance',[159] the application of which would not assist in meeting the objections here mentioned.

Determining the probative value of similar facts cannot be other than a speculative exercise and, except in very rare instances,[160] it is likely to cause undue prejudice. Courts and reformers may remain prepared to countenance continued use of such evidence on the basis of pragmatism and perceived necessity. If so, efforts would be more appropriately directed towards coherent articulation of such factors, accompanied by an explanation of how they are to be reconciled with the need for consistent application of justice standards to all who stand accused of crimes.

---

151. E.g., *Noor Mohammed* v. *R* [1949] AC 182, at 191-2; *Harris* v. *DPP* [1952] AC 694, at 706-7; *R* v. *Sims* [1946] KB 531, at 539.
152. E.g., *R* v. *Bond* [1906] 2 KB 389, at 417; *Thompson* v. *R* [1918] AC 221, at 232.
153. See view of Neasey J (dissenting) in ALRC 26, Vol. 1, para. 814.
154. The incompatibility of such an approach with the presumption of innocence is noted in some American decisions — see e.g., *US* v. *Foskey* 636 F (2d) 517 (1980), at 523.
155. Per Neasey J, *supra*, n.153. See also *Perry* v. *R* (1983) 57 ALJR 110, at 116.
156. For detailed consideration of psychological materials pertinent to this point, see ALRC 26, Vol. 1, paras 795-800. See also M. Saks and R. Hastie, *Social Psychology in Court* (1978), at 162-3; Kaplan, 'Character Testimony' in Kassin and Wrightsman (eds), *supra*, n.120, Ch. 6.
157. E.g., *DPP* v. *Boardman* [1985] AC 427, at 462. Compare *R* v. *Rance* (1976) 62 Cr. App. R 118, at 121.
158. Kaplan, *supra*, n.156, at 166.
159. E.g., US Federal Rule 404(b); ALRC 38, Draft Bill, Cll. 87-9; CLRC 11th Report, Draft Bill, Cl. 3.
160. *R* v. *Straffen* [1952] 2 QB 911 is often cited as an example.

Cross-examination of the accused

Accused persons of previous bad character are also disadvantaged by risk of loss of a shield against cross-examination thereon,[161] where (*inter alia*), the nature or conduct of the defence involves 'imputations' on the character of prosecution witnesses.[162] In some jurisdictions this proviso is not activated where the accused is seeking to establish or support a defence by means of such imputations.[163] A majority of the CLRC favoured such an approach[164] whereas a minority favoured total abrogation of the proviso.[165]

In England, under present rules, a loss of the protective shield will be triggered by any imputation, whatever the motive therefor.[166] Reasoning relating to shield loss on this and other grounds[167] is objectionable. Evidence so elicited is said to be relevant only to credibility of the accused and not to issues. The CLRC regarded this distinction as 'a genuine one which can be applied in practice'.[168] Application of the approach requires a judicial exhortation to the jury to avoid a prohibited chain of reasoning by only inferring guilt on the basis of a conclusion that the accused's courtroom evidence is discredited. To infer guilt directly from the fact of bad character is ostensibly forbidden. Assuming that such a direction is understood at all,[169] empirical studies[170] highlight its limited effectiveness. The virtual impossibility of the required mental

---

161. Criminal Evidence Act 1898, s.1(f).
162. Criminal Evidence Act 1898, s.1(f)(ii).
163. See, e.g., Thomson Report, *supra*, n.98, para. 50.24, approving *O'Hara* v. *HM Advocate* [1948] JC 90; Evidence Act 1929 (SA), s.18(2); Crimes Act 1900 (NSW) s.413 A (4).
164. 11th Report paras 128–9 and Draft Bill Cl. 6(4). Legislation in New South Wales *supra*, n.163 is based on this proposal.
165. 11th Report, para. 130.
166. *Selvey* v. *DPP* [1970] AC 304. This decision preserved the exception relating to the defence of consent in cases of alleged rape: see at 339, 344, 355.
167. Criminal Evidence Act 1898, s.1(f)(ii)(iii).
168. 11th Report, para. 120. See also op. cit., para. 129 and *Scott* v. *R* [1989] 2 WLR 924, at 931.
169. See, e.g., Severance and Loftus, 'Improving the Ability of Jurors to Comprehend and Apply Criminal Jury Instructions' (1982) 17 Law and Soc. Review 153. Similar distinctions in other contexts have been referred to by a member of the CLRC as 'gibberish' — see Cross, 'A Very Wicked Animal Defends the 11th Report . . .' [1973] Crim. LR 329, at 333–4. See also R. Cross, *An Attempt to Update the Law of Evidence* (1974).
170. Hans and Doob, 'Section 12 of the Canada Evidence Act and the Deliberations of Simulated Jurors' (1976) 18 Crim. LQ 235; Doob and Kirshenbaum, 'Some Empirical Evidence on the Effect of s.12 Canada Evidence Act upon the Accused' (1972) 15 Crim. LQ 88; Wissler and Saks, 'On the Efficacy of Limiting Instructions' (1985) 9 Law and Human Behaviour 37; Saks and Hastie, *supra*, n.156, at 39, 63. Compare results in A. Sealy and W. Cornish, *supra*, n.58. Note that revised juror instructions may assist comprehension in some instances — see Severance and Loftus, *supra*, n.169.

feat has also received judicial recognition.[171] Accomplishment of the feat is particularly unlikely where a close similarity exists between the former bad conduct and offences presently charged.[172] The Court of Appeal, however, has departed from its own earlier decision by ruling that in such cases trial judges are not obliged to exercise discretion so as to exclude cross-examination upon such conduct.[173]

Even if it were possible to confine usage of elicited evidence in the manner expounded, it would be unjustifiable to conclude that the accused's credibility is necessarily impaired by virtue of past conduct. As it is, the position is more disquieting in view of the likelihood that such evidence will be used to infer guilt directly.

The failure of English courts consistently to exercise protective discretion in cases where undue prejudice inevitably arises, emphasizes the need for radical reappraisal of this area of the law. Total protection of the accused from this means of eliciting character evidence, as advocated by the CLRC minority,[174] would both address the problems here outlined and conform to customary antipathy to collateral issue evidence displayed by the courts in other contexts.

Expert evidence

Expert evidence is assuming increasing significance in litigation, but evidence rules impede its usage in some significant contexts.

In criminal cases, expert opinion evidence on ultimate issues[175] is prohibited.[176] Despite a modern tendency to desist from strict enforcement, the rule's availability as a makeweight reason for exclusion of unfavoured types of evidence makes its formal abolition desirable. Such an approach has been recommended by the CLRC[177] and a number of

---

171. *R v. Watts* [1983] Crim. LR 541, at 542, per Lane CJ. See also *R v. Braithwaite* (unrep., 24 November 1983); *Krulewitch v. US* 336 US 440 (1949), at 433, per Jackson J; *Nash v. US* 54 F (2d) 1006 (1932), at 1007, per Learned Hand J; J. Frank, *Law and the Modern Mind* (1930), at 184.
172. See *R v. Watts* [1983] Crim. LR 541, at 542; and *R v. Braithwaite* (unrep., 24 November 1983).
173. *R v. Powell* [1986] 1 All ER 193.
174. *Supra*, n.165.
175. For consideration of doubts over the precise meaning of this term, see I. Freckelton, *The Trial of the Expert* (1987), at 68–70 and ALRC 26, Vol. 2, App. C, para. 105.
176. The rule was abolished in civil cases by the Civil Evidence Act 1972, s.3(1). See Law Reform Committee 17th Report, *Evidence of Opinion and Expert Evidence*, Cmnd 4489 (1970), paras 26–7.
177. 11th Report, para. 268; Draft Bill Cl. 43(1).

other reform bodies,[178] and was incorporated in the original draft of the United States Federal Rules.[179]

The rule requiring expert opinions to be based on admissible facts[180] also has an inhibitory effect. There is again here scope for discriminatory treatment of unfavoured evidence to which the rule may be applied with uncustomary rigour. Attempts to introduce evidence from experts in social science or psychology for example, may be rebuffed on the technical ground that it rests on a hearsay basis.[181] Whilst it might be contended that data obtained by customary professional methodologies should be classified as 'fact',[182] or that such basis is not used for a 'hearsay' purpose in the course of evidence,[183] such arguments are likely to meet with an uncertain reception in English courts.[184] A further problem facing psychological experts stems from the requirement of full disclosure of the basis of opinion. Such disclosure is incompatible with the need to maintain confidentiality of testing methodologies in order to preserve their validity.

A possible approach to reform of the basis rules is found in US Federal Rule 703 which permits expert opinions based on inadmissible facts. Since, however, adjunct Rule 705 reserves discretion to order full disclosure of basis, the Federal Rules approach is not entirely satisfactory in the psychological context. A preferable approach is that recommended by the ALRC, involving total abolition of the common law rules,[185] with exclusion resting only on discretionary restraint of, (*inter alia*), unnecessary or misleading evidence.

The potential value of increased use of expert evidence relating to credibility of identification evidence, confessions and children's evidence

---

178. E.g., Ontario Law Reform Commission, *Report on the Law of Evidence* (1976), at 153–8; Canadian Federal/Provincial Task Force, *Report on Uniform Rules of Evidence* (1982), paras 8–10; Scottish Law Commission Memorandum No. 46, *Law of Evidence* (1980), R.01–R.06; Criminal Law and Penal Methods Reform Committee of South Australia, *3rd Report on Court Procedure and Evidence* (1975), para. 6; ALRC 26, Vol. 1, para. 473.

179. Rule 704; note comments in the Official Advisory Committee's Note (1975) SR 98-225, 98th Cong. 2d Sess., at 230–1. On the nature and effect of the amendment to Rule 704 enacted by Congress in the Insanity Defence Reform Act 1984, see R. Simon and D. Aaronson, *The Insanity Defence* (1988), Ch. 3 and *US* v. *Edwards* 819 F (2d) 262 (1987); *US* v. *Dotson* 817 F (2d) 1127 (1987).

180. It has been questioned whether cases usually cited as establishing the rule do in fact have that effect — see Freckelton, *supra*, n.175, at 83.

181. Note remarks of Lawton LJ in *R* v. *Turner* (1974) 60 Cr. App. R 80, at 82 and see *R* v. *MacKenny* (1980) 72 Cr. App. R 78, at 81, per May J. Compare remarks of Blackburn J in *Milirrpum* v. *Nabalco Pty Ltd* (1971) 17 FLR 141, at 162–3.

182. *Milirrpum* v. *Nabalco Pty Ltd* (1971) 17 FLR 141, at 162–3.

183. See, e.g., *R* v. *Dietrich* [1971] 1 CCC (2d) 49, at 65–6; *Lewis* v. *Southmore* 480 SW (2d) 180, (1972) at 187.

184. Although some exceptions have emerged in English cases (e.g., see *R* v. *Abadom* [1983] 76 Cr. App. R 48), their scope is uncertain.

185. ALRC 38, Ch. 11; Draft Bill Cl. 68.

has been recognized by some courts[186] and reform bodies[187] in other jurisdictions. Such evidence is likely to be precluded if common law rules excluding collateral issue evidence are strictly applied. A further impediment is the principle excluding expert evidence concerning mental states or cognitive processes which do not conform to legal concepts of 'abnormality'.[188] This approach is justifiably viewed as archaic by the ALRC.[189] The Commission rightly concludes that justice will be enhanced by unrestricted reception of such expert evidence, subject only to considerations which include possible unfair prejudice and undue waste of time.[190]

General issues in evidence reform

The prodigious outpourings of reform bodies in all jurisdictions indicate the extent of necessary change in the law of evidence. As Fox J notes, the time has come to stop adding to the superstructure and to examine the foundations.[191] Attention must necessarily be directed at identification of appropriate fundamental objectives and development of principles effectively furthering those aims. Examination is also required of procedural dimensions of legal and investigatory processes where they have direct bearing on the type, quality and impact of evidence adduced at trial.

Some defects examined in this chapter are illustrative of continued application of rules described by the American Law Institute as 'so defective that instead of being the means of developing truth, they operate to suppress it'.[192] The extent to which the tendency towards truth suppression may be reversed depends not merely on evidence rule reform but also on reappraisal of the adversary context within which litigation occurs. System tenets such as the norm of judicial passivity at trial, unbridled party autonomy and absence of independent investigatory mechanisms in criminal cases, detract from the goal of truth ascertainment to a degree often inimical to satisfactory standards of justice. The thesis that the adversary system better promotes crucial testing of

---

186. E.g., *US* v. *Downing* 753 F (2d) 1224 (1985).
187. E.g., New Zealand Department of Justice Report, *supra*, n.72; ALRC 26, Vol. 1, para. 743. See also Scottish Law Commission, *supra*, n.63, para. 4.62. Note also recommendation in 'Justice', *supra*, n.126, para. 3.18.
188. See, e.g., *R* v. *Turner* (1974) 60 Cr. App. R 80; *R* v. *MacKenny* (1980) 72 Cr. App. R 78; *R* v. *Masih* [1986] Crim. LR 395; *R* v. *Reynolds* (1975) 29 CRNS 141.
189. ALRC 26, Vol. 1, para. 743. As the Commission here notes, many mental health professionals feel unease over the postulated dichotomy between mental 'normalcy' and 'abnormality'.
190. ALRC 38, Draft Bill Cl. 117.
191. *Supra*, n.53, at 175.
192. Introduction to *Model Code of Evidence* (1942), at viii.

evidence than inquisitorial systems,[193] is belied by miscarriages of justice attributable to partisanship in gathering[194] and presentation[195] of evidence. Continuation of the adversary system may have less to do with perceived potentiality for forensic exactitude than conformity to tradition and latent political doctrine.[196] If so, such features require re-evaluation in the face of the need for modification on other grounds.

Also in need of reappraisal is the primacy of orality as the dominant forensic medium.[197] A broader spectrum of trial and presentational modes may provide more appropriate contexts for modern litigation than the currently utilized range. A more cosmopolitan selection of options, incorporating some aspects of inquisitorial procedures and methods of evaluation, is worthy of consideration.[198]

Reform of evidence law should be preceded by ample analysis of the extent to which exclusion of probative evidence is justifiable on extrinsic policy grounds. Little consensus has emerged within or between jurisdictions with regard to such issues as the appropriate nature and scope of evidential privileges and exclusion of illegally and improperly obtained evidence. In the latter sphere, some approaches accord priority to relevance[199] and necessity of evidence. Others, however, accord overriding significance to the moral probity of trial processes[200] or the educative effects of judicial censure.[201] There is much room for legitimate disagreement over the nature, scope and evaluative content of such concepts, and the appropriateness of their use to suppress probative evidence in individual cases may be questioned. Moreover, recent English experience illustrates the unsatisfactoriness of exclusionary discretions

---

193. See J. Thibaut and L. Walker, *Procedural Justice* (1975), Ch. 5. Compare Lind, 'The Psychology of Courtroom Procedure' in N. Kerr and R. Bray (eds), *The Psychology of the Courtroom* (1982), at 21–4.
194. See, e.g., Fisher Report, *supra*, n.129, para. 23.13.
195. See, e.g., Smith, 'Forensic Pathology, Scientific Expertise and the Criminal Law' in R. Smith and B. Wynne (eds), *Expert Evidence* (1989), at 70–90 for a discussion of recent miscarriages of justice in this context. See also Sarjant and Hill, *supra*, n.140, at 5–6 and Chs 3, 4.
196. See, e.g., L. Friedman, *A History of American Law* (1973), at 350; Frank, *supra*, n.14, at 92.
197. Differing opinions have been expressed in this connection in official reports. Compare, e.g., CLRC 11th Report, para. 239; *Final Report of Committee on Supreme Court Practice and Procedure* (Evershed Committee), Cmd 8878 (1953), para. 251; Home Office, *The Use of Videotaped Technology at Trials of Alleged Child Abusers* (1987), para. 13, with *Fraud Trials Committee Report* (1986), paras 5.4–5.5; *Report of Review Body on Civil Justice*, *supra*, n.112, para. 76.
198. See, e.g., Consultation Paper, *supra*, n.109, para. 231. Compare Evershed Committee, *supra*, n.197, para. 251.
199. E.g., *Kuruma* v. *R* [1955] AC 197.
200. E.g., *Bunning* v. *Cross* (1978) 141 CLR 54; Canadian Charter of Rights and Freedoms 1982, s.24(2).
201. E.g., *Olmstead* v. *US* 277 US 438 (1928).

based on elastic concepts such as 'fairness',[202] particularly when appellate reversals are unaccompanied by clear guidelines for trial judges.[203]

Rule evaluation and reform from the crucial perspective of truth ascertainment requires attention to modern psychology.[204] With some exceptions,[205] there remains a lingering judicial willingness to cling to constructs fashioned from anecdote, 'common sense' and non-deterministic notions of behaviour and motivation. Applied psychological research provides an appropriate medium for refutation or verification of such notions where incorporated into evidence rules. Jury research, for example, has already yielded information of relevance to rule appraisal as well as findings indicating the possibility of significant enhancement of jurors' memory and fact-processing capacities in consequence of revised modes of evidence presentation and procedural adjustments.[206]

The importance of psychological research as a component in reform analysis has already received recognition from the Law Reform Commissions of Canada and Australia and some legislatures in the United States, whose deliberations on aspects of evidence reform have been directly influenced by data from specifically appointed psychological consultants. In England and Scotland in contrast, only sporadic attention has been given to such material and the scope of such input has been relatively limited. Psycho-legal research of suitable quality requires greater encouragement than is currently forthcoming in England, particularly in the area of criminal justice.[207]

Results of psycho-legal research may ultimately indicate the extent to which exclusionary rules could be regarded as dispensable following development of alternative techniques of evidence evaluation. In the meantime, however, the most suitable objective is the formulation of principles and procedures grounded on a sound empirical and theoretical base. In the present state of knowledge, this presents better prospects of rectitude of decision than immediate transition from formalism to open-ended standards.

Evidence reform should proceed by the impact analysis method, which involves commitment to post-reform monitoring.[208] In a task as multi-faceted and complex as evidence reform, an appropriate degree of

---

202. Police and Criminal Evidence Act 1984, s.78.
203. E.g., *R v. Mason* [1987] 3 All ER 481.
204. See ALRC 38, para. 8.
205. See, e.g., Judge Brian Clapham, 'Introducing Psychological Evidence in the Courts' in Lloyd-Bostock (ed.), *supra*, n.54, Ch. 7.
206. For a recent review see S. Kassin and L. Wrightsman (eds), *The American Jury On Trial* (1988). Note also Fraud Trials Committee *Improving the Presentation of Information to Juries in Fraud Trials* (1986); Australian Institute of Criminology Seminar Proceedings No. 11, *The Jury* (1986).
207. Note remarks in M. Zander, *A Matter of Justice* (1988), at 296-7.
208. See ALRC 38, para. 19.

open-mindedness is needed and it will be necessary in many areas to continue to accommodate new knowledge. With the integrity of the justice system at stake, such efforts cannot but be worthwhile.

7 National security versus civil liberty

Richard Stone

Introduction

There is no doubt that wide acceptance of the view that the rights of the individual must at some point succumb to claims of the state based on 'national security'. The European Convention on Human Rights, for example, recognizes that the interests of national security can justify restrictions on privacy (Article 8), freedom of expression (Article 10)[1] and freedom of assembly and association (Article 11).

Recent English case law has, however, served to bring more clearly into focus the question of where and how this balance should be struck. For example, in *Secretary of State for Defence* v. *Guardian Newspapers*[2] the House of Lords was interpreting section 10 of the Contempt of Court Act 1981, which allows a journalist to refuse to disclose the source of information, unless it is necessary (*inter alia*) in the interests of national security. The House gave a broad interpretation to the phrase, and compelled disclosure. One month later, an almost identically constituted House again considered national security, not in the context of the interpretation of a statute, but in deciding the scope of judicial review of the exercise of the prerogative powers.[3] Once again the individual's freedom, in this case to belong to a trade union (or more precisely, the right of his union to be consulted about the removal of his right to belong), fell before an executive claim of national security.

More recently there has been the reform of section 2 of the Official Secrets Act 1911, by the Official Secrets Act 1989, partly as a result of criticism of the fact that the scope of section 2 extended beyond 'national security' issues.[4]

---

1. But not freedom of thought, conscience and religion under Article 9.
2. [1984] 3 All ER 601. This case is discussed more fully below: see text accompanying n.38.
3. [1985] 1 AC 374.
4. As happened in relation to the prosecutions of the civil servants Clive Ponting (1985) and Sarah Tisdall (1984). See also comments of the Franks Committee, Cmnd 5104 (1972).

All this demonstrates the current concern over the relationship between national security and civil liberties. Much of the discussion has centred on the extent to which the courts should involve themselves in the process of balancing individual rights against the interests of the state. The most extreme view is that the issue is 'non-justiciable', as exemplified by Lord Denning in *R* v. *Home Secretary, ex parte Hosenball*:

There is conflict here between the interests of national security on the one hand and the freedom of the individual on the other. The balance between these two is not for a court of law. It is for the Home Secretary.[5]

As will be seen later,[6] other judges have been more prepared to consider the issue, either at the procedural level (that is, 'Did the Minister genuinely act for reasons of national security?') or even at the substantive level (that is, 'Was the restriction of liberty based on considerations properly categorized as being concerned with national security?') There is no consistency of approach, however, and part of the purpose of the analysis of the case law here is to suggest the best way forward. Whatever the outcome of the 'justiciability' issue, however, another, more fundamental question also needs answering. That is, what exactly is 'national security'? If our judges are going to regard a claim of 'national security' on the part of the government as a trump card which cancels out all individual rights, then we ought to know what the phrase means. This is particularly so if the courts are going to say, not so much 'I can't define an elephant, but I know one when I see one', but 'I'm not going to look at this animal, but if someone (that is, the Minister) tells me that it is an elephant, then I will agree'.

At times this attitude is forced on the courts by Parliament through a statutory provision that the certificate of the Minister is conclusive of the issue (for example, the Data Protection Act 1984, section 27). But at other times the courts have shown themselves only too willing to accept the constraint. This could only be acceptable if there were a clear consensus on all sides on the meaning of the phrase. That is not so. In the debates on the Interception of Communications Act 1985, for example, the opposition made repeated attempts to remove the phrase 'national security' because they were convinced that a Conservative Home Secretary would have a different view of the scope of that phrase from their own. They saw it being used to justify, for example, the interception of the communications of the Campaign for Nuclear Disarmament (CND),[7] whereas Mr Robin Corbett expressed the view that 'possession of American nuclear weapons by this country is the gravest threat to our national security'.[8]

---

5. [1977] 1 WLR 766, at 783.
6. Below, p.131.
7. HC, Vol. 76, col. 1116, 2 April 1985.
8. HC, Vol. 77, col. 301, 17 April 1985.

Two issues, then, are under consideration. First, what is the scope of the phrase 'national security'? Second, to what extent should the courts involve themselves in deciding whether national security is at risk in any situation before them? The use of the phrase 'national security' in legislation will be considered first, and then the existing case law. Finally a scheme for the future development of the law in this area will be discussed.

National security in statutes

The phrase 'national security' has a fairly recent history as regards use in statutes. It is only since 1945 that it has been used with any frequency. Prior to that the phrase 'interests of the state' was used.[9] Despite this short history, a search of the LEXIS library of statutes and statutory instruments reveals about a hundred current instances of its use. Some typical examples of how it is used will be considered to illustrate the statutory influences on the justiciability issue, and the question of definition.

Looking first at justiciability, the most clear-cut situation arises in those statutes which make the issue of a ministerial certificate conclusive. Under section 27 of the Data Protection Act 1984, for example, personal data are exempt from the Act's registration and right of access provisions if this is required for the purpose of safeguarding national security. A certificate signed by a Cabinet Minister, the Attorney-General or the Lord Advocate is conclusive evidence that the exemption is required for such a purpose.[10]

Similarly, section 42 of the Race Relations Act 1976 states that nothing in parts II and IV of the Act 'shall render unlawful an act done for the purpose of safeguarding national security'. Section 69 then provides that in any proceedings under the Act 'a certificate signed by or on behalf of a Minister of the Crown and certifying . . . that any act specified in the certificate was done for the purposes of safeguarding national security, shall be conclusive evidence of the matters certified'. Apart from the fact that the power under the Race Relations Act is not limited to a particular type of Minister, these provisions are of identical effect. They leave no room for judicial consideration of any kind. It is purely a matter of the Minister's discretion. Even if the court or tribunal can

---

9. A similar development in the United States has been noted by Harold Relyea (184) 4 in *Media Law and Practice* 238. 'Interests of the state', which has attracted attention from its use in the Official Secrets Act 1911, can clearly have a wider meaning than 'national security', though it must surely encompass everything that is included within the more modern phrase. The concentration in this chapter is on the use and meaning of 'national security', with 'interests of the state' receiving only secondary consideration.
10. The section deals in the same way with exemption from the non-disclosure provisions — s.27(3), (4).

see no way in which national security could possibly be involved in the case before it, it must bow to the Minister's certificate and find accordingly.

Another provision which in theory allows more scope for judicial intervention, though in practice it is difficult to see when it would occur, is the fairly common one to be found in connection with the publication of Annual Reports by bodies such as the British Steel Corporation. Section 6 of the Iron and Steel Act 1982 states that the Corporation's Annual Report shall set out any direction given by the Secretary of State during that year (for example, under section 3) unless 'the Secretary of State has notified to the corporation his opinion that it is against the interests of national security to do so'.[11]

Presumably it is conceivable that a court might be prepared to consider whether any reasonable Secretary of State could possibly have held such an opinion, but it is hard to imagine circumstances where a court would ever be appraised of the issue. In practice, the Corporation, or other body, will censor its report on the Secretary of State's notification, and no one will be any the wiser. At least in this type of case there is no direct attack on an individual's rights of freedom, just a risk of undue secrecy about the actions of the Executive.

The same cannot be said of another provision which has similarly limited scope for challenge. Section 2 of the Interception of Communications Act 1984 provides that the Home Secretary may issue a warrant for the interception of post or telephone communications if 'he considers that the warrant is necessary — (a) in the interests of national security'. This allows national security considerations to justify serious infringements of an individual's privacy. As with the Iron and Steel Act, the Secretary of State's view is not stated to be conclusive of the issue, but the provisions in the rest of the Act mean that consideration of the basis for the Secretary's view is highly unlikely to come before any court. In particular, section 7, which establishes a special tribunal with exclusive jurisdiction to consider complaints that the Act has not been followed, and section 9, which prohibits evidence of cross-examination in any part or tribunal (other than 'the tribunal' established under the Act) which might show that a warrant has been issued, appear effectively to rule out court supervision of the Secretary of State's exercise of discretion.[12] The Tribunal, in considering complaints, has to apply 'the principles applicable by a court on an application for judicial review'. The government stated during the debates on the Act that:

the task of the tribunal is to decide whether interception had been properly authorised, in the sense of whether the material placed before the Secretary of

---

11. S.6(3)(a). A similar provision is to be found in the London Regional Transport Act 1984, s.34.
12. See s.7(8) and s.9(1).

State was such that he could properly come to the conclusion that the warrant was within the specified criteria.[13]

No specific comment was made, however, about whether the issue of the existence of national security grounds is within the Tribunal's competence. At best, then, the Interception of Communications Act indicates that, on the justiciability issue, decisions on national security questions may be susceptible to a judicial process, but that this is not to be trusted to the ordinary court system.

A more relaxed approach is sometimes evident where it is someone other than a government minister who is claiming the protection of national security. For example, under the Prevention of Terrorism (Temporary Provision) Act 1984, Schedule 3, paragraph 4, a police superintendent was given the power to make an order equivalent to a search warrant if he had 'reasonable grounds for believing that the case is one of great emergency and that in the interests of the State immediate action is necessary'. Assuming that the existence of 'reasonable grounds' applies to the belief in the necessity for immediate action in the interests of the state, the basis for the superintendent's belief would clearly be subject to judicial review. It is true that the superintendent might say: 'I was told by a Minister that the interests of the state required me to act', and that the court might simply accept this as 'reasonable grounds' for the officer's belief. It is possible to envisage circumstances, however, where the court would have to become more directly involved. If, for example, the basis of the superintendent's action was that he had received information that plans and equipment to be used in a demonstration outside a nuclear power-station were on the premises to be searched, the court would have to consider what the interests of the state were, as well as whether the superintendent could reasonably have believed that his action was necessary to further them. There is nothing in the statute which would compel acceptance of a Ministerial view of this issue.[14]

As a final contribution to the statutory provisions relating to the justiciability issue, the Industrial Tribunal (Rules of Procedure) Regulations 1985,[15] provides an interesting contrast to the more restrictive sectors examined. Rule 7(1) provides that hearings are to be in public,

unless *in the opinion of the tribunal* a private hearing is appropriate for the purposes of hearing evidence which relates to matters of such a nature that it would be *against the interests of national security* to allow the evidence to be given in public.[16]

---

13. HL, Vol. 463, col. 1259, 16 May 1985.
14. But the approach of the House of Lords to a similar issue in *Chandler* v. *DPP* [1964] AC 763, see below, p.127.
15. SI 1985: 16.
16. Emphasis added. A similar provision applies to the Employment Appeal Tribunal SI 1980.

The interesting thing about this provision is that the Industrial Tribunal is allowed to decide for itself whether national security is involved. That, of course, includes deciding that evidence does *not* effect national security. Recognition of such issues is therefore not a skill which only Ministers can possess. Moreover, the Industrial Tribunal itself is allowed to hear the sensitive material, albeit in camera. If clients and their advisers, together with the members of the Industrial Tribunal can be trusted to listen to matters affecting national security, it is strange that at other times it is felt that such matters are too sensitive to be discussed in court.

There is no consistent pattern to the statutory provisions as far as justiciability is concerned. But the statutes do not universally exclude the courts' supervision. Indeed, it can be argued that the fact that at times Parliament has gone to considerable lengths to oust the jurisdiction of the courts means that, in the absence of such provisions, jurisdiction must exist. This suggests that for an issue to be 'off limits', it must not merely relate to national security, it must have some additional characteristics which make it particularly sensitive. This brings us back to the problem of definition.

There is no statute or statutory instrument in which a full definition is attempted. The nearest thing is perhaps section 106 of the Telecommunications Act 1984, which states that the power of the Secretary of State to give a direction under the Act in the interests of national security or relations with a foreign government includes a power to do so to carry out the government's obligations as member of an international organization, or party to an international agreement. But this seems to have more to do with defining 'relations with a foreign government' than with the phrase with which we are primarily concerned.

Nor does an examination of the subject-matter of the statutes and statutory instruments in which national security is mentioned provide any clear indication of its scope. It is true that its use is often in areas where it might be expected to be important, such as enactments concerned with terrorism or nuclear power.[17] However, it also appears in unexpected places such as employment, or the Planning Inquiries (Attendance of Public) Act 1982. This Act does, in fact, provide some rather tangential assistance with the definitional issue. Section 1 empowers the Secretary of State to give directions regarding the secrecy of evidence if he is satisfied that it would be likely to result in the disclosure of matters of 'national security' *and* 'that the public disclosure of that information would be contrary to the national interest'. This twofold test clearly implies the existence of a class of material, probably identified by subject-matter, which deals with 'national security', but not all of which needs to be kept secret. It should, then, be possible to produce a list of topics

---

17. E.g., Atomic Energy Authority Act 1971, s.9.

coming under the wider category,[18] even if the issue of what within that category is required to remains secret remains nebulous. Unfortunately, neither this statute, nor any other, gives any further assistance with defining even the wider category.

Statutory material, then, reveals a range of approaches on the justiciability issue, but gives little help by way of definition. Much scope is left to the courts to lay down rules and guidelines. How has this scope been used?

National security in the cases

In this section the English case law related to national security issues is considered, both as regards justiciability and definition. The two aspects will be looked at in parallel, rather than sequentially, but some separate conclusions will be drawn at the end.

The starting point for consideration of the justiciability issue must be the First World War cases of *In Re a Petition of Right*[19] and *The Zamora*.[20] It was in the latter case that Lord Parker made the following statement:

Those who are responsible for the national security must be the sole judge of what the national security requires. It would be obviously undesirable that such matters should be made the subject of evidence in a court of Law or otherwise discussed in public.[21]

This has often been quoted subsequently as authority for a strict rule of non-justiciability of questions of national security. However, as is not uncommon with well-used quotes, the context in which it was made gives it a slightly different flavour.[22] Lord Parker was discussing the conditions which must exist to allow a belligerent power, under international law, to requisition vessels or goods in the custody of its Prize court. The first of these is identified as being when the vessel or goods in question are urgently required in connection with 'the defence of the realm, the prosecution of war, or other matters of national security'.[23] He then goes on to state that it was the view of the members of the Judicial Committee that

the judge ought, *as a rule*, to treat the statement on oath of the proper officer of the Crown to the effect that the vessel or goods which it is desired to requisition are urgently required for use in connection with the defence of the realm,

---

18. This possibility is explored further below, pp.135–36.
19. [1915] 3 KB 649.
20. [1916] 2 AC 77.
21. Ibid. at 107.
22. See the comments of Lord Scarman in *Secretary of State for Defence* v. *Guardian Newspapers* [1984] 3 All ER 601.
23. [1916] 2 AC 77, at 106.

the prosecution of the war, or other matters involving national security, as conclusive of that fact.[24]

This statement of the principle seems to leave the door open for judicial consideration of the national security issue, at least in exceptional cases. It should also be noted that the principle was not applied, since the affidavit of the Director of Army Contracts omitted to state that the copper in question was urgently required for national purposes.[25] The statements quoted are thus strictly speaking *obiter dicta*.[26]

Lord Parker used as partial authority for his views in *The Zamora* the judgment of Warrington LJ in the case of *In Re a Petition of Right*.[27] This concerned the power of the Crown, in time of war, to occupy land and premises, without paying compensation. Warrington LJ took the view that there was such a power, not limited to the conduct of actual military operations against an enemy. He said that the only condition for the exercise of the power was

that the act in question, having regard to existing circumstances, must be necessary for public safety and the defence of the realm, and on this matter the opinion of the competent authorities who alone have sufficient knowledge of the facts, provided they act reasonably and in good faith, should be accepted as conclusive.[28]

Once again, a statement which at first sight excludes the courts, on closer examination lets in what would nowadays be called a *Wednesbury* test of reasonableness. This is confirmed by the next paragraph, where Warrington comments:

In the present case, having regard to the attacks which have been actually made upon our shores, it cannot, I think, be denied that the authorities might reasonably come to the conclusion to which they have in fact arrived, that it was necessary to take and use the land in question.

The court was thus assessing the reasonableness of the decision, and deciding that, on the facts, there were reasonable grounds for it. Since there was no suggestion that the actions were not done in good faith, they were justified as an exercise of this prerogative. This was a matter on which the court could decide.

The First World War cases, then, are not as strongly supportive of the non-justiciability of issues of national security as they are sometimes claimed to be. As to the definition of national security, the statements by Lord Parker quoted above[29] indicate that the defence of the realm, and the prosecution of war are certainly within its scope, but that other

---

24. Ibid. Emphasis added.
25. Ibid. at 108.
26. But cf. the comments of Lord Diplock in *Council of Civil Service Unions* v. *Minister for the Civil Service* [1985] 1 AC 374.
27. [1915] 3 KB 649.
28. Ibid. at 666.
29. *Supra*, n.23.

matters are as well. Unfortunately these cases give no indication of what those other matters might be.

From 1916 there is a surprising lack of discussion of the matters under consideration for nearly fifty years. It is not until 1964 that we find the House of Lords getting to grips with them again. This was in *Chandler v. DPP*,[30] on section 1 of the Official Secrets Act 1911. Some members of the CND were charged with conspiracy to commit an offence under that section by entering an airfield (a 'prohibited place' under section 3) for a 'purpose prejudicial to the safety or interests of the state'. The defence wished to challenge prosecution evidence that the intended disruption would have been prejudicial to the safety or interests of the state, and to introduce their own evidence that their 'purpose' was to eradicate nuclear weapons, which would be beneficial to the state. The judge refused to allow evidence on either issue, and the Court of Appeal and House of Lords unanimously affirmed his decision. The reasoning behind the decision differs slightly between their Lordships, but it seems likely that the following statement by Viscount Radcliffe would have been generally accepted:

[T]he disposition and equipment of the forces and the facilities afforded to allied forces for defence purposes constitute a given fact and it cannot be a matter of proof or finding that the decisions of policy on which they rest are or are not in the country's best interests.[31]

On the other hand, there was no general acceptance that the government should always have the last word on the interests of the state. For example, Lord Reid stated: '"State" is not an easy word. It does not mean the government or the Executive ... I would be prepared to accept the organised community as coming as near to a definition as one can get'.[32] Viscount Radcliffe was of the view that it is not the case that 'Ministers of the state have any general authority to prescribe to the courts what is or is not prejudicial to the interests of the State'.[33] Even Lord Devlin, who equated the state in this context with 'the organs of government of a national community', which as far as the armed forces and defence are concerned means the Crown,[34] and took the view that the Crown is the best judge of its own interests, does briefly recognize that this presumption is not irrebuttable: 'Men can exaggerate the extent of their interests, and so can the Crown'.[35]

Although there are these caveats placed by their Lordships, the effect of the *Chandler* decision has been towards non-justiciability, particularly in Official Secrets Acts cases. Its influence in this direction was felt in

---

30. [1964] AC 763.
31. Ibid. at 798.
32. Ibid. at 790.
33. Ibid. at 798.
34. Ibid. at 807.
35. Ibid. at 811.

the trials of Sarah Tisdall[36] and Clive Ponting[37], civil servants charged under section 2 of the Official Secrets Act 1911 with unauthorized disclosure of information related to defence matters.

On the definition of national security, *Chandler* is no help since this phrase is not used in the statute. In *Secretary of State for Defence* v. *Guardian Newspapers*,[38] which arose out of the Tisdall case, 'national security' was central to this dispute. Miss Tisdall had given a photocopy of a document carrying the classification 'SECRET' to *The Guardian* newspaper, which published it. The Secretary of State sought its return, in order to identify the source of the leak (Miss Tisdall at that time not having been discovered). *The Guardian* resisted, basing its defence in part on section 10 of the Contempt of Court Act 1981, which allows for the non-disclosure of sources of information, except where, *inter alia*, such disclosure is *necessary* in the interests of national security. The judge in the first instance thought that section 10 was not relevant to an action for the recovery of property, but would have held for *The Guardian* on the national security issue. The House of Lords held unanimously that section 10 was potentially available to *The Guardian*, but was divided over whether the newspaper could on the facts take advantage of it. The majority agreed that the disclosure of the source of information was necessary in the interests of national security.[39] This was not because the specific document published by *The Guardian* disclosed information which it was contrary to the national interest to reveal. There was general agreement that this was not the case. However, as Lord Donaldson put it:

> The maintenance of national security requires that untrustworthy servants in a position to mishandle highly classified documents passing from the Secretary of State for Defence to other ministers shall be identified at the earliest possible moment and removed from their positions.[40]

Although this case does not give any positive definition of national security, the following conclusions are implicit:

1. Documents can be overclassified. The document in this case was labelled 'SECRET'. This means, according to the Civil Service's classification system, that it contains 'information and material the unauthorised disclosure of which would cause serious injury to the interests of the nation'.[41] As we have seen, there was general agreement that the disclosed document was not of this character.

---

36. See also 6 Cr. App. Rep. (S) 155; and *Secretary of State for Defence* v. *Guardian Newspapers* [1984] 3 All ER 601.
37. See, C. Ponting, *The Right To Know*, (1985).
38. [1984] 3 All ER 601.
39. Lord Scarman and Lord Fraser dissented on the basis that the affidavit presented to the judge did not reveal that national security was involved.
40. In the Court of Appeal, [1984] 1 All ER 454, at 458.
41. [1984] 3 All ER 601, at 610.

The civil service classification of SECRET was unjustified, and the fact of the classification was not conclusive of the document's status for the purpose of section 10 of the Contempt of Court Act.
2. Documents concerned with nuclear weapons (in this case *Cruise* missiles) are not necessarily concerned with matters of national security (despite the comments of Lord Roskill on page 622).
3. 'The interests of national security' can be affected not only by an act which is itself prejudicial, but also by an act which raises the potential of prejudicial acts in the future.

Further assistance on the definition issue is to be found in the breach of confidence cases, which at times also lay stress on the importance of potential rather than actual risks to national security. The first of these cases is *Attorney General* v. *Jonathan Cape*.[42] Lord Widgery had to consider whether Richard Crossman's diaries, containing detailed descriptions of his life as a Cabinet Minister, could be published. Once again, the indication of the scope of national security to be drawn from the case is negative rather than positive. There was agreement that there was nothing in the material proposed for publication, which had been 'vetted', which would prejudice national security. By implication, then, the actual content of the diaries, dealing with detailed descriptions of meetings of the Cabinet, and Cabinet committees, and discussions with Crossman's own department, was not concerned with national security. Such discussions are thus not, without more, matters of national security.[43] They are, however, confidential, and disclosure would have been restrained but for the fact that, in Lord Widgery's view, the lapse of time since the events described occurred meant that the balance of public interest was in favour of publication.

The same balancing of the public interest was involved in the *Spycatcher* case, *Attorney General* v. *Guardian Newspapers Ltd* (No. 2).[44] The proposed publication in this case was of a book of memoirs by a former member of one of the security services. It was accepted by all the judges involved that disclosure of information about the activities of the security or intelligence services was, by its nature, harmful to national security, and that this did not depend on the precise nature of any particular information to be disclosed.[45] This clear statement of at least one category of information which is always within the scope of national security, has, however, been undermined by the later case of *Lord Advocate* v. *Scotsman Publications Ltd*.[46] A former member of the

---

42. [1975] 3 All ER 484.
43. Unauthorized disclosure might nevertheless be contrary to the 'interests of the state': *supra*, n.8. On the facts of the case, Crossman had to be regarded as having 'authorized' the disclosures.
44. [1988] 3 All ER 545.
45. Though by the time the case reached full trial, publication of the book elsewhere in the world meant that no further damage to national security was possible.
46. [1989] 2 All ER 852.

Secret Intelligence Service (MI6), privately published a book about his period with the service (1948–53).[47] In an action to prevent the *Scotsman* from publishing material from the book, it was considered by the Crown that it did not contain any material damaging to national security. In the absence of such a concession it is clear that the House of Lords would have proceeded on the basis that such a book was, by its nature, directly prejudicial to national security. It is not clear why the Crown concession was made. If it was because the information in the book had already been published elsewhere, and that no further harm would result from further publication, then it was consistent with the *Spycatcher* decision, but it becomes difficult to understand why the action was brought in the first place. Any other explanation, however, leaves a conflict between the position taken in *Spycatcher* and in the Scottish case.

The justiciability issue is not discussed in any detail in the breach of confidence cases. It was much more central in the GCHQ case, *Council of Civil Service Unions* v. *Minister for the Civil Service*.[48] Here the conflict was between the right to belong to a trade union, and the requirements of national security. The Prime Minister, as Minister for the Civil Service, had issued an order under prerogative powers, by virtue of an Order in Council, that government employees working at the communications headquarters of the intelligence service (GCHQ) could not any longer belong to a trade union. The House of Lords held unanimously that the use of such prerogative powers was susceptible to judicial review, but that in this case the failure to consult the trade unions before instituting the ban (which would otherwise have been challengeable as an unfair procedure), was justifiable because it was done on the basis that it was in the interests of national security. The government feared that a campaign of industrial action, which would have seriously disrupted the work of GCHQ, would have followed any attempt to involve the trade unions in negotiation in this issue.

The House of Lords had no difficulty in accepting that such disruption was likely, and that it would prejudice national security. Once again, the work of the security and intelligence services is seen as an area where there is little doubt that national security considerations arise. There was less unanimity, however, on the justiciability issue. Lord Fraser, citing *The Zamora*,[49] took the line that 'the judicial process is unsuitable for reaching decisions on national security'.[50] Similarly Lord Diplock thought that national security 'is *par excellence* a non-justiciable question' on which the executive and not the courts must have the last word.[51] Lord Roskill, on the other hand, while agreeing that national

---

47. Authorization for publication had been refused by the government.
48. [1985] 1 AC 374.
49. [1916] 2 AC 77.
50. [1985] 1 AC 374, at 402.
51. Ibid. at 412.

security is a matter which is 'not amenable to the judicial process',[52] thought that there must be some evidence before the court that national security is involved, and that this must be more than 'mere assumption' on the part of the Executive.[53] However, that evidence may not be challengeable by cross-examination or counter-evidence.[54]

Lord Scarman was prepared to go even further. Building on an analysis which he began in his speech in the *Secretary of State for Defence* v. *Guardian Newspapers*,[55] he pointed out that it was important to consider the type of issue that was before the court. Although he recognized that there are limits, dictated by law and common sense, which the courts must observe in dealing with the question of what is required in the interests of national security, the court does not abdicate its judicial function.[56] If, as was the case in relation to section 10 of the Contempt of Court Act, the court was being asked to decide as a matter of fact whether national security justified an exception being made, this must be established to the satisfaction of the court. Evidence must be given and considered. The position is slightly different where the issue arises, as in the *GCHQ* case, as a matter of judicial review. Evidence is again needed, not to establish that national security was as a fact involved, but that, for instance, the person exercising the power reasonably believed that national security was involved.

This also seems to be the opinion of Lord Brightman, who in the course of a very short speech, said that:

[T]he evidence is compelling that the Minister for the Civil Service acted without prior consultation with the unions concerned because she believed, *and reasonably believed*, that such process of prior consultation might result in disruption that would pose a threat to the security of the nation.[57]

Lord Brightman's opinion thus falls somewhere between those of Lord Scarman and Lord Roskill. He is requiring evidence for the Minister's belief that national security was prejudiced, and also that the court should be able to assess whether that evidence was sufficient to found a reasonable belief. He does not, however, commit himself on the broader approach taken by Lord Scarman as regards issues of fact such as those raised by section 10 of the Contempt of Court Act.

A line very similar to Lord Brightman's was taken by Taylor J in the subsequent case of *R* v. *Secretary of State for the Home Dept, ex parte Ruddock*.[58] The vice-president of the CND, Mr John Cox, was complaining that his telephone calls had been intercepted on the authority of a warrant unlawfully issued by the Home Secretary. He

---

52. Ibid. at 420.
53. Ibid. at 421.
54. Cf. *Chandler* v. *DPP* [1964] AC 763.
55. [1984] 3 All ER 601, at 619.
56. [1985] 1 AC 374, at 404.
57. Ibid. at 423. Emphasis added.
58. [1987] 2 All ER 518.

sought judicial review of the issue of the warrant. The Home Secretary refused, on grounds of national security, to confirm or deny the existence of a warrant. He claimed that this policy of silence had to be maintained consistently, since to breach it could be of assistance to those involved with espionage and subversion. Further, he argued that the court should, for the same reason, refuse to hear the case. The judge, however, refused to exercise his discretion in this way. Basing his authority on *The Zamora*[59] and the *GCHQ* case,[60] he said that there must be evidence before the court that national security was involved, and ruled that the existence of the Home Secretary's policy of silence was not enough to establish this: 'I do not accept that the court should never inquire into a complaint against a minister if he says his policy is to maintain silence in the interests of national security'.[61]

He went on to find as a matter of fact, on the basis of evidence provided by a former member of the intelligence services, that a warrant had been issued to tap John Cox's telephone. But there was no evidence that the Home Secretary had acted unreasonably, in the *Wednesbury* sense, in issuing the warrant, and so he refused to grant a declaration that its issue was unlawful. On this last point Taylor J, who until then had taken a similarly vigorous line on the national security issue to that taken by Lord Scarman, became rather more favourable to the Executive. Rather than seeking evidence that there were national security considerations justifying the phone-tapping, he required evidence from the applicant that there were *no* national security considerations involved. As long as it was possible to envisage a situation where the Home Secretary had before him information justifying the tap, it could be said that he had acted reasonably.[62]

Where, then, does the case law leave us on the two issues under consideration? On justiciability there is a range of views. There is probably majority support, however, for requiring the Executive to produce some evidence that national security is involved in the case. Mere assertion will not be enough. However, there is no general agreement on how closely this evidence should be scrutinized, and whether it may be challenged by the defence. Despite several decisions by the House of Lords in this area, no consistent line has as yet emerged.

On the definition issue, we have some hints and suggestions, but few clear guidelines. 'National security' covers the defence of the realm and the prosecution of war;[63] the disposition of the armed forces in general,[64] and, probably, nuclear weapons in particular;[65] and the

---

59. [1916] 2 AC 77.
60. [1985] 1 AC 374.
61. [1987] 2 All ER 518, at 526.
62. Such information could have related to Mr Cox's activities as a leading member of the Communist Party, Great Britain.
63. *The Zamora* [1916] 2 AC 77.
64. *Chandler* v. *DPP* [1964] AC 763.
65. *Secretary of State for Defence* v. *Guardian Newspapers* [1984] 3 All ER 601.

activities of the security and intelligence services.[66] On the other hand, cabinet documents and discussion are not, *per se*, within its scope.[67] Nobody has suggested that the areas listed above are exclusive, and there are vague references at times to other matters of national security. The specific examples do, however, suggest a fairly limited scope for the concept. The more limited the scope, the easier it should be to define. What direction, then, should the law take, for its future developments?

Future development of national security

Looking first at the issue of the extent to which the courts should involve themselves with decisions about national security, it is submitted that the Scarman approach is the best way forward. That is, that when the issue comes before the court as one of fact, the court should give it full consideration. This would apply to the breach of confidence cases, the Official Secrets Act 1911, s.1, the Contempt of Court Act, section 10, and any other statutory or common law dispute, where one of the parties claims that national security is involved.

Where the challenge is an application for judicial review of an Executive decision which is claimed to be based on national security considerations, then the court should require evidence that the person who took the decision genuinely believed that national security justified it. As to whether that belief was reasonably held, there is no reason why the question of whether merely *Wednesbury* reasonableness, or something more substantial, must be shown should not depend on the normal rules for judicial review. There is no reason for any special rules just because national security is, or may be, involved.

There are two arguments for favouring judicial involvement, one political, the other legal.

The political argument is based on the view that in a liberal democracy, with a separation of powers, to allow the Executive to cloak its activities behind a screen of national security is a recipe for disaster. Evidence of this is easily found on the other side of the Atlantic, where the Watergate affair has been described as 'resulting quite directly from the corruption of Presidential power in the "national security" era'.[68] This episode showed that 'we must . . . assume that if the President has authority to violate laws and Constitution for reasons he must justify only to himself, the chances are that the laws and the Constitution will be violated'.[69] This cynicism about Executive claims of national security is probably more healthy than the rather complacent attitude to be found

---

66. *Spycatcher* [1988] 3 All ER 545; *Council for Civil Service Unions* v. *Minister for the Civil Service* [1985] 1 AC 374.
67. *Attorney General* v. *Jonathan Cape* [1975] 3 All ER 484.
68. Harry Cleveland and Stuart Gerry Brown, 'The Limits of Obsession: Fencing in the "National Security" Claim' (1976) 28 Admin. Law Rev. 327, at 339.
69. Ibid.

at times among the English judiciary, and perhaps best exemplified by Lord Denning:

> In some parts of the world national security has on occasion been used as an excuse for all sorts of infringements of individual liberty. But not in England. Both during the wars and after them, successive ministers have discharged their duties to the complete satisfaction of the people at large . . . They have never interfered with the liberty or the freedom of movement of any individual except where it is absolutely necessary for the safety of the state.[70]

The legal argument for judicial intervention stems from the fact that Parliament has at times, as we have seen, gone to considerable lengths to ensure that in certain situations the courts do not consider matters relating to national security. It follows, then, that in those areas where Parliament has not found it necessary to take such steps, the courts should feel free to give whatever consideration is appropriate to the issue. There is no reason why the courts should wish to place themselves under tighter restrictions than necessary.

The definition issue is more difficult. The possibility of finding an alternative to the phrase 'national security' which would be more precise in its application, and avoid the problems associated with it, was given lengthy consideration during the debates on the Interception of Communication Act 1985. Typical of the definitions proposed was that put forward by Mr Douglas Hogg at the committee stage. He proposed to substitute 'defence of the realm' for 'national security' in section 2. This phrase would then be further defined thus:

> [T]o defend the U.K. from external and internal dangers arising from attempts at espionage or sabotage, or from the actions of persons and organisations whether directed from within or without the country which may reasonably be considered to be subversive to the state.[71]

The difficulty with this lengthy definition is that it creates as many problems as it solves. The phrases it uses, in particular 'subversive to the state' are as vague as the one it is trying to replace. Mr Hogg therefore proposed a further definition which limits a subversive action to one 'which can reasonably be regarded as one which threatens the safety and well-being of the state and which is intended to undermine or overthrow parliamentary democracy by unlawful political or unlawful industrial or by violent means'.[72] Mr Hogg was of the view that this would at least have the merits of removing protesters against nuclear weapons or nuclear power from the scope of the Act.[73] The Home Secretary, however, found the definition too limited, particularly in its failure to

---

70. *R* v. *Home Secretary, ex parte Hosenball* [1977] 1 WLR 766, at 783. Lord Denning was still of the same view in 1985 when he quoted this passage during the debates on the Interception of Communications Act; HL, Vol. 464, col. 869, 6 June 1985.
71. HC, Vol. 76, col. 1112, 2 April 1985.
72. This adopted the definition given by a Home Office Minister, Lord Harris, in a debate on subversive activities on February 26 1975; HL, Vol. 357, col. 947.
73. HC, Vol. 76, col. 1116, 2 April 1985.

deal with the 'foreign aspect' of national security.[74] For reasons of this kind the government had concluded that no 'portmanteau' definition was possible. Nevertheless, attempts were made, both at the Report stage in the Commons, (by Mr Robin Corbett),[75] and in the House of Lords (by Lord Mishcon)[76] to insert definitions each time phrases such as 'defence of the realm' or 'subversion, terrorism, or espionage' were used. If the experiences of these debates is accepted, it appears that the difficult phrase 'national security' can only be replaced, or defined, by using other equally difficult and ambiguous phrases.[77]

This does not mean, however, that national security is totally incapable of definition, as was suggested at some points during the debates.[78] If that were the case there would be no point in having the phrase at all, and provisions that, for example, the Secretary of State may act in such and such a way 'if he believes that it is necessary in the interests of national security', could end after the word 'necessary'. What needs to be done is, not to look for an alternative 'portmanteau', but rather to unpack the existing portmanteau and make an inventory of its contents. In other words, if national security is to be defined, it will have to be by making detailed lists of the subjects and activities that are within its scope. The resulting definition might be long and cumbersome. But that should not deter us from attempting the task. Indeed, we already have a model of how it might be tackled. Section 2 of the Official Secrets Act was for many years criticized as being a catch-all provision of unnecessarily wide and indeterminate scope. In 1972 the Franks Committee[79] had the perspicacity to see that reform of section 2 could not be achieved by a single substitution of an alternative definition. They recommended that replacement legislation should categorize the different types of official information. This has now been done in the Official Secrets Act 1989. Whereas the old section 2 occupied half a page of the statutes, its replacement, though narrower in scope, runs to sixteen sections and eleven pages.

A statutory definition of 'national security' would not need to be quite as long as this. If we 'unpack' the concept in the way suggested above, we find, as we have seen:

1. the defence of the realm;
2. the prosecution of war;
3. the disposition of the armed forces;
4. nuclear weapons;

---

74. HC, Vol. 77, col. 300, 17 April 1985.
75. Ibid.
76. HL, Vol. 464, col. 865, 6 June 1985.
77. The US experience with defining national security has been equally unsuccessful, see Thomas I. Emerson, 'National Security and Civil Liberties', (1982) 9 *Yale Journal of World Public Order* 78.
78. E.g., by Lord Denning, HL, Vol. 464, col. 869, 6 June 1985.
79. Cmnd 5104, 1972.

5. the activities of the security and intelligence services;
6. other matters of national security.

As for 'other matters of national security', any area that has not been specifically mentioned as relating to national security over the past fifty years surely does not need that status now. This general category can safely be deleted. Of the remaining five, one to four could all come under the general heading of 'defence'. So we are left with 'defence', and 'security and intelligence'. These also happen to be two of the categories of 'official information' defined in the Official Secrets Act 1989.[80] The others are 'international relations', 'crime and special investigation powers', and confidential information. None of these are, however, without more, matters concerning national security. They will only be so in so far as they relate to security, intelligence, or defence. If it is felt that these areas themselves need further definition, this is to be found in sections 1 and 2 of the 1989 Act.

The proposed definition of national security, then, whether contained in a statute, or stated by the courts, should start by limiting the phrase to the two areas mentioned. Whenever a court is required by statute, or common law, to consider whether national security is concerned in a case, it should first ask, does it concern the security or intelligence services, or defence? This would have to be established as a fact by evidence. There is no reason to allow the Executive to hide behind ministerial certificates at this point. If the court finds as a fact that none of the areas specified is involved, then it need consider national security no further. If, however, it answers the first question in the affirmative, a further question will arise. For although it is a necessary condition that defence, security or intelligence matters are involved, it is not sufficient. For example, some information relating to defence may be out of date, or, as in the document considered in the *Tisdall* case, concern questions of political presentation, rather than the disposition of nuclear weapons. The further question that must be asked is whether serious damage will be caused to the area concerned if the court finds against the party claiming the protection of 'national security' (which will normally be the Executive). The Official Secrets Act 1989, with its definition of 'damaging' disclosures, again provides a model for how this part of the definition could be put into statutory language. It is inevitably a more subjective issue than the first part of the definition, and it may be that here the courts will at times have to take a government minister's word regarding the damage that might arise. But, as has been suggested above, they should be reluctant to do so, and should only take this course where it is forced on them by clear statutory provisions.

If the courts had adopted the approach outlined above, a different outcome might have been expected in *Chandler*, the *Guardian* case, and

---

80. Ss.1 and 2.

Ruddock. The *GCHQ* decision, however, would probably still have gone the same way.

Conclusion

The restriction of civil liberty on the basis of national security is too important to be left in the control of the Executive. It is also too important to be founded on vague notions and assumptions that 'we all know what we mean'. The relatively short statutory and case law history of the concept of national security has shown its power, but has not produced clarity or certainty. There comes a point in the development of any legal concept (and 'national security' is in the process of becoming, if it has not already become, a legal concept rather than simply a question of fact), when there is a need to step back from particular cases and attempt to delineate its overall shape. This is what has been attempted in this chapter.

Although definition is difficult, as we have seen, it is not impossible if it is approached by taking the concept and cataloguing its components rather than trying to deal with it as a unified whole. The most satisfactory way of doing this would be for Parliament to enact a Definition of National Security Act, which would set out the approach to be adopted, and provide subsidiary definitions of the phrases used. This would then be used by the courts as a basis for interpreting statutory provisions, and for guiding the development of the common law. It is, however, unlikely that parliamentary time would be found for such a measure, particularly as its main effect would be to limit Executive discretion. It will be up to the courts then, and the House of Lords in particular, to take an appropriate opportunity to define the concept in the way outlined. Only once this has been done will the balance between national security and civil liberty, which has been tending to tip upwards restriction, be restored to equilibrium. It is important that this should happen, for if we weight security too highly against liberty, we may end up with a very secure society, but one in which our liberties, which allow us to enjoy the security, have evaporated.

8 Changing attitudes: the case of racial discrimination

David Bonner

Introduction

Our Jubilee is also the twenty-fifth anniversary of the passage of the Race Relations Act (RRA 1965),[1] Britain's first attempt to deal with racial discrimination within its shores by legislative curtailment in the public interest of the traditional freedom of contract cherished by the common law. In a University city which has become culturally and ethnically more heterogeneous in those twenty-five years,[2] this dual anniversary is a welcome opportunity to survey and appraise attempts to combat racial discrimination through the creation of legal rights, remedies and enforcement machinery in a succession of laws which, while aimed at changing behaviour rather than attitudes, none the less reflected aspirations that the educational impact of law and its enforcement might also, in the longer term, play some role in the reduction of racial prejudice. The period reveals changing attitudes and approaches amongst policy-makers, legislators and the courts to the role and effectiveness of anti-discrimination law, to the concept of discrimination, to the areas of life amenable to legal intervention, and to the methods of enforcement likely to be most effective in tackling an endemic rather than a transient feature of British society. The case of racial discrimination is an instance of the increasingly interventionist role of law in industrial relations and reveals some hostile judicial attitudes, occasionally expressed in emotive language[3] to novel administrative agencies.

---

1. The RRA 1965 received Royal Assent on 8 November 1965.
2. See V. Marett, *Immigrants Settling in the City*, Leicester University Press (1989), at 1–10, and sources cited there.
3. See esp. Lord Denning MR in *Science Research Council* v. *Nasse* [1979] QB 144, at 170, 172, CA.

Origins, developments and aims of the legislation

Several Private Members' Bills of varying scope to deal with racial discrimination failed in Parliament but succeeded in drawing attention to the problem.[4] The first legislative step, the RRA 1965, was a limited measure applying only to discrimination in specified places of public resort. The then Home Secretary hoped it would be the last.[5] However, its glaring inadequacies in the face of widespread discrimination in other areas of life, particularly employment and housing, produced the Race Relations Act 1968 (RRA 1968), weakened by compromises made to win the grudging support of both sides of industry. The current measure, the Race Relations Act 1976 (RRA 1976), which repealed its predecessors, was in part made possible by the passage of the similar Sex Discrimination Act 1975, whose gestation had taken full account of the weaknesses of its sister legislation.[6]

Legislation making racial discrimination unlawful was for Britain a novel use of the law to deal with a new social situation which was the product of post-World War II non-white immigration from the Commonwealth and the difficulties encountered by those immigrants and their descendants.[7] Initially the motivating concern was with public order problems, something which shaped the limited response in and character of the RRA 1965. The subsequent responses, while conscious of the public order dangers of not providing legal remedies for aggrieved individuals, emphasized much more the moral, social and economic imperatives of dealing with a problem more complex, subtle and widespread than had been thought in 1965.[8] Ironically for a country which had exported both the common law tradition and slavery (a root of the racial problem) across the Atlantic in its imperial heyday, Britain's legislative intervention to remedy the deficiencies of the common law in providing protection against racial discrimination, was heavily influenced by the United States' experience. All three legislative schemes were brought forward by Labour governments, the Conservative opposition appearing less sanguine about the role of law, rather than persuasion, education and voluntary action, in this area, concerned also about the appropriateness of singling out racial discrimination as an evil against which to provide legal protection, and somewhat ill at ease with the nature and mode of regulation of business (particularly small business) activity involved.[9] The measures were not populist but elitist in the

---

4. A. Lester and G. Bindman, *Race and Law*, Penguin Books (1972), at 107–10.
5. HC Debs, Vol. 716, cols 1055–6 (Sir F. Soskice MP, Home Secretary).
6. *Racial Discrimination*, Cmnd 6234 (1975), paras 48–50 (cited in this chapter as 'White Paper').
7. Ibid., para. 128.
8. Ibid., para. 4.
9. See for example HC Debs, Vol. 711, cols 943, 950 (Mr P. Thorneycroft, MP); Vol 716, col. 1059 (Mr Sharples MP); Vol 763, cols 67–81 (Mr Q. Hogg MP), cols 147–57 (Mr R. Maudling MP); Vol. 906, cols 1574–5 (Mr W. Whitelaw MP); HL Debs, Vol 373, cols 739–49 (Lord Hailsham).

sense of reflecting and proceeding from 'the moral concern of a relatively small number of individuals, within and outside government'.[10] As Home Secretary in two Labour governments, Roy Jenkins was a key architect of both the RRA 1968 and the RRA 1976.[11]

Race discrimination legislation is more than an unequivocal declaration of public policy on the illegitimacy of racial discrimination. It also gives protection and redress to minority groups, thereby enabling peaceful and orderly adjustment of grievances and the release of tensions. It further encourages those who would rather not discriminate but feel impelled to do so because of social and economic pressures exerted by others (for example, customers, work-force or neighbours) by setting up the countervailing pressure of their traditional respect for the law. Its purpose is not to enforce moral attitudes by law, but rather to seek to discourage the behaviour in which prejudice finds expression and through that, hopefully, to reduce prejudice itself.[12]

Expanding concepts of discrimination

As sociological, economic, political and policy perceptions of racial discrimination have evolved, so they have found reflection, albeit distorted by the constraining precision of legal language, in widening legal concepts. Initially concern centred on prejudice, on deliberate adverse treatment by the prejudiced or by the non-prejudiced so acting to appease the prejudiced, and on avoiding segregation. As the 1970s loomed, this approach was seen as too limited; emphasis instead shifted to institutional and structural reasons for the exclusion of ethnic minorities from sectors of socio-economic life.[13] This perspective had little concern with motive and more with the effect of, for example, access requirements on ethnic minority applicants so that in employment the focus was on the effect of 'seniority' or 'experience' requirements for entry or promotion, in a context of past prejudiced discrimination in that employment or such discrimination, past or present, in society at large. The concern was with 'institutional discrimination' or 'institutional racism'. The validity of testing inevitably came under close scrutiny. Even more so than with prejudiced discrimination, the concern was for the consequences for the individual of his group membership, a factor apt to pose problems for a legal system laying stress on individuals and

---

10. L. Lustgarten, *Legal Control of Racial Discrimination*, London, Macmillan (1980), at xiii.
11. Even though he had ceased to be Home Secretary when the RR Bill 1968 was introduced to Parliament: see Lester and Bindman, *supra*, n.4, at 149.
12. Ibid. at 85; HC Debs, Vol. 763, cols 55–6 (Mr J. Callaghan MP, Home Secretary).
13. For detailed consideration see McCrudden, 'Institutional Discrimination' (1982) 2 OJLS 303, at 305–17.

ill at ease in dealing with collectivities, when these perceptions of social reality were translated into legal concepts.[14]

All three statutes have encompassed direct discrimination — in essence, less favourable treatment of a person on racial grounds — the RRA 1965 and the RRA 1968 solely so. The RRA 1976 goes further in embracing as indirect discrimination some element of this wider perception of discrimination, and catching unjustifiable conditions or requirements which disproportionately disadvantage a particular racial group. That Act also encapsulates as discrimination victimization in a specialized, narrower than common-parlance sense — essentially treating someone less favourably for laying or supporting a complaint or action under the legislation or for doing something in relation to any person by reference to it.[15] That concept has been less important than the others and is not further examined herein.[16] In this chapter, references to discrimination cover, according to context, only direct and indirect discrimination.

Since some exclusionary barriers can be justified under the RRA 1976, the British approach to discrimination remains, despite the expansion afforded by indirect discrimination, essentially rooted in an 'equal opportunity' rather than a 'fair shares' approach.[17] The 'equal opportunity' approach is process-oriented in the sense of emphasizing the irrelevance and illegitimacy of racial grounds as a determinative factor in decision-making on the allocation of resources, rather than dictating equality of result as would be the case with a results-oriented 'fair shares' approach. At its most extreme, the latter looks to results in terms of mere proportionality, and leads inexorably to the remedy of racial quotas where discrimination is found.[18] British courts appear quite comfortable dealing with direct discrimination, and their interpretation and development of the concept has been positive both in terms of substance and in aiding matters of proof. In marked contrast, despite some encouraging and positive aspects, judicial handling of the cumbersome and restrictive wording of indirect discrimination, coupled with some ill-concealed antipathy to the mode of its enforcement by the Commission for Racial Equality (CRE), have made it a weaker weapon in tackling racial disadvantage than had been hoped.

The RRA 1965 made it unlawful to practise discrimination on racial grounds, defining discrimination as refusal or neglect to afford access to, for example, services to a person in the like manner and on the like terms as were afforded to members of the public.[19] Its successors have

---

14. Lustgarten, *supra*, n.10, at 11–12; 'Racial Inequality and the Limits of the Law' (1986) 49 MLR 68, at 69, 72–6.
15. RRA 1976, s.2.
16. It should be reformed as recommended by the CRE in its *Review of the Race Relations Act 1976: Proposals for Change* (1985), proposal 2, p.6.
17. Lustgarten, *supra*, n.10, at 6–7.
18. Ibid.
19. RRA 1965, s.1(1), (3).

defined direct discrimination less restrictively as treating someone less favourably than another on racial grounds[20] and, *ex abundante cautela* to dispose of any 'separate but equal' argument, have expressly declared that segregation on racial grounds *ipso facto* ranks as less favourable treatment.[21] Although it will feature often in direct discrimination, prejudice is neither a necessary nor a sufficient component,[22] the racially prejudiced employer who, while considering them inferior beings, none the less hires non-white workers and treats them as badly as his other employees, is not caught, while the non-prejudiced personnel officer who rejects a non-white applicant in the belief that the applicant would suffer working with prejudiced colleagues, thereby directly discriminates. The courts have affirmed that direct discrimination embraces A treating B less favourably because of some racial attribute of C, even where C has no real relationship with B; the definition is not linked to the victim's racial attributes.[23]

Racial grounds in the RRA 1965 and the RRA 1968 covered only race, colour, ethnic or national origins,[24] 'rubbery and elusive' language[25] not defined in the legislation. In consequence of what some regarded[26] as the unnecessarily restrictive view of 'national origins' taken by a House of Lords[27] antipathetical to the aims of the legislation, the RRA 1976 extends also to nationality, including citizenship.[28] With direct discrimination, what matters is not whether scientifically the victim is a member of a particular race etc., but rather whether the discriminator believed him to be a member and for that reason treated him less favourably.[29]

Matters of proof are crucial. The burden rests on the complainant on the usual civil standard. Discovery is available, with safeguards to delete material in the interests of privacy and confidentiality.[30] The RRA 1976 established a questions procedure; failure to answer questions or giving evasive answers can ground a finding of unlawful discrimination by the court or tribunal which considers the responses.[31] The courts have stressed the need to draw inferences from the available facts in a context

---

20. RRA 1968, s.1(1); RRA 1976, s.1(1)(a).
21. RRA 1968, s.1(2); RRA 1976, s.1(2).
22. McCrudden, *supra*, n.13, at 304.
23. *Wilson* v. *TB Steelwork Co. Ltd, The Times*, 21 January 1978 (IT); *Applin* v. *Race Relations Board*, [1973] QB 815, CA; *Zarcynska* v. *Levy*, [1979] 1 All ER 836, EAT; *Showboat Entertainment Centre* v. *Owen*, [1984] 1 All ER 836, EAT.
24. RRA 1965, s.1(1); RRA 1968, s.1(1).
25. Per Lord Simon in *Ealing LBC* v. *Race Relations Board*, [1972] AC 342, at 362-3, HL.
26. Hucker, 'The House of Lords and the Race Relations Act' (1975) 24 ICLQ 284.
27. *Ealing LBC* v. *Race Relations Board*, [1972] AC 342, HL.
28. RRA 1976, ss.3(1), 78(1).
29. Per Lord Fraser in *Mandla* v. *Dowell Lee*, [1983] 2 AC 548, at 563, HL; B. Hepple, *Race, Jobs and the Law in Britain*, Penguin Books (2nd edn, 1970), at 37.
30. *Science Research Council* v. *Nasse*, [1980] AC 1028, HL.
31. RRA 1976, s.65.

in which clear proof will often be lacking,[32] have stated past and subsequent conduct of the alleged discriminator to be relevant within limits,[33] and have permitted inferences to be drawn from a racial imbalance identified through monitoring the ethnic breakdown of a work-force pursuant to the Code of Practice on Employment drawn up by the CRE.[34] That body has proposed that once the complainant has established that the circumstances are consistent with less favourable treatment on racial grounds, the burden of proof should pass to the respondent to establish non-racial grounds for that treatment.[35] Such a reform, resting on the basis that the respondent is the person best able to show the grounds for his actions, in part because he is in possession of relevant records and documentation, would put an appropriate finishing touch to the practical effectiveness of a legal concept wide enough to penalize overt discrimination, especially if matters were conducted before special discrimination tribunals.

Indirect discrimination is a 'persuasive definition', 'one which gives a new conceptual meaning to a familiar word without substantially changing its emotive meaning, and which is used with the . . . purpose of changing, by this means, the directions of people's [attitudes]'.[36] It represents an attempt 'to capture and retain the repugnance and abhorrence of the older meaning of discrimination while at the same time applying it to a conceptually wider set of circumstances',[37] that is to unjustifiable barriers which disproportionately exclude ethnic minorities whether these were erected consciously for that purpose or not. Its narrow interpretation may in some measure spring from the association inherent in this persuasive definition which, one might speculate, may have inhibited the full development of the new concept by causing some reluctance to attach too readily to familiar practices which unintentionally exclude ethnic minorities a label redolent of notions of racial prejudice. The concept, which recognizes a group interest rather than a group right,[38] derives from the interpretation of discrimination given by the United States' Supreme Court which stated, with respect to justifying exclusionary criteria: 'The touchstone is business necessity. If an employment practice which operates to exclude Negroes cannot be shown to be related to job performance the practice is prohibited'.[39]

Formulated in convoluted terms,[40] indirect discrimination occurs

---

32. *Owen and Briggs* v. *James*, [1982] ICR 618, CA; *Khanna* v. *Ministry of Defence*, [1981] IRLR 333, EAT.
33. *Chattopadhay* v. *Headmaster of Holloway School*, [1982] ICR 132, EAT.
34. *WMPTE* v. *Singh* [1987] ICR 837, EAT.
35. CRE, *supra*, n.16, proposal 8, p.14.
36. McCrudden, *supra*, n.13, at 345–6.
37. Ibid. at 346.
38. Lustgarten, *supra*, n.10, at 11–12.
39. *Griggs* v. *Duke Power Co.*, (1971) 401 US 424, at 331.
40. RRA 1976, s.1(1)(b).

where a condition or requirement, applicable to all applicants for the prize on offer (for example, housing, employment), disproportionately disadvantages a particular racial group and cannot be justified by the person applying it on grounds other than racial grounds. An individual victim member of the disadvantaged racial group can challenge it if it works to his detriment because he cannot comply with it.[41] Under its powers to deal with discriminatory practices, the CRE can challenge indirectly discriminatory conditions or requirements without the need for a victim.[42] The concept, and the CRE's powers, were intended to be the vehicle which eliminated unjustifiable practices which were fair in a formal sense but discriminatory in operation and effect by excluding racial minorities.[43] Dismantling of barriers was not to be achieved through litigation and enforcement alone; their existence would encourage those who distributed or controlled society's prizes to undertake in their own enlightened self-interest a radical self-appraisal of their determinative arrangements to remove voluntarily those barriers which were not justifiable. Elimination of irrelevant determinative criteria would work to the benefit of minority and majority alike. Success would depend on the interpretation given to the constraining legal language of the new concept.[44] While some judicial interpretation has been positive, some has limited the scope of the concept in a manner which, while understandable in the face of the statutory language, is not in the public interest given these aims.

Indirect discrimination looks to the effect of a condition or requirement on a particular racial group, to social facts about broader societal relationships, something with which British judges appear uncomfortable.[45] The House of Lords' expansive definition of group defined by ethnic origins as one means of constituting a racial group[46] avoided the unedifying prospect that Jews and Sikhs as such might not be protected by the legislation, and it has provided the vehicle for protecting gypsies[47] and Rastafarians.[48] Equally sensible and appropriate was their Lordships' decision that 'can comply' in the context of disproportionate disadvantage meant ability to do so consistently with the customs and practices of the racial group to which the complainant belongs.[49] The aim of the legislation is not a levelling integration into some *café au lait* oneness but equality of opportunity within cultural diversity. On the limiting side, an understandable judicial interpretation of 'condition or

---

41. RRA 1976, s.1(1)(b)(iii).
42. RRA 1976, s.28.
43. White Paper, *supra*, n.6, para. 35.
44. Lustgarten, *supra*, n.10, at 12.
45. Lustgarten, *supra*, n.14, at 72.
46. *Mandla* v. *Dowell Lee*, [1983] 2 AC 548, esp. Lord Fraser at 562–3.
47. *Commission for Racial Equality* v. *Dutton*, [1989] 1 All ER 306, CA.
48. (1989) 139 *New LJ* 459.
49. *Mandla* v. *Dowell Lee*, [1983] 2 AC 548, esp Lord Fraser at 565–6.

requirement' as something that must be satisfied if the applicant is to obtain the prize[50] means that indirect discrimination leaves untouched disadvantaging preferences or factors to be taken into account. Legislative amendment to cover 'practices, policies and situations' is desirable if unjustifiable disadvantaging barriers are to be dismantled, if the status quo is to be altered as was the aim. The courts' approach to the justification issue has been damaging, at one stage diluting a 'business necessity' test,[51] calling for the closest scrutiny of conditions or requirements, to a lower-order one of advancing reasons which reasonable people would accept as sound and tolerable.[52] This dilution was the more unfortunate in that the issue is one of fact. In the employment context, where most cases arise, decisions can vary from one industrial tribunal to another with little opportunity for appellate correction.[53] It was inappropriate that a body whose composition reflects the perspective of both sides of industry, which must appraise the justifiability of familiar and established employment arrangements, should have been required only to conduct such a low degree of appraisal. A necessity test (proving that what is causing the adverse impact is necessary and that the same end cannot be achieved in a less discriminatory manner) is preferable.[54] There may be a judicial move towards this; the Court of Appeal has recently stated that 'justifiable' requires an objective balance to be struck between the discriminatory effect of the condition and the reasonable needs of the person who applies it.[55]

In the areas within its scope, the legislation has permitted few exceptions to its central theme of colour/racial blindness; 'racial classifications must not generally be acted upon, whether they are benign or malignant'.[56] One exception is where membership of a particular racial group is a legitimate job requirement. The RRA 1968 allowed the selection of a person of a particular nationality or descent for employment 'requiring attributes especially possessed by persons of that nationality or descent'.[57] The RRA 1976 achieves the same end with the more precisely formulated 'genuine occupational qualification' exception, applying only to jobs which require membership of a particular racial group either for reasons of authenticity (for example, actor, artist's or photographic model, waiter in a genuine ethnic restaurant) or because the holder of the job provides persons of a particular racial group with

---

50. Perera v. Civil Service Commission, [1983] IRLR 166; CA: Meer v. Tower Hamlets LBC, The Times, 3 June 1988, CA.
51. Steel v. Union of Post Office Workers, [1988] 1 WLR 64, EAT.
52. Ojutiku v. Manpower Services Commission, [1982] ICR 661, CA.
53. Clarke v. Eley (IMI) Kynoch Ltd, [1982] IRLR 482, CA.
54. CRE, supra, n.16, proposal 1, pp.5–6.
55. Hampson v. Dept of Education and Science, [1989] IRLR 69, CA.
56. Lester and Bindman, supra, n.4, at 175.
57. RRA 1968, s.8(11).

personal services promoting their welfare which can best be provided by a fellow-member.[58] A 'racial balance' exception in the RRA 1968,[59] designed to counteract *de facto* segregation of immigrant workers in particular jobs or on particular shifts in a workplace, ambiguously worded and deploying a grotesque definition of racial group,[60] was not incorporated into the RRA 1976; little used, it was thought capable of abuse and detracted from the overall non-discrimination massage of the legislation.[61]

Reverse discrimination, using racial classifications to favour a racial group, has been a prominent feature of the United States' experience as a means of redressing the effects of past discrimination and assisting the advancement of racial minorities who had thereby been unable to compete on an equal footing. In employment or in law/medical school admissions, for example, this response would typically involve establishing minimum qualifications for the job or the place, lack of which would exclude anyone, and then to prefer minority applicants who satisfy them over whites with higher qualifications.[62]

Constitutionally and politically controversial in the United States,[63] such an approach has been eschewed by policy-makers in Britain and the legislation condemns it as direct discrimination. This rejection may reflect fears of awakening or intensifying white resentment, particularly in a time of high unemployment and economic difficulty, which would make more difficult the cause of good race relations,[64] or a feeling that the British situation is different from that in the United States with its legacy of slavery and legally-sanctioned segregation;[65] or the view that the remedial measures inherent in reverse discrimination are unjust in so far as they make an innocent victim, the white applicant who loses out, suffer for the wrongful acts of others.[66] Instead the RRA 1976 sanctions as exceptions to its general rule of non-discrimination certain special assistance measures, particularly in the employment sphere, designed to alleviate some of the disadvantages suffered by ethnic minorities.[67] For example, where a particular racial group is not represented at all or is underrepresented in his work-force or part of it,

---

58. RRA 1976, s.5.
59. RRA 1968, s.8(2)–(4).
60. Lester and Bindman, *supra*, n.4, at 208–13; Hepple, *supra*, n.29, at 112–20.
61. White Paper, *supra*, n.6, para. 62.
62. Lustgarten, *supra*, n.10, at 14.
63. See, *inter alia*, A. Cox, *The Role of the Supreme Court in American Government*, Oxford, Clarendon Press (1976), Ch. 3; R. Dworkin, *Taking Rights Seriously*, London, Duckworth (1977), Ch. 9; *University of California Regents* v. *Bakke* (1978) 438 US 265.
64. *The Brixton Disorders 10–12 April 1981: Report of an Inquiry by the Rt Hon. the Lord Scarman, OBE* Cmnd 8427 (1981), para. 6.32.
65. Lustgarten, *supra*, n.10, at 23–4.
66. Ibid. at 16–7.
67. RRA 1976, ss.35–8.

an employer may encourage only persons of that racial group to take advantage of opportunities for doing particular work at his establishment or may restrict training opportunities, designed to equip people for particular work, to those of his employers who are members of that racial group,[68] a provision that could usefully be extended to non-employees.[69] Such provisions are purely permissive and facilitatory. A useful reform would be to enable a tribunal to order such steps to be taken by an employer whose discrimination against a particular racial group had contributed to its non- or underrepresentation.[70] More controversially, the CRE has proposed that, in underrepresentation, an employer may be permitted to carry out a policy of preferring a member of the underrepresented group for employment in the narrowly confined situation where the competing applicants for a post are otherwise equally well-qualified for it.[71] There would be merit in exploring further Lustgarten's suggestion that an additional concept of discrimination be devised to penalize a body's attitude of *laissez-faire* in the face of manifest racial inequality,[72] but the nature and degree of resource distribution that might entail would hardly commend itself to a government of the current complexion.

The expanding scope of the legislation

The range of areas of life subjected to the legal norm of non-discrimination has expanded considerably. This has reflected increasing awareness of the pervasive nature of racial discrimination but scope has also been governed by careful consideration of the areas in which anti-discrimination law could play a positive rather than counterproductive role. This consideration has particularly been linked with the wider issue of the proper role of law in industrial relations and with keeping the law out of areas involving 'private and intimate relations'. The application of the law to certain parts of the public sector has also proved problematical.

Apart from dealing with discriminatory restrictions on the disposal of tenancies,[73] the RRA 1965, reflecting its origins in concern with public order, was confined to discrimination in specified places of public resort:[74] hotels (narrowly defined, possibly not covering 'private' hotels[75]), restaurants, cafés, public houses or other places where food

---

68. RRA 1976, s.38.
69. CRE, *supra*, n.16, proposal 23(i), p.38.
70. Ibid., proposal 16, p.27; Lustgarten, *supra*, n.10, at 36–7.
71. CRE, *supra*, n.16, proposal 23(ii), p.38.
72. Lustgarten, *supra*, n.10, at 31–7.
73. RRA 1965, s.5.
74. RRA 1965, s.1.
75. RRA 1965, s.1(5); Lester and Bindman, *supra*, n.4, at 263.

and drink was supplied for consumption on the premises; theatres, cinemas, dance halls, sports grounds, swimming pools or other places of public entertainment or recreation; premises, vehicles, vessels or aircraft used for the purpose of a regular service of public transport; and places of public resort maintained by a local or other public authority. In effect it extended only marginally beyond areas covered by the common law mandate of non-discrimination by those following a common calling (for example, innkeepers, common carriers), while not covering other places of public resort such as shops.[76]

The Political and Economic Planning (PEP) Report (1967) on the extent of racial discrimination made manifest its scale in areas not covered by the RRA 1965, particularly in employment and housing.[77] Not only did its extent vary from 'the massive to the substantial', it was both serious and growing and, since it was based more on colour than on foreign origin, it was unlikely to disappear as the passage of time saw the coloured community change character from immigrant to indigenous.[78] The first Report of the Race Relations Board[79] and that of the Street Committee[80] on the North American experience both made clear that an anti-discrimination law, with enforcement founded on conciliation, could play a positive role in these spheres. Accordingly the RRA 1968 covered employment, housing accommodation, business and other premises, the provision of goods, facilities and services to the public or a section thereof (a wider notion than the specified places of public resort in the RRA 1965), and discriminatory advertisements. The RRA 1976 additionally expanded the notion of employment (for example, to cover the role of qualifying bodies regulating entry to a profession[81]), made education the subject of specific provision,[82] and embraced most clubs and associations in their treatment of members, associate members and prospective members.[83]

The tradition of 'voluntarism' in British industrial relations — the notion that matters should be regulated by free collective bargaining, with law, legal regulation and enforcement viewed with suspicion as inferior substitutes — may seem somewhat quaint, given the last twenty years of legal intervention in the industrial relations sphere, but adherence to it by both sides of industry required concessions to be made in the enforcement aspect of the employment provisions to win grudging

---

76. Lester and Bindman, *supra*, n.4, at 258; Hepple, *supra*, n.29, at 162.
77. W.W. Daniel, *Racial Discrimination in England*, Harmondsworth, Penguin Books (1968).
78. Lester and Bindman, *supra*, n.4, at 80–2.
79. Cited ibid. at 128.
80. H. Street, G. Howe and G. Bindman, *Report on Anti-Discrimination Legislation*, Political and Economic Planning (1967), Ch. 12 (cited in this chapter as 'Street').
81. RRA 1976, s.12.
82. RRA 1976, ss.17–19.
83. RRA 1976, s.25.

support for the RRA 1968.[84] The comparative lack of opposition to the wider coverage of employment in the RRA 1976 and the mode of individual enforcement there adopted is perhaps some indication of the sea-change in the role of law in the employment sphere in such a short time. Concern for small businesses won temporary and decreasing protection from the employment provisions of the RRA 1968 — four years for firms with fewer than eleven employees, two years for those with fewer than twenty-six.[85] Lord Hailsham's attempt to win protection for small businesses in respect of the RRA 1976 was unsuccessful.[86] Reluctance to overcome by law established traditions of discriminatory crew segregation (some of which had had statutory recognition) in the shipping industry (said to be justified to avoid racial conflict in the lengthy, close-quarters living characteristic of seafaring life), permitted under the RRA 1968 racial discrimination in hiring to avoid persons of different colour, race, ethnic or national origins being compelled to share sleeping-rooms, mess rooms or sanitary accommodation.[87] Concern to protect the viability of the British shipping industry and for the economies of India and Bangladesh produced an employment exception with respect to seamen recruited abroad, one which still survives in the RRA 1976 and ought now to be removed.[88]

Some of these exceptions may reflect a principle, exhibited in the North American experience and reflected in other spheres of the British anti-discrimination legislation, that 'some relationships may be so personal and intimate that legal intervention is either likely to be ineffective or politically or socially unacceptable'.[89] This basis may explain the peculiar exception from the accommodation provisions of the RRA 1968 permitting discrimination in the allocation of sleeping-cabins on ships.[90] It has excepted in both the RRA 1968 and the RRA 1976 employment for the purpose of a private household,[91] the provision or disposal of residential accommodation in 'small premises'[92] and a very limited notion of 'private' sales of owner-occupied property.[93] Where to draw the line engenders disagreement, nowhere more so than with respect to clubs and voluntary associations in their treatment of members, associate members and prospective members.[94] If a club or association is so organized that in reality there is no concern with the personal attributes

---

84. Lester and Bindman, *supra*, n.4, at 126–30; Hepple, *supra*, n.29, at 170–1, 179–201.
85. RRA 1968, s.8(1).
86. HL Debs, Vol. 374, cols 144–57.
87. RRA 1968, s.8(10); see further Hepple, *supra*, n.29, at 120–2.
88. RRA 1968, s.8(7), (8); RRA 1976, s.8, 9; CRE, *supra*, n.16, proposal 7, p.12.
89. Street, *supra*, n.80, at 63.
90. RRA 1968, s.7(6); see further Lester and Bindman, *supra*, n.4, at 254–5.
91. RRA 1968, s.8(6); RRA 1976, s.4(3).
92. RRA 1968, s.7(1)–(5); RRA 1976, s.22.
93. RRA 1968, s.7(7), (8); RRA 1976, s.21(3).
94. HC Debs, *Standing Committee A* (1975–6), cols 333–96.

of 'members', so that in fact its facilities and services are open, if not to the public at large, then to at least a section of the public, the legislation could catch them either as a specified place of public resort (RRA 1965) or as a provider of facilities or services to the public or a section thereof (RRAs 1968, 1976). For the House of Lords, what removed a club or association from the category of provider to the public or a section thereof was its operation of a genuine system of personal selection of members.[95] Where such existed, the club or association could discriminate in its selection and treatment of members. Where it was part of a union of clubs under which members of clubs affiliated to the union had associate member rights in other affiliated clubs, it could also discriminate in its treatment of such associate members from clubs operating genuine selection schemes.[96] Governmental concern that this line drawn by the judiciary could adversely affect the impact of the legislation as a whole[97] prevailed over opposition concern that this was an area in which voluntary action was preferable to legal coercion which would, in forcing the pace of change, be resented, prove counterproductive, ineffective and thus tarnish the general reputation of legal protection.[98] The RRA 1976 effectively limits the 'private' sphere of activity with respect to clubs and associations to such bodies with less than twenty-five members.[99] The principle of equality of opportunity without homogeneity, produced a degree of protection for associations aimed at conferring membership benefits on particular racial groups defined otherwise than by colour (for example, London Welsh), by allowing them to discriminate in this sphere on racial grounds other than colour.[100]

Although the RRA 1968 applied,[101] and the RRA 1976 applies,[102] to the Crown and to the public sector generally in much the same way as to the private sector and to individuals, the important role of government in taking a lead and setting a good example to others has been weakened by a too wide exception for the protection of national security;[103] by the protection afforded to acts done under statutory authority, to certain acts done with ministerial approval or at ministerial direction;[104] by the exception for certain discriminatory employment rules in the Crown Service and specified public bodies;[105] and by the limitation effected

---

95. *Charter* v. *Race Relations Board*, [1973] AC 868, HL.
96. *Dockers' Labour Club and Institute Ltd* v. *Race Relations Board*, [1976] AC 285, HL.
97. White Paper, *supra*, n.6, para. 72.
98. HC Debs, *Standing Committee A* (1975–6), cols 333–96.
99. RRA 1976, ss.20, 25 read together.
100. RRA 1976, s.26.
101. RRA 1968, s.27.
102. RRA 1976, s.75.
103. RRA 1976, s.42; see CRE, *The Race Relations Act 1976 — Time for a Change?* (1983), at 23.
104. RRA 1976, s.41; see CRE, *supra*, n.16, proposal 5, p.9 and *Hampson* v. *Dept of Education and Science*, (1990) 140 *New LJ* 853, HL.
105. RRA 1968, s.27(9); RRA 1976, s.75(5).

through interpretation of 'facilities and services' to cover only the provision in the public sector of facilities and services akin to those which can be provided by the private sector.[106] That planning authorities and their services are now caught is welcome.[107] The general duty on local authorities with respect to the elimination of discrimination and the promotion of equality of opportunity and good relations between persons of different racial groups, admirable as a statement of what a good local authority should do,[108] is too vague to enforce against laggardly local authorities.[109] Instead all bodies carrying on a service or undertaking of a public nature should be under the same duty as the CRE to 'work towards the elimination of discrimination and to promote equality of opportunity and good relations between persons of different racial groups generally'.[110] To enable proper monitoring of their response in the equal opportunity field, such bodies should be required by law to publish annual reports and programmes on their work in the field of race.[111]

Changing methods of enforcement

Since the race relations legislation represented for Britain a novel use of the law, it is not surprising that the relatively short period since the Race Relations Bill of 1965 initially proposed dealing with the matter by the wholly inappropriate means of criminal sanctions,[112] should have witnessed quite radical changes in modes of enforcement. It was perhaps equally to be expected that the creation under the RRA 1976 of the CRE, a body combining promotional, rule-making, investigatory and adjudicatory functions (less charitably viewed as the role of prosecutor and judge), should be viewed with suspicion and its role curtailed by a conservative judiciary.

The RRA 1965 and the RRA 1968 envisaged court proceedings very much as a matter of last resort and in no way as the prerogative of the individual victim of discrimination.[113] Rather matters were placed in the hands of an administrative agency, the Race Relations Board (RRB) which, following the North American model, carried out investigations, deployed processes of conciliation as a method of law enforcement, using

---

106. *Amin* v. *Entry Clearance Officer, Bombay*, [1983] 2 AC 818, HL.
107. RRA 1976, s.19A.
108. RRA 1976, s.71.
109. CRE, *supra*, n.16, at 35-6.
110. Ibid., proposal 22.
111. Ibid.
112. Jowell, 'The Administrative Enforcement of Laws Against Discrimination' [1965] PL 119, at 164.
113. For a detailed consideration see Lester and Bindman, *supra*, n.4, Chs 8 and 9; Hepple, *supra*, n.29, Chs 8-10.

techniques of persuasion, backed ultimately by the threat of court proceedings (what Tarnopolsky has described in the Canadian context as 'the iron hand in the velvet glove'[114]), to win from the discriminator apologies, monetary compensation and assurances of his future conduct. The hope was that conciliation would resolve disputes by avoiding the polarization inherent in coercive legal proceedings and would have an educative and calming effect.[115] Legal proceedings could only be brought under the RRA 1965 by the Attorney General,[116] reflecting the perceived public character of the wrong done, and under the RRA 1968, by the RRB. Despite being given in the RRA 1968 a limited power to investigate on its own initiative, the enforcement activities of the RRB revolved almost exclusively around individual complaints.[117] Although the Street Report had recommended the creation of special race relations tribunals,[118] the RRA 1968 instead provided for proceedings in designated county courts where the judge had the advice of assessors consisting of persons experienced in race relations matters.[119] The threat of legal proceedings as the ultimate weapon backing up investigation and conciliation was weakened by the limited range of remedies available — under the RRA 1965, restraining injunctions only,[120] under the RRA 1968, declarations, restraining injunctions, special damages and damages for loss of opportunity, and the revision of discriminatory terms in contracts.[121] The effectiveness of the RRB was hampered by lack of power to compel the production of documents or the attendance of witnesses, power (erroneously, given the North American experience) thought inconsistent with the ethos of the conciliation process.[122] Enforcement was rendered even more cumbersome by the relationship between the RRB and its local conciliation committees (although this was eased in the RRA 1968),[123] and, in the employment sphere, by the concession made to win support from both sides of industry — that employment complaints should first be dealt with by suitable voluntary machinery within the industry itself. Such machinery varied in nature and effectiveness, but was subject to safeguards in that the Department of Employment and Productivity had to approve and evaluate its suitability and in the right of appeal to the RRB.[124] Such defective enforcement, with the carrot of conciliation not backed by a sufficiently strong stick, too dependent on winning the support of the alleged discriminator, made

---

114. Tarnopolsky, 'The Iron Hand in the Velvet Glove' (1968) 46 Can BR 565.
115. Ibid., at 572-3; Jowell, *supra*, n.112, at 129.
116. RRA 1965, s.3.
117. RRA 1968, s.17; see Lester and Bindman, *supra*, n.4, at 311-13.
118. Street, *supra*, n.80, Ch. 17.
119. RRA 1968, s.19(2).
120. RRA 1965, s.3(1).
121. RRA 1968, ss.19, 21-3.
122. Lester and Bindman, *supra*, n.4, at 305.
123. Ibid. at 294.
124. Ibid. at 295, 313-23; Hepple, *supra*, n.29, Ch. 8.

it difficult for the Board to press the individual victim's rights too far (whatever might be his wishes on the matter) without clear-cut evidence, and placed at risk its support among ethnic minorities.[125] The weaknesses in a complaints-based procedure (for example, non-typicality, too few complaints), with no power in the RRB to conduct strategic investigations into patterns of discrimination, meant that the RRB was unable to tackle effectively important areas of discrimination.[126]

Following the precedent of the Sex Discrimination Act 1975, the framing and passage of which had taken account of these weaknesses, the RRA 1976 took a markedly different approach, although one that still utilized as a central feature a North American-style administrative agency, the CRE. The former heavy reliance on conciliation was gone. The individual was made master of his own destiny in that, in most situations, he could take action in respect of his grievance (conceived of clearly as a statutory tort) in respect of employment matters, after ACAS conciliation had failed to resolve the complaint, in an industrial tribunal,[127] and, in respect of other matters, in a designated county court.[128] The difficulties which beset all private litigants were to be in part offset by the power in the CRE to provide assistance, although it was expected that this would tend to come more in cases which raised issues of more general importance.[129] As for remedies, declarations, restraining (rather than mandatory) injunctions, and damages are available (except for unintentional indirect discrimination), including damages for injured feelings and exemplary damages.[130] There is still, however, no power to order that the discriminator redress the wrong by giving the victim the next job, the next house etc.

Only the CRE can take action in respect of discriminatory practices, discriminatory advertisements, pressures and instructions to discriminate.[131] It can deal with persistent discrimination by seeking injunctive relief in a designated county court.[132] Freed of responsibility for individual complaints, a key role for the CRE was to be a pro-active, strategic one of wide-ranging formal investigation of patterns of discrimination, backed up by powers to make recommendations,[133] and to issue a non-discrimination notice requiring its subject not to contravene specified provisions of the RRA 1976, which is enforceable in the courts.[134] The courts, elevating what appeared to be intended as a

---

125. Lester and Bindman, *supra*, n.4, at 309.
126. Ibid. at 305.
127. RRA 1976, ss.54–6.
128. RRA 1976, s.57.
129. RRA 1976, s.66. For instances of success, see CRE, *Annual Report 1988*, at 9.
130. RRA 1976, s.57; *Alexander* v. *Home Office*, [1988] 1 WLR 968, CA; *Noone* v. *North-West Thames Regional Health Authority*, [1988] IRLR 195, CA.
131. RRA 1976, ss.29–31, 63.
132. RRA 1976, s.62.
133. RRA 1976, s.51.
134. RRA 1976, ss.58–61.

procedural constraint to a substantive one, have, however, reduced the types of formal investigation open to the CRE to two.[135] First, it can investigate the activities of a named person whom it reasonably suspects to have discriminated. Powers to obtain documents and compel the attendance of witnesses are available as of right, but the terms of reference of the formal investigation must be confined to the acts of discrimination reasonably suspected, and to verifying the possibility of other discrimination of a similar kind reasonably inferable from such acts. The second type of formal investigation (aimed at making recommendations) is a general investigation not dealing with named persons, where *subpoena* powers to obtain documentary evidence and witness evidence are available only with the assent of the Secretary of State. The process of investigation and enforcement has been rendered lengthy and convoluted by procedural constraints attached by the courts,[136] and by the addition to the respondent's right to appeal the terms of a non-discrimination notice to the courts, of judicial review of the factual basis for the notice's issue.[137] For a while, judicial limitations on its formal investigation role saw the CRE proceeding to settlements by negotiation and consent.[138] In order to reduce racial discrimination, statutory amendment should ensure the CRE has the ability, backed by *subpoena* powers, to investigate a named person (e.g. a large employer) without suspecting unlawful discrimination.[139] Flexibility of response would be enhanced were the CRE given the power to accept legally binding undertakings instead of proceeding to the final stage of enforcement.[140] Its role as adjudicator rather than investigator should, however, be transferred to special discrimination tribunals, suitably composed of decision-makers acquainted with the realities and mechanisms of discrimination. The CRE would bring before those tribunals for adjudication and action evidence of discrimination, which evidence would largely flow from formal investigations.[141] Those tribunals should have power in appropriate cases to order the discriminator to take a specified range of corrective action (e.g. in the employment sphere, engagement or reinstatement).[142]

---

135. Appleby and Ellis, 'Formal Investigations: The Commission for Racial Equality and the Equal Opportunities Commission as Law Enforcement Agencies' [1984] PL 236; *Hillingdon LBC* v. *Commission for Racial Equality*, [1982] AC 779, HL; *In Re Prestige Group PLC*, [1984] 1 WLR 337, HL.
136. Appleby and Ellis, *supra*, n.135 *passim*.
137. *Commission for Racial Equality* v. *Amari Plastics*, [1982] 1 QB 1194, CA.
138. McCrudden, 'The Commission for Racial Equality: Formal Investigations in the Shadow of Judicial Review' in R. Baldwin and C. McCrudden (eds), *Regulation and Public Law*, Weidenfeld and Nicholson (1987), 227, at 261.
139. CRE, *supra*, n.16, proposal 12, p.21.
140. Ibid., proposal 21, p.35. Cf. Fair Employment (Northern Ireland) Act 1989, ss.12, 13, 33.
141. CRE, *supra*, n.16, proposal 13, p.24. For a specialist tribunal see Fair Employment (Northern Ireland) Act 1989, ss.2-6.
142. CRE, *supra*, n.16, proposals 14, 16, pp.24, 27.

Appraisal and future prospects

While the anti-discrimination legislation has seen off some of the cruder racism once manifest in advertisements and in insurance,[143] its effects in terms of reducing racial inequality appear minimal: the incidence of racial discrimination seems undiminished;[144] there is little evidence of a significant *in terrorem* effect on employers' behaviour;[145] the rate of success of individual complaints before industrial tribunals reluctant to draw inferences of discrimination is not encouraging, although success is greater where aided by the CRE;[146] and while the CRE's enforcement effort, hampered by judicial interference, is numerically and qualitatively quite impressive,[147] the precise extent of its influence has been questioned.[148] The case of racial discrimination must inevitably make lawyers and policy-makers more humble and cautious about the shaping, social engineering role of legislation. While current governmental commitment to non-discrimination is clearly stated, much of its force is blunted, as were statements of its predecessors of different political hues, by discriminatory immigration and nationality laws and policies (most recently evidenced in the response to the fears of Hong Kong), the corrosive propaganda effect of which seems more powerful than that of legislation promoting racial equality.[149] Conservatives have always appeared less sanguine about and committed to the role of law, as opposed to education, persuasion and voluntary action in the sphere of discrimination. Without a change in government, radical transformation of the anti-discrimination legislation is unlikely.[150] The Fair Employment (Northern Ireland) Act 1989 indicates that no change can be expected in the definitions of discrimination since those in the RRA 1976 have merely been adapted to deal with religious discrimination.[151] The Northern Ireland model gives more hope in the enforcement sphere in that it equips its Fair Employment Agency with powers envied by the

---

143. White Paper, *supra*, n.6, para. 31.
144. See CRE, *Annual Report 1984* at 1; *Annual Report 1987* at 6; Brown and Gay, *Racial Discrimination 17 Years After the Act*, Policy Studies Institute (1985).
145. Lustgarten, *supra*, n.14, and sources cited there.
146. CRE, *supra*, n.16, at 18.
147. But nor should its valuable less public work in the field of encouragement and promotion be ignored.
148. Lustgarten, *supra*, n.14, at 68–9.
149. Lester and Bindman, *supra*, n.4, at 13–14; I. McDonald, *Race Relations: The New Law*, Butterworth (1977), at iv.
150. The governmental approach seems to be one of permitting piecemeal amendment in suitable statutes from time to time; see the insertion of RRA 1976, s.19A by the Housing and Planning Act 1986, s.55; and the creation of a code-making power for the CRE with respect to the rented sector by the Housing Act 1988, s.137.
151. Fair Employment (Northern Ireland) Act 1989, s.49.

CRE.[152] That legislation, however, was in part prompted by American pressure firmly linking investment to action in accordance with the MacBride principles on equality of opportunity in employment in the Province.[153] It is not easy to identify a potentially similarly effective catalyst for change in the racial sphere. It is, of course, possible, perhaps likely, that ethnic minority (especially youth) concern at their perceived role in society, at continuing or increasing disadvantage, and at the perceived failure of law, government and society to redress it, could produce serious public order problems in inner cities so as to act as a catalyst for renewed action, including a reappraisal of the RRA 1976. Reform in response to such pressure could have the dual disadvantage of being resented as a concession to violence and being viewed by those it is intended to assist as a diversionary sop[154] or 'too little, too late'. It would be better to conduct in a calmer atmosphere a full reappraisal and reform of the role of anti-discrimination law in the achievement of genuine equality of opportunity within the cultural diversity of a multi-racial society, and to provide the necessary tools in the context of a wider range of socio-economic policies to redress racial disadvantage and alienation, including a non-discriminatory immigration and nationality regime. There is no shortage of models of anti-discrimination law to consider. The CRE's 1985 proposals, drawn on in this chapter, could usefully be dusted off. A fresh look across the Atlantic at the United States' far wider range of regulatory techniques than Britain has drawn on so far would be valuable.[155] Experience with the new Fair Employment model in Northern Ireland, where problems of politico-religious discrimination are firmly entrenched, will doubtless be instructive. Perhaps it is also time to reconsider whether laws on racial discrimination should be enforced by a Human Rights Commission as part of a Human Rights Code outlawing discrimination on a broader range of grounds than racial:[156] sex, religion, political affiliation, age. After all, is it not the general goal that individuals should usually be treated on their merits as individuals rather than on the basis of the group to which they belong? Or is such traditional liberalism now an irrelevance?

---

152. Whitmore, 'A helping hand's weak arm', *The Guardian*, 16 June 1989, at 25. The powers cover *inter alia* giving directions, accepting binding undertakings, setting goals and timetables for affirmative action, requiring the monitoring of the religious composition of work-forces. The government mistakenly regards religious discrimination in Northern Ireland as essentially different from racial discrimination in Britain. But both are deep-seated and require effective equipment for their eradication.
153. See W.D. Flackes and S. Elliott, *Northern Ireland: A Political Directory 1968–88*, The Blackstaff Press (1989), at 122–3.
154. On the 'pacification' theory see Lustgarten, *supra*, n.10, at xiii and sources cited there.
155. McCrudden, *supra*, n.138, at 264–6.
156. See, for example, the Ontario Human Rights Code; Hartley, 'Race Relations Law in Ontario' [1970] PL 20 and 175.

9 Making social security law simpler

David Pollard

Introduction

Jubilee essays are often a time for reflection over the period being celebrated. This chapter conforms with that tradition. The jubilee period more or less coincides with the period over which I have had a love–hate relationship with a subject, namely, social security law, which at the commencement of that period could hardly be said to exist in terms of coherent exposition but which now is the subject of academic attention and has found its way into the curricula of many law schools.

It is not the purpose of this chapter to discuss the substance of the law — that has been done elsewhere.[1] The purpose of this chapter is to comment on the presentation of the law to the users of the law. Jubilee essays on the topic of reform often attempt to show how, during the jubilee period, reform has been achieved. This chapter in no way conforms with that tradition. It concentrates on a pressing need for reform, shows how poorly the users of the law have been served by statutory draftsmen, makes a plea for the better presentation of the rules which regulate entitlement to and the administration of social security benefits, and makes some modest suggestions for reform, in the form of a Users' Code, which might, possibly, be the subject of a next jubilee essay.

A wide-ranging examination of the drafting and public presentation of legislation was made during the early years of the jubilee period by the Renton Committee[2] and the following conclusion[3] may form the scriptural text for this chapter:

It is of fundamental importance in a free society that the law should be readily

---

1. *Social Welfare Law*, London, Longman, (1977–90).
2. *The Preparation of Legislation* (Chairman, the Rt Hon. Sir David Renton) (1974–5) Cmnd 6053, referred to below as '*Renton*'.
3. *Renton*, paras 7.4, 7.6.

ascertainable and reasonably clear. To the extent that the law does not satisfy these conditions, the citizen is deprived of one of his basic rights and the law itself is brought into contempt. [The] user of the statute book who turns to it for information about the way in which the law affects his or his client's interests should be able to find this information without undue trouble. There will of course be certain Acts which are not readily intelligible and it will usually be necessary for the layman to seek the advice of a professional lawyer. It should be possible for the professional adviser to find his way in the statute book without difficulty, and unnecessary obstacles ought not to be placed in his path. He has a right to expect that statutes should be drafted and arranged in a way which makes plain to him the relevance of the law, even of complex provisions, to the problems of his client. [If] lawyers find the law difficult, how can the laymen expect to fare?

Developments in social security provision during the jubilee period

I have examined the development and presentation of social security rules during the jubilee period from a number of viewpoints — as a writer explaining the law to lawyers and laymen, as a teacher of the law to students, solicitors, social workers and members of appeal tribunals, as an adviser to and representative of claimants for benefit, and as a member of a social security appeal tribunal. At the start of the jubilee period, life was much simpler. Social security law was mostly based on the post-war scheme created following the Beveridge Report,[4] a comprehensive scheme for those days of insurance-based benefits for unemployment, sickness, retirement and widowhood, together with non-contributory family allowances and a scheme of industrial injuries benefits for incapacity, disablement and death caused at work, and a 'safety net' of national assistance which would 'eventually diminish'.[5]

Much reform has been achieved in the substance of social security law and, coinciding roughly with the jubilee period, the basics of the Beveridge scheme have been extended to cover many groups of disadvantaged persons who were outside that scheme of insurance-based benefits since they had never (or had only partly) entered the labour market, and for whom there were sufficiently strong pressure groups to ensure that they had at least some share in the post-war prosperity of a time when so many had 'never had it so good'. New targets for income maintenance and new disadvantaged groups arising from demographic changes have been identified (such as the elderly, the lone parent, the low-waged family and the disabled) and these have augmented the move towards non-contributory benefits, the development of social assistance by way of a guaranteed right to a minimum subsistence income, and limited moves towards replacing social security provision as hitherto understood with

---

4. *Social Insurance* (1944) Cmd. 6550, 6551.
5. Ibid., para. 369.

self-help and employment protection. Some, but not all, of the key milestones are listed below.

With regard to the move towards non-contributory benefits, the jubilee period saw the introduction of non-contributory retirement pensions for those excluded under Beveridge,[6] invalidity benefit as a long-term benefit for those incapable of work,[7] attendance allowance for those needing substantial attendance in relation to bodily functions,[8] invalid care allowance for those giving up work to look after a disabled person,[9] mobility allowance for those unable or virtually unable to walk,[10] non-contributory invalidity pension (later severe disablement allowance) for those incapable of work but who had not paid sufficient contributions for an insurance-based benefit,[11] one-parent benefit as an increase of child benefit for lone parents.[12] With regard to the development of social assistance by way of a guaranteed right to a minimum subsistence income, the jubilee period saw an increasing number of persons depending on means-tested subsistence-level benefits (either in whole or to supplement low incomes and low insurance-based benefits), such as supplementary benefit, available as of right to provide a minimum income,[13] family income supplement to help those in low-paid work who were responsible for the upbringing of children,[14] rent allowances and rent rebates administered by local authorities,[15] a new supplementary benefit system, based on a complex set of legal provisions designed to measure and meet individual needs,[16] a detailed national system of housing benefit,[17] and, replacing the above, an immensely complex scheme of 'income-related benefits' (income support, family credit and housing benefit, together with grants and loans from a social fund).[18] With regard to moves towards replacing social security provision as hitherto understood with self-help and employment protection, there was new provision for a basic retirement pension, supplemented by an earnings-related addition and the opportunity to contract out of the state retirement pension scheme and to rely on private occupational pensions,[19] rudimentary schemes of guaranteeing at least a minimum

---

6. National Insurance Acts 1970 and 1971.
7. National Insurance Act 1971.
8. National Insurance Act 1970.
9. Social Security Benefits Act 1975.
10. Social Security Pensions Act 1975.
11. Social Security Benefits Act 1975.
12. Child Benefit Act 1975.
13. Ministry of Social Security Act 1966.
14. Family Income Supplements Act 1970.
15. Housing Finance Act 1972.
16. Social Security Act 1980.
17. Social Security and Housing Benefits Act 1982.
18. Social Security Act 1986.
19. Social Security Pensions Act 1975.

amount of employment,[20] statutory sick pay, administered by employers,[21] and statutory maternity pay, administered by employers.[22]

Whether one describes the above as a development of a comprehensive system to meet 'need' or as a series of happenings which cumulatively have resulted in a comprehensive system, we now, at the end of the jubilee period, have a series of benefits relied on by immense numbers of beneficiaries.[23] However, if newly defined and widely differing categories of need are to be accommodated and in social, economic and political contexts differing from those pertaining at the beginning of the jubilee period, the relative simplicity of those days must, inevitably, give way to a degree of complexity hitherto unknown. Some of the factors contributing to this inevitable complexity are discussed in outline below. However, as will be emphasized below, there is a fundamental distinction to be drawn between a complex system and an incomprehensible system.

The inevitability of a complex system

It is a long-recognized feature of the United Kingdom constitution that the raising of taxes and the spending of monies so raised must be authorized by Parliament. A social security system which redistributes so high a percentage of money raised by taxation, including national insurance contributions, can be no exception. Any desire to limit public expenditure inevitably means that the redistribution of taxes by way of social security benefits can be accomplished only by precise (and complex) legislation to authorize the payment of these benefits. Each time a new group of beneficiaries is defined, the scheme must provide not simply for the conditions of entitlement to be defined and placed in an appropriate position, if any, in the overall scheme of things, but provision must be made for ancillary and procedural matters, such as contributions conditions, where appropriate, residence conditions, claims rules, payments rules, rules designed to ensure that beneficiaries cannot accumulate entitlement to a multiplicity of benefit, rules to decide how disputes over entitlement should be resolved, and so on. The growth of the scheme, as mentioned above, has been spasmodic. Some developments fitted into the

---

20. National Insurance Act 1966, Employment Protection Act 1975, Employment Subsidies Act 1978.
21. Social Security and Housing Benefits Act 1982.
22. Social Security Act 1986.
23. Latest available (end of 1987) figures for beneficiaries of the more important social security benefits are: attendance allowance (641,000), child benefit (6,712,000), family income supplement (220,000), industrial injuries disablement benefit (183,000), invalidity benefit (968,000), maternity allowance (109,000), mobility allowance (512,000), one-parent benefit (681,000), retirement pension (9,764,000), severe disablement allowance (260,000), supplementary benefit (4,900,000), unemployment benefit (675,000), widows' benefits (367,000). Source: *Social Security Statistics* 1988 (HMSO, 1989).

existing scheme with ease but some show the joints very clearly.[24] General propositions designed to target beneficiaries have to be translated into precise terminology and the draftsman has to define with care for the purposes of social security the meaning of both everyday words and phrases, such as 'unemployed', 'incapable of work', 'one-parent family', 'disabled', 'the elderly' and 'unable to walk' (to cite but a few), and also words and phrases which already have a known meaning within the legal system, such as 'rent', 'insurance policy' and 'tenant' (again to cite but a few). The jubilee period has seen considerable changes in attitude to a fundamental concept of any system of social security, namely, how does one define 'poverty', the state of affairs which social security is designed to alleviate? The system has ceased to define poverty in terms of subsistence poverty and has recognized the existence of 'relative poverty',[25] although it may not yet have devoted sufficient resources towards its elimination. This has had considerable and inevitable effects on income-related benefits (as they are now called), where a basic feature is that a person with capital above a specified limit should spend his or her capital above this limit before looking to the state for support and that a person who has income should look to the state only to supplement that income up to the current threshold of the poverty level. Nowadays, many people who look to income-related benefits are relatively rich in terms of subsistence poverty and especially in terms of the standards pertaining before and just after Beveridge. They may own a house, have an insurance policy, have money set aside for funeral expenses, have part-time earnings and consumer durables. However, they may be relatively poor in 'relative poverty' terms because modern views of acceptable lower limits of poverty will not dictate the compulsory sale of the home, a wedding ring, the cashing-in of an insurance policy, or the spending of a charitable gift for children in order to achieve a level of subsistence poverty before entitlement to social security support is achieved. Therefore, value judgments have to be made of what capital and income resources a 'relatively poor' person should be allowed to keep without affecting title to benefit and, again inevitably, those value judgments have to be translated into complex rules. Other value judgments have been inserted into the scheme as a result of the passionate debates which have occurred during the jubilee period on the modern State being a 'caring' State, based on the prayer of St Francis, and the 'nanny State', which is said to inhibit economic growth and to reduce the amount of money which can be redistributed to the 'really deserving poor'. The Beveridge system was based on the simple concept that a thriving economy would continue from the war

---

24. One welcome reform of substance was the introduction of common Regulations for Adjudication (SI 1986 No. 2218) and Claims and Payments (SI 1987 No. 1968).
25. R. Townsend, A Survey of Household Resources and Standards of Living: *Poverty in the United Kingdom*, Penguin (1979), p.31.

economy and would mean that work, and wages or salary, would be available to all capable of working, and that such workers would contribute to an insurance scheme which would then redistribute earnings to those unable or not required to work. There was, therefore, inherent in the scheme an obligation (continuing from the days of the first Elizabeth) to work and to finance the scheme. This 'work ethic', as it is usually called, if not universally accepted, was readily understandable at the commencement of the jubilee period. However, the jubilee period has seen the abolition of the simplicity of the work ethic in times of high unemployment and demographic changes and has heard debates which can be summarized by a series of questions which any designer of a social security scheme must answer and translate into legal provisions. How, then, can and indeed should social security be used as a state mechanism to create a thriving economy, and should it be used to do this by means of withholding benefits from those who abstain from the labour market, by means of forcing people into a low-wage economy or by means of incentives? Should the system withhold benefits from those who abstain from the labour market because of trade disputes, or who leave employment for 'invalid' reasons, or who are not actively seeking work (and what of their families)? Should 16 to 17 year olds stay at home and be supported by the family rather than by the State (and what if they are responsible for a child, estranged from their parents, or have been in the care of a local authority rather than a family)? If employment is unavailable locally (or for the particular work skills or physical or mental capacity of an individual), should an unemployed, or incapable, person be made to leave home and family (or change his or her normal occupation for one of which he or she is capable)? Should a person be entitled to keep wages from part-time employment as part-time employment is often a way of entering or re-entering the labour market, an escape from the home for a lone parent, a therapeutic measure for a disabled person, and a means of being useful for a retirement pensioner? These and other questions generate complexity within the scheme and demand the drawing of yet more borderlines between the modern deserving and undeserving poor.

Whether deserving or undeserving, those seeking, or seeking to enforce, social security benefit entitlement will today enter a system far removed from the relative simplicity of that laid down at the beginning of the jubilee period. Their numbers include, very significantly, many individuals whose ability to know of, to claim, and to enforce any benefit entitlement may be impaired by physical and mental disability, by low educational attainment and literacy skills, by language difficulties and by a general inability to cope with the modern complex world. Their world can be made more complex by the legislation providing for their benefits and many, but not all, will be confronted with the need to use that legislation.

Who uses the legislation?

The Renton Committee concluded that 'in principle the interests of the ultimate users should always have priority over those of the legislators'.[26] Who, then, are the 'users' of social security legislation? In one sense, the users are countable in millions. Retirement pensioners 'use' the law relating to retirement pensions each time they visit a Post Office to draw their pension. However, this is to take the notion of 'user' to an extreme extreme. I would prefer to suggest the phrase 'active user' or 'direct user', in other words, someone who may need to be brought into direct contact with the words of the legislation and who has to use those words to undertake a number of tasks discussed below, and active users are counted in very many thousands.

Persons who come within the notion of the 'active user' include welfare rights officers, trade union officials, certain claimants, certain employers, lay members of Citizens' Advice Bureaux, solicitors for whom social security law is a minor part of everyday practice, expert advisers in law centres, DSS officials who prepare and conduct cases for a tribunal hearing, and lay and legally qualified members of the appeal tribunal. Their tasks include giving initial advice to someone contemplating a claim, then, when an initial decision has been made which is unfavourable, the scrutiny of the legislation and an explanation to the claimant to see if the claimant can give facts (not previously disclosed or thought important) which might support an appeal, showing that a decision, although unwelcome, has been made in exact conformity with the legislation and that an appeal will not succeed, preparing for and conducting an appeal. So often the task is to act as an interpreter to someone whose reading age is below that of the draftsman.

With regard to appeals against unfavourable decisions, it is possible to give some quantifiable indication of the direct use of the statutory provisions.[27] A large number of appeals are registered each year.[28] When an appeal is registered, the case is normally reviewed by the DSS internally and a good number of appeals lapse after such a review (which may be favourable or where it may be shown to the claimant that the original decision was correct).[29] A good number of appeals are subsequently withdrawn[30] for unascertainable reasons, although, in my experience an appeal is usually withdrawn when, on receiving the detailed summary of

---

26. *Renton*, para. 10.3.
27. Figures for the years 1985 and 1987 are taken from *Social Security Statistics* (HMSO, 1986 and 1988, respectively). However, the figures may be somewhat distorted by reason of the fact that many appeals in recent years related to provisions permitting an element of value judgment (now substantially eliminated) and to the award of supplementary benefit single payments (now abolished).
28. 1985: 290,485; 1987: 430,715.
29. 1985: 73,667; 1987: 79,322.
30. 1985: 44,431; 1987: 46,590.

facts and law and the argument of the DSS, the claimant realizes, or is advised, that an appeal would not succeed. A very large number of appeals are heard[31] by many appeal tribunals, and at about half of the appeals the appellant and/or a representative attends the hearing.[32]

Problems with social security legislation

The problems with which the many active users of social security legislation have so often been confronted during the jubilee period are legion but may conveniently be analysed under three headings, each with its own subordinate problems.

The problem of availability to the user of an up-to-date and accurate legislative text

As has been seen above, the present social security scheme operates in a complex social and economic context and, inevitably, there must be many rules whose translation into statutory provisions must occupy much legislative space. There are very many statutory sources and, at the time of writing, there are over thirty separate statutes and over 450 statutory instruments dealing wholly or in part with social security.[33] These provisions are constantly being amended. For example, the scheme for income-related benefits (income support, family credit and housing benefit) came into existence in April 1988, and by the time I had submitted the manuscript for a second edition of a work on income-related benefits in October 1989, I had, not counting the uprating of figures, which is inevitable in time of high inflation, noted nearly 600 amendments to the scheme. Six hundred amendments do not simplify a system. The frequent amendment of the legislation is compounded by the fact that such legislation is particularly plagued by the use of what is known as 'non-textual amendment' as opposed to what is known as 'textual amendment'. Textual amendment means the substitution of a whole new paragraph or sentence, either by the amending section (or regulation) stating that henceforth the new section or regulation shall read as follows, or by stating that the amended text of the section or regulation shall have effect as it appears in a Schedule. Non-textual amendment means that the amending section or regulation directs the insertion of a word or phrase between two existing words or directs that existing words

---

31. 1985: 114,550; 1987: 165,307.
32. 1985: appellant only: 38,440, representative only: 5,140, appellant and representative: 20,588 (total 64,168); 1987: appellant only: 50,067, representative only: 7,085, appellant and representative: 27,471 (total 84,623).
33. At the time of publication, there will have been many more.

be deleted. When a section or regulation is non-textually amended several times by several different amending sections or regulations, the result is, at the very least, an inelegant and confusing hotchpotch.[34] A constitutional device to counter this problem is that of consolidation and reissue of all the statutory provisions, but, in the absence of such consolidation, the current problem is then of the availability of an up-to-date and accurate text containing what currently exists of the original Queen's Printer's copies of the many statutes and statutory instruments.

Efforts have been made to reproduce the statutory provisions as enacted and as so often amended in order to provide an authoritative and up-to-date text of those provisions. A compendium of the law relating to social security is published by HMSO as a loose-leaf work (in 11 large volumes and known colloquially as the Blue Volumes). As a means of presenting an accurate text to the user, the Blue Volumes are extremely useful, showing whether, how, when, and by what, the text as enacted has been amended and indicating enacted amending provisions not yet in force. They are made available to the public at DSS offices and appeal tribunal buildings (but their bulk and price limit their availability elsewhere). In an attempt to overcome the problems of bulk and price a number of other, smaller, compilations have been produced and have achieved a semi-offical status. However, although some individual contributions are indeed extremely good, there is elsewhere an unacceptably high rate of inaccuracy.

Take, for example, the treatment of child benefit in the 1988 edition of one compilation,[35] where it is stated[36] that there has been provided 'an authentic text of the statutes and regulations as at April 11 1988'. In the operation of child benefit it is important to know who is a child, and, in addition to those persons under the age of 16, a child includes certain persons staying on at school or college in 'full-time education'. In the comment on the appropriate section,[37] there is a General Note to the effect that the 'following are deemed to be in receipt of full-time education . . . (a) those receiving education otherwise than at a school under special arrangements made by the local education authority' and this is followed by a reference to a regulation,[38] which indeed, when made, made a reference to otherwise than at a school under 'special arrangements'. Alas, however, and to the confusion of the user, that regulation was revoked (and substituted by another regulation) over a year before the 'authentic text' date.[39] As from 6 April 1987, the

---

34. The Income Support (General) Regulations 1987 (SI 1987 No. 1967), Sched. 7, has been non-textually amended 105 times and textually amended 3 times.
35. *Non-Means Tested Benefits.*
36. Preface.
37. Child Benefit Act 1975, s.2.
38. The Child Benefit (General) Regulations 1976 (SI 1976 No. 965), reg. 5(a).
39. By SI 1987 No. 357, reg. 4.

Regulations relating to child benefit were changed to take account of a particular situation affecting persons who stop attending classes at school but return there to take examinations and an amendment[40] was made to clarify the position. The amendment is omitted.[41] In some ways the omission is more worrying than a mere clerical error since the problem raised was already well known. Furthermore, the omission is made all the more strange because the same amending Regulation[42] added other regulations[43] to the same Regulations and the latter are faithfully reproduced.

The 'authentic text' date, 11 April 1988, was the date on which supplementary benefit was replaced by income support. Everyone knew this, even the government, and throughout the social security statutory provisions changes were made to replace references to supplementary benefit by references to income support. The rules relating to child benefit were so amended,[44] as from that date, but the 'authentic text' simply takes no notice of this.[45] Finally, the text[46] reproduces another regulation,[47] but since this was revoked,[48] as from 6 April 1987, its continued reproduction and the commentary thereon would appear to be superfluous, to say the least.

To echo the words of the Renton Committee,[49] if a learned compiler of an authentic text cannot reproduce the statutory provisions with accuracy, what chance has the ordinary user of such work? So the user is left with the Blue Volumes, where the user is faced with not the problems of accuracy but with the additional problem of currency.

It is suggested that any norm of constitutional behaviour should contain a principle that legislation should be available to the user before it comes into force. This principle is recognized, in part, by the publication of a bill before enactment; by provisions governing the laying of certain statutory instruments before Parliament; by the printing and sale of statutory provisions when enacted or made; and, with regard to statutory instruments, by a general rule of practice that as far as possible such instruments will not come into force until three weeks after laying before Parliament. Despite this, it can happen that statutory provisions may be in force for a considerable time before the user can obtain them.

---

40. SI 1987 No. 357, reg. 5(4), added The Child Benefit (General) Regulations 1976, regs 7(4)–(6).
41. P.465.
42. SI 1987 No. 357, regs 5(2) and 5(3).
43. Regs 7(1A) and 7(2A), respectively.
44. SI 1988 No. 521, reg 12, appropriately amended The Child Benefit (General) Regulations 1976, reg. 7C.
45. P.466.
46. Pp.470–1.
47. The Child Benefit (General) Regulations 1976, reg. 15.
48. By SI 1987 No. 491, reg. 19(1).
49. *Supra*, n.3.

So far as social security law is concerned, it is important to note that the above constitutional safeguards only provide for the public availability of the original measures and that to so many users it is impracticable to have recourse to the originals. The 'real availability' of the statutory provisions may, in practice, only be provided by the Blue Volumes but this 'real' availability is considerably reduced by the fact that many statutory provisions have been in force for many months before they have been published in the Blue Volumes. Perhaps it would be a pious hope to suggest, as a constitutional safeguard, that the statutory provisions should not come into force until they have been published in the official text of the Blue Volumes, which could become a 'Users' Code'. However, the presentation of an accurate and up-to-date text is not enough and a 'real' Users' Code should, it is suggested, go further, because 'insufficient assistance is given to the reader in the task of collation which results from the purely chronological arrangement'.[50]

The problem of insufficient assistance being given to the user

As has already become obvious, it is inescapable that social security law contains much detail and this may be enacted by enacting details in the sections of a statute, in Schedules to a statute, or by statutory instruments. Obviously, Governments prefer to use statutory instruments because rules can be made quickly and without the need for special Parliamentary enactment. As far as the user is concerned, it does not matter. The user must go to and use the detailed rules relevant to the case in hand and regardless of the hierarchical ancestry of the rule. Provided that the user is told where to go, it does not matter that the rules which govern entitlement to or disqualification from, for example, sickness benefit are contained in a section, a Schedule or a statutory instrument.

Constitutional propriety demands that statutory instruments implementing a principle stated in a statute be authorized by that statute, but so often there is little overt co-relation between the parent section and the implementing regulations. What the user needs, and what could be provided by a 'real' Users' Code, is a series of signposts. Statutes often refer to 'subject to prescribed conditions' but there is no signposting to pin-point which regulation or paragraph of a regulation of which Regulation is appropriate and lays down the prescribed conditions.

For example, entitlement to 'reduced earnings allowance' (a benefit for persons, *inter alia*, injured by accident at work whose earning capacity is thereby reduced) depends, *inter alia*, on the person's 'regular occupation'. The statute[51] states that:

---

50. *Renton*, para. 6.13.
51. Social Security Act 1975, s.59A(2).

the Secretary of State may by regulations provide that in prescribed circumstances employed earner's employment in which a claimant was engaged when the relevant accident took place but which was not his regular occupation is to be treated as if it had been his regular occupation.

There is no signpost to the appropriate implementing regulation and the finding of that regulation may take the uninitiated some time and considerable effort. Even to state in (or at the end of) the enabling section something to the effect that 'the prescribed circumstances for the purposes of this section will be found in the [name] Regulations' would provide a signpost.

A Users' Code could, without committing any constitutional impropriety, take the matter further and give real assistance to the user by collating both enabling section and implementing regulation into an 'article' to use a neutral word, always stating the constitutional ancestry and hierarchy of each 'rule' in the article. For example, the problem of 'regular occupation' described above could be solved by the creation of article, say 99, as follows:

Article 99: Regular occupation for the purposes of reduced earnings allowance.

Art. 99(1). The Secretary of State may by regulations provide that in prescribed circumstances employed earner's employment in which a claimant was engaged when the relevant accident took place but which was not his regular occupation is to be treated as if it had been his regular occupation (Social Security Act 1975, s.59A(2)).

Art. 99(2). Employed earner's employment in which a claimant was engaged when the relevant accident took place but which was not his regular occupation shall be treated for the purposes of art. 99(1) as if it had been his regular occupation where the claimant, at the time the relevant accident took place, had no regular occupation but was pursuing a course of full-time education (Social Security (Industrial Injuries and Diseases) Miscellaneous Provisions Regulations 1986 (SI 1986 No. 1561), reg. 2).

Further problems of insufficient assistance being given to the user arise from the too frequent lack of linking between substantive provisions and ancillary provisions in that important provisions relating to one benefit are not found in the normal Regulations relating to that benefit but in ancillary Regulations (and without a signpost). For example, regulations relating to child benefit[52] provide for a higher rate of child benefit for single parents, known as 'one-parent benefit'. In a certain number of cases, an increase of another specified social security benefit on account of the relevant child will be reduced by the amount of one-parent benefit payable. This rule is not to be found in the Regulations governing one-parent benefit but in ancillary Regulations relating to what are known as

---

52. The Child Benefit and Social Security (Fixing and Adjustment of Rates) Regulations 1976 (SI 1976 No. 1267), reg. 2(2).

'overlapping benefits' (the 'Overlapping Benefits' Regulations).[53] To take another example, there is a rule that where entitlement to family credit is less than 50p a week, that amount will not be payable. This rule is not to be found where it might be expected to be found, namely, in the Regulations dealing with assessment of family credit, but in a separate set of Regulations (the 'Claims and Payments' Regulations).[54] The transfer of the 'one-parent benefit rule' and the 'family credit rule' from the Overlapping and Claims and Payments Regulations, respectively, would create the problem that those Regulations would then be incomplete. A horrifyingly simple solution would be to place each rule within both sets of relevant Regulations.

To give sufficient assistance to the user of the statutory provisions relating to social security, therefore, demands at the very least a series of signposts to point the user in the correct direction, a guide or index to the complete statutory provisions, either in the statutory provisions themselves or by means of an extra statutory publication, such as a Users' Code. However, even the limited suggestions for reform mooted above will only partially aid the user. Once the user has been guided to the detailed rule relevant to the case in hand, that detailed rule may be incomprehensible.

The problem of incomprehension

Much social security legislation is incomprehensible even to those who may claim some familiarity with the subject-matter of that legislation. Statutory provisions 'should not only be clear and unambiguous, but readable. It ought not to call for the exercise of a cross-word/acrostic mentality which is able to ferret out the meaning from a number of sections, schedules and regulations.'[55] As Sir Ernest Gowers so aptly wrote:[56]

Acts of Parliament, statutory rules and other legal instruments have a special purpose, to which their language has to be specially adapted. The legal draftsmen ... have to ensure to the best of their ability that what they say will be found to mean precisely what they intended, even after it has been subjected to detailed and possibly hostile scrutiny by acute legal minds. For this purpose they have to be constantly aware, not only of the natural meanings which their words convey to the ordinary reader, but also of the special meaning which they have acquired by legal convention and by previous decisions of the Courts. Legal drafting must therefore be unambiguous, precise, comprehensive and largely conventional. If it is readily intelligible, so much the better; but it is far more important that it

---

53. The Social Security (Overlapping Benefits) Regulations 1979 (SI 1979 No. 597), reg. 8.
54. The Social Security (Claims and Payments) Regulations 1987 (SI 1987 No. 1968), reg. 27(2).
55. *Renton*, para. 6.3.
56. *The Complete Plain Words*, HMSO (1986), p.6.

should yield its meaning accurately than that it should yield it on first reading, and legal draftsmen cannot afford to give much attention, if any, to euphony or literary elegance. What matters most to them is that no one will succeed in persuading a court of law that their words bear a meaning they did not intend, and if possible, that no one will think it worth while to try.

Might anyone think is 'worth while to try' to elicit the meaning of:

the amount mentioned in paragraph (1)(a) shall be one-sixth of the weekly amount for normal requirements for the time being applicable to a person to whom paragraph 3 of the table in paragraph 2(3) of Schedule 1 to the Act (long-term rate for householders) applies, that one-sixth being, where it is not a multiple of 10 pence, rounded to the nearest such multiple or, if it is a multiple of 5 pence but not of 10 pence, the next higher multiple of 10 pence.[57]

At the time the regulation was made, this could have been expressed quite simply as £6.30.

I am fortunate to possess a 'cross-word/acrostic mentality', an aptitude which came in very useful when undertaking the task of finding out the current rate of a widow's pension under the industrial injuries scheme. The current rates of many benefits are to be found in the Social Security Act 1975,[58] which is normally uprated each year and the user may have to seek the current uprating statutory instrument.[59] There are three rates of widow's pension: an initial rate, a higher permanent rate, and a lower permanent rate. The current uprating instrument is very helpful with regard to the first two. The initial rate is stated to be £57.65 per week and the higher permanent rate is stated to be £43.60 per week. The lower permanent rate is not quite so easy to find as it is stated to be '30 per cent. of the sum specified in section 6(1)(a) of the Pensions Act'. The trail starts here. According to Schedule 20 to the Social Security Act 1975, 'the Pensions Act' means the Social Security Pensions Act 1975. The next move is to find section 6(1)(a) of the Social Security Pensions Act 1975 which refers to '6(1)(a) a basic component of £11.60'. Back to the current uprating order which causes some initial discomfort as it inserts into section 6(1)(a) two, yes two, sums. However, a careful scrutiny of the uprating order shows that one sum is solely for the purposes of sickness benefit. Therefore we take the other sum which is £43.60. A calculator is, therefore, needed and this valuable instrument shows that 30 per cent of £43.60 equals £13.08. A lot of time would have been saved if, instead of '30 per cent. of the sum specified in section 6(1)(a) of the Pensions Act', the draftsman had simply stated '£13.08'.

Finally, from my ever-increasing collection of 'all-time favourites' may be cited:

---

57. The Supplementary Benefit (Duplication and Overpayments) Regulations 1980 (SI 1980 No. 1580), reg. 7(2).
58. Schedule 4.
59. At the time of writing, SI 1989 No. 43.

17(1) Regulation 16 [which relates to recovery of wrongly paid sums by deduction from specified benefits] shall apply without limitation to any payment of arrears of supplementary pension or allowance other than any arrears caused by the operation of regulation 8(1) of the Supplementary Benefit (Determination of Questions) Regulations 1980 (suspension of payments), but shall apply to the amount of pension or allowance to which a person is presently entitled only to the extent that there may, subject to regulation 18 of the Supplementary Benefit (Claims and Payments) Regulations 1981 (priority as between certain debts), be recovered in respect of any one benefit week —

(a) in a case to which paragraph (2) applies, not more than the amount there specified; and

(b) in any other case, 3 times 5 per cent. of the single householder rate, that 5 per cent. being, where it is not a multiple of 5 pence, rounded to the next higher such multiple.

(2) Where —

(a) the person to whom the supplementary pension or allowance is payable is a person to whom —

(i) paragraph 1(a) of the table in paragraph 2(3) of Schedule 1 to the Supplementary Benefits Act 1976 (normal requirements for person over pensionable age who has a partner) applies,

(ii) paragraph 3(a) of that table (normal requirements for householders over pensionable age) applies,

(iii) regulation 7 of the Supplementary Benefit (Requirements) Regulations 1983 (long-term rate for normal requirements) applies, or

(iv) regulation 9(12)(a)(i) or (b)(i) of those Regulations (long-term rates for normal requirements of boarders) applies; or

(b) the person responsible for the misrepresentation of or failure to disclose a material fact has, by reason thereof, been found guilty of an offence under section 55 of the Act or under any other enactment, or has made a written statement after caution in admission of deception or fraud for the purpose of obtaining supplementary benefit,

the amount mentioned in paragraph (1)(a) shall be one-sixth of the weekly amount for normal requirements for the time being applicable to a person to whom paragraph 3 of the table in paragraph 2(3) of Schedule 1 to the Supplementary Benefits Act 1976 (long-term rate for householders) applies, that one-sixth being, where it is not a multiple of 10 pence, rounded to the nearest such multiple or, if it is a multiple of 5 pence but not of 10 pence, the next higher multiple of 10 pence.

(3) Where in the calculation of the resources of the person to whom the supplementary pension or allowance is payable the amount of earnings or other income falling to be taken into account is reduced by regulation 10(5) or 11(5) of the Supplementary Benefit (Resources) Regulations 1981 (partial disregard of earnings or other income respectively) the weekly amount applicable under paragraph (1) may be increased by not more than half the amount of the

reduction, and any increase under this paragraph has priority over any increase which would, but for this paragraph, be made under regulation 17(3) of the Supplementary Benefit (Claims and Payments) Regulations 1981 (regular payments to third parties for fuel items).

The regulation continues for several paragraphs . . .[60]

Incomprehension is compounded by the frequent use of 'legislation by reference' whereby statutory provisions are made shorter (but less certain) by incorporating, by reference to other provisions, the substance of those other provisions. Legislation by reference may necessitate searching out legislation not always readily at hand. For example:

No single payment shall be made in respect of . . . any repair to property of any body mentioned in section 28(4) of the Housing Act 1980 or section 10(2) of the Tenants' Right etc (Scotland) Act 1980 (public sector housing bodies);[61]

and

Where earnings to which regulation 35(1)(i)(i) applies are paid in respect of or on the termination of any employment which is not part-time employment, the period over which they are to be taken into account shall be . . . a period equal to such number of weeks as is equal to the number (less any fraction of a whole number) obtained by dividing the net earnings by the maximum weekly amount which, on the date on which the payment of earnings is made, is specified in paragraph 8(1)(c) of Schedule 14 to the Employment Protection (Consolidation) Act 1978.[62]

When the legislation by reference is not even as specific as the above examples, the user of the legislation may feel that he or she has reached some legislative limbo. For example:

'"Benefit week" has the meaning assigned to it by regulations made pursuant to section 14(2)(f) of the Act';[63]

and

a claimant shall be treated as actively seeking employment in any week if, and only if, he takes such steps in that week as he would be required to take under regulations made under subsection 2(aa)(i) of section 17 of the Social Security Act in order to be regarded as actively seeking employed earner's employment in that week for the purposes of that section.[64]

Incomprehension is compounded by the frequent use of overcompressed wording. Clarification of statutory provisions does not always necessitate fewer statutory provisions since, so often, simplicity can be

---

60. The Social Security (Payments on Account, Overpayments and Recovery) Regulations 1987 (SI 1987 No. 491), reg. 17.
61. The Supplementary Benefit (Single Payments) Regulations 1981 (SI 1981 No. 1528), reg. 6(2)(m).
62. The Income Support (General) Regulations 1987, reg. 29(4B), as inserted by SI 1989 No. 1323, reg. 9(c).
63. The Supplementary Benefit (Duplication and Overpayments) Regulations 1980, reg. 2(1).
64. The Income Support (General) Regulations 1987, reg. 10A(3), as inserted by SI 1989 No. 1323, reg. 6.

achieved by creating a larger number of provisions, together with the adequate signposting mentioned above. For example, the income support scheme makes provision for extra money to be granted to a 'severely disabled person'. A person will, *inter alia*, be treated as a severely disabled person if:

(a) [deals with a single claimant or lone parent];

(b) if he has a partner —

(i) he is in receipt of attendance allowance; and

(ii) his partner is also in receipt of such an allowance or, if he is a member of a polygamous marriage, all the partners of that marriage are in receipt thereof; . . .

and, either an invalid care allowance is in payment to someone in respect of caring for only one of the couple or, in the case of a polygamous marriage, for one or more but not all the partners of the marriage or, as the case may be, such an allowance is not in payment to anyone in respect of caring for either member of the couple or any partner of the polygamous marriage.[65]

In the view of the author, whose experience of claims for income support from members of a polygamous marriage is rather less than his experience of claims from married or unmarried couples, the compression of the two situations (one usual and the other rather rare) and the two social security benefits mentioned (attendance allowance and invalid care allowance) is potentially confusing. Simplicity could have been achieved by dividing the claimants into couples and members of a polygamous marriage and treating them separately. Consequently, a person will, *inter alia*, be treated as being a severely disabled person if:

(a) [deals with a single claimant or lone parent];

(b) if he is one of a couple and he is in receipt of attendance allowance and his partner is also in receipt of attendance allowance . . . and, either an invalid care allowance is in payment to someone in respect of caring for only one of the couple or, as the case may be, invalid care allowance is not in payment to anyone in respect of caring for either of the couple;

(c) if he is one of a polygamous marriage and he is in receipt of attendance allowance and all the partners of that marriage are in receipt of attendance allowance . . . and, either an invalid care allowance is in payment to someone in respect of caring for only one or more but not all the partners of the marriage, or, as the case may be, invalid care allowance is not in payment to anyone in respect of caring for any partner of the marriage.

In operating the law relating to social security, the writer, adviser, representative and teacher may need to insist that the reader, client, DSS personnel, appeal tribunal member and student must accept the exact

---

65. The Income Support (General) Regulations 1987, Sched. 2, para. 13(2)(*b*), as amended by SI 1989 No. 1678, reg. 6(*f*).

wording of the legislation. Sometimes this will be to gain a benefit or increased benefit for a client by pointing out words to an adjudication officer; sometimes the converse is true and all that can be done is to show a client or appellant that the exact words disqualify him or her from a benefit.

It is, to say the least, disconcerting to have to climb down from this lofty proposition when it is found that the statutory provision contains an obvious mistake. For example, what are referred to as the 'night workers regulations' are designed to deal with the situation where a person works a night shift and becomes unemployed or incapable of work. Earlier forms of the regulations[66] used the phrases 'where a period of employment begun on any day extends over midnight into the following day' and 'where a period of employment commencing on any day extends over midnight into the following day'. However, a subsequent form[67] mistakenly used the phrase 'where a period of unemployment commencing on any day extends over midnight into the following day' and the obviously incorrect wording was not amended for quite some time.

Another example comes from the statutory maternity pay scheme, which provides for compensation for women who give up work during pregnancy, provided that they are 'employees' and regulations deem certain women to be or not to be treated as an employee. The following caused some confusion:

A woman who is in employed earner's employment within [the normal meaning of that phrase for social security purposes] but whose employer —

(a) does not fulfil [prescribed conditions] as to residence or presence in Great Britain, or

(b) is a woman who, by reason of any international treaty to which the United Kingdom is a party or of any international convention binding the United Kingdom —

(i) is exempt from the provisions of the [Social Security Act 1975], or

(ii) is a woman against whom the provisions of the [Social Security Act 1975] are not enforceable,

shall not be treated as an employee for the purposes of [statutory maternity pay].[68]

It would appear either that the sex of the employer is for some obscure reason of vital importance (with the consequence that in many cases a sex-change operation for the employer should be arranged by women who

---

66. SI 1948 No. 1277, reg. 5; SI 1975 No. 564, reg. 5.
67. SI 1983 No. 1598, reg. 5.
68. The Statutory Maternity Pay (General) Regulations 1986 (SI 1986 No. 1960), reg. 17(3).

wish to avoid this provision) or that the draftsman has made an error.

The picture, therefore, at first sight is of a

complex and closely inter-related drafting [which is] proving to be full of pitfalls ... The regulations cannot be adequately applied without the most careful scrutiny. Each phrase, indeed each word must be carefully considered ... There is a legislative labyrinth through which the [user] must pick [his or her] path with consumate care.[69]

The suggested solutions to the problems of availability to the user of an up-to-date and accurate legislative text and of insufficient assistance being given to the user, by means of a Users' Code will not, unfortunately, solve the problem of incomprehension, since all that would happen would be that the user arrived at the labyrinth more quickly. Might not the Users' Code be elaborated with assistance from the user? Consultation with representatives of the various categories of user mentioned above or the monitoring of draft proposals by a group or committee of user experts (who would play a specialized 'proof-reading' exercise but would, naturally, have no policy role to play), might reduce the occurrence of problems of obscurity *simpliciter* and of obscurity resulting from legislation by reference, by overcompression and by obvious mistakes, and might (to use a phrase which has emerged during the jubilee period) render the system of social security law more 'user friendly'.

Fanfare for a simple system

In 1985 it looked, for a fleeting moment, that this jubilee chapter might be rendered otiose when the government turned radical attention to social security reform. The Government recognized 'piecemeal development' resulting in a 'system of bewildering complexity, with different benefit levels, different eligibility rules and different rules of assessment',[70] and that 'because rules are complex and vary from benefit to benefit mistakes are made and the public is bewildered'.[71] The government promised great things:

The starting point for reform is to create a benefit structure which is simpler, clearer and fairer.[72]

The Government's aim has been to set in place a system which, because it can be more easily understood and operated, provides a better service to the public.[73]

---

69. *R(SB) 2/82*, para. 5. J. Mitchell, Commissioner.
70. *Reform of Social Security, Programme for Action* (1985) Cmnd 9691, para. 1.27.
71. Ibid., para. 1.1.
72. Ibid., para. 6.13.
73. Ibid., para. 6.7.

Governments should be judged by the results they achieve and not by their stated intentions. The question has to be raised as to whether the statutory legislative programme for social security does achieve that simplicity. Alas, in the very last sentence of this jubilee chapter comes a simple answer, namely, 'no'.

10 Jurisdiction agreements: time for a change

Jan Grodecki

Introduction

In international commercial practice it is common for the contracting parties to agree on a tribunal in which any dispute arising out of their contract should be resolved. Such a *prorogatio fori* is an indispensable part of modern trade since the choice of a court, like the choice of law to govern the contract, brings much needed certainty to international transactions. The parties' choice of a court may form a clause which is an integral part of the contract itself or it may take the shape of a collateral contract. Either way the validity and effect of the jurisdiction agreement is of immense practical and theoretical importance and fully justifies the attention given to it by courts and writers on the Continent[1] and, to a lesser degree, in England.[2] The agreement may, of course, refer to the English or to a foreign tribunal and the problems which either choice creates are not the same nor are the ways in which the courts deal with them. In this country most decisions concern the choice of a foreign tribunal. If in such a case the plaintiff brings an action in England in defiance of the agreement, the defendant may either ask for a stay or, as the case may be, oppose an application for leave to serve the writ out of jurisdiction under RSC, Order 11. Where the defendant does not raise any objections there is much discussion in civilian countries as to whether the court is bound *ex officio* to decline to assume jurisdiction. The discussion is largely sterile since in most instances the defendant's attitude will amount to submission and as such provide an alternative basis of the court's competence.

---

1. See generally Gaudemet-Tallon, *La Prorogation volontaire de juridiction en droit international privé* (1965); Kaufmann-Kohler, *La clause d'élection de for dans les contrats internationaux* (1979).
2. Cowen and Mendes da Costa (1965) 43 Can. B. Rev. 453; Bissett-Johnson (1970) 19 ICLQ 541; Pryles (1976) 24 ICLQ 543; Kahn-Freund (1977) 26 ICLQ 825; L. Collins (ed.) *Dicey and Morris on the Conflict of Laws*, Stevens (11th edn, 1987), at 402–17.

In a well-known statement in the case of *The Fehmarn*,³ Lord Denning, referring to the parties' choice of a foreign tribunal, said:

> It is a matter to which the courts of this country will pay much regard and to which they will normally give effect, but it is subject to the overriding principle that no one by his private stipulation can oust these courts of their jurisdiction in a matter that properly belongs to them.

That this 'overriding principle' represents old common law need not be doubted although early cases do not yield any such categorical formulation of the 'no ouster' rule. Reasons for it can also only be guessed at: national pride and a feeling of judicial superiority, jurisdiction seen as an aspect of national sovereignty, fear of the foreign court applying the 'wrong' law or applying the 'right' law in the wrong manner, public policy, loss of fees,⁴ etc. However this may be, the 'no ouster' rule in an absolute form was abandoned at least as early as 1796 in the case of *Gienar* v. *Meyer*⁵ in which Eyre CJ paid heed to the parties' choice of Dutch courts (which he described as 'not unreasonable') and ordered a stay of the English proceedings. In 1811, in *Johnson* v. *Machielsne*,⁶ Lord Ellenborough was equally deliberate in saying that a foreign jurisdiction clause was not void and should be given the same construction and effect as it would have received in the foreign country in question. Both these early pronouncements show a remarkable liberalism which is regrettably absent from many subsequent decisions. In some of them in the nineteenth century, to justify the court's action in giving effect to a foreign jurisdiction clause, a somewhat spurious resort was made to arbitration legislation.⁷ In the case of *Racecourse Betting Control Board* v. *Secretary of State for Air*,⁸ Mackinnon LJ criticized this as wrong and unnecessary and added that: 'in truth [the power and duty of the court to stay the action] arose under a wider general principle, namely that the court makes people abide by their contracts.'

Whilst it cannot be doubted that today prima facie the courts will respect the parties' choice of a foreign tribunal and stay the English proceedings, the emphasis on the court's discretion not to do so shows no sign of abating and the burden of proof, which rests on the plaintiff, to persuade the court that it is just and proper not to stay shows no sign of increasing. This stands in great contrast with the position in the majority of the civil law countries, where it is accepted that the local court must decline jurisdiction inconsistent with a foreign jurisdiction clause,⁹ but is paralleled in other common law countries.

---

3. [1958] 1 WLR 159, CA, at 162.
4. Or of a valuable invisible export in more modern times, *supra*, n.1.
5. (1796) 2 HB1 603.
6. (1811) 3 Camp 44.
7. *Law* v. *Garrett* (1878) 8 Ch. D 26.
8. [1944] Ch. 114, CA, at 126.
9. See Kahn-Freund, op. cit., n.2; Gaudemet-Tallon, *supra*, n.2. Exceptions are Spain and Italy.

In the United States judicial hostility towards jurisdiction clauses continued virtually undiminished until the decision of the Supreme Court in *M/s Bremen* v. *Zapata Off-Shore Company (The Chaparral)*[10] in 1972. The majority of the American decisions until then were based on the grounds that such clauses were contrary to public policy. Some exceptions can be found in the reports: where the American court was not regarded as 'convenient',[11] or the clause was 'reasonable',[12] or where although the clause was not enforced damages for its breach were awarded.[13] Limited change came with the Second Restatement of the Law: Conflict of Laws, section 80, providing that 'the parties agreement as to the place of the action cannot oust a state of judicial jurisdiction, but such an agreement will be given effect unless it is unfair or unreasonable'. However, many courts remained faithful to the 'no ouster' doctrine and only the *Zapata* case, with the judgment of Burger CJ notable for its liberal and internationalist spirit, marked a real change.[14] The position in Australia remains closely similar to that in England,[15] and whilst in Canada decisions differ, a somewhat greater hostility towards jurisdiction agreements is apparent even in recent cases.[16]

Validity of the jurisdiction agreement

A jurisdiction clause has a contractual as well as a procedural element within it. Normally it is an integral part of the contract, one of its numerous clauses and its validity like that of the rest of the contract should be regarded as a matter of substance and submitted to the proper law of the contract. In some countries at one time its equally clear procedural element tended to dominate and under a procedural classification the matter was subjected to the *lex fori*.[17] Today, however, there is an almost universal consensus that the validity of the clause must be governed by the proper law of the contract and only its effects left to

---

10. (1972) 407 US 1; [1972] 2 Lloyd's Rep. 315.
11. *Gulf Oil Corp.* v. *Gilbert*, 330 US 501 (1947).
12. *Wm. Muller & Co. Inc.* v. *Swedish American Line Ltd* 224 F 2d 806 (US Court of Appeals 2d Cir) (1955). Contrast *Carbon Black Export* v. *The SS Monrosa* 254 F 2d 297 (5th Cir) (1958).
13. *Nute* v. *Hamilton Mut. Ins. Co.* 72 Mass. (6 Gray) 174 (1856). An odd decision. See generally Pryles, *supra*, n.2.
14. Much will depend on the extent to which the state courts will adopt the new federal rule.
15. See Bissett-Johnson, *supra*, n.2; Pryles, *supra*, n.2; Sykes and Pryles, *Australian Private International Law* (1987) at 77–9.
16. E.g. *Khalij Commercial Bank Ltd* v. *Woods* (1985) 17 DLR (4th) 358. Compare with an equally inward-looking decision of the Court of Session in *Scotmotors (Plant Hire) Ltd* v. *Dundee Petrosea Ltd* [1982] SLT 181. See text accompanying n.37.
17. E.g. Germany and Italy. See Kahn-Freund, *supra*, n.2, at 830.

the *lex fori* of some chosen court. No other law can determine the latter but this should not and does not mean that the validity of the agreement should be treated alike.

English law reached this position at a remarkably early date, as the words quoted above[18] from the judgment of Lord Ellenborough in *Johnson* v. *Machielsne* show, and it is now well established.[19] A jurisdiction agreement invalid by its proper law will not be given effect by an English court. Proper law of the contract is determined according to the normal rules and since the decision of the House of Lords in the case of *Compagnie Tunisienne de Navigation SA* v. *Compagnie d'Armement Maritime SA*,[20] the express choice by the parties of the court of a country is not taken to imply the choice of its law, but in most cases it will prove to be the decisive factor. If the law of the chosen forum is not the proper law of the contract then the court will not take it into account on the validity issue. Proper law alone will be applied to pleas such as mistake, misrepresentation, undue influence, inequality of bargaining power, frustration, illegality and uncertainty,[21] regardless of whether the effect of any such plea is to render the contract void or voidable.

The House of Lords considered the matter at some depth in 1982 in the case of *Trendtex Trading Corporation* v. *Crédit Suisse*.[22] The contract was expressed to be subject to Swiss law and contained a Swiss jurisdiction clause. The plaintiff, who instituted proceedings in this country in defiance of the clause, claimed that the contract was contrary to public policy and of no effect since the assignment of the English right of action for which it provided offended against the English rules relating to champerty and maintenance. Robert Goff J (as he then was) granted a stay on the ground that by Swiss law the contract and the jurisdiction clause remained valid.[23] The Court of Appeal affirmed this judgment, holding that even if the contract were invalid by English law (which the court thought not to be the case), the question whether the agreement gave rise to enforceable rights and duties was for the proper law to determine.[24] The House of Lords differed from the Court of Appeal in deciding that the assignment did offend against the rules of champerty and maintenance and was therefore contrary to English public policy but that this did not conclude the matter. The effect of the

---

18. *Supra*, n.6.
19. *Hoerter* v. *Hanover etc. Works* (1893) 10 TLR 103, CA; *Evans Marshall & Co. Ltd* v. *Bertola* [1973] 1 WLR 349, CA; *Trendtex Trading Corp.* v. *Crédit Suisse* [1982] AC 679; *The Iran Vojdan* [1984] 2 Lloyd's Rep. 380; *The Frank Pais* [1986] 1 Lloyd's Rep. 529.
20. [1971] AC 572.
21. *The Iran Vojdan* [1984] 2 Lloyd's Rep. 380.
22. [1982] AC 679.
23. [1980] 3 All ER 721.
24. [1980] QB 629.

invalidity of the assignment on the agreement as a whole was a matter for the proper law of the contract, i.e. Swiss law.[25]

All this is well settled and there are only two matters which require some comment: interpretation of the clause and non-existence of the contract.

Interpretation of the clause: exclusive or non-exclusive

Doubts may exist as to whether the jurisdiction clause is intended to be exclusive and as to its scope.

The parties may have intended that the chosen tribunal was to have sole competence to deal with the dispute or they may have merely wished to name the tribunal of one or more countries as entitled to deal with the dispute without depriving any other court which may have jurisdiction from assuming it. A non-exclusive clause does little more than ensure that the defendant will not object to the jurisdiction of any one of the named tribunals. As such it is obviously far less significant than an agreement to submit disputes to the exclusive jurisdiction of one court. It is difficult to say just how significant it is since most cases concern either exclusive clauses or those in which the clause was held to be non-exclusive. This led to the court immediately and without additional explanation refusing the stay. In a rare instance where the matter did receive some, albeit brief, mention, Kerr J (as he then was) thought that such a clause might at best constitute a ground for not exercising the court's discretionary jurisdiction under RSC, Order 11, but where the defendant had been duly served within the jurisdiction the action should not be stayed on that ground alone.[26]

English decisions from quite an early date[27] show a remarkable consistency in submitting all questions of construction to the proper law of the contract.[28] In most cases that law will apply to the jurisdiction clause as well as to the substantive provisions, but in the very infrequent

---

25. Hence just because some aspect of the contract was void under the English doctrine of public policy did not justify the court in refusing to honour the foreign jurisdiction clause. However, the position may have been different (although the judgments do not say this) if the entire contract and above all the jurisdiction clause itself did offend the English doctrine. One may wonder why so much of the Court of Appeal's and the House of Lords' attention was devoted to the examination of the English rules of champerty and maintenance, since it was agreed that it was for the proper law to determine whether the clause was operative and there would be no reason for a Swiss court to take English law into account on the issue of validity.
26. *Evans Marshall & Co. Ltd* v. *Bertola SA* [1973] 1 WLR 349 at 361.
27. *Johnson* v. *Machielsne* (1811) 3 Camp 44, *supra*, n.6.
28. 'The clause was in a German contract and it must be construed according to German law,' per Lord Esher MR in *Hoerter* v. *Hanover etc. Works* (1893) 10 TLR 103 at 104. Cf. *Trendtex Trading Corp.* v. *Crédit Suisse* [1982] AC 679; *The Iran Vojdan* [1984] 2 Lloyd's Rep. 380; *The Frank Pais* [1986] 1 Lloyd's Rep. 529.

case of a *dépecage* the proper law will be that applying to the jurisdiction clause. The only exception to the general application of the proper law appears to be the case, discussed later, where interpretation by the *lex fori* is imposed on the court by local mandatory legislation.[29]

This consistency is, however, marred in two respects. First, in a number of cases the court engaged in the process of construction without specifying the law by reference to which this was done and, in effect, applied English law.[30] The case of *Carvalho* v. *Hull, Blyth (Angola) Ltd*[31] is an example which is all the more interesting since the interpretation issue was here extremely important. The Court of Appeal refused a stay on the ground, *inter alia*, that the 'District Court of Luanda' chosen by the parties at the time when Angola was a Portuguese colony was not the same as the court sitting in Luanda following the creation of an independent Angolan state. The court did not indicate what was the proper law of the contract nor by reference to what law it reached its conclusion and clearly applied English law. It would be difficult to argue on the facts of the case that English law was the proper law of the contract and interpretation by Portuguese or Angolan law would have been more troublesome, especially as a time conflict was involved, but the result might well have been different. Occasionally resort to English law is justified on the ground that as there was no evidence of the foreign proper law before it, the court proceeded on the basis that it was the same as English law.[32] It must be assumed that, although the court remained silent on the point, this was what was done in *Carvalho* and the other cases.[33]

Second, in some earlier decisions the courts insisted that a clause could not be construed as exclusive unless it contained express terms to this effect.[34] Apart from being inconsistent with the rule that proper law governs interpretation, this insistence appeared as little more than a device to protect the jurisdiction of the court. The better view must be that this approach is now abandoned by the courts which, on a number of later occasions, have stressed the need to give the words of the

---

29. *The Hollandia* [1983] 1 AC 565, *infra*, n.59 where the issue was treated as one of the effect and not validity of the agreement. In Germany at one time interpretation was left to the law of the court whose jurisdiction the clause sought to exclude. See Kahn-Freund, *supra*, n.2.
30. *The Makefjell* [1976] 2 Lloyd's Rep. 29, CA, where the *contra preferentem* rule and domestic cases were relied on; see S. Knight (1977) 26 ICLQ 664; *Austrian Lloyd SS Co.* v. *Gresham Life Assurance Society Ltd* [1903] 1 KB 249, CA; *The Sennar* (No. 2) [1985] 1 WLR 490, HL.
31. [1979] 3 All ER 280, CA.
32. *The Frank Pais* [1986] 1 Lloyd's Rep. 529. The old fiction which refuses to go away was relied on by Sheen J.
33. Cf. Pryles, *supra*, n.2.
34. *Hoerter* v. *Hanover etc. Works* (1893) 10 TLR 103; *Westcott* v. *Alsco Products of Canada Ltd* (1960) 26 DLR (2d) 281; *Contractors Ltd* v. *MTE Control Gear Ltd* [1964] SASR 47.

jurisdiction clause their 'common sense'[35] or 'plain meaning'.[36] In Scotland and in Canada, however, it is still very much alive. As late as 1982 the Court of Session in *Scotmotors (Plant Hire) Ltd* v. *Dundee Petrosea Ltd*[37] held that its jurisdiction cannot be ousted unless the provision therefor had been 'expressly specified' or 'distinctly expressed'. Yet the language of the clause was quite clear: 'the parties thereto submit to the jurisdiction of the English courts.' The decision causes all the greater disquiet since in the process of construction the Court of Session appeared to be applying English law and cited some English decisions.[38] The even later decision of the High Court of Ontario in *Khalij Commercial Bank Ltd* v. *Woods*[39] exhibits an equally parochial attitude.

Interpretation of the clause: the scope of the clause

It is for the proper law to determine whether, as a matter of construction, the jurisdiction agreement applies to delictual as well as contractual claims. A very clear authority is provided by the case of *The Sindh*[40] where the Court of Appeal called in aid in construing the jurisdiction clause in a contract governed by French law the doctrine of *non-cumul*. In the words of Lord Denning MR:

This is a French contract to be construed in accordance with French law. According to that law the claim of the cargo-owners rests in contract and in contract only. According to that law, the exclusive jurisdiction clause requires this dispute to be determined by [the French courts]. The plaintiffs cannot avoid that clause by bringing an action in England and framing it in tort.[41]

In the later case of *The Sennar (No. 2)*,[42] the House of Lords held that the Sudanese exclusive jurisdiction clause was wide enough to cover claims in both contract and tort and stayed the English action but, unfortunately, nothing was said in the judgments about the law by reference to which this conclusion was reached. The New South Wales court dealing with the same issue in *Hanessian* v. *Lloyd Triestino SA di*

---

35. *The Makefjell* [1976] 2 Lloyd's Rep. 29, at 33 per Cairns LJ.
36. *Austrian Lloyd SS Co.* v. *Gresham Life Assurance Society Ltd* [1903] 1 KB 249, at 252 per Mathew LJ. See Kahn-Freund, *supra*, n.2, at 828–9; Dicey and Morris, *supra*, n.2, at 404, n.93.
37. [1982] SLT 181.
38. Ibid. at 182. The court also relied on two Scottish arbitration cases *Calder* v. *Mackay* (1860) 22 D 741 at 744 per Lord Justice-Clerk Inglis and *McConnel and Reid* v. *Smith* [1911] 1 SLT 333 at 334 per Lord Dundas.
39. (1985) 17 DLR (4th) 358. Contrast *G and E Auto Brokers Ltd* v. *Toyota Canada Inc.* (1981) 117 DLR (3d) 707.
40. [1975] 1 Lloyd's Rep. 372.
41. Ibid. at 373.
42. [1985] 1 WLR 490.

Navigazione[43] was quite specific in holding that the issue of interpretation was for the proper law which was Italian and by that law the clause was wide enough to cover both claims. Consequently the plaintiff's action in tort was duly stayed.

Another aspect of determining the ambit of the jurisdiction agreement is the applicability of the agreement to a subsequent contract between the parties or to a subcontract between one of the parties and a third party. This has rarely come before the courts but an example is provided by the case of *The Forum Craftsman*[44] where the court denied to the defendant the right to rely on the jurisdiction clause, since he could not show that he was a party to the contract nor that under the Japanese proper law of the contract he had an enforceable right to rely on the clause.

Non-existence of the contract

Whilst it is well settled that the validity of the jurisdiction agreement depends on its proper law, where one of the parties pleads that there was no *consensus ad idem* between them, a question of some difficulty is said to arise. A number of solutions can be offered; the matter can be left to the *lex fori*, or to the law of the chosen court or to the putative proper law of the contract or to the putative proper law of the jurisdiction clause, if different from that of the contract of which it forms a part.[45]

Perhaps the difficulties have been exaggerated. It is not disputed that the proper law of the contract and of the jurisdiction clause (and the two will normally be the same) governs validity and that a jurisdiction clause which is valid by that law will be given effect in England. The distinction which is often discussed in this context between void and voidable contracts is of little significance,[46] and the attempt to give varying legal consequences to various pleas such as illegality, fraud, misrepresentation, mistake, duress, etc., is particularly sterile.[47] Theoretical distinctions must not stand in the way of a practical solution which should be consistent, if this is attainable, with the general approach to contractual validity. The one relevant question is whether under its proper law the jurisdiction agreement is operative. It may well be that the contract itself is invalid but the jurisdiction clause may be severed from it. Severability of the clause is the key to the solution of the problem and that key must be provided by the proper law. Approached in this way the plea of non-existence may have to be treated differently from other pleas challenging

---

43. (1951) 68 WN NSW 98. The contract for sea travel provided that 'disputes arising from this contract or in connection therewith shall be put before the law court in Trieste or Genoa'.
44. [1985] 1 Lloyd's Rep. 291, CA.
45. See Dicey and Morris, *supra*, n.2, at 405–6.
46. See *Trendtex Trading Corp.* v. *Crédit Suisse* [1982] AC 679.
47. E.g. by Diplock and Russell LJJ in *MacKender* v. *Feldia* [1967] 2 QB 590 at 602–3 and 605. See Kahn-Freund, *supra*, n.2, at 840.

the validity of the contract, but only in so far as it may be said that if the contract is deemed to be non-existent, it is not possible either in law or common sense for the jurisdiction clause to be severed from it and left intact.[48]

This may have been what Lord Denning MR had in mind when he said in the case of *Mackender* v. *Feldia*:[49] 'I can well see that if the issue was whether there ever had been any contract at all, as, for instance, if there was a plea of *non est factum*, then the foreign jurisdiction clause might not apply at all.' He did not say what law should decide this but Diplock LJ (as he then was) in the same case suggested that 'it may well be that the question has to be determined by English law.'[50] The court did not have to decide the matter since the case did not involve the plea of non-existence of the contract and the better view points to the proper law or the putative proper law.[51] The Court of Appeal's decision itself is a very strong reaffirmation of the dominant role of the proper law wherever validity of the contract is in question. The court was concerned with a plea that an insurance policy subject to Belgian law and containing a Belgian jurisdiction clause was void and unenforceable as illegal and contrary to public policy. The court held that the fact that the policy itself may have been void or unenforceable did not necessarily mean that the jurisdiction clause could not be severed and left intact and whether it was so severable was a matter for the Belgian proper law to determine.[52]

Effects of the jurisdiction agreement

Whilst the contractual element of the jurisdiction agreement is placed almost in its entirety within the domain of its proper law, its effects which constitute the procedural element must be governed by the law of the chosen court. Only that law can determine whether the effect of the agreement, in the positive sense, can found its own competence or, in the negative sense, can restrict or exclude it.

---

48. Kahn-Freund, *supra*, n.2, at 840.
49. [1967] 2 QB 590, at 598.
50. Ibid., at 603. The distinction made in this respect by Cheshire and North, *Private International Law*, Butterworths (11th edn, 1987) at 241 between invalidity of the clause and that of the main contract is unconvincing and so are the authorities cited in support.
51. See also *The Iran Vojdan* [1984] 2 Lloyd's Rep. 380; *The Frank Pais* [1986] 1 Lloyd's Rep. 529. See Dicey and Morris, *supra*, n.2, at 406. Whilst agreeing that this is the best solution, the editors express the worry that 'for the English courts to decide the question whether there was a contract between the parties at the jurisdictional stage would be, in effect, in all but the clearest case, to try the merits'. But is the court's task really different when it has to deal with any other plea of invalidity? Surely in both cases all that the court needs to be satisfied by is that by reference to the proper law there is an arguable case in favour of the clause being operative. Cf. *Attock Cement Co. Ltd* v. *Romanian Bank for Foreign Trade* [1989] 1 Lloyd's Rep. 572, CA.
52. See also *Trendtex Trading Corp.* v. *Crédit Suisse* [1982] AC 679.

The question which arises in some countries[53] of whether the agreement by itself provides a sufficient jurisdictional basis for the chosen court, does not arise in England. Submission by the defendant is a fundamental basis of jurisdiction at common law and, in the event of a previous agreement where the defendant is not in England at the time of the dispute, the writ can be served on him abroad under RSC, Order 11, rule 1(1)(d)(iv) (formerly Order 11, rule 2).

English and foreign jurisdiction clauses

Whether the agreement refers to the choice of the English court or that of a foreign one, its effects should be the same. In the case of *The Chaparral*,[54] both Diplock and Willmer LJJ thought that 'the court should apply the same principle whether the forum of contractual choice is England or some other country'. It is in fact difficult to justify any differential treatment — after all an English jurisdiction clause should be seen as the ouster of the jurisdiction of a foreign one. Yet, whatever the theory of the matter, in practice it is unlikely that an English court would refuse to give effect to an English jurisdiction clause by staying the English action or granting leave for service abroad.[55] Diplock LJ (as he then was) admitted that the question arises 'more frequently'[56] where the contractual choice is of a foreign court and there does not appear to be any instance in which an English court refused to exercise its jurisdiction in the presence of a valid English jurisdiction clause in response to a plea by the defendant that it was just and proper to stay the action.[57] In *The Chaparral*, the only case in which there is any discussion of the matter, leave for service out of the jurisdiction was granted. There is also little scholarly interest which may seem surprising since, in theory at any rate, an English jurisdiction clause should present similar problems to those of a foreign one. The conclusion appears to be that, despite Diplock and Willmer LJJ's words, an English jurisdiction clause is effective as a rule of law and is not subject to judicial discretion in the same manner as a clause choosing a foreign tribunal.

The legal potency of the two sorts of jurisdiction agreements is also

---

53. See Pryles, *supra*, n.2, at 580.
54. [1968] 2 Lloyd's Rep. 158 at 164 per Diplock LJ. See also Willmer LJ ibid., at 162.
55. Cf. Dicey and Morris, *supra*, n.2, at 411.
56. Part of the reason is that if the defendant is content, his submission will give the court jurisdiction and the jurisdiction agreement will not need to be considered.
57. Nor will a stay be granted on the ground that the English court is a *forum non conveniens*: see *The Hida Maru* [1981] 2 Lloyd's Rep. 510, CA. This is right since the parties' choice determines the issue of convenience. See also *Tracomin SA v. Sudan Oil Seeds Co. Ltd* (No. 1) [1983] 1 WLR 1026, CA which shows that proceedings in a foreign court brought in defiance of an English jurisdiction clause are more likely to be stayed.

different when one considers the effect on the clause of a mandatory provision (common law or statutory) of the *lex fori* which limits the parties' freedom of choice under the proper law by either precluding the local court from exercising jurisdiction[58] or providing that its competence is compulsory.[59] It is obvious that if such a provision is express, certain and direct, the court must enforce it and no amount of jurisdiction agreement can make any difference. An example is offered by the Australian Sea Carriage of Goods Act 1925, section 9(2) of which makes it illegal to make an agreement excluding or lessening the competence of Australian courts in a bill of lading relating to the carriage of goods to Australia from abroad. Any such agreement will be 'illegal, null and void and of no effect'. Where the provision is not so specific it is questionable if it is right to resort to it in order to limit the parties' freedom of choice by a process of extensive interpretation. One may well doubt that an English jurisdiction clause would ever be subjected to such treatment, yet it was meted out by the House of Lords to a foreign clause in the case of *The Hollandia*.[60] The court held that the effect of article 3 of the Hague–Visby Rules scheduled to the Carriage of Goods by Sea Act 1971 was to prohibit the submission of the dispute to the courts of Holland (as chosen by the parties) because Dutch courts would give effect to the original Hague Rules which set a lower maximum limit on the liability of the carrier.

The decision which at the time was criticized by some writers[61] and accepted with apparent approval by others,[62] has not grown in stature with the passage of time. Lord Diplock thought that if it was clear that the foreign court would award less than the Hague–Visby Rules provided for, then 'an English court is in my view commanded by the [Carriage of Goods by Sea] Act to treat the choice of forum clause as of no effect'.[63]

The weakness of this approach is that there is no specific provision banning jurisdiction clauses or those which might lead to lesser liability either in the Rules or in the Act. Article III, paragraph 8 of the Rules which provides that 'any clause lessening [the carrier's] liability shall be null and void and of no effect' does not refer to jurisdiction clauses at all, yet through (in Lord Diplock's words) a 'purposive' as opposed to a

---

58. See Kahn-Freund, *supra*, n.2, at 837 for a list of statutes most of which implement international conventions. A common law example would be absence of competence to determine title to foreign land.
59. See Bissett-Johnson, *supra*, n.2, at 545; Pryles, *supra*, n.2, at 548; Consumer Credit Act 1974, s.140(1); Employment Protection (Consolidation) Act 1978, s.140.
60. [1983] 1 AC 565.
61. See especially the trenchant criticism by Mann, (1983) 99 LQR 376 at 402–4.
62. Dicey and Morris, *supra*, n.2, at 413; Cheshire and North, *supra*, n.49, at 241–2; J. Morris, *The Conflict of Laws*, Stevens (3rd edn 1984), at 99; J. Collier, *Conflict of Laws*, Cambridge University Press (1987) at 150–2.
63. [1983] 1 AC 565 at 574.

'narrow and literalistic'[64] interpretation, the court attributed to this article such an effect. As a purely domestic statute would not be interpreted in such a way, the agreement seems to envisage a new extra-potent legal category of uniform statutes, which are to prevail over the parties' choice of a tribunal and of a proper law, over the fact that the jurisdiction clause is valid by that proper law and over the general rule that the process of construction is a matter for the proper law and not the *lex fori*. In the House of Lords no reference was made to a passage in Lord Denning MR's judgment in the Court of Appeal in which he invoked a 'higher public policy' which 'demands that in international trade, all goods carried at sea should be subject to uniform rules'.[65] Such a 'positive' use of public policy at least provides some principle on which to rest the decisions, albeit one can obviously object that it goes beyond the normal ambit of the doctrine.

Lord Diplock's use of the word 'purposive' invites a questioning of the purpose. Uniformity may be a worthy goal but becomes less self-evident when many states do not subscribe to a convention or, what is even more important, those which do take a different line by treating a jurisdiction clause such as the one which came before the court in *The Hollandia* as valid and fully effective.[66] One should not, furthermore, lose sight of the fact that jurisdiction clauses are not only freely agreed but are perfectly normal, legitimate and widely used throughout the world, and consequently the 'purposive' interpretation leads to the defeat of the parties' trading expectations. In these circumstances Lord Diplock's description of them as 'colourable devices' and of the court as a 'court of convenience'[67] is surprising and shows that behind the overprotective attitude towards international conventions coupled with unwillingness to look at comparative evidence, one can see traces of the old hostility towards foreign jurisdiction clauses. Fortunately the decision in *The Hollandia* was not extended in *The Benarty*[68] where a different provision of the Hague–Visby Rules was invoked, nor in the case of *Amanuel v. Alexandros Shipping Co.*[69] where there was doubt about whether the foreign court would or would not apply the Rules.

---

64. Ibid. at 572. It is doubtful that such an interpretation is imposed on the courts by the Vienna Convention on the Law of Treaties of 1969, articles 31 and 32, which, on the contrary, provide for the ordinary meaning of the words used in the uniform statutes to be the main principle of construction. See, however, *Fothergill* v. *Monarch Airlines* [1981] AC 251 at 282 per Lord Diplock. As to the applicable law in *Rustenburg Platinum Mines Ltd* v. *South African Airways* [1979] 1 Lloyd's Rep. 19, Eveleigh LJ thought that the Warsaw Convention scheduled to the Carriage by Air Act 1961 should be construed in accordance with the law which governed the contract of carriage. On the question of interpretation of uniform statutes see Mann (1979) 95 LQR 346 and (1983) 99 LQR 376 *contra* Morris (1979) 95 LQR 59.
65. [1982] QB 872 at 884.
66. See Mann, *supra*, n.61.
67. [1983] 1 AC 565 at 573 and 574.
68. [1985] QB 325 CA.
69. [1986] QB 464.

The court's discretion

Whilst an English court should in principle stay an English action brought in breach of a foreign jurisdiction agreement, strong emphasis continues to be laid on the court's discretion to come to a different conclusion. The most authoritative statement of the law and of the circumstances which should be taken into account by the court when exercising its discretion was formulated by Brandon J (as he then was) in the case of *The Eleftheria*:[70]

The principles established by the authorities can, I think, be summarised as follows:

(1) Where plaintiffs sue in England in breach of an agreement to refer disputes to a foreign Court, and the defendants apply for a stay, the English Court, assuming the claim to be otherwise within the jurisdiction, is not bound to grant a stay but has a discretion whether to so or not.
(2) The discretion should be exercised by granting a stay unless strong cause for not doing so is shown.
(3) The burden of proving such strong cause is on the plaintiffs.
(4) In exercising its discretion the Court should take into account all the circumstances of the particular case.
(5) In particular, but without prejudice to (4), the following matters where they arise, may be properly regarded:
   (a) In what country the evidence on the issues of fact is situated, or more readily available, and the effect of that on the relative convenience and expense of trial as between the English and foreign Courts.
   (b) Whether the law of the foreign Court applies and, if so, whether it differs from English law in any material respects.
   (c) With what country either party is connected, and how closely.
   (d) Whether the defendants genuinely desire trial in the foreign country, or are only seeking procedural advantages.
   (e) Whether the plaintiffs would be prejudiced by having to sue in the foreign Court because they would
      (i) be deprived of security for that claim;
      (ii) be unable to enforce any judgement obtained;
      (iii) be faced with a time-bar not applicable in England; or
      (iv) for political, racial, religious or other reasons be unlikely to get a fair trial.

The starting point is that the court should stay the English action and make parties abide by their contracts. The action should be allowed to continue only if the plaintiff convinces the court that it is 'just and proper' that it should do so. Other expressions have been used to describe the position. In the early case of *Law* v. *Garrett*,[71] the Court of Appeal referred to a 'prima facie' duty to respect the clause. Diplock

---

70. [1970] P 94. Confirmed by the same judge in the Court of Appeal in *The El Amria* [1981] 2 Lloyd's Rep. 119 and in the House of Lords in *The Sennar* (No. 2) [1985] 1 WLR 490.
71. (1878) 8 Ch. D 26.

LJ (as he then was) in *Mackender* v. *Feldia*[72] required 'very strong reasons' to permit one of the parties to go back on his word, and Lord Denning MR in a later case thought that the full effect should be given to the clause 'unless its enforcement would be unreasonable and unjust'.[73]

In *YTC Universal Ltd* v. *Trans Europa SA*[74] Lord Denning MR used yet another formulation referring to 'exceptional circumstances' needed to justify the refusal of a stay. This was echoed by Brandon J himself in the case of *The Makefjell*[75] decided some seven years after *The Eleftheria*. In the Court of Appeal, however, neither Cairns LJ nor Sir Gordon Willmer thought that Brandon J's intention was to introduce 'a further and unwarrantable' test.[76] It is, however, unfortunate and perhaps symptomatic of the state of the law that the Court of Appeal took objection to the use of the word 'exceptional' as being unduly restrictive of the court's discretion.[77] The courts also stress that the burden of proof, which rests on the plaintiff to persuade the court not to stay the English proceedings, is heavy and particularly so in cases of the court's jurisdiction under RSC, Order 11 where the defendant is not present in England or the ship is not in an English port.[78]

These judicial statements are, however, overshadowed by others which lay stress on the court's discretionary powers and many decisions are not easy to reconcile with the court's 'prima facie duty' to give effect to the clause.[79] One would have expected that in cases involving Order 11, the conjunction of what is an exorbitant jurisdiction with a foreign forum clause, would reduce the court's discretion to a vanishing point. However, the decision of the Court of Appeal in the case of *Evans Marshall & Co. Ltd* v. *Bertola SA*[80] shows that this is far from being

---

72. [1967] 2 QB 590 at 604.
73. *Trendtex Trading Corp.* v. *Crédit Suisse* [1980] QB 629 CA at 658. See also *Limerick Corporation* v. *Crompton and Co.* (1910) 2 Ir R 416 at 418: unless some 'paramount reason to the contrary' is shown.
74. (1968) 112 SJ 842; [1973] 1 Lloyd's Rep. 480 n. CA, at 481.
75. [1975] 1 Lloyd's Rep. 528 at 532.
76. [1976] 2 Lloyd's Rep. 29 at 38.
77. The fact that 'exceptional circumstances' were found to exist in as dubious an authority as *Evans Marshall & Co. Ltd* v. *Bertola SA* [1973] 1 WLR 349, CA shows that these different formulae do little to explain the exercise of judicial discretion, *infra*, n.80.
78. See Kerr J in *Evans Marshall & Co. Ltd* v. *Bertola SA* [1973] 1 WLR 349 at 362.
79. *The Fehmarn* [1958] 1 WLR 159 CA; *Evans Marshall & Co. Ltd* v. *Bertola SA* [1973] 1 WLR 349, CA; *The Adolf Warski* [1976] 2 Lloyd's Rep. 241 CA; *The Visha Prabha* [1979] 2 Lloyd's Rep. 286; *The Atlantic Song* [1983] 2 Lloyd's Rep. 394; *The Frank Pais* [1986] 1 Lloyd's Rep. 529.
80. [1973] 1 WLR 349. The decision is difficult to understand. The situation that arose was clearly foreseeable by the parties and the stay was refused on the ground of highly questionable 'exceptional circumstances'. In *The Chaparral* [1968] 2 Lloyd's Rep. 158, CA and in *Mackender* v. *Feldia* [1967] 2 QB 590, CA, both Order 11 cases, the agreement was honoured. Contrast *Ellinger* v. *Guinness Mahon and Co.* [1939] 4 All ER 16 which, however, provides a rare example of a case where service out of jurisdiction in defiance of the agreement was justified.

so and that the courts are loath to limit their discretion even in this situation.

The most important part of Brandon J's formulation concerns his guidelines to the manner in which the court's discretion should be exercised. The care with which these have been compiled cannot obscure the fact that most of them are directed towards discovering which is the most convenient court to try the case — an inquiry which seems out of place where *ex hypothesi* the parties themselves have resolved the matter. The court is thus to take into account the convenience of parties and witnesses, expense, situation of evidence, even some procedural advantages, etc. — all of which tend to establish the *forum conveniens*. What is involved is a balancing act, a weighing of all the factors mentioned by Brandon J which are present in any given case, and the ultimate decision rests, as he himself said in the case of *The Adolf Warski*,[81] on a 'balance of convenience' or 'argument'. In the case of *The El Amria*[82] in the Court of Appeal, it was argued that the acceptance by Sheen J in the court below of the test used by Lord Denning in *The Fehmarn*[83] of the court of the country mostly concerned with the dispute was inconsistent with the 'principles' stated in *The Eleftheria*. Brandon LJ (as he then was) said that that could have been the case if the judge directed himself solely by reference to Lord Denning's test. Whether in truth there is a great deal of difference between this test and that of a balance of convenience or argument may well be open to doubt.

The present position is very unsatisfactory. Robert Goff J (as he then was) remarked in *Trendtex Trading Corp.* v. *Crédit Suisse*[84] that Brandon J did not state the principle on which the court should exercise its discretion, and a balance of convenience or argument will scarcely serve as one in the face of a deliberate choice by the parties of a forum in which they agreed that the dispute should be tried. They have, or must be presumed to have, taken into account all such factors as the geographical location of the court, its procedure, costs, languages, expense and inconvenience of witnesses' travel, etc.[85] The multiplicity of factors which are to be taken into account and the lack of a principle on which to base them lead to the court's discretion being used too often and on inadequate grounds. In the case of *The Makefjell*[86] Brandon J himself spoke of

---

81. [1976] 1 Lloyd's Rep. 107 at 112. The judge refused the stay (and the Court of Appeal [1976] 2 Lloyd's Rep. 241 affirmed his decision) taking into account such factors as expense of witnesses and experts in having to travel to the foreign court as well as linguistic difficulties of an action in that court. The case, like *The Fehmarn* and *Evans Marshall & Co. Ltd* v. *Bertola SA*, goes to the verge of the law.
82. [1981] 2 Lloyd's Rep. 119.
83. [1958] 1 WLR 159 CA.
84. [1980] 3 All ER 721 at 733.
85. See *The Kislovodsk* [1980] 1 Lloyd's Rep. 183.
86. [1975] 1 Lloyd's Rep. 528 at 535.

a danger that such exceptions would be so frequent as to undermine the generality of the rule; or to put it another way, that the rule will be nearly as much honoured in the breach as in the observance. Such an outcome would, in my view, involve a departure from the basic principle that foreign jurisdiction clauses of this kind should be enforced save only in cases which can truly be described as exceptional.

One specific example of such danger is provided by the cases, of which the decision of Sheen J in *The Atlantic Song*[87] is the latest, in which the court reached its decision mainly on the grounds that the defendant was merely seeking a procedural or tactical advantage in objecting to the English action. Except perhaps in cases of particularly glaring behaviour, it does seem wrong to punish the defendant in this manner for insisting on his contractual rights and somewhat inappropriate to coin a maxim: 'where the court has a discretion, the applicant must come with clean procedural hands'.[88] The applicant is surely the plaintiff and not the defendant and in so far as the plaintiff is in breach of his word his hands will seldom be entirely clean.

The position causes all the more concern in view of the considerable reluctance on the part of the Court of Appeal in the absence of a very serious error to interfere with the exercise of discretion by the judge below. In the case of the *The Makefjell*[89] Cairns LJ stated the position thus:

the court should not interfere with the exercise of the judge's discretion unless he had gone wrong in law or in the basis on which he exercised his discretion or was plainly wrong in the way in which he exercised it.

In *The Adolf Warski*[90] a highly questionable decision, the Court of Appeal decided against such interference. Willmer LJ remarked that he was 'unable to say that [the judge's] exercise of discretion was plainly wrong'.

Conclusion

In many neighbouring areas of private international law the last fifteen years have seen a marked change in the judicial attitude towards foreign courts. The emergence of the doctrine of *forum non conveniens*, greater readiness to order a stay of the English proceedings in cases involving a substantial foreign element, increasing restraint in the grant of leave for service out of jurisdiction under RSC, Order 11 — all provide evidence

---

87. [1983] 2 Lloyd's Rep. 394. See also *The Visha Prabha* [1979] 2 Lloyd's Rep. 286 and *The Frank Pais* [1986] 1 Lloyd's Rep. 529 both decided by Sheen J.
88. Collins (1973) 22 ICLQ 339 at 343.
89. [1976] 2 Lloyd's Rep. 29 at 35.
90. [1976] 2 Lloyd's Rep. 241 at 247. The judge in question was Brandon J.

that former judicial chauvinism is being replaced by judicial comity.[91] Furthermore, in the very area of jurisdiction agreements two recent statutory provisions have greatly enhanced their status. Article 17 of the Brussels Convention of 1968, which is given effect by the Civil Jurisdiction and Judgments Act 1982, provides (where the case falls within the scope of the Convention) for the exclusive jurisdiction of the court chosen by the parties even where none of the parties is domiciled in a Contracting State.[92] The same Act in section 32 bars recognition or enforcement of a foreign judgment if proceedings were brought in violation of an agreement between parties to settle their dispute otherwise than by proceedings in that country's courts.[93]

Paradoxically these changes not only have not made any impact on the treatment of jurisdiction agreements at common law but, on the contrary, appear to be leading to a lessening of their effect in England. The paradox is largely due to an increasing tendency to confuse the problem with that of the discovery of an appropriate or convenient court to deal with the dispute. This tendency, as has already been noticed, derives in part from the formulation of Lord Brandon's guidelines but is being clearly strengthened by the growth of the doctrine of *forum non conveniens*. Danger signs can not only be seen in the the reports but also in legal literature. A French writer, Mme Gaudemet-Tallon in a monograph published in 1965 wrote: 'The Anglo-American world through the medium of the doctrine of *forum conveniens* demands that the court chosen by the parties should have a reasonable relation or substantial connection with the dispute'.[94] This is not an accurate statement of English law at the time but it strangely foreshadows the present dangers and a recent suggestion that the jurisdiction clause can be ignored and proceedings permitted to continue in England if this country is shown to be 'the natural forum' for the dispute and the plaintiff would suffer 'substantial injustice' by being deprived of the opportunity of bringing proceedings in England.[95]

Such suggestions must be resisted.[96] The two situations are quite

---

91. See Lord Diplock in *The Abidin Daver* [1984] AC 398 at 411, and Lord Reid in *The Atlantic Star* [1974] AC 436 at 453.
92. Unless the chosen court or courts have declined jurisdiction.
93. See *Tracomin SA v. Sudan Oil Seeds Co. Ltd* (No. 1) [1983] 1 WLR 1026.
94. *Supra*, n.1, at 199. The present writer's translation.
95. Barma and Elvin (1985) 101 LQR 48 at 65–6. But if there is danger of 'substantial injustice' there should be no necessity to show that England is 'the natural forum', e.g. *Ellinger v. Guinness Mahon and Co.* 83 SJ 924; [1939] 4 All ER 16, see text at n.105. See also Cheshire and North, *supra*, n.49, at 239 where it is stated that 'the law has not yet reached the stage where the two forms of discretion can be assimilated' without an indication that such a development would be highly undesirable.
96. Cf. *The El Amira* [1981] 2 Lloyd's Rep. 119 at 129 per Stephenson LJ:

> I would go no further towards assimilating the court's duty in considering a stay to enforce a foreign jurisdiction clause to its duty in considering a stay sought for a different purpose . . . The parties to the contract incorporating the foreign jurisdiction clause, above all, agreed to the jurisdiction of the foreign court, presumably with knowledge of how it works and what it cannot do, and to go any further would weaken Lord Justice Brandon's cardinal principle, which prevents the court from treating the question whether to stay as one of convenient forum and brings this case so close to the border line.

different because where there is a jurisdiction agreement the convenient or natural forum is indicated by the parties themselves. As Burger CJ said in the *Zapata* case: 'The contract by the forum clause had expressly resolved the issue of convenient forum'.[97] The jurisdiction clause is part of the contract and many other clauses may have been agreed on the assumption of its inclusion. It may well be that any one of these clauses turns out to the disadvantage of one of the parties. It has never been suggested that, in the absence of such things as the plea of mistake, fraud or undue influence, he should be rescued from the consequences of his agreement. There is no reason to treat the jurisdiction clause differently. On the contrary, there is every reason to give it full effect. In doing so this country, instead of becoming increasingly isolated, would come closer to the prevailing civilian acceptance of jurisdiction agreement as binding. Furthermore, it would recognize that the right to choose a forum brings vital certainty to international transactions, that such forum clauses are habitually used in international trade and are included in standard forms in the expectation that the courts will treat them as fully effective.

It is suggested that the more liberal, less nationalistic and more hospitable attitude the English courts are now showing should be reflected in a changed attitude towards jurisdiction agreements. If 'the overriding principle'[98] that the parties cannot by their bargain alone oust the jurisdiction of the courts is still to be retained, then at the very least it should be accompanied by an affirmation that the search for a natural or convenient or most closely connected forum is not legitimate and the only principle on which the evidence of discretion should be based is that of grave injustice. Furthermore, 'great caution'[99] should accompany its use.[100]

Another, preferable, suggestion is, however, timely and appropriate. As traditional hostility towards foreign tribunals is receding and litigation in this country needs no longer to be seen as a valuable invisible export,[101] the 'no ouster' principle increasingly appears as an

---

97. [1972] 2 Lloyd's Rep. 315 at 321.
98. *The Fehmarn* [1958] 1 WLR 159 AC at 162 per Lord Denning.
99. *The Makefjell* [1976] 2 Lloyd's Rep. 29, CA at 34 per Cairns LJ referring to discretion under RSC, Order 11 but denying that this necessarily applies to jurisdiction agreements.
100. Robert Goff J (as he then was) in *Trendtex Trading Corp.* v. *Crédit Suisse* [1980] 3 All ER 721 at 733 thought that the principle on which the court should exercise its jurisdiction should be that it would be 'unjust' to stay the proceedings. It is submitted that if this is to be the basis of jurisdiction then the court should insist on proof of grave injustice.
101. See Kerr (1978) 41 MLR 1. Speaking at the 1989 Bar Conference, *The Times*, 2 October 1989, Mr Justice Hirst said that London was the world centre for commercial and shipping litigation and that the immense volume of work of the Commercial Court was in part explained by the fact that nearly 30 per cent of the cases involved no English litigant and jurisdiction of the court was founded on the presence in most of them of an English jurisdiction clause.

anachronism.[102] Instead, it is suggested, foreign jurisdiction clauses should be regarded as effective as a matter of law to exclude jurisdiction of English courts.[103] This suggestion is not as radical as it may seem. The court already refuses to use its theoretical discretionary powers in relation to the choice of the English forum nor does it allow any discretion to the foreign court whose judgment given in breach of a jurisdiction agreement is presented for recognition or enforcement in England. The possible, albeit very rare, difficulty of a negative jurisdictional conflict in which the chosen forum does not regard the agreement as a valid basis of its own competence could be solved, as it is in civilian countries, by holding that in such circumstances the jurisdiction clause loses its effect.[104] The rule making foreign jurisdiction clauses effective in ousting the jurisdiction of the English court would, as any other conflictual rule, be subject to the doctrine of public policy in its accepted sense of a threat to fundamental tenets of justice and morality. Where, as in the case of *Ellinger* v. *Guinness Mahon and Co.*[105] the plaintiff would be unable to get a fair trial in the chosen forum because of political, racial or religious reasons, the court would be entitled to disregard the agreement and allow the English action to proceed. No amount, however, of inconvenience or embarrassment, procedural, financial or otherwise should be sufficient to deprive the parties' agreement of its force.[106]

---

102. 'A vestigial legal fiction', per Burger CJ in *M/s Bremen* v. *Zapata Off-Shore Co.* [1972] 2 Lloyd's Rep. 315 at 320.
103. This would not affect the court's right to order *interim* relief.
104. In this situation an English court could use its discretion to refuse a stay. This is claimed by Kahn-Freund, *supra*, n.2, at 849 as an advantage of the present system.
105. 83 SJ 924; [1939] 4 All ER 16.
106. Note even in the situation envisaged by Burger CJ in *M/s Bremen* v. *Zapata Off-Shore Co.* [1972] 2 Lloyd's Rep. 315 at 322 where the trial in the chosen forum 'will be so gravely difficult and inconvenient that [the plaintiff] will for all practical purposes be deprived of his day in court'.

11 United Kingdom barriers to a common market in legal development

Malcolm Ross

Introduction

Not, perhaps, since common law succumbed to the wiles of equity has there been such a catalyst for all-pervasive legal change as that presented by membership of the European Community. The *sui generis* features of Community law are sufficiently well known to make otiose detailed discussion of the structure and powers of the Community institutions, the supremacy of Community law over conflicting national provisions, or the doctrine of direct effect invented by the European Court of Justice to entrench Community law by allowing individuals to pursue such rights in their national courts.[1]

Instead, this chapter will examine the possible divergence between *communautaire* perceptions of the legal instruments for market integration and the application in practice of Community law by United Kingdom courts and tribunals. The scale of any discrepancy will be measured against three principal criteria: the effectiveness of the use by national courts of the reference procedure under Article 177 EEC, the extent to which fresh interpretative techniques and novel legal concepts have permeated the national judicial consciousness, and the nature of the response to direct effect in terms of the classification and availability of national remedies.

Each of these considerations presents its own novelties. Article 177, the pivotal provision of the EEC Treaty concerning dialogue between national courts and the European Court, offers the challenge of a relationship which is co-operative and equal rather than appellate and hierarchical. The handling of Community law, with its emphasis upon the

---

1. For general discussion of these issues, see D. Wyatt and A. Dashwood, *The Substantive Law of the EEC*, Sweet & Maxwell (2nd edn 1987), and T. Hartley, *The Foundations of European Community Law*, Clarendon Press (2nd edn 1988).

balancing of economic concepts and objectives, may be especially demanding for an English judicial structure and tradition not hitherto heavily imbued with such elusive and overtly political considerations. Flexibility and adaptability, supposedly the strengths of the common law, must also be stretched if domestic courts are to give proper and full protection to rights derived from Community provisions. In particular, the reorganization of existing national remedies or the creation of new ones will affect the long-established, if sometimes hazy, division between public and private law.

These institutional, conceptual and historical processes make it hardly surprising that the response of United Kingdom courts to Community law and methodology has been characterized by cautious under-utilization rather than zealous participation. Nevertheless, as will be seen below, this apparently studied indifference should not disguise the substantial changes already wrought by the short period of United Kingdom membership. Separation of 'national' from 'Community' issues has been made increasingly tenuous, if not quite yet impossible. United Kingdom courts have already discovered that Community implications may exist in, for example, the choice of sentencing method in criminal cases,[2] the opening of shops on Sundays,[3] the making-up of prescriptions under the National Health Scheme,[4] and the grant arrangements for students.[5] Of course, recognition that such Community dimensions exist depends upon litigants and, more especially, legal advisers as much as upon judges. Finding a 'Euro-defence' remains a skill in its infancy, partly perhaps because of the uneven treatment accorded to Community law in the stages of higher legal education and professional training courses.

The use of Article 177

The naïve bystander, or even the drafters of the EEC Treaty, might have thought that a connection between national courts and the European Court of Justice could easily and fruitfully be made. As an engine for legal change, Article 177 EEC offers disciplined direction by way of uniform development of Community law principles and also a learning curve for national judges.[6] But an engine needs ignition, and the United Kingdom courts have so far failed to spark the Article 177 machinery

---

2. Case 175/78, *Saunders*, [1979] ECR 1129.
3. See, *inter alia*, *Rochdale BC* v. *Stewart John Anders*, [1988] 3 CMLR 431 and *London Borough of Waltham Forest* v. *Scott Markets*, [1988] 3 CMLR 773.
4. Cases 266 and 267/87, *R* v. *Pharmaceutical Society of Great Britain*, [1989] 2 All ER 758.
5. Case 197/86, *Brown*, [1988] 3 CMLR 403.
6. On Article 177 generally, see Asser Institute: *Article 177 — Experiences and Problems*.

into life very often.[7] However commendable their record may be for subsequently applying the preliminary rulings made in those cases actually sent to Luxemburg, serious doubts remain about the courts' progress on the learning curve towards 'Euro-consciousness'.

One obvious explanation of the comparatively low number of references made by United Kingdom courts is the ghost of *Bulmer* v. *Bollinger*.[8] However inconsistent Lord Denning's guidelines in that case may be with the most *communautaire* view of Article 177,[9] they have had a lasting impact upon domestic courts. Even in 1989, courts faced with the decision whether to refer still put a premium on the *Bulmer* approach,[10] although subject to the exegeses provided by later cases. Of these, probably the fullest and most influential have been the judgments of Bingham J in *Customs & Excise Commissioners* v. *ApS Samex*[11] and Kerr LJ in *R* v. *Pharmaceutical Society of Great Britain*.[12]

Certainly, the following words of Bingham J represent a most *communautaire* analysis of the advantages to be gained from making references to the European Court:

It has a panoramic view of the Community and its institutions, a detailed knowledge of the treaties and of much subordinate legislation made under them, and an intimate familiarity with the functioning of the Community market which no national judge denied the collective experience of the Court of Justice could hope to achieve. Where questions of administrative intention and practice arise the Court of Justice can receive submissions from the Community institutions, as also where relations between the Community and non-member states are in issue. Where the interests of member states are affected they can intervene to make their views known . . . Where comparison falls to be made between Community texts in different languages, all texts being equally authentic, the multinational Court of Justice is equipped to carry out the task in a way which no national judge, whatever his linguistic skills, could rival. The interpretation of Community instruments involves often not the process familiar to common lawyers of laboriously extracting the meaning from words used but the more creative process of supplying flesh to a spare and loosely constructed skeleton. The choice between alternative submissions may turn not on purely legal considerations, but on a broader view of what the orderly development of the Community requires. These are matters which the Court of Justice is very much better placed to assess and determine than a national court.

Given such a crystal-clear perception of the benefits to be derived from the preliminary rulings system, the question therefore remains of the reasons for the low level of uptake by domestic courts. Two principal

---

7. Evidence in a forthcoming report by the University Institute Florence into the quality of dialogue between national courts and the European Court indicates that there is a low rate of referral by United Kingdom courts compared with other member states.
8. [1974] Ch. 401.
9. See the European Court's view in Case 166/73, *Rheinmuhlen*, [1974] ECR 139.
10. E.g., *Barkworth* v. *Customs and Excise Commissioners*, [1988] 3 CMLR 759.
11. [1983] 3 CMLR 194.
12. *Supra*, n.4.

explanations merit closer scrutiny: the special characteristics of the reference process in the United Kingdom, and the extent to which United Kingdom courts rely, mistakenly or otherwise, upon their own skills of interpretation.

As far as the decision to refer is concerned, there seems to have been an inhibiting emphasis placed upon the wishes of the parties and their legal advisers. After all, Article 177 EEC confers the discretion to refer upon the court or tribunal in question. But in *Bulmer*, Lord Denning observed that:

If both parties want the point to be referred to the European Court, the English court should have regard to their wishes, but it should not give them undue weight. The English court should hesitate before make a reference against the wishes of one of the parties, seeing the expense and delay which it involves.

Although there have been some notable declarations of judicial independence in deciding whether to refer, the historical link between judge and counsel may be detrimental to liberal usage of Article 177 EEC. Certainly, it appears that the closeness of the relationship spills over from the decision to refer into the framing of the questions themselves. Even though ultimate responsibility for the reference remains with the court, a set of questions agreed in this way may deflect the purpose of sending off the case to Luxemburg.

The real fear about attaching too much significance to the views of counsel and the parties is that Article 177 ceases to be measured by its essential criterion, the interpretation of Community measures. An illuminating and, it is suggested, typical, approach can be seen from the judgment of Taylor J in *R* v. *Secretary of State for Social Services, ex parte Schering Chemicals Ltd.*[13] In deciding not to refer, he noted:

at one stage I was exercised as to whether or not this case ought to have been referred . . . But counsel on both sides, who are most experienced in such matters, urged me to give my decision. I concluded that it was right to do so, since it seems to me that I have clear guidance from the cases cited and from counsel themselves.

Here the reliance upon counsel is also linked with the notion of *acte clair*, an approach which parties seeking to avoid expense and delay are likely to endorse. There is thus a sense in which the relationship with counsel doubly works against the chances of a reference being made to Luxemburg.

It is perhaps too easy to criticize the use of *acte clair* by national judges, since the benefit of hindsight normally allows identification of those cases which should have been resolved by a reference. However, care must be taken to distinguish those cases which could merely have provided earlier opportunities for the Court of Justice to embark upon what have subsequently proved to be thorny jurisprudential issues from

---

13. [1987] 1 CMLR 277.

the genuinely pathological case in which there were doubts already in existence about the meaning of a Community provision at the time the decision not to refer was made.

In the former category, for example, might be placed several cases dealing with the application of the free movement of goods provisions of the Treaty to price controls, advertising and other marketing arrangements.[14] Illustrations of the second category can be found throughout the period of United Kingdom membership and at all levels of the court hierarchy, facts which themselves are disturbing in their implications regarding lack of adaptation by the judiciary. Thus, to take an early case, the magistrate in *R* v. *Secchi*[15] refused to refer a case involving the potential use of Article 48(3) on the grounds that the migrant involved 'obviously' was not a worker within the meaning of the Treaty. This was despite the fact that at that stage of its jurisprudence the Court of Justice had not pronounced upon the margins of the 'worker' concept where occasional and part-time activities were in issue.

Whereas *Secchi* effectively demonstrates the dangers of *acte clair* in the context of the meaning of a Community provision identified as such by the national court, other instances are open to criticism for failing to accept the possible relevance of Community sources altogether. The question of the impact of the Treaty upon the grants and training support available to students was particularly under-recognized in early United Kingdom cases. In *R* v. *ILEA, ex parte Hinde*[16] Taylor J refused a reference ostensibly on pragmatic grounds rather than any obvious interpretative security. The Chancery Division in *MacMahon* v. *DES*[17] declined to make a reference in a similar case but on the basis that the issues involved application, not the interpretation of covert discrimination. As a result, in the court's view, the matter was one for domestic resolution only.

At the top of the judicial tree, the House of Lords refused to refer the case of *Duke* v. *GEC Reliance Ltd*[18] and instead applied its own controversial view of the interface between Community and national competence. But, it may be claimed, the very exercise of drawing such lines raised matters of interpretation, either of the substantive scope of primary and secondary Community legislation, or of the general principles on Community interpretation which may derive from the *Von Colson* case.[19] To decide that a matter is domestic, and thus immune from Article 177, is a conclusion which may actually on occasion

---

14. E.g., *Potato Marketing Board* v. *Robertsons*, [1983] 1 CMLR 93, *Potato Marketing Board* v. *Drysdale*, [1986] 3 CMLR 331, *R* v. *Secretary of State for Social Security, ex parte Bomore Medical Supplies*, [1986] 1 CMLR 34.
15. [1975] CMLR 383.
16. [1985] 1 CMLR 716.
17. [1982] 3 CMLR 91.
18. [1988] 1 All ER 626.
19. Case 14/83, *Von Colson* v. *Land Nordrhein Westfalen*, [1984] ECR 1921.

demand reference as part of its prior reasoning. It should not be a question of mere assertion (especially bearing in mind the factors itemized by Bingham J in the *Samex* case as the strengths of the European Court of Justice).

The picture that emerges of United Kingdom usage of Article 177 is that the need for interpretation is restrictively viewed. Other, mainly pragmatic, considerations may offset any doubts which the court would otherwise recognize about the meaning or relevance of particular provisions of Community law. In addition to the judge–counsel relationship already discussed, arguably excessive weight is also given to the institutional structure. It has become increasingly common for lower courts to take the view that a decision not to refer can always be overturned later. Nevertheless, there are still exceptions such as *Newstead* v. *Dept of Transport*,[20] where the Employment Appeal Tribunal voiced the view that there may be a saving of costs or time (or both) to be achieved by making the reference sooner rather than later. This was a case in which both sides were publicly funded, and there was no doubt that the issue fell to be determined solely by the meaning of the Community provisions. Despite, in the EAT's opinion, it being 'normally appropriate' for references to be left to the Court of Appeal or House of Lords, the balance of convenience was in favour of an early reference. The subsequent importance of the ruling by the European Court[21] has amply vindicated this decision, if any further justification were needed.

Interpretation and conceptual novelty

The main question here is the extent to which the so-called teleological approach of the European Court, with its concomitant dynamism and inventiveness, has rubbed off on United Kingdom courts, either in their approach to Community measures or to domestic legislation. The striking feature of the response is that an attempt appears to have been made to maintain the division between 'European' and 'national' styles of interpretation. Indeed, a more cynical approach might suggest that there has been a conscious avoidance of the more flexible model offered by the European Court of Justice. Lord Diplock, in the first House of Lords reference, *R* v. *Henn and Darby*,[22] hardly encouraged widespread use of such a style when he observed that it was usually at the expense of the letter of the law! Nevertheless, Lord Diplock did warn English judges not to be too ready to hold that the meaning of the English text seems so plain that no question of interpretation can be involved. This warning

---

20. [1986] 2 CMLR 196.
21. Case 192/85, [1988] 1 All ER 129.
22. [1981] AC 850.

was particularly timely, given that the Court of Appeal[23] in the same case had managed to hold that a total ban on the imports of certain allegedly pornographic material did not constitute a quantitative restriction or measure of equivalent effect for the purposes of Article 177 EEC.

Several consequences flow from any resistance to changes in interpretative style. First, and most obviously, the pigeonholing of matters as 'European' or 'national' can only reinforce any existing prejudices or misperceptions of the proper relationship between these legal sources. The further penetration of Community measures into the consciousness of ordinary local lawyers is likely to be inhibited. Second, and perhaps ironically, the retention of interpretative divisions actually places a premium on the proper and effective use of the Article 177 process. The use of *acte clair* is likely to be more prevalent and run a greater risk of being misplaced as a result of demarcation between interpretative styles. There is also a sense in which reluctance to refer also prevents the acquisition by the national court of the experience of teleological approaches necessary to enable it to give judgment in future cases. Knowing whether a case requires a reference only properly flows from familiarity with the tools of assessment which the Court of Justice might apply.

A more specific challenge posed by Community law concerns the nature of the judicial task. This is not just a question of measuring the meaning of words in a new way; the very object of that evaluation may be qualitatively different in some areas of the EEC Treaty. Of course, English courts are not without skills or experience in some analogous fields. However, it should be remembered that probably the most important comparison, competition law, is a creature very different in its scope and application from its counterpart under the EEC Treaty. An exploration of some of the differences between the two approaches may explain the difficulties which United Kingdom courts face in handling the economic issues directly raised by Community law.

It is generally accepted that English competition law statutes have been characterized hitherto by their adherence to formalism and definitional rigidity. The performance of the Restrictive Practices Court (in which there is assistance from specialist lay assessors) has been criticized for its strong stance against agreements and arrangements falling within the Restrictive Trade Practices Acts, particularly its unwillingness to countenance any effective use of the so-called 'gateways' and 'tailpiece' to defend such practices. In part, this outcome may be explicable by the very nature of the Acts in question, which set out in detail the restrictions and arrangements which are to be prohibited. However, the specific and narrow view engendered by the domestic legislation hardly acts as a suitable springboard from which to analyse the more broadly expressed prohibitions of Articles 85–6 EEC.

---

23. [1978] 1 WLR 1031.

Similarly, the common law contribution to English competition law development has been minimal, with the doctrine of restraint of trade as one of the few obviously still influential areas. Attempts to invent new torts have been conspicuously unsuccessful,[24] although some of the classically recognized actions, such as passing off, clearly have enjoyed some recent resurgence. The important implication of these developments, or rather lack of them, is that there has been an absence of dynamism and creativity which, coupled with the demarcation noted above concerning interpretative styles, does not augur well for the ability of English courts to adapt fully to the demands of Community competition provisions.

This fear can be demonstrated by the problems experienced already in translating such measures into effective rights. On the one hand, it is clear from the House of Lords ruling in *Garden Cottage* v. *Milk Marketing Board*[25] that breach of Article 86 EEC constitutes the tort of breach of statutory duty for the purposes of analysis under domestic law. Whilst is is clear that the availability of remedies (explored more fully below) requires such classification to be undertaken, it is less obvious why the *right of action* had to be viewed in English terms at all. It may be said that the right stems from Article 86 as a directly effective provision, enforceable by virtue of the European Communities Act 1972. By analysing the plaintiff's claim in terms of breach of statutory duty, the House of Lords may have stultified progress towards entrenchment of Community rights. Certainly, the emphasis of the judgments upon English analogies subsequently gave the majority of the Court of Appeal in *Bourgoin SA* v. *Minister of Agriculture, Fisheries and Food*[26] the ammunition with which to limit further the enjoyment by individuals of full protection against breaches of Article 30 EEC.

Movement towards harmonization may, of course, provide some incentive for the development of teleological styles. The proposals, for example, to rewrite restrictive practices legislation in the United Kingdom along the lines of the Community model, with an exemption system analogous to Article 85(3), would at least demand that the courts turn their attention to concepts similar to those required by the EEC Treaty. In so far as this reduces the gulf in objectives between Community and domestic measures, some beneficial effects may occur in terms of interpretative maturity. Hitherto, the separation between an overriding emphasis upon 'public interest' under United Kingdom law and the promotion of market freedom and penetration in the Community has potentially increased the risk of legal conflict. Moving the goalposts so that domestic and Community litigants at least play on the same pitch

---

24. See *Lonrho plc* v. *Shell*, [1981] 2 All ER 456 and *Lonrho plc* v. *Fayed*, [1989] 2 All ER 65.
25. [1984] AC 130.
26. [1986] QB 716.

might encourage national courts to accept that they should referee the game in a new spirit too.

This is not to say that all aspects of Community law and policy should come as total surprises to United Kingdom lawyers and judges. The problem is really one of purposive usage. For example, the Competition Act 1980 introduced the notion of the 'anti-competitive practice' to control behaviour by parties with market strength. This emphasis on behaviour and market effect clearly corresponds to the structure of Community regulation. However, by creating an institutional structure built around the Director-General of Fair Trading and the Monopolies and Mergers Commission, the United Kingdom system plays down the significance of individual litigation and court participation. Instead, the model is one of accountability via judicial review of the acts of these administrative authorities. Nearly a decade after the passing of the Competition Act, no case law *in the courts* exists to explain the meaning of an anti-competitive practice. This lacuna is all the more important even in domestic terms, since the cumulated investigations of the Director-General and MMC do not yield a particularly uniform picture.[27]

There is thus something of an historical void in the domestic justiciability of concepts such as excessive or predatory prices, the objective criteria which might justify one party's denial of market access to another or, more widely still, the whole notion of unfair competition. Yet, somewhat curiously and alarmingly, there have been very few references under Article 177 by United Kingdom courts concerning matters of competition law.[28]

Of course, it must be recognized that not all failures to exploit or utilize Community law can be laid at the national judiciary's door. On the one hand, there is the need for clarity by the European Court of Justice when giving preliminary rulings. It might be asked, for example, whether the opaque nature of some decisions, such as that in *Jenkins* v. *Kingsgate (Clothing Products) Ltd*[29] is such as to encourage the use by national courts of the reference procedure. On the other hand, there are sometimes hazy borders to the scope of national courts' jurisdiction. In theory, the response should be to refer such matters for clarification, but the reality may be to ignore or retreat from the difficulty.

For example, there are several references in the EEC Treaty to the balancing of Community interests. The derogation from the free movement of goods provisions in Article 36 EEC requires that any prohibitions or restrictions which would otherwise fall foul of Articles 30–4 'shall not constitute a means of arbitrary discrimination or a disguised

---

27. See N. Green, *Commercial Agreements and Competition Law*, Graham & Trotman, (1986), Ch. 3.
28. Case 51/75, *EMI* v. *CBS*, [1976] ECR 811 remains a rare example of referral.
29. Case 96/80, [1981] ECR 911.

restriction on trade between member states'. This assessment appears to fall squarely within the competence of national courts in the light of the case law of the European Court of Justice.[30] Yet, in contrast, the derogation provided by Article 90(2) EEC in favour of undertakings entrusted with the operation of services of general economic interest or having the character of a revenue-producing monopoly appears to be only partly applicable by national courts. Whilst it seems that the latter may identify whether a body has sufficient status to qualify under the provision, and whether application of the normal Treaty rules would obstruct the performance of that body of its tasks, it appears[31] beyond the competence of the national court to rule on the final element of Article 90(2), requiring that 'The development of trade must not be affected to such an extent as would be contrary to the interests of the Community.' The national court can thus be faced with a case brought by an individual against a public body for breach of, say, Article 86 EEC, in which the defendant invokes the derogation of Article 90(2). Assuming no prior intervention by the EC Commission, the national court appears incapable of providing an immediate solution, even though it may decide that there has been a prima facie abuse of a dominant position. It may be tempting to offer the parties an answer without making a reference, even if this means avoiding a real point of Community law.

Giving effect to direct effect: changing national remedies

The *communautaire* view of the doctrine of direct effect identifies two principal virtues. First, there is the entrenchment of Community law at the most basic and widespread level by allowing individuals to pursue Community law rights through their national courts. Second, and associated with the first point, direct effect removes dependence upon Community institutions or member state governments for the enactment or supervision of Community measures possessing the well-known characteristics for direct effect.[32]

However, the achievement of the first of these goals requires the co-operation of national courts. The European Court of Justice has itself not been entirely explicit in its views of their obligations under the doctrine. Most of its comments have been confined to the need for 'protection' of individual rights by national courts, without explaining whether this necessitates the creation of new national rights, remedies or

---

30. This seems to flow from the answer given by the European Court of Justice to the reference made by the House of Lords in Case 34/79, *R* v. *Henn and Darby*, [1979] ECR 3795.
31. Case 10/71, *Hein*, [1971] ECR 723. See Wyatt and Dashwood, *supra*, n.1, Ch. 19.
32. Namely, that the provision is clear, precise and unconditional. See Case 26/62, *Van Gend en Loos*, [1963] ECR 1.

procedures, or whether protective consequences flow automatically as a matter of Community law.

The difficulties of ensuring protection of individuals' Community rights have recently starkly arisen before the House of Lords in the case of *Factortame Ltd* v. *Secretary of State for Transport*.[33] The appeal arose from interim relief sought by the Spanish owners of various fishing vessels against the relevant government department for enacting national rules which allegedly contravened the Community fisheries policy. A preliminary reference had already been made by the Divisional Court on the substantive matter of whether the national rules were in conflict with Community law. That court's decision to grant interim relief to the plaintiffs, who faced economic losses if deprived of their fishing rights, was then overturned in the Court of Appeal. Thus the central issue on appeal to the House of Lords was whether any interim relief was available pending the outcome of the substantive preliminary ruling, either as a matter of national or Community law.

Lord Bridge, giving the unanimous judgment of the House of Lords, summarized the arguments in favour of the existence of an overriding principle of Community law obliging national courts to secure interim protection as follows:

Directly enforceable Community rights are part of the legal heritage of every citizen of a member state of the EEC. They arise from the Treaty itself and not from any judgment of the European Court declaring their existence. Such rights are automatically available and must be given unrestricted retroactive effect. The persons entitled to the enjoyment of such rights are entitled to direct and immediate protection against possible infringement of them. The duty to provide such protection rests with the national court. The remedy to be provided against infringement must be effective, not merely symbolic or illusory. The rules of national law which render the exercise of directly enforceable Community rights excessively difficult or virtually impossible must be overridden.

However, counsel succeeded in persuading the House that all the relevant European Court of Justice decisions on securing protection involved actual, and not putative, Community law rights. As a result, the House used Article 177 EEC procedure to refer questions concerning the possible existence of a Community law obligation to secure interim protection of putative rights.

Before examining the implications of the *Factortame* judgement in detail, the various options open to the House should be considered. For example, there might be available remedies under domestic law which would adequately serve to protect the individual's position. Such a conclusion would, of course, involve no conflict with Community law and be largely uncontroversial. Alternatively, domestic remedies might be interpreted, or even created, by reference to an independent, and higher, rule of Community law. The effect would be to maintain the appearance

---

33. [1989] 2 All ER 692.

of national rules, albeit interpreted in conformity with the doctrine of supremacy of Community law. A further possibility would be to discover, or request from the Court of Justice the invention of, a directly effective Community principle conferring protection on individuals. Such a principle, whilst requiring some procedural implementation, would make the remedy itself a matter of Community law.

In effect, the House of Lords in *Factortame* chose the third path, having rejected the first and not really discussed the second. Crucially, the House authoritatively discounted the existence of any appropriate relief for the plaintiffs as a matter of English law. In so doing, it overruled two cases[34] which had been seen by some commentators as offering a method of protection for individuals seeking interim injunctive relief against public authorities.

It is, perhaps, a matter of some relief that the House of Lords did not consider the possibility of interpreting existing English remedies in the light of Community objectives. Had it done so, then from the evidence of *Duke* v. *GEC Reliance* and the other cases discussed above in connection with interpretative styles it would seem likely that a ruling against interim relief might firmly have been made instead of the lifeline offered by way of a reference under Article 177 EEC.

The idea of a compromise solution in the form of English remedies interpreted in European mode and tailored to secure the full enjoyment of Community rights depends largely upon the scope and status of the *Von Colson* ruling by the European Court of Justice. Although made in the context of an individual seeking to rely upon a directive, the exhortation to interpret implementing domestic legislation in the light of the contents and objectives of the directive could be extrapolated into a general statement about the need to avoid conflict with the doctrine of supremacy by ensuring the conformity of domestic measures with Community requirements.

Any such move was forcefully resisted by the House of Lords in the *Duke* case. Lord Templeman sought to limit the scope of the *Von Colson* case, observing:

The ruling of the European Court did not constrain the national court to construe German law in accordance with Community law but ruled that if under German law the German court possessed the power to award damages which are adequate and which fulfilled the objective of the equal treatment directive then it was the duty of the German court to act accordingly.

The *Von Colson* case is no authority for the proposition that the German court was bound to invent a German law of adequate compensation if no such law existed and no authority for the proposition that a court of a member state must distort the meaning of a domestic statute so as to conform with Community law which is not directly applicable. If, following the *von Colson* case, the German

---

34. *R* v. *Secretary of State for Home Dept, ex parte Herbage*, [1986] 3 All ER 209 and *R* v. *Licensing Authority, ex parte Smith Kline & French Laboratories Ltd*, [1989] 2 All ER 113.

court adhered to the view that under German law it possessed no discretion to award adequate compensation, it would have been the duty of the German government in fulfilment of its obligations under the EEC Treaty to introduce legislation or evolve some other method which would enable adequate compensation to be obtained.

Seen in these terms, the position in *Factortame* would have involved the House of Lords in the invention of an English law of adequate compensation where none existed.

However, it should not be assumed too lightly that the *Duke* approach is either itself justifiable or on all fours with the problem which arose in *Factortame*. In particular, great emphasis was placed in *Duke* upon the lack of horizontal direct effect possessed by the provision of the directive in question. This allowed the House of Lords to argue that s.2(4) of the European Communities Act 1972 neither enabled nor constrained English courts to give effect to it. This approach would not suffice to dispose of *Factortame*, since the Community regulations involving fishing rights would be directly effective if the Divisional Court's original Article 177 EEC reference is decided on the basis that the national regulations are incompatible with the Community fisheries regime.

The ruling by the House of Lords in *Factortame* that no interim relief was available under English law reinforces doubts about the quality of leadership being offered at the top of the judicial hierarchy concerning the effective application of Community rights in the United Kingdom. In its earliest dealings with Community law, the House seemed to offer a clear acceptance of the twin pillars of supremacy and direct effect.[35] But it has not wished to venture further and mould domestic law to avoid threats to the effective enjoyment of those principles.

It should be stressed that *Factortame* is hardly the first authority to invite the question whether remedies adequately support rights. In the *Bourgoin* case, discussed above, a majority of the Court of Appeal ruled that damages were not available as of right for an infringement of Article 30 EEC. Parker LJ found himself seeking refuge in the hitherto shadowy area of misfeasance in public office to limit financial compensation to situations where the relevant minister or body had knowledge of the nature of the breach. Even Oliver LJ, who would have allowed damages in *Bourgoin* for breach of statutory duty by analogy with the *Garden Cottage* ruling under Article 86 EEC, still couched his argument in English terms. There was no attempt to base the remedy on the breach of the directly effective Community rule itself. By referring the question of a possible Community law requirement for remedies, the House of Lords in *Factortame* has at last met the issue directly.

Certainly, it should be recognized that any affirmative answer from the European Court of Justice to the question whether Community rules demand the creation of national remedies would go significantly further

---

35. *Garland* v. *British Rail Engineering Ltd*, [1982] 2 All ER 402.

than its explicit position in previous cases. Hitherto, the Court of Justice has confined itself to comments such as these in *Rewe* v. *Hauptzollamt Kiel*:[36]

Although the Treaty has made it possible ... for private persons to bring a direct action, it was not intended to create new remedies in the national courts to ensure the observance of Community law ... On the other hand ... it must be possible for every type of action provided for by national law to be available for the purpose of ensuring observance of Community provisions having direct effect, on the same conditions as would apply were it a question of observing national law.

In effect, this approach amounts to a restatement of the principle of non-discrimination central to the EEC Treaty as a whole. The European Court has paid less attention to the meaning of the 'real and effective' remedies which should be available on this non-discriminatory footing.

From policy and legal points of view, the case for confirming a Community rule is strong. As Green and Barav[37] have argued: 'What would be unfortunate would be a situation whereby a directly effective provision were denied admission as a proper cause of action on the ground that it failed to satisfy some eccentric technicality of English laws.' Put in merely pragmatic terms, incomplete enjoyment of rights by individuals in a particular member state hinders the development of the very freedoms which the EEC Treaty seeks to promote.

More substantively, it may be argued that several specific characteristics and provisions of Community law may be invoked to support a Community law duty regarding remedies. The clearest starting-point is provided by Article 5 EEC, which establishes a duty of solidarity between member states and demands that they 'take all appropriate measures ... to ensure fulfilment of the obligations arising out of this Treaty' and that they 'abstain from any measure which could jeopardise the attainment of the objectives of this Treaty.' National courts undoubtedly form part of the member states for this purpose.

Taking a teleological view of this provision, fulfilment of obligations can only be done by the provision of effective remedies, not just the recognition of the existence of rights. In other words, direct effect is not just about *locus standi*; it is about substantive enjoyment of rights. Even without resorting to policy-oriented interpretation, the partial or inconsistent availability of remedies within and across member states can be seen as measures jeopardizing the attainment of objectives since they constitute disincentives to the taking-up of conferred rights.

Moreover, the arguments in favour of Community law obligations upon national courts do not depend exclusively upon Article 5 EEC which, it must be conceded, has not been accepted by the European

---

36. Case 158/80, [1981] ECR 1841.
37. 'Damages in the national courts for breach of Community law' in (1986) 6 *Yearbook of European Law* 55.

Court of Justice as a directly effective provision in its own right. The principle of non-discrimination, already articulated by the Court of Justice in the context of access to remedies, does not have to be a maximum standard. Indeed, the European Court has displayed the ability in the past to create obligations extending beyond a non-discriminatory base. Under Article 30 EEC, for example, the existence of a measure equivalent to a quantitative restriction should be ascertained by reference to the deprivation of competitive advantage, at least in the area of national price controls allegedly constituting trade barriers.[38] Even in those cases where the European Court has limited itself to the concept of discrimination, there is ample evidence that protection exists for individuals on the basis of the substance rather than the form of the allegedly unlawful activity. It is therefore suggested that the attitude towards remedies should develop in parallel. After all, remedies must be 'real and effective', clearly indicating a substantive approach.

However, it should be recognized that there has been no systematic attempt at legislative level within the Community to initiate a homogenous set of remedies for infringement of directly effective rights. Nevertheless, the history of Community case law suggests that the European Court of Justice has never been overburdened by the need to avoid treading on institutional or governmental toes. Indeed, it would be consistent with the short history of the Community if the principal impetus for the development of a Community principle concerning establishment of remedies were to be invented by the European Court.

A clear illustration of the reticence of the Community institutions can be seen from the provisions of the Directive on mutual recognition of professional qualifications.[39] This legislation, aimed at simplifying free movement of professionals, encountered particular problems at the drafting stage when trying to take account of the peculiar position of the United Kingdom.[40] Any specific legal basis for the protection of the exercise of a trade or profession was very hard to pin down as a result of the piecemeal development of a limited range of statutory and common law remedies. The final legislative solution adopted was to lay down a specific obligation upon professional bodies to communicate their decisions about migrants' applications to pursue their calling in the host state. According to Article 8, paragraph 2 of the Directive, 'A remedy shall be available against this decision, or the absence thereof, before a court or tribunal in accordance with the provisions of national law.'

This provision may be compared with the position already reached by the European Court of Justice before the enactment of the directive. In

---

38. See, *inter alia*, Case 13/77, *GB Inno* v. *ATAB*, [1977] ECR 2115.
39. Directive 89/48/EEC OJ 1989 L19/16.
40. See Ross, (1989) 14 ELRev 162.

Case 222/86, *Heylens*,[41] involving the refusal of the relevant French authorities to recognise the qualifications of a Belgian football trainer, the European Court ruled that in the context of the right of free movement of workers under Article 48 EEC, 'the *existence of a legal remedy* against any decision by a national authority refusing to recognise such right is *essential* to guarantee the individual *effective* protection of his right.' [emphasis added]

It is therefore interesting to speculate upon the proper interpretation of Article 8 of the mutual recognition directive in the light of the *Heylens* judgment. How should an English court react to, say, an application by a Community national holding qualifications rejected as adequate by an English professional body listed in the Annex to the Directive?

In the event of a reference to the European Court of Justice (which, it is suggested, would be obviously appropriate in such circumstances), the principal difficulty would be the extent of the member state's obligation to introduce a remedy if none existed. Article 8 of the Directive recognizes a relationship between the remedy and national provisions but, it may be argued, only in the sense that some procedural device at national level is essential to allow the remedy to be enforced. In other words, the remedy shall be available as a matter of Community law as demanded by the directive. The mechanics of facilitating it are left to national law. This interpretation is preferable to making the existence of the remedy subject to national law, and would be consistent with the *Heylens* ruling adopted by the European Court of Justice.

Of course, it would still have to be conceded that the effect of such an interpretation would be limited to the meaning of the particular directive, since the ultimate obligation would be to impose upon the member state the duty to create a remedy. To this extent, the ruling in *Heylens* is further-reaching since it may represent a general principle which the European Court of Justice is seeking to promote. Any claim that the judgment only governs Article 48 EEC may be met by the argument that all the other fundamental freedoms created and protected by the EEC Treaty should be accorded the same treatment.

The development of a principle of Community law obliging the creation, where necessary, of new remedies is thus at a crucial stage. Having first demanded that migrants shall not be discriminated against where national remedies are available, the European Court of Justice has apparently progressed in *Heylens* to requiring that the legal remedies must exist in the first place where protection of directly effective Community law rights is at stake. The stage to be explored further is the quality of that existence: in the United Kingdom context, a public remedy against breach of Article 30 exists, but it may arguably be ineffective or inadequate.

---

41. [1987] ECR 4097.

It is to be hoped that the European Court of Justice takes the opportunity offered by the *Factortame* reference to clarify its stance on these issues. The question of the protection of putative rights can hardly be discussed without reference to the effective remedies for undisputed rights. If there is no Community law basis for the latter, then clearly there will be no hope for the protection of the former. The House of Lords does at least emerge with credit for having given the European Court of Justice the opportunity to pronounce.

Conclusions

The response of the United Kingdom courts to Community law has been largely unambitious and, more importantly, lacking in *communautaire* spirit. Faced with new and challenging justiciable concepts, there has not been a strong uptake of the helpline offered by the Article 177 EEC reference procedure. Somewhat paradoxically, the common law spirit of inventiveness and flexibility is precisely what is missing from the reaction to Community law. By neither utilizing the discretion to refer nor embarking on a programme of development and adjustment of domestic provisions in the light of Community influences and obligations, the United Kingdom courts have achieved a double setback to the progress and entrenchment of the directly effective rights designed to protect individuals. Whilst some exports in legal thinking have occurred from the common law tradition, most notably in the adoption by the European Court of Justice of the essentially English concept of a right to a hearing,[42] there has yet to be a similar lifting of the barriers to the import of *communautaire* doctrines. This unwritten free movement is the key to the proper enjoyment by Community citizens in domestic courts of the rights revealed by the European Court of Justice.

---

42. See Hartley, *supra*, n.1, p.147.

12 The reform of the legal profession or the end of civilization as we know it

Fiona Cownie

Introduction

On Tuesday 21 February 1989, Sir Stephen Brown, President of the Family Division of the High Court, gave a speech to the Family Law Bar Association, in which he is reported as saying that the proposals recently put forward by Her Majesty's government for the reform of the legal profession raised issues that threatened 'the administration of the law on which our civilisation depends.'[1] Such howls of outrage are not unique in the history of a profession which has been quick to defend itself against any interference from those outside its ranks. In 1833 the government of the time introduced a bill establishing a national system of county courts. The legal profession was up in arms; many barristers thought that they would lose part of their business if the new courts were introduced; in addition, litigation was likely to be taken away from the Assizes, where young barristers gained experience of advocacy. Lord Lyndhurst told the House of Lords that

> If he [Lord Lyndhurst] had been fortunate enough to possess the powers of eloquence that belonged to his noble and learned friend [the Lord Chancellor], he would have placed before them a picture of such hideous deformity on this topic as would have caused them to turn from it with shuddering and horror.[2]

Over a century later, the legal profession would still like to persuade reformers to turn away from their proposals as if from a Gorgon.

The phoney war — the troublesome decade

My learned friends have found the last decade a particularly trying one, since it has seen an almost constant pressure for reform of the legal

---

1. *The Times*, 23 February 1989.
2. Hansard 3rd Series, HL, Vol. XVIII, col. 881, 17 June 1833.

profession; reform which, for the most part, they would rather not see implemented.

The decade began well: in 1979 the Royal Commission on Legal Services published its Report[3] and lawyers heaved a collective sigh of relief when they learned that as far as the legal profession was concerned, the Benson Committee had concluded that the status quo should be preserved; the Bar should retain its monopoly over rights of audience in the higher courts, solicitors should retain their monopoly over conveyancing work and the two branches of the legal profession should not be fused into one.

Commentators outside the profession were not so sanguine about the conclusions reached by Benson. *LAG Bulletin* commented, 'The Report is characterised by an over-anxiety not to offend the professional establishment'.[4] It was certainly true that the Royal Commission appeared happy to leave the regulation of the legal profession to the profession itself and that it hoped that this situation would continue for the foreseeable future. 'The profession should have a period of orderly development free, so far as possible, from external interventions.'[5] It was this attitude which prompted William Twining to make the following remarks when commenting on the Royal Commission's Report in the *Modern Law Review*: 'The legal profession can breathe freely for at least another decade — its autonomy strengthened, the fusion issue buried, the conveyancing monopoly confirmed, although the latter may be a continuing source of complaint'.[6] While this was a perfectly reasonable view to take at the time, the decade which followed was to see the legal profession subject not merely to complaints about their conveyancing activities, but to what the profession was to regard as a wholesale onslaught on its professional status.

It was the solicitors who came under attack first, when in 1983 Austin Mitchell MP introduced a Private Member's bill into the House of Commons with the aim of allowing licensed conveyancers to undertake the conveyancing of residential property in competition with solicitors. Negotiations between Mr Mitchell and the government resulted in him withdrawing his bill; the government then introduced its own bill with the same objective. Overriding all the protestations from the Law Society, Part II of the Administration of Justice Act 1985 permitted licensed conveyancers to undertake conveyancing work in competition with solicitors.

Solicitors were extremely concerned at the loss of their conveyancing monopoly, regarding it as a major threat to the livelihood of many members of their profession. Consequently, they looked for areas into

---

3. Benson Committee, Cmnd 7648 (1979).
4. [1979] LAG Bulletin 251.
5. Benson Committee, *supra*, n.2, R 3.2.
6. (1980) 43 MLR 558, 559.

which they could expand their activities. A prime target for expansion was advocacy; solicitors began to press for the removal of the barristers' monopoly of rights of audience in the higher courts. The Law Society's campaign was given some welcome publicity in the case of *Abse* v. *Smith*;[7] Mr Leo Abse, together with twenty-four other Members of Parliament sued Cyril Smith MP for libel after remarks he made in a radio interview about their attitude to the Falklands crisis. The action was settled on the basis that an apologetic statement would be read out in open court. Mr Smith's solicitor regarded the fee charged by counsel for performing this task as 'unnecessarily expensive' and therefore decided to seek the leave of the court to appear before it himself in order to read out the statement. Leave was refused, both at first instance and on appeal, but the Court of Appeal held that the judges of the High Court as a collegiate body could exercise their inherent power to alter the rules regarding rights of audience, which gave further impetus to the Law Society's campaign. A few months later, a Practice Direction was issued to the effect that solicitors could appear in the Supreme Court in formal or unopposed proceedings.[8]

Following this victory for the Law Society, tension between the two branches of the profession continued to grow, and it was revealed in an increasingly vitriolic series of public interchanges, not only over rights of audience, but also over the question of the possible fusion of the two branches of the profession. Clearly, such internecine squabbles could only damage the public image of the profession. Recognizing this, the Bar proposed that a joint committee should be set up by both parts of the profession to consider their future. However, when this was done, the Marre Committee was to prove a great disappointment. Its credibility was seriously undermined by the fact that it had far too few resources to deal with anything but the most minimal amount of evidence, it had no research capacity of its own and when its final report was published, it contained a strong Note of Dissent from the barrister members of the Committee, supported by some independent members, about rights of audience.[9]

The Marre Committee did make some recommendations for change, agreeing, for instance, that professions other than solicitors should be permitted direct access to counsel and that solicitors should be eligible for appointment as High Court judges. However, in general, this report, like that of Benson, was firmly in favour of the status quo and the Committee felt able to conclude unanimously that 'Any changes which weaken the ability of the Law Society and the General Council of the Bar to regulate the conduct and competence of their members are

---

7. [1986] 1 All ER 350.
8. [1986] 2 All ER 226.
9. *A Time for Change, Report of the Committee on the Future of the Legal Profession*, General Council of the Bar and the Council of the Law Society (July 1988).

unlikely to be in the public interest'.[10] As far as the profession was concerned, that was their final word on their future. Change, if it was to take place, was an internal matter which lawyers wished to implement by themselves.

However, by the end of the decade which had begun in such a promising fashion, with the Benson Committee recommending that the legal profession should regulate itself in the manner in which it thought best, there was to be a final surprise attack.

Let battle commence — the Green Papers

In October 1988, with the troublesome decade near to an end, the legal profession was faced with its most serious challenge; a fundamental appraisal of the profession which would emphatically deny that lawyers were to be left to their own devices to administer their profession. In that month, much to their amazement, lawyers were catapulted into a full-scale confrontation with the government, when the Lord Chancellor announced that he would be publishing a Green Paper on the future of the legal profession. In the event, three Green Papers were published: one on conveyancing,[11] one on contingency fees,[12] and one on the work and organization of the legal profession;[13] it is with the last item that this chapter is mainly concerned and which will be referred to as the 'Green Paper'.

The basic premise of the Green Paper was that the public should have the best possible access to efficient and effective legal services provided by competent practitioners. Thus there should be as free and efficient a market in legal services as possible, enabling the discipline of the market to provide consumers with a wide choice of services at the most economical price. However, at the same time the expertise of the providers of legal services must be maintained at the right level to ensure competence.[14] The Green Paper made it clear that the legal profession was to be subject to the same government policy objectives as actors in other aspects of economic life; there was no reason to exclude it from the discipline of competition which applied to the rest of the economy.[15] However, the market was not to be allowed total freedom, since 'the interests of justice and the needs of those who make use of or are affected by the law' were to be safeguarded,[16] and there was an acknowledged need to maintain a balance between competition and regulation.[17]

---

10. Ibid., para. 4.23.
11. Cm 572.
12. Cm 571.
13. CM 570.
14. Ibid., paras 1.1–1.3.
15. Ibid., para. 1.9.
16. Ibid., para. 1.9.
17. Ibid., para. 1.4.

The government proposed to introduce market forces to the legal profession in various ways, but some of their proposals were to play a crucial part in the debate which followed. First, the role of the new Lord Chancellor's Advisory Committee on Education and Conduct became the focus of much attention. The government was keen to see more specialization within the profession, so that the public would have a wide choice of practitioners who were acknowledged to be competent in particular areas of law. In order that members of the public would know that recognition as a specialist had real value, it was proposed that the rules relating to the education, training and qualifications of specialists would be approved by the Lord Chancellor, after taking advice from his new Committee.[18] The Committee itself was envisaged as 'a vigorous and active standing committee'[19] composed of a judge as chairman, two barristers, two solicitors, two academics and eight lay representatives.[20] It was intended to play an important role, both in ensuring the provision of legal services of good quality and in maintaining the standards of conduct expected of practitioners, since its other major task would be to advise the Lord Chancellor on the principles to be embodied in the codes of practice under which the profession would in future operate. The profession would be required to produce codes of conduct embodying these principles in relation to the provision of legal advice and assistance and in relation to advocacy.[21] The government proposed to impose these two sets of principles on the profession, subjecting the Council of the Law Society and the Bar Council to the same procedures as any other professional body whose members wished to offer such services. All such bodies would be required to submit their codes of conduct to the Advisory Committee, which would have to be satisfied that the codes embodied the approved principles as laid down by the Lord Chancellor in a statutory instrument.[22]

The other change proposed in the Green Paper, which was to prove equally contentious, was that in future, rights of audience should depend only on whether advocates had had the correct training and were bound by the appropriate codes of conduct, rather than on whether the lawyer in question was a solicitor or barrister. In effect, this would allow solicitors full rights of audience in all courts.[23] The Green Paper contained many other proposals in relation to the work and organization of the legal profession, but it was these two proposals in particular, coupled with what was seen as a 'free market' approach, which were to be the focus of the ensuing debate.

---

18. Ibid., para. 3.11.
19. Ibid., para. 3.12.
20. Ibid., para. 3.14.
21. Ibid., paras 4.11–4.15.
22. Ibid., paras 4.11–4.13.
23. Ibid., para. 5.8.

Deploying the troops — the 'free market' approach

Many commentators focused on the application of the government's free market philosophy to the legal profession as if it were the major theoretical underpinning of the proposed reforms. They tended to identify the proposals with the idea that the provision of legal services should be open to free competition and to comment on them in those terms. The judges, in their response to the Green Papers, remarked 'We preface our comments on advocacy by noting that in this field great care must be exercised in the application of simple principles of competition'.[24] The Bar, in its response, identified freedom of competition as one of two major themes to which the government was committed in its programme of reform,[25] but saw this as an unsatisfactory perspective: 'The legal system and the legal profession cannot be viewed solely as an economic activity'.[26] Writing to *The Times*, the Chairman of the Bar Council argued that regarding justice as a consumer durable would undermine the integrity of the English legal system: 'Justice cannot be measured in terms of competition and consumerism; justice is not a consumer durable; it is the hallmark of a civilised and democratic society'.[27]

The thrust of such comments is that the government, when forming its proposals, has concentrated solely on its belief in the efficacy of market forces as a means of reform; there is a vision of a legal profession regulated solely by the demands of the market. This view might be thought to be unsurprising, given that the proposals emanate from a government whose economic policies arguably owe much to the work of economists such as Hayek and Friedmann. It has been said of this group of economists:

> Monetarists [such as Hayek and Friedmann] . . . tend to be libertarian in their social philosophy. Their aim is to get government off the backs of the people; to reduce the scope of bureaucratic meddling and decision making; to return freedom of choice (via the market) back to individuals and to give only the minimalist nightwatchman role to the state.[28]

Under such a regime, lawyers might reasonably have expected to have been left alone to deal with the cold winds of competition which were to be allowed to blow through their profession. Margaret Thatcher herself had promised in her keynote address to the Conservative Party Conference in 1979, 'If you ask whether the next Conservative Government will cut controls and regulations and keep interference in people's

---

24. *Judges' Response*, para. 31.
25. *Quality of Justice - The Bar's Response*, General Council of the Bar 1989, para. 3.19.
26. Ibid., para. 4.4.
27. *The Times*, 3 July 1989.
28. P. Jackson, 'Policy Implementation and Monetarism', in P. Jackson (ed.) *Implementing Government Policy Initiatives: The Thatcher Administration 1979-1983*, Royal Institute of Public Administration (1985), at 26.

lives to a minimum, my answer is "Yes, that is exactly what we shall do."[29]

Yet it is apparent from the start that the government was not committed to an entirely free market in legal services; even as it stated its belief at the very beginning of the Green Paper that legal services should be subjected to the discipline of the market, it was giving equal prominence to its belief that 'the public must also be assured of the competence of the providers of those services.'[30] So, while competition is to provide efficient legal services, it will still be necessary to use other means to maintain the standards of competence and conduct which are needed in order to safeguard the interests of the public when they consult lawyers. The government's position appears to be that while it believes in the free market, it practices regulation of that market. Of course, the regulation of the market is an economic position which can be justified, though not generally by reference to the ideas of Hayek or Friedmann, but the Green Paper does not offer any guidance on its theoretical basis; it has departed from its perceived attachment to the free market, but it fails to explain what is to be the ordering principle behind its proposals. Perhaps this is because, more than a coherent philosophy, 'Thatcherism' is a mixture of different ideas which appeal to a particular strand of Conservatism found in Britain today. It has been said that, '"Thatcherism" may mean different things to different people, but essentially it embodies related values, attitudes and beliefs which favour the free market rather than the state as the means of allocating resources'.[31] This is too simplistic an analysis, however, as is the search for one underlying economic philosophy in the reform of the legal profession.

'Thatcherism' is prepared to be eclectic, to grab from diverse sources that which it finds conducive:

The Thatcher Government's strand of monetarism was more than just setting monetary targets, it included a package of structural readjustments, trades union reforms and a fiscal strategy which would be compatible with financial stability. Based upon a neo-liberal counter-revolution, . . . it embraced an idealisation of the market-place and the writings of neo-liberal economists such as Milton Friedmann and Frederick von Hayek, along with the new classical economists such as Robert Lucas in the U.S.A. and Patrick Minford in the U.K. The economic philosophy was, therefore, a pot-pourri of different strains of right-wing economic thinking.[32]

The effect of this eclecticism is that 'Thatcherism' is inherently contradictory; whilst trumpeting its belief in the free market, it is prepared to indulge in regulation to achieve what it believes is right.

---

29. Margaret Thatcher, 'Conference Speech 1979', excerpted in F. O'Gorman, *British Conservatism* (1989), at 221.
30. *Supra*, n.13, para. 1.2.
31. G. Peden, *British Economic and Social Policy: Lloyd George to Margaret Thatcher*, Oxford, Philip Alan (1985).
32. Jackson, 'Perspectives on Practical Monetarism', in Jackson *supra*, n.28, at 36.

The contradictory nature of 'Thatcherism' can be seen most clearly in its attitude to the City. Here, in the temple of Capitalism, surely the market would reign supreme? Here above all one might reasonably have expected a lack of regulation and control, freedom to operate constrained only by the discipline of the market. Not a bit of it; the Thatcher government's treatment of the City and its financial institutions throws into stark reality the contradictions which lie at the heart of 'Thatcherite' economics.

[A] close examination of the City's revolution in regulation soon reveals puzzling features. We might naively expect that competition and deregulation would cause the State to retreat and controls to disappear. The contrary has happened. Mrs Thatcher's second administration subjected the financial community to historically unprecedented state-based controls. The sum total of regulatory change increased the number of rules, the formality and variety of the institutions concerned with their enforcement, and the sanctions supporting enforcement.[33]

So the government's approach to the reform of the legal profession should not, in terms of its apparently contradictory economic approach, have caused any surprise. Commentators, both economic and political, can see such contradictions in many areas of government policy. Mrs Thatcher, the devotee of Hayek and Friedmann, has presided over a government which has been prepared to interfere in the market as it pleases. As far as the reform of the legal profession is concerned, it is therefore unsurprising that it contemplated a free market in legal services which was to be subject to a number of apparently arbitrary state controls; of these, proposals aimed at ensuring the competence of the profession were to provide a focus for much of the ensuing debate.

A bitter skirmish — regulating the profession

It was the government's attempt to impose standards of competency on the legal profession which produced the most anguished reaction from practitioners, and on this point in particular they were supported by the judiciary, who perceived both the proposals relating to codes of conduct and those concerning rights of audience for advocates as a threat to their constitutional position. In their response to the Green Papers, the judges summarized their views as follows:

The Government is proposing that in future the Lord Chancellor should make the final decision on standards of education and training for advocates, prescribe the principles to be embodied in codes of conduct for advocates, and be empowered to make decisions on rights of audience in the High Court and Court of Appeal by means of subordinate legislation. **These proposals represent a grave breach of the doctrine of separation of powers.**[34] [Judges' emphasis]

---

33. Moran, 'Thatcherism and Financial Regulation' (1988) 59 *Political Quarterly* 20, at 20.
34. *Judges' Response*, 'Summary', para. 3.

This sort of statement illustrates the seriousness with which the judiciary reacted when faced by proposals which they clearly regarded as a threat to their zealously guarded independence. It is interesting that, while they were happy to call in aid such weighty concepts as the doctrine of separation of powers, the judges did not feel it necessary to elaborate on their understanding of what the doctrine involves; in its crudest form, it might just be thought to refer to the separation of the judiciary from the Executive and the legislature, yet, with a Lord Chancellor who is not only the head of the judiciary but also a Cabinet Minister, we are already faced with a situation which the doctrine would not encompass. The judges might be thought to be extending the doctrine beyond its crude boundaries when they assert that, in relation to the Lord Chancellor's position as final arbiter of codes of conduct for advocates, 'We regard this as a grave breach of the doctrine of separation of powers even though it does not directly threaten the independence of the judges themselves'.[35] The *Judges' Response* had the appearance of a measured response by the judiciary to government proposals which were criticized as allowing only a short time for comments,[36] and yet their Lordships apparently did not think it necessary to define the terms which they were using to criticize what they clearly regarded as ill-thought-out government proposals.

Yet the judges made some serious points; their concern that the proposals might undermine the independence of advocates, because the Lord Chancellor would wield ultimate control over the profession via his control over their rules of conduct, is not to be taken lightly. Judicial review of the Lord Chancellor's decisions is not an entirely satisfactory method of curbing abuse of power, should it occur, and there are good arguments for 'transforming the Lord Chancellor's Department into a Ministry of Justice, with a Minister answerable to the House of Commons and a Commons Select Committee considering its activities'.[37] Such an arrangement, whilst it might have its drawbacks, would go much further to meeting criticisms, such as those made by the judges, than bland reassurances from Lord Mackay that such fears are unfounded, because 'the powers and duties of the Lord Chancellor will be provided for in a tightly drawn Act of Parliament'.[38] The danger that some future Lord Chancellor might use his powers in such a way as to deter advocates from representing clients who wished to challenge decisions made by the government of the day should not be dismissed too lightly.

It is clear, too, even from their corporate response, that the proposals aroused a considerable amount of emotion among their Lordships, for

---

35. *Judges' Response*, 'Independence of the Judiciary', para. 20.
36. *Judges' Response*, 'Introduction', para. 2.
37. Pannick, 'Howls of Fury at the Bar', *The Observer*, 19 February 1989.
38. Lord Mackay, writing in *The Times*, 14 April 1989.

the tone of the document is quite vehement in places; a little further on in their response we find them declaring 'The Government should recognise that it has gone too far in making these proposals'.[39] However, it was in the reactions of individual judges that we were to see just what a raw nerve the government had touched. Some of the remarks made by their Lordships were, to say the least, intemperate; on one occasion, Lord Hailsham accused the government of 'thinking with its bottom' in relation to the Green Papers, 'The one thing that has worried me about the whole exercise is that one does not know if the Government is sitting on its head or its bottom. Its trouble is that it is thinking with its bottom and sitting on its head'.[40] Meanwhile, Lord Lane, the Lord Chief Justice, felt able to describe the Green Paper as 'one of the most sinister documents ever to emanate from Government',[41] and Lord Ackner thundered, 'threatening and deeply depressing stormclouds are hanging over the entire legal profession and the judiciary'.[42] In the House of Lords debate on the reforms Lord Hailsham commented that the legal profession could not be regulated like a grocer's shop in Grantham, while Lord Lane is reported as having accused the Lord Chancellor of publishing the Green Papers without previously consulting the judges, referring to a 'failure of courtesy'. Lord Mackay replied that he had offered to consult the judges when he was preparing the proposals and they had turned him down, preferring to remain at arm's length. Lord Lane, he explained, had now withdrawn his accusation.[43]

How would their Lordships regard advocates who appeared before them in courts using such Rumpole-style rhetoric? How might the most junior barrister be regarded by his/her colleagues were he/she to ignore in such a wholesale manner the advice given in that worthy tome 'The Art of the Advocate'? In a chapter devoted to 'Style in Speeches' the author (himself a Queen's Counsel) begins by warning us that 'The advocate does not live by style alone'. He goes to great pains to tell us that 'The modern advocate must practice moderation if not in all things, then at least in the use of ... verbal condiments ... Arguments should seem to rely more on force of logic than extravagances of language'.[44] Their Lordships have apparently forgotten the basic rules of advocacy in a way which would shame the humblest novice in their erstwhile profession.

Whilst their Lordships were prepared to use such colourful language and overblown rhetorical devices in defence of the status quo, the reaction of the legal profession as a whole was equally vehement. The day after Lord Mackay published his Green Papers the Chairman of the

---

39. *Judges' Response*, 'Summary', para. 5.
40. *The Times*, 15 April 1989.
41. *The Guardian*, 17 February 1989.
42. *The Guardian*, 2 February 1989.
43. *The Guardian*, 8 April 1989.
44. Richard Du Cann, *The Art of the Advocate*, Penguin Books (1980), at 179.

Bar Council stated that control of justice would go 'from the judges and be entrusted to civil servants'. This would give rise to 'grave constitutional dangers.'[45] In fact, when the Bar mounted its infamous advertising campaign against the government's reforms, loss of self-regulation was one of the 'wrongs' highlighted: 'The Government's proposals could mean a defendant could be prosecuted by *state* prosecutors, tried by a Judge drawn from the ranks of *state* prosecutors, and represented by an advocate licensed by a body controlled by — you've guessed it — the *state*.'[46] [Italics as in original]

Many people will find it unsurprising that the legal profession has leapt to defend its privilege of self-regulation with such alacrity and with such ferocious energy. In particular, those sociologists of the professions who follow the functionalist tradition of scholarship would regard self-regulation as one of the distinctive characteristics of a profession. Structural functionalists, whose tradition of scholarship can be traced right back to the work of Emile Durkheim, 'the father of sociology', focus on the question of social order as their central concern; given that society is composed of individuals, what is it that prevents humankind from degenerating into anarchy? Professions are seen as a valuable source of community, operating as an antidote to individualistic tendencies. Furthermore, 'If functionalism had to identify professions by a single characteristic, self-regulation would be near the top of the list.'[47] It is self-regulation which sets a profession apart from a mere occupation, which is invariably regulated by outsiders. Such scholars would find it entirely predictable that, when the privilege of self-regulation is threatened, it is perceived by lawyers as an attack upon their very status as professionals and arouses their passionate opposition. It is a question of power, as well as status; the proposed reforms would take the important power of regulation away from the profession and give it to the state. The reaction of the legal profession was not just a fit of pique, brought on by an attack upon their privileged status as professionals who regulate their own conduct; it was the reaction of a group within society which realized that if the reforms went through, power would be concentrated most effectively in the hands of the state.

In defending its right to self-regulation, the legal profession faced an uphill struggle, for whilst self-regulation is clearly to the advantage of the profession which enjoys this privilege, the advantages for those outside the profession, and in particular the clients who wish to be assured of protection from malpractice, are less obvious. If the lawyers' desire for continued self-regulation were to gain support outside the confines of the legal profession, it had to be seen to be effective. Clearly, for the independent observer, the efficacy of the disciplinary system is one

---

45. *The Times*, 26 January 1989.
46. *The Times*, 17 March 1989.
47. R.L. Abel, *The Legal Profession in England and Wales*, Basil Blackwell (1988), at 29.

means by which a judgment can be made of whether the profession deserves to keep this particular privilege, together with the status it bestows. Richard Abel comments that the ultimate test of such a system of social control 'is the extent to which it punishes those who have committed offences. By this criterion, barrister discipline is highly suspect'.[48] He goes on to point out that in the years between 1968 and 1985 less than one-quarter of all complaints against barristers went to a formal hearing. Further, in the small number of cases that did receive a formal hearing, very few barristers were punished. In the period under examination, only 3 per cent of complaints led to disbarment and only 1 per cent resulted in suspension.[49] An examination of the record of solicitors' attempts at self-regulation does not reflect any better on the profession's efforts to discipline its members. While surveys have shown quite a high level of satisfaction with solicitors, given the large numbers of practitioners, even a small level of dissatisfaction would involve many thousands of grievances.[50] More importantly, only 2 per cent of those who are dissatisfied with the service they receive complain to the Law Society.[51] The system has come in for a lot of criticism because the concerns of complainants are so different from those for which the Law Society is prepared to take action; consequently, most lay complaints are rejected. It does not instil confidence in the effectiveness of the system. Even the Law Society has had to acknowledge that there are problems in this area, and it has implemented some reforms, including the setting-up in 1986 of the Solicitors Complaints Bureau as a separate body. However, as the Green Paper made clear,[52] the disciplinary machinery of the solicitors' profession is a source of continuing concern, and it is not at all clear that the reforms which have been undertaken are sufficient to persuade either the government or the public that the profession can effectively police its members, and thus legitimately claim that self-regulation is not just a matter of self-interest.

As Lord Mackay pondered over the reaction to his proposals, he must have felt a little beleaguered. *The Guardian* commented:

Lord Mackay must have found his working life rather lonely in the last few months. The judges, who he needs to be in contact with daily over court administration and appointments, have turned into an alien force. The Bar is even more glacial. And as a final throw, Sir Patrick Mayhew, his closest professional colleague in government, has threatened to resign as Attorney General unless the Lord Chancellor drops his plan to give solicitors full rights of audience in the higher courts.[53]

---

48. Ibid., at 135.
49. Ibid., Table 1.46b.
50. Ibid., at 251.
51. Ibid., at 251.
52. *Supra*, n.13, paras 4.16–4.29.
53. *The Guardian*, 'Comment', 30 June 1989.

It was the last issue, the end of the Bar's monopoly of rights of advocacy in the higher courts, which proved to be the other issue which grabbed the headlines and provided another major focus for the debate.

Rallying to the flag — rights of advocacy

If the profession as a whole faced an uphill struggle in defending its right to self-regulation, then barristers faced an even greater challenge in defending their monopoly of rights of audience in the higher courts. The proposals contained in the Green Paper which would effectively end the Bar's monopoly of advocacy rights in the higher courts were those which suggested that, in future, rights of audience should depend not on whether a lawyer happened initially to qualify as a barrister or a solicitor, but solely on whether they had gained one of the proposed advocacy certificates and were bound by the relevant code of conduct.[54] The Green Paper made it abundantly clear that 'the present distinctions in the treatment by courts of the different branches of the profession would disappear.'[55]

For the two branches of the legal profession, this issue lies at the heart of their differences. It is not a new problem; in 1833, when Lord Lyndhurst was opposing a bill attempting to introduce a system of county courts, he remarked that he had

> found [the] fees to be so low, that none but very needy attorneys would work for them. The effects of the Bill, therefore, would be to place within the lower departments of the profession a set of men on whose honour and integrity you could place no reliance; you would have them promoting chicanery and encouraging litigation, for no other object than to recompense themselves by the multitude for the small amount of their fees; and thus you would degrade the legal profession from its highest member to the lowest, by involving judges, barristers and attornies in one common poverty and ruin.[56]

The arguments put forward by the Bar in more recent times may be more subtle, but the strident tone used by Lord Lyndhurst is never far below the surface. In the Marre Report[57] the views of the General Council of the Bar on this topic were set out in detail;[58] they canvassed a wide variety of altruistic reasons for the retention of the status quo, from the superior ability of members of the Bar to discharge their duty to the court because they do not have a close relationship to the client, to the suggestion that it is to the client's advantage to have two lawyers with different skills and experience when there is a need to discuss tactical

---

54. *Supra*, n.13, paras 5.7 and 5.8.
55. *Supra*, n.13, para. 5.8.
56. Hansard 3rd Series, HL, Vol. XVIII, col. 881, 17 June 1833.
57. *Supra*, n.9, Ch. 18.
58. Ibid., para. 18.24.

questions or settlement proposals. Yet even among these worthy reasons, others, perhaps less altruistic, were also put forward as being of equal importance: 'If extended rights of audience were granted to solicitors, young barristers could not make a living;' 'any extension of the rights of audience of solicitors would undermine the Bar'.[59] At the heart of all their concern lies the frightening possibility, stated in stark terms by the Bar itself in the Marre Report, that 'if solicitors had rights of audience [in the higher courts] the client would inevitably be represented by an advocate in the solicitor's firm'.[60]

Perhaps because they were aware that the Bar was only too vulnerable to accusations of self-interest, the Bar's leaders placed considerable emphasis, in their campaign against the Lord Chancellor's proposals, on the benefits to the public of the retention of a separate Bar. From the beginning, a central part of their strategy was an appeal to members of the public, 'who have benefited from the Bar's services, believe it works well and can speak from their knowledge in its support'.[61] However, the insistence by the leaders of the Bar that the defence of the advocacy monopoly was undertaken because it was in the public interest (rather than a matter of self-interest) was to lose them much-needed support for their opposition to the government's proposals: 'The Bar Council's starting point is that the public will best be served by continuance of the independent barristers' and solicitors' professions with their separate and specialised functions.'[62] 'We feel strongly that the voice of the high street solicitor has not been heard so far in the debate. It is the general public, who rely on high street solicitors for access to the skills of the Bar, who will suffer.'[63] It appeared patronizing and supercilious, and tended to arouse resentment in those very members of the public whose interests the Bar apparently had at heart. Letters to *The Times* revealed that some members of the public were not impressed with the Bar's attitude:

I have noted the tendency of members of the legal profession to invoke the interests of the consumer when arguing in defence of their own. They thereby strain the consumer's credulity and do themselves a disservice. There is really no need for them to try to disguise the fact that they are defending their own corner. I for one see nothing shameful in that and would be surprised if they did otherwise. That is the honest and straightforward approach. On the other hand, when they seek to identify my interests with theirs I begin to feel uneasy. In less polite language, I small a rat.[64]

---

59. Ibid.
60. Ibid.
61. *The Times*, 30 January 1989.
62. *Supra*, n.25, para. 2.2.
63. Desmond Fennell QC, Chairman of the Bar Council, reported in *The Times*, 6 March 1989.
64. Sir John Leahy, *The Times*, 'Letters', 4 March 1989.

It was unfortunate that the attitude of those members of the Bar who represented their profession during this time, when they wished to gain public sympathy for their position, managed to alienate many of the very people whom they wished to impress. It also meant that such altruistic arguments as the Bar was able to rely on were effectively lost because they were subsumed in those arguments which were based on self-interest.

Predictably, the Bar was not alone in defending its monopoly of advocacy rights in the higher courts. Those erstwhile members of the profession, the judges, also favoured the retention of the status quo: 'There are advantages in the present system which derive mainly from the distinct functions of the preparation and presentation of cases being in separate professional hands.'[65] However, for the judges it was not just an attachment to tradition. They regarded the Green Paper's proposal that it should be the Lord Chancellor who was the final arbiter of who could appear in which court[66] as another grave constitutional threat:

> Until now, no Government Minister has had, and no Government has sought power to exercise ultimate control of the profession of advocacy in the courts. Once such power is given, the risk that it may be misused by some future Government cannot be ignored.[67]

Clearly, the risk of an unacceptable abuse of power should not be disregarded, but in extending their constitutional concerns to encompass the existence of an independent Bar, the judiciary could all too easily be seen as merely defending their cousins at the Bar.

The final frontier – the White Paper and the Courts and Legal Services Bill

As far as 'Thatcherite' economics were concerned, the White Paper which followed the furious debate, which was entitled 'Legal Services: A Framework For The Future',[68] was to prove far less controversial than the Green Paper — not because its content *was* less controversial, but because its tone was much less strident. Gone were the insistent references to competition and the discipline of the market. The White Paper appeared, on first glance, to have different concerns. Its references were to 'access to justice' and the provision of 'legal services to meet clients' needs'.[69]

The apparent difference in the approach of the two documents was reflected in the statements made about their overall objectives. The

---

65. *Supra*, n.34, at 3–4.
66. *Supra*, n.13, para. 5.13.
67. *Supra*, n.34, at 1.
68. Cm 740.
69. Ibid., paras 2.3 and 2.4.

Green Paper's objectives were said to be to ensure that the public had the best possible access to legal services of the right quality and for any particular legal need. It stated that the best way of achieving this aim was not only to ensure that the services were supplied by persons having expertise in the relevant area, but also to ensure that 'a market providing legal services operates freely and efficiently so as to give clients the widest possible choice of cost effective services.'[70] The White Paper, in stating its overall objectives, emphasized the need to lay down standards of education and training to ensure that those who provide legal services are competent to do so, but equally important was the need to lay down standards in the conduct of advocacy and litigation, 'which are required in the interests of the proper and efficient administration of justice.'[71] Surely this was a White Paper which had taken on board the criticisms about justice not being a consumer durable and the unsuitability of market forces being applied to legal services? Certainly the perception of some members of the Bar was that the Lord Chancellor was beating a hasty retreat from the application of 'Thatcherite' economics to the work of the legal profession. The Chairman of the Public Accounts Committee of the Bar wrote:

> Our major concern in all this was not our own interests, but the interests of justice — i.e. that the courts and tribunals should come to the right decision with people being properly and well represented . . . When the White Paper was published, that concern about the interests of justice was duly recognised. The objectives were expressly stated in paragraph 2.3 to be competence, maintenance of standards and conduct, and thirdly the removal of unnecessary obstacles, but there was the vital addition of the proper and efficient administration of justice and the interests of justice, so that the interest of the person being judged at law and by the law was predominant.[72]

It was not surprising that members of the Bar took heart after the publication of the White Paper; they were certainly encouraged to do so by the media, who soon pounced on what they believed to be a softer attitude on the part of the government. *The Guardian*'s report of the matter was typical. Under the headline 'Mackay takes softer line on law reform', the paper's legal correspondent wrote: 'The changes . . . are noticeably less radical than the shake-up outlined in the original Green Paper.'[73] The Bar was not alone in its belief that Lord Mackay was retreating from his original proposals; 'Solicitors', screamed the headlines, were also 'angry at Mackay retreat'[74] and the President of the Law Society was said to be 'alarmed' at the apparent inability of Lord Mackay to push his proposals through in the face of all the opposition from the Bar and the judiciary.

---

70. *Supra*, n.13, para. 1.1.
71. *Supra*, n.68, para. 2.3.
72. *The Times*, 'Letters', 12 December, 1989.
73. *The Guardian*, 20 July 1989.
74. *The Guardian*, 30 June 1989.

Certainly, references to 'the interests of justice' imbued the White Paper with a very different tone from the Green Paper, but it was perhaps a little optimistic of the Bar to assume that those references amounted to a fundamental change of heart. Immediately following those heartwarming references to justice, the White Paper continued: 'The statute will make it clear that the framework it will create has the express purpose of ensuring the development of fresh ways of providing legal services . . . and of ensuring that clients have a wider choice of providers of such legal services.'[75] Surely such statements should have sounded a warning bell in the ears of those who hoped that the government had executed a U-turn?

If the measured tones of the White Paper had lulled the Bar into thinking that the government had retreated from its intention to introduce market forces to the provision of legal services, then the Courts and Legal Services Bill[76] left the Bar in no doubt that market forces were still at the forefront of the government's mind. Clause 14 of the Bill sets out the statutory objective of the legislation, which is said to be 'the development of legal services in England and Wales . . . by making provision for new ways of providing such services and a wider choice of persons providing them.'[77] Gone are the comforting references to justice, which the Bar had hoped would prevent the implementation of the most radical reforms, and we are returned, quietly but insistently, to the world of free markets and competition between actors on the economic stage. As *The Times* Legal Correspondent commented, 'Although the White Paper's aim was to widen the consumer's choice of lawyer, the Bar drew comfort from its insistence that changes should be made only in the "interests of justice", believing this radical reform could be shown to damage these interests. What now emerges, in undoubtedly the most controversial part of the Bill, is that a statutory objective of greater public choice is to be overriding.'[78] Faced with this new statutory objective, it seems that there is little comfort for the Bar here; no reassuring references to 'the interests of justice' remain to encourage a belief that change, is not, after all, on the way. We have returned to the principles, if not the hectoring tone, of the Green Paper. The cold winds of competition will blow through the Temple and Lincoln's Inn.

However, if competitive forces remained to chill the hearts of many lawyers up and down the country, the legal profession as a whole could breathe a sigh of relief in relation to the issue of self-regulation. This jealously guarded privilege was to suffer a glancing blow at the hands of the White Paper, but not the body-blow that had been feared, and this

---

75. *Supra*, n.68, para. 2.4.
76. The version referred to is the original HL Bill ordered to be printed 6 December 1989.
77. HL Bill 13, cl. 14.1.
78. *The Times*, 14 December 1989.

state of affairs was to continue with the publication of the Courts and Legal Services Bill.

The Lord Chancellor's Advisory Committee on Education and Conduct would still exist, and it would still retain its lay majority,[79] but it was not to be the fearsome body whose appearance had caused so much consternation when the Green Paper was debated. Its role, in all the areas which fall within its jurisdiction, is purely advisory.[80] It appears that the government has acknowledged the force of the criticisms which were made of the original conception of the Advisory Committee and has drawn the teeth of its 'monster'. The constitutional arguments put forward with such vehemence by the judiciary have been heeded and the new Committee will not destroy the profession's right of self-regulation.

However, the Committee still retains the ability to 'give advice to the General Council of the Bar, the Law Society and other authorised bodies on all aspects of their qualification regulations and rules of conduct, whether or not relating to advocacy or the conduct of litigation',[81] and those bodies 'shall have regard to it to the extent that it applies in relation to matters connected with advocacy or the conduct of litigation'.[82] Despite this duty, the Committee's role is clearly that of advisor, making suggestions to the professional bodies, who have a central role.

Not that the legal profession emerges entirely unscathed, since it does not retain complete control over matters of training and conduct. Both the White Paper and the Bill adopted the same pattern for dealing with the regulation of the profession. As far as solicitors and barristers are concerned, the rules of conduct and regulations for education and training which presently exist will continue to apply. Only if provision is required for new areas of work will these bodies have to comply with the new arrangements laid down for all professional bodies which wish to grant advocacy rights or rights to conduct litigation to their members. These new arrangements require that draft rules are referred to the Lord Chancellor's Advisory Committee, which will then pass them on, together with its comments, to the Lord Chancellor and 'designated judges'.[83] The new rules will not become effective until they have gained the approval of the Lord Chancellor and the designated judges, although if any of them refuse their approval, the Lord Chancellor must specify who refused and the reason given for refusal,[84] so that the decision can be challenged in the courts by way of judicial review. Reliance on judicial review as a means of curbing any tendency on the part of the

---

79. HL Bill 13, cl. 16.
80. Ibid., Sch. 2.
81. Ibid., Sch. 2, para. 5(3).
82. Ibid., Sch. 2, para. 5(4).
83. 'Designated judges' are the Lord Chief Justice, Master of the Rolls, President of the Family Division and Vice-Chancellor — HL Bill 13, cl. 8.
84. HL Bill 13, Sch. 4, Part 11.

judges to favour the status quo might be thought to be one of the most significant features of the new arrangements, revealing the extent of the Lord Chancellor's desire to placate the other members of the judiciary. It would have been possible to provide a special remedy for those who were dissatisfied by the refusal of approval for new rules of conduct, but instead there is only provision for a reasoned decision which can be challenged by judicial review. The inadequacies of judicial review as a means of curbing abuse of power have been well documented and the Bill's reliance on this remedy is significant.

If Lord Mackay can be accused of giving in to the judges on the regulation of the profession, he appears at first sight to have taken a much firmer stand on rights of audience. Both the White Paper and the Bill make it abundantly clear that the judges have lost their absolute power to decide who may appear before them in the courts: 'The Government considers that it is for the professional bodies ... to satisfy the courts and the public that their members can meet the high standards of competence and conduct required for rights of audience.'[85] In the Bill, we find alongside the statutory objective, the following 'general principle':

As a general principle, the question whether a person should be granted a right of audience, or be granted the right to conduct litigation, should be determined only by reference to — a) whether he is qualified ... and b) whether he is a member of a professional ... body.[86]

It appears at first sight that Lord Mackay is determined to ensure that the Bar's monopoly of advocacy rights in the higher courts is done away with. The Bill appears to state in emphatic terms that any lawyer will be able to appear in any court, provided that he/she is qualified to do so. On consideration, however, the Bill may not be as radical as many solicitors had hoped that it would be. Barristers will have rights of audience in all courts; only if the Bar wishes to work in additional areas will they need to gain the approval of the Lord Chancellor and 'designated Judges'[87] (the Lord Chief Justice, the Master of the Rolls, the Vice-Chancellor and the President of the Family Division).[88] The same conditions are then applied to solicitors, and there lies the rub; solicitors' existing rights of audience are preserved, but any changes, including extended rights of audience, will have to be approved by the Lord Chancellor and the designated judges.[89]

It is the process by which approval for change is to be gained which has caused concern, and in particular the need to gain the concurrence of the four senior judges. Concern increased dramatically after one of

---

85. *Supra*, n.68, para. 3.9.
86. HL Bill 13, cl. 14.3.
87. HL Bill 13, cl. 81.
88. HL Bill 13, 24, 28, 26.3 and Sch. 4, Part 11.
89. HL Bill 13, 24, 29, 26.3 and Sch. 4, Part 11.

those judges, Lord Donaldson, made a speech to the Bar Council, stating his belief that the interests of justice might require that certain types of case were conducted by full-time advocates. Lord Donaldson is reported as having drawn a distinction between those cases with a direct public interest in the outcome, such as crime, cases involving children and judicial review of the decisions of public bodies, and all other cases, where the public interest lies solely in securing an adequate system of justice. In the first type of case, 'the interests of justice may demand special requirements, such as, for example, that the preparation and presentation of the case be in separate hands.'[90] As Lord Donaldson went on to point out, his suggestion does not necessarily mean that one pair of hands must belong to a barrister and another pair to a solicitor, but given their present patterns of work, many solicitors feel that Lord Donaldson was implying that the preservation of the status quo would be in order. Solicitors were also quick to note that the designated judges include not only Lord Donaldson, but also the Lord Chief Justice, Lord Lane, the judge who described the Green Paper as 'one of the most sinister documents ever to emanate from government'.[91] Those who hoped for radical changes in the legal profession might reasonably be thought to have some cause for concern at the amount of influence these two fierce opponents of reform now possess.

In giving the senior judges a major role to play in the granting of rights of audience, Lord Mackay was clearly attempting a compromise between the initial hard-line proposals in the Green Paper, which would have left the ultimate decisions about rights of audience solely within the responsibility of the Lord Chancellor,[92] and the judges' desire to maintain the status quo,[93] whereby the judiciary decided which lawyers they would permit to appear in which courts. Lord Donaldson's speech undermined any notion that Lord Mackay had managed to stick to his guns in the face of fierce opposition from the combined forces of the Bar and the judiciary. Solicitors felt that the Lord Chancellor had bowed to the pressure exerted by his judicial brothers, and had given them a veto over the exercise of advocacy rights, which some judges, at least, were prepared to use to ensure that solicitors are effectively kept out of the higher courts. Given that the Bill envisages that the approval of all four designated judges will be necessary before changes can be implemented,[94] it will only take one judge to sabotage reform. Of course, the Bill provides that if the Lord Chancellor or any one of the designated judges refuses to approve a proposal, then the Lord Chancellor must, if asked to do so in writing, specify 'who refused and the reason

---

90. *The Guardian*, 2 October 1989.
91. *Supra*, n.41.
92. *Supra*, n.13, paras 4.11–4.13.
93. *Supra*, n.24, para. 46.
94. HL Bill 13, Sch. 4, Part 11, para. 11(7).

given for refusing'.[95] The question then must be how onerous a burden the giving of reasons will prove to be. Is it a reason to state merely that 'the interests of justice require it', or will their Lordships have to go on and explain *why* the interests of justice require that a proposal should be turned down? If the duty consists of the former approach, then the Bar and the judiciary really have won this particular battle, and solicitors are right to feel pessimistic about the prospects for real reform of their rights of audience.

It will be open to the Law Society, if it is dissatisfied with any reasons given by the senior judges as part of the process of approval, to challenge those reasons by way of judicial review. The process of judicial review will then involve judges reviewing reasons given by other judges. Will they be more liberal in their interpretation of what amounts to a 'reason' than they would be if the decision-maker were not a judge? It is possible that some of the litigation will go as far as the House of Lords; the House of Lords will then be reviewing the reasons given by judges lower down the judicial hierarchy; will we then see who really are the senior judges? Perhaps we should also acknowledge the role politics has to play in this area; as *The Financial Times* commented:

In debating the issues and trying to predict the outcome, the one factor that seems to have been underestimated is the part politics has to play in the implementation of reform. If the whispers are to be believed, it may yet have the last word.[96]

The aftermath — facing the future

As the battle draws to a close and the legal profession faces an uncertain future, is it likely to entail the end of civilization as they know it? Undoubtedly there will be changes; already the Bar has realized that if it is to compete effectively with solicitors for bright young graduates, it will have to make alterations to the system of pupillage.[97] Pupils may stand a greater chance of being paid, but will the profession which they seek to join really be very different from the one which existed before the Green Papers were published. The answer to that question largely depends on the effectiveness with which the designated judges wield their veto over advocacy rights. If solicitors can act as advocates in the higher courts, then major change appears inevitable. Already there are signs that City solicitors would like to set up their own advocacy service. A spokesman for Herbert Smith told *The Lawyer* magazine that

Obviously, we shall continue to use counsel, but the immediate change I foresee will be a speeding-up of the current tendency for junior counsel work to be dealt

---

95. HL Bill 13, Sch. 4, Part 11, para. 11(8).
96. *The Financial Times*, 27 June 1989.
97. 'Changing Face of the Bar', *The Times*, 25 January 1989.

with by solicitors . . . We believe that young people joining the profession will want to become advocates . . . and we intend to give them that opportunity . . . We shall begin advocacy training courses next year.[98]

If the big City firms hold back work from junior counsel and give it to their own staff, many young lawyers will think more than twice about whether it is worth taking all the risks which a career at the Bar entails. For all the Bar's protestations, there is still no guarantee that a pupil will be paid; pupils still have to rely on a mixture of grants, pupillage awards and loan schemes.[99] If solicitors' firms are able to offer interesting advocacy work, together with a regular income, many will reject the option of risky self-employment at the Bar. It is not only those who are at the beginning of their career who may decide to forego the pleasures of life at the Bar, as the well-publicized departure of a senior tax barrister to a large firm of accountants has revealed.[100]

However, neither of these changes could be regarded as heralding the end of legal civilization as we now know it. Of all the possible changes which the legal profession faces as a result of Lord Mackay's onslaught, it is the Bar's loss of its monopoly of advocacy in the higher courts which could, at least for the Bar and the judiciary, signal the end of life in its current form. A crucial factor in the future development of the legal profession will be the decisions made by those four designated judges; they are likely to find themselves at the centre of whatever controversy lies ahead and, like it or not, they will probably be catapulted out of their current civilized obscurity into the rough and tumble of legal politics, as the two branches of the legal profession continue their battle.

The centrality of the judges in all this is something which would have come as little surprise to that hard-line legal realist, Karl Llewellyn. Reviewing Campbell's *Cases on Mortgages of Real Property* in the Harvard Law Review in 1926, Llewellyn wrote:

The reviewer holds that the time has passed when the study of law could profitably be centred on legal doctrine. At the present juncture, the only serviceable focus of law study is law in action; law in action not only in the sense of . . . what the courts and all quasi-judicial bodies actually do; but also [in the sense of] the actual ordering of men's actions.[101]

As we survey the battlefield on which the legal profession is engaged in fighting for its future, it is this dimension, the actual ordering of men's actions and in particular the actions of those four judges, which is likely to take our attention for some time to come and to prove the decisive factor in deciding whether or not Lord Mackay has presided over the end of legal civilization as we know it.

---

98. *The Lawyer*, October 1989.
99. *Supra*, n.97.
100. *The Lawyer*, 3 October 1989.
101. (1926) 40 Harv. LR 142, at 144.

13 'And that man dying'

Tony Bradney

Introduction

According to a myth that is rapidly developing a significant body of believers, the Critical Legal Studies movement has 'undermined the central ideas of modern legal thought and put another conception of law in their place'.[1] Rejecting the idea that legal argument is a discrete enterprise, carried through by means of technical tools of legal analysis, the Critical Legal Studies movement has shown, it is said, that legal argument, even in the most arcane reaches of the law, is political argument.[2]

Myths are, of course, things that are true. They are also things that are not true simply as narratives. The most interesting aspects of their truth do not lie in a superficial analysis of the literal veracity of their content.[3] This chapter will argue that one of the more illuminating features of the progress of the Critical Legal Studies movement is not the question of whether or not it can be said to have undermined previous legal thought, but rather, what the nature of some of the arguments advanced for such a contention says about the general level of understanding of previous legal thought. What is revealed, it will be argued, adds strength to the view expressed by Geoffrey Wilson:

---

1. R. Unger, 'The Critical Legal Studies Movement' (1983) 96 Harv. L Rev. 561 at 561. Identifying what is, and what is not, a piece of work within the Critical Legal Studies genre is a hazardous task. Even more difficult is accurately representing complex and ambiguous arguments in a short chapter (see n.6 below). Whilst I hope not to have misrepresented anyone, this chapter, like any other academic or intellectual production, is primarily intended to set out what I, as author, think. In this context, when referring to and discussing the work of others, I am conscious of the strength of Italo Calvino's comment that 'everyone mines every book for the things that are useful to him' (I. Calvino, *The Uses of Literature* (1986) at 50).
2. Unger, *supra*, n.1 at 602–48.
3. C. Levi-Strauss, *Structural Anthropology* Penguin (1977) Ch. XI.

The words 'English legal scholarship' though high sounding have a similar function to the words 'disposable paper cup'. Each adjective strengthens the message that one can not expect much in terms of quality or long-term utility from it.[4]

Finally it will be argued that consideration of the Critical Legal Studies movement and that which preceded it suggests that in both there is an obeisance to authority which is inimical both to scholarship and the pursuit of knowledge which frustrates an understanding of the subject of this volume, flux in law.

Critical Legal Studies

Advancing the merits of a theoretical position involves two simultaneous processes. First, something must be said about the content of the position being advanced. Second, perhaps implicitly, something must be said about an absence in content in previous theoretical positions. Critical Legal Studies undermines previous positions, if it does, both by virtue of what it says and by virtue of what was not said before.

Whilst the Critical Legal Studies genre is broad, one important strand of argument within it directly concerns the status of technical tools of legal analysis. In essence this strand can be stated quite straightforwardly:

> In sum, *stare decisis*, while integral to the language of legal discourse and the mystique of legal reasoning, serves a primarily ideological rather than functional role. Nor is there any more validity to the notion of legal reasoning when the source of law is a statutory or constitutional provision or the language of an agreement. Courts determine the meaning and applicability of the pertinent language; similar arguments and distinctions are available; and the ultimate basis is a social and political judgment. Indeed, even the facts relevant to a particular controversy (largely reduced to uncontroversial givens in law schools) are not capable of determination by any distinctly legal or nonpolitical methodology. Law is simply politics by other means.[5]

The use of any particular formulation of an argument generally used amongst a group of scholars is often unfair to other scholars in that group. Those adhering to the tenets of the Critical Legal Studies movement are no more in agreement than any other group with the details of the position they uphold.[6] However the general tenor of the quotation

---

4. G. Wilson, *English Legal Scholarship* (1987) 50 MLR 818 at 819.
5. D. Kairys, 'Legal Reasoning', in D. Kairys (ed.) *The Politics of Law: A Progressive Critique*, Pantheon (1982) at 16–17.
6. Arguably, it is more difficult to state adequately a Critical Legal Studies 'position' by relation to just one comment than in the case of other legal theories. Adherents of the movement have noted its constant attention to contradiction (for example, Mark Kelman has written, '[w]hat strikes me as most distinctive about Critical Legal Studies ... is its focus on ambiguity, its resolute refusal to see a synthesis in every set of contradictions' (M. Kelman, 'Trashing' (1984) 36 Stan. L Rev. 293 at 296)). Critics, even relatively friendly critics, have seen this 'refusal to see a synthesis' as a lack of coherence in conceptual analysis. In answer to the question, 'does critical legal theory achieve new,

above will serve as an illustration of the view taken, within the Critical Legal Studies movement, of what would traditionally be regarded as formal legal reasoning.

Several features of the position above are important. First, *stare decisis* and statutory interpretation are taken seriously:

> It is true that there is a distinctive lawyers' body of knowledge of the rules in force. It is true that there are distinctive lawyers' argumentative techniques for spotting gaps, conflicts, and ambiguities in the rules, for arguing broad and narrow holdings of cases, and for generating pro and con policy arguments.[7]

There is no attempt to suggest that these matters are simply a veil which mask the features of law which are important for scholarship, professional training or whatever other task is set. On the contrary great weight is placed on the importance of such techniques. However, the material is not seen as being important in the manner it would indicate itself, but rather, in other ways:

> ... we would stress that the law is open to numerous different readings and thus that the entire tradition of western law can plausibly be seen as a complex amalgamation of religious, political, economic and ethical discourses concerned precisely to provide models for contemporary social relations. If such is accepted to be the case, then time and again legal judgement and the rhetoric of legal reasoning hides the complex economic, political and ethical choices that the judiciary are inevitably making in their decisions as to how to apply the law.[8]

Whilst in its own terms formal legal reasoning is seen as a neutral means of analysing and formulating legal propositions, the Critical Legal Studies movement sees it as being subservient to wider forms of discourse. Formal legal reasoning is seen as a form of rhetoric rather than as being analogous to syllogistic logic.[9] To say this is not to detract from the seriousness with which formal legal reasoning is treated. Rhetoric need not be mere rhetoric.[10] It is persuasive speech but not

---

imaginative and liberating theoretical synthesis or is its work marred by a jumbled, incoherent eclecticism?', Alan Hunt's answer appears to be yes and yes (A. Hunt, 'The Theory of Critical Legal Studies' (1986) 6 OJLS 1). This is not to say that there are no coherent theories advanced within the Critical Legal Studies movement (see, for example, a sketch of 'A constitutive theory of law' in K. Klare 'Law Making as Praxis' (1979) 40 *Telos* 123), but these theories do not seem to play, at least as yet, a central role in the Critical Legal Studies movement. This makes abstracting a 'position' difficult, if not impossible.

7. D. Kennedy, 'Legal Education as Training for Hierarchy' in Kairys (ed.) *supra*, n.5 at 47.
8. P. Goodrich, *Reading the Law*, Blackwell (1986) at 87.
9. Legal reasoning is sometimes treated as rhetoric in the ordinary sense of the word (see, for example, Kelman *supra*, n.6 at 320-6), and sometimes in a technical sense (see, for example, W. Murphy and R. Rawlings, 'After the *Ancien Régime*' (1982) 45 MLR 34 at 58; and P. Goodrich, 'Rhetoric as Jurisprudence: An Introduction to the Politics of Legal Language' (1984) 4 OJLS 88).
10. See T. Campbell, 'Realizing Human Rights' in T. Campbell et al. (eds) *Human Rights: From Rhetoric to Reality*, Blackwell (1986) at 1-2.

necessarily cant. On the other hand, in order to accept that a form of speech is highly organized and effective, one does not have to accept that it works in the way in which it claims to work.

If one takes seriously formal legal reasoning, but does not accept it on its own terms, the challenge is then to react to it. In the case of Critical Legal Studies this is done by an attempt 'to describe — to make maps of — some of these interlocking systems of belief [that constitute the law]'[11] and thus, 'to delegitimate legal process by documenting the incoherence of legal doctrine'.[12] Munger and Seron have identified three different strands of work within this attempt.[13] The strand which is most exemplary of the Critical Legal Studies genre is that which Munger and Seron characterize as 'the nihilistic strand'. In this, doctrine is examined in isolation; its incoherence and contradictions demonstrated merely by reference to the legal texts themselves. In the strand which Munger and Seron describe as 'totalistic', the connections between legal reasoning and the structures of consciousness within society are traced. This strand seeks to connect analysis of legal doctrine with the wider presence of structures such as capitalism or class in the analysis of the political economy. Finally, there is the strand that tries to bring together doctrinal evidence and theoretical propositions about the relationship between 'historically situated social relations and legal ideology'.[14] Whilst these different strands offer various explanations of the importance of legal doctrine they are at one in dwelling on the importance of legal doctrine as opposed to law.

What Critical Legal Studies offers then is a new concern with legal doctrine; a concern which seeks to put the analysis of doctrine in a new light.

The traditional stance

What difference is there between Critical Legal Studies and the work of those concerned to provide a theoretical background to, and statement of principle for, the traditional notions of formal legal reasoning? At first glance the answer seems to be that the gulf is wide.

Work within the Critical Legal Studies genre emphasizes the openness of the legal text. Traditional formulations appear to do the converse. At the beginning of his 'Preliminary Statement', in his book on precedent, Rupert Cross notes that '[t]he peculiar feature of the English doctrine of precedent is its strongly coercive nature'.[15] In his book on statutory

---

11. R. Cross, *Precedent in English Law*, Clarendon Press (3rd edn, 1977) at 4.
12. R. Gordon, 'New Developments in Legal Theory' in Kairys (ed.) *supra*, n.5 at 287.
13. F. Munger and C. Seron, 'Critical Legal Studies versus Critical Legal Method' (1984) 6 *Law and Policy* 257 at 262.
14. Ibid., at 263-9.
15. Ibid., at 266.

interpretation the same writer observes that '[c]ourts spend more of their time applying words of undisputed meaning to facts which have been disputed than in interpreting statutory words of disputed meaning'.[16] Explaining the rationale for what he perceived as the determinant nature of precedent in English law, A.L. Goodhart wrote: '[i]t is as desirable to determine definitely the law of crimes and of torts as it is to establish the law of property or of contracts'.[17] The emphasis in such works appears to be on the concrete nature of legal doctrine.

For those who rest their work on the foundation of writers like Goodhart or Cross, the conceptual emphasis is also on the clarity of law. Text writers rarely note their theoretical presuppositions before commencing their work (perhaps not recognizing that they have any), but when they do there seems to be a belief in the internal logic of the law, for example: 'In the main, the English law of real property rests on the logical development of clear principles, and it is these principles that throughout we have sought to emphasise'.[18]

Most pages of most texts are lists of legal rules, together with appropriate authorities. For the authors, the clarity of the law seems to be apparent at a superficial level. The majority of cases are merely referred to for the rule for which they are thought to be authority. No lengthy consideration of the argument in the judgments is necessary. The case is authority and for what it is authority is obvious — an approach far removed from Critical Legal Studies.

At this point it seems that we have both what is novel in the approach of Critical Legal Studies (the analysis of legal doctrine in terms other than its own) and what is missing in traditional theories of legal doctrine (the failure to appreciate the formlessness of legal argument). However, halting the characterization of traditional theories of legal doctrine at the stage of the paragraphs above would be making two mistakes. First, it

---

16. R. Cross, *Statutory Interpretation*, Butterworths (1976) at 41. In the second (1987) edition of this book, John Bell, with Sir George Engle responsible for editing the work, has substantially amended this part of the text. The passage quoted has been omitted.
17. A.L. Goodhart, *Essays in Jurisprudence and the Common Law* (1972) at 56. As with Critical Legal Studies, it is necessary to emphasize the difficulties of accurately describing a theory by relation to the work of only a few of its adherents. However, the writers cited in this section of this chapter are not casually chosen. This theory of judicial reasoning is the one to which the judiciary themselves subscribe (at least in their public writings). In this respect it is worth recalling that during Alan Paterson's study of the Law Lords, he was told by them that Goodhart and Cross were two of very few academics whom they held in high regard. (A. Paterson, *The Law Lords*, Macmillan (1982) at 14-20.) Paterson cites Lord Wilberforce's question in oral argument in *Morgans* v. *Launchbury*, when counsel read a passage from the *Law Quarterly Review*: 'Is it by any particular authority? By A.L. Goodhart or Professor Cross?' (Paterson, p.19). This may be said to give these writers an authority as purveyors of a tradition that others do not have. That is not to say that their work is any more accurate than others.
18. Re Megarry and H.W.R. Wade, *The Law of Real Property*, Stevens (1966) Preface to the first edition at vii.

would assume that any single statement from a writer would fully capture the width of their theoretical enterprise. Second, it would assume that those who used theories (especially those who used them unconsciously or without attribution) properly understood or represented them.

In describing the process by which one determines whether a judicial pronouncement constitutes part of the *ratio decidendi* of a case or not, Cross, in the course of analysing the importance of the judge (the speaker of the judgment) in this matter, observes that 'it is trite learning that the interpreter has nearly as much to say as the speaker so far as meaning of words is concerned.'[19] Comparisons of the descriptions above of Critical Legal Studies and traditional theories of legal doctrine suggest that such a comment is more redolent of a writer within the Critical Legal Studies genre than a stalwart of the traditional approach to formal legal reasoning. Yet the passage cited is not out of place in Cross's general theory. This can be illustrated by reference to Cross's discussion of the central question in any traditional theory of precedent: '[i]s it possible to do appreciably more than say that propositions of law which a judge appears to consider necessary for his decision are *ratio* and all other legal propositions that emerge from his judgments are *dicta*?'[20] To this Cross answers, '[i]t will be submitted that it is not possible to do appreciably more than this, although some valiant attempts have been made to go further'.[21] Such comments subvert the idea that Cross's theory is a simple antithesis of writers within the Critical Legal Studies genre.

One writer cannot represent a tradition, especially when one turns to the details of that writer's thought. However, the refusal to accept determinancy in *stare decisis* that one finds in Cross is mirrored in the work of Goodhart.

Goodhart offers one of the more minutely detailed (and thus seemingly precise) descriptions of how to abstract the *ratio* from a case. His essay, 'The *ratio decidendi* of a case',[22] covers twenty-six pages and (in Cross's analysis) provides six separate propositions concerning the construction of a *ratio*.[23] Goodhart's thesis rests in large part on the reader's ability to identify the material facts of a case as the judge sees them. Goodhart states that '[i]t is by his choice of the material facts that the judge creates law'.[24] For Goodhart, 'the first and foremost essential step is . . . to determine what were the material facts on which the judge based his conclusion'.[25] His essay provides a series of rules for determining what

---

19. Cross (1977) *supra*, n.11 at 42.
20. Ibid., at 49.
21. Ibid.
22. In Goodhart, op. cit.
23. Cross (1977) *supra*, n.11 at 66-9.
24. Goodhart, *supra*, n.17 at 10.
25. Ibid.

is and what is not a material fact. However, before stating these rules, Goodhart writes of them, 'none can be found which will invariably give us the desired result [the ability to isolate what the judge thinks is a material fact]'.[26] The rules he provides are, in his view, merely 'tentative suggestions', which may be of 'some aid to the student'.[27]

Thus, at its very base, Goodhart's thesis has formlessness built in. The traditional theory of precedent rests on the outside observer's ability to identify a *ratio* and, for Goodhart, there will be some cases where no rule can delineate how this can be done. Nor is this the only point in Goodhart's thesis where formlessness is noted. On the important point (for Goodhart) of distinguishing material from immaterial facts, Goodhart notes that only strong judges identify what the material facts are in a judgment. In the majority of cases the judge states both material and immaterial facts in the judgment and does not distinguish between the two categories.[28] Goodhart offers 'guides' for identifying the two categories in such instances.[29] These 'guides' are just that. They are couched in the language of suggestion, not prescription.[30]

To argue the above is not to argue that the views of writers within the Critical Legal Studies genre and traditional theorists of doctrine replicate one another or are even similar. It is simply to note that what divides the two groups is not, on the one hand, a belief in the indeterminacy of legal doctrine and, on the other hand, a belief that legal doctrine can be reduced to simple logic; to argue that the doctrinal conception is not, as has been suggested, 'of legal regulation as a rigidly scientific and peculiarly rational enterprise in the exegesis of legal texts'.[31]

To make such a simple point, at such length, might seem excessive. When, in a monograph on contract law, Hugh Collins wrote that 'classical contract law appears as a mass of technical rules,' and that

---

26. Ibid., at 10-11.
27. Ibid., at 11. Goodhart's view of the potential use of his thesis is similar to Cross's observation that although a formula for determining a *ratio* cannot be found, 'a tolerably accurate description' of the lawyer's use of the term can be given (Cross (1977) *supra*, n.11 at 76).
28. Goodhart, *supra*, n.17 at 15.
29. Ibid.
30. For example, 'in discussing the principle of a case in which there is no opinion, the facts of person, time, place, kind and amount are *presumably* immaterial. This is true to an even greater extent when there is an opinion' (Goodhart *supra*, n.17 at 16); or 'omitted facts are *presumably* held to be immaterial' (Goodhart *supra*, n.17 at 17) (emphasis added).
31. P. Goodrich, 'Law and Modernity' (1986) 49 MLR 545 at 545. Of course the accuracy of the statement quoted depends in part on the weight to be given to the phrases 'rigidly scientific' and 'peculiarly rational' as descriptions of legal doctrine's view of itself. If these should be read as 'more rigidly scientific and peculiarly rational than other systems of communication within society', then the statement takes on more force. As Goodrich suggests, '[t]he faith which the legal community places in the doctrinal ideal of the foundational rationality of law . . . has always been a matter of degree' (Goodrich, ibid. at 546), and he is well aware of Cross's own appreciation of doctrinal limitations in his work. (See P. Goodrich, *Reading the Law* (1986) at 76.)

there was 'no greater error in the history of legal thought than the belief that the technical rules are exhaustive of the standards guiding judicial action and determining the law's content',[32] one reviewer protested that '[n]o writer is named as entertaining this very bizarre idea . . . [T]he picture is, of course, an Aunt Sally, a thing propped up as a target.'[33] In another review of the same book, Francis Reynolds quoted Ronald Dworkin writing that when one searched for 'mechanical jurisprudence', 'All specimens captured . . . have had to be released after careful examination of their texts.'[34] From these comments, one might extrapolate the proposition that nobody has ever believed that doctrinal study would admit of one right answer in all cases or could provide a complete picture of law. Critical Legal Studies provides nothing new in its 'discovery' of the open-ended nature of legal reasoning; it seems that theoreticians of traditional legal reasoning were already well aware of it, as were practitioners of doctrinal study.

Despite the above, does Roger Brownsword's comment that '[b]lack-letterism does, it must be granted, presuppose truth, in the sense that one can come up with the right answer when asked to advise on the legal position'[35] have no descriptive force? Is it not true that for the doctrinal lawyer, the case is all? It would seem difficult to deny this when, for example, J.C. Smith, in one of his books on the law of contract, writes that he seeks 'to elucidate the fundamental principles of the subjects from the authorities'.[36] If the protests of the reviewers of Hugh Collins are to be taken seriously, and at the same time statements like that from J.C. Smith treated as honest reflections of their endeavour, clearly there is a need for a more sophisticated understanding of what adherence to doctrinal theory means. What exactly do academics (and indeed judges) think they do when they purport to practise traditional legal reasoning?

The practice of traditional legal reasoning

The word *ratio* was used by judges in 215 of the 4,125 cases recorded on LEXIS after 1987. The word *obiter* was used in 244 cases in the same period.[37] This information is both trivial and suggestive.

---

32. H. Collins, *The Law of Contract*, Weidenfeld & Nicolson (1986) at 16.
33. T. Weir, 'Book Review of H. Collins: *The Law of Contract*' (1986) 45 CLJ 503 at 504.
34. F. Reynolds, 'Book Review of H. Collins: *The Law of Contract*' (1986) 102 LQR 628 at 633.
35. R. Brownsword, 'Book Review of J. Eekelaar and J. Bell: *Oxford Essays in Jurisprudence*, Clarendon Press (1987), W, Twining: *Legal Theory and Common Law*, Blackwell (1986) and P. Fitzpatrick and A. Hunt: *Critical Legal Studies*', Blackwell (1988) 104 LQR 329 at 334.
36. J.C. Smith, *The Law of Contract* (1989) at v. The Preface of Megarry and Wade's *Law of Real Property* has already been quoted in similar vein (see text accompanying n.18).
37. The details of the search results, together with the actual searches used, are reproduced in the appendix to this chapter.

If traditional theories of legal reasoning accurately reflect the conceptual basis upon which judgments are constructed then, prima facie, in any judgment one would expect detailed discussion of *ratios* which might bind and *obiter* remarks which might persuade. Moreover, one would expect not just discussion of the substance of these matters but also close analysis of whether previous judicial utterances were *ratio* or *obiter* and whether in fact they bound or not. Cross and Goodhart dwell on the difficulties of identifying the *ratio* of a case; of distinguishing it from *obiter* remarks. Thus, when cases are referred to in a judgment, one might expect prolonged consideration of what exactly constitutes the *ratio* in any previous judgment thought relevant and what is merely *obiter*. Equally, as Cross suggests, the hierarchy of precedent is by no means straightforward.[38] Thus, having established what the *ratios* of previous cases were, one might expect to find frequent discussion of whether or not they were *ratios* that bound. Clearly it does not follow from any of this that either the word *ratio* or *obiter* need to be used in a judgment. There are other ways of referring to, and discussing, the legal rule that might be derived from a case. Nevertheless it is surprising, to say the least, that the judiciary themselves so rarely use the words describing the basic conceptual categories of the theory which they say forms the foundation for their work.

Goodrich has written that precedent, in the sense of looking at previous judgments before making the one at hand, is a feature common to all classical and medieval Western legal traditions.[39] What distinguishes the system of precedent currently said to pertain to the United Kingdom is the rigidity with which it is applied. It is the detailed problems and principles which Cross and Goodhart describe which give the system this rigidity. However, from the information derived from the LEXIS database, it seems questionable whether an examination of the minutiae of the principles of precedent form part of the average judgment. The law reports abound with references to previous cases but not with discussion of *stare decisis*.

Assessing the way in which academics use doctrinal theory (even in the rather perfunctory manner of the assessment of judges above) is very difficult. There is too much writing, addressed to too many different audiences, to allow of anything but a few tentative observations.

First, doctrinal lawyers write mainly about the substance of law. This might seem unsurprising. It is the explication of law which they see as their task. However, despite the comment by Megarry and Wade quoted above,[40] most doctrinal lawyers do not believe that they should simply devote themselves to expounding that part of the law which they think is clear. Their work is concerned to query, compare and order conflicting

---

38. Cross (1977) *supra*, n.11 at Ch. III.
39. Goodrich, *Reading the Law* at 127.
40. See text accompanying n.18.

or obscure authorities. But, as has been shown above, their chosen method is not, even on its own terms, without serious problems. Plainly there are pragmatic reasons why one might not wish to postpone discussion of the content of law until all the details of one's theory of interpretation are fully worked out. Nevertheless, this does not fully explain why so little is written about doctrinal theory. There is, of course, far more writing about doctrinal theory than the work of Cross and Goodhart chosen as exemplars in this essay. However, there is far less writing about doctrinal theory than about contract or tort or land law or any other single substantive area. Equally, very few people write about doctrinal theory, and some of those who do are themselves theoreticians rather than practitioners of the art.[41] Doubtless all of this is due in part to the vagaries of what publishers and editors consider worthy of publication. But it might also be in part the result of the degree of seriousness with which doctrinal lawyers treat doctrinal theory. An awareness of the internal problems of doctrinal theory does not become a pressing intellectual problem if, in the examination of substantive law, the doctrinal lawyer uses that theory with the lightest of hands.

A second point that may be pertinent to the description of the doctrinal lawyer's use of doctrinal theory is that, as was shown above, doctrinal theory holds itself out merely as a partial theory. It does not purport to provide either positive or normative explanations for all forms of legal argument.[42] Thus a doctrinal lawyer must necessarily look to some other theory to form the foundation of at least part of their exegesis of the law. Yet where, within the work of most doctrinal lawyers, is this supplementary theory to be found?[43]

When considering the advent of Critical Legal Scholarship, this then might be the significant opposition to be drawn: on the one hand the concentration of Critical Legal Scholarship on the details of judicial reasoning and on the other hand the very broad brush which both judges and doctrinal lawyers bring to the traditional principles from which this reasoning is said to spring. What Critical Legal Scholars are saying about the formlessness of legal reasoning is not as new as the stress that is put on this notion.[44] Cross and Goodhart may, in general terms, be said to

---

41. See, for example, the work of Neil MacCormick.
42. See pp.238–242 above.
43. There are some exceptions. The work of Patrick Atiyah is a good example of sustained attention to both doctrinal theory and other forms of analysis.
44. Hutchinson and Monahan are correct in observing that the Critical Legal Studies analysis of indeterminacy in legal reasoning springs from a larger view of indeterminacy in social relationships generally, and thus they are right to say that '[t]he CLSers' main claim to originality is their refusal to shrink back from the implications of social contingency' (A. Hutchinson and P. Monahan, 'Law, Politics and the Critical Legal Scholars' (1984) 36 Stan. L Rev. 199 at 216). However, the point argued in this chapter is that within the legal community, it is the narrower insistence on legal indeterminacy within this theory which is of importance. From the perspective of the legal community the theoretical basis for this insistence is irrelevant.

have made similar observations to some of the central points being put by authors within the Critical Legal Studies genre but the manner of the writing of Cross and Goodhart did not challenge doctrinal study in the same way.

It is this conclusion which supports Wilson's comment about the low quality and short-term utility of English legal scholarship. Although Robert Goff has argued that the role of the legal academic is to identify legal principles of long-term merit which might not be apparent to a judge concerned only with the short-term interests of the individual litigants in a case,[45] it is precisely this role which doctrinal lawyers seem least well-equipped to fulfil. How, without any overarching theory against which to measure their comments and provide coherence to the invention of their arguments, can the practice of the doctrinal lawyer, described above, be anything more than a series of momentary points of illumination? If such lawyers use doctrinal theory without reference to the details of that theory, supplement that theory with ad hoc references to such disparate and loaded terms as 'commercial convenience' or 'hardship' (to take a random, illustrative example from the first page of the first chapter of a leading text on contract law,[46]) without any attempt to elucidate their understanding of the conceptual background of those terms, that which results will almost necessarily be imprecise and contradictory in form.[47] In such work the explicit or implicit reference to doctrinal theory, which gives an air of intellectual respectability to that which is done, turns out to be specious. Whilst the reference appears to raise the work from the anecdotal and ephemeral, legitimating its claim to be founded on and leading to principle, in fact, as has been shown such work seems to have little connection with theory.

Such points take on greater force the larger the project undertaken. Thus they have an especial force when the topic is one of reform, evolution or change in law.

---

45. 'Judge and jurist, conditioned by their experience, adopt a very different attitude to their work. For the one, the overwhelming influence is the facts of the particular case; for the other it is the idea' (R. Goff, 'The Search for Principle' (1983) *LXIX Proceedings of the British Academy* 169 at 171). See also 183–4. In the same paper Goff also puts forward the antithetical proposition that '[in] the development of legal principles, the dominant power should, I believe, be that of the judge' (p.185).
46. G. Treitel, *The Law of Contract*, Stevens (7th edn, 1987) at 1.
47. Atiyah is of course correct when he writes that 'there can be no practice without theory', and that even those who insist that there is no value in theory are themselves acting on an implicit theory (P. Atiyah *Pragmatism and Theory in English Law*, Stevens (1987) at 143). However, a theory can either be something like measles or something like a guide. Both affect behaviour but it is only the latter which can produce complete harmony between intellect and behaviour. Implicit theory is like measles; the behaviour that results is as arbitrary as involuntary itching. Explicit theory is a self-conscious attempt to achieve a complete understanding of the matter under consideration.

Flux in law

Each different idea of movement in law has its own cadences: its implications, connotations and reverberations requiring investigation. Legal scholarship has come further in recognizing this than the polemics of 'Law Reform Now'[48] or the constant updating of factual information which reaches its apogee in *Halsbury's Laws of England*. Is, for example, law 'reform' inevitably imbued with some vague liberal philosophy of ameliorating the general lot or is it merely a technical term describing the way by which one ideology engineers a social change towards it own arbitrary preferences? Does the concept of evolution in law contain within it merely the idea of change in legal rules or does it imply progress and improvement so that law now is 'better' than law before? Does law change at all or is all law, no matter what the content of the legal rules, '[b]orn of violence and superstition, and established in the interests of the consumer, priest and rich exploiter';[49] the superficial change in detail concealing the real and unchangeable matter of substance? Is it legal rules that change or those who administer them?

There is, of course, the obvious Heraclitian sense in which law changes: that you can never step into the same river twice, that one case, one statute, succeeds another and law is never the same from one moment to the next. However, although law does change thus, merely to portray the shimmer on the stream is a task for a photographer and the photograph merely of nostalgic interest. For those concerned with changes in case law, what has happened is of interest because of inferences which can be made about what will happen. However, as this chapter has argued, to draw those inferences properly demands far more than a chronology of case law or statute. Similarly, to use the socio-legal methods to describe a process of change in law is not enough in itself. As John Baldwin and Michael McConville have noted, such researchers need to be aware that evidence will always fall short of proof,[50] and as Colin Campbell and Paul Wiles have suggested, to make their work complete there always needs to be attention to the necessity for conceptual clarification of the premises for both research and the conclusions to research.[51] Even to make limited suggestions about the advantages of one form for legal rules as opposed to another form is to imply much about the way changing form changes content and application. It is the whether, the how, the why, the when and the to what about law changing

---

48. Lord Gardiner and A. Martin, *Law Reform Now*, Gollancz (1963).
49. P. Kropotkin, 'Law and Authority', in R. Baldwin (ed.) *Kropotkin's Revolutionary Pamphlets* (1970) at 206.
50. J. Baldwin and M. McConville, 'The English Legal Profession and the Politics of Research: A Case Study', in R. Luckham (ed.) *Law and Social Enquiry: Case Studies of Research*, Scandinavian Institute of African Studies (1981) at 153.
51. C. Campbell and P. Wiles, 'The Study of Law in Society in Britain' (1976) 10 *Law and Society Review* 548, particularly at 551-3.

that excites interest. From Wilson's comments, cited at the beginning of this chapter, it seems there has been little progress in even beginning to answer such questions. To see how true this is, it is necessary to consider the production of knowledge in British university law schools.

Strong poets

Why are there no 'strong poets' in British university law schools?[52] Why do British university law schools not produce the figures whose work because of its depth of innovation, excites the attention of people other than those concerned with the parochial problems of law?[53]

Edmund Husserl wrote:

Philosophy — wisdom (*sagesse*) — is the philosopher's quite personal affair. It must arise as *his* wisdom, as his self-acquired knowledge tending towards universality, a knowledge for which he can answer from the beginning, and at each step, by virtue of his own absolute insights.[54]

If we do not do this our work is merely a series of contingent remarks, dependent for its truth, accuracy or utility on presuppositions which we leave to others to inquire into. It is the challenge to avoid this which is met most successfully by the strong poets and which seems largely ignored in British university law schools. As 'radically beginning philosophers',[55] each must begin again, putting in doubt all convictions previously accepted. The most basic requirements of scholarship verifying your sources, if understood as an intellectual task rather than a mere challenge to the accuracy of citations, makes this demand of all who seek knowledge not merely those who follow the professional discipline of

---

52. By a strong poet is meant someone who produces a uniquely distinctive approach to what they say; someone for whom it is not true to say that '[t]he words (or shapes, or theorems, or models of physical nature) marshaled to one's command . . . seem merely stock items, rearranged in routine ways' (R. Rorty, *Contingency, irony and solidarity*, Cambridge University Press (1989) Ch. 2). I take the term 'strong poets' from Richard Rorty (Rorty, ibid. at 24). He in turn derived it from Harold Bloom (see H. Bloom, *The Anxiety of Influence: A Theory of Poetry*, Oxford University Press (1973)). Like Rorty, I take the phrase to refer potentially to any intellectually or artistically creative worker and not just to poets (even if that term is widely referred to literary figures in general). For this purpose I reject the distinction drawn by George Steiner between 'executants' and 'the reviewer, the literary critic and the academic vivisector' where only the former has access to the 'authentic experience of understanding' (G. Steiner, *Real Presences: Is There Anything In what We Say?*, Faber and Faber (1989) at 8), although I accept the contrast Bloom makes between 'the poet in every reader' and 'the critic in every reader' (Bloom, at 25).
53. This situation is not unique to British law schools. Mark Tushnet has commented, 'I cannot imagine . . . an intellectual history of contemporary America in which legal thought would play an important part' (M. Tushnet, 'Legal Scholarship: Its Cause and Cure' (1981) 90 Yale LJ 1205 at 1205.
54. E. Husserl, *Cartesian Meditations: An Introduction to Phenomenology*, Nijhoff (1960) 2.
55. Ibid., at 16.

philosophy.[56] It is always necessary to look at the forms within which we claim to be working, to place ourselves

> inside these dubious unities in order to study their internal configuration . . . to ask . . . what unities they form . . . by what right they can claim a field that specifies them in space and a continuity that individualizes them in time; according to what laws they are formed; against the background of which discursive events they stand out; and whether they are not, in their accepted and quasi-institutional individuality, ultimately the surface effect of more friendly unities.[57]

Even for those who do not consider the search for apodictic certainty necessary, or possible, there is still the need to establish the continued utility of the language they use.[58]

One immediate answer to the question why British university law schools lack strong poets might be the parasitic and professional nature of law as a discipline in the United Kingdom. Historically, law departments and legal scholars in Great Britain have been primarily concerned with training lawyers, and legal writing with serving the perceived immediate, pragmatic needs of lawyers. The only distinctive feature of the discipline has been formal legal reasoning. If this feature is as limited as is suggested in this chapter, and its application even more limited, it is scarcely surprising that those in the discipline have had only a slight influence outside the discipline. Outside formal legal reasoning there is, in law, only that which has been borrowed and adapted from elsewhere. Law has played the role of the younger sister, trailing in the wake of her wiser, more experienced elder siblings. British law schools have tended to be more geographically than intellectually a part of the universities which have been their nominal hosts.[59] As they have sought to change their nature, seeking a more academic role, they have naturally turned to older disciplines, such as philosophy, sociology and economics, for both their model and their schemes of analysis.[60]

To point to the professional and parasitic nature of law, cannot, however, be to provide a complete answer to the question asked at the beginning of this final section. For law is, and for some time has been, more than a professional discipline. Nor is it unique in its parasitic nature. Indeed it could be argued that to refer to law as parasitic is to

---

56. 'Philosophy as synoptic vision is obviously not the province of a single academic discipline' (R. Rorty, *Consequences of Pragmatism* (1982) 30).
57. M. Foucault, *The Archaeology of Knowledge*, Tavistock (1972) 26.
58. This would be true for those who agree that '"true" resembles "good" or "rational" in being a normative notion, a compliment paid to sentences that seem to be paying their way and that fit in with other sentences which are doing so' (*Consequences of Pragmatism*, Rorty (1982) xxv).
59. See A. Bradney, 'Legal Education in the 21st Century' in J. Grant el al. (eds) *Legal Education: 2000*, Avebury (1988).
60. Even if they have mainly used such disciplines in a subsidiary role merely to validate preconceived ideas derived from doctrinal study (Munger and Seron *supra*, n.13 at 261.

imply a false dichotomy between 'pure' and 'derivative' disciplines. Such a dichotomy could be maintained only if a pure discipline can be identified. Whilst some might argue for the purity of disciplines such as science,[61] others would respond that such attribution of purity misrepresents those very disciplines.[62] Disciplines are pure only in an institutional sense, pure only to the accountant who subdivides the various departments: intellectually, they are interdependent; symbiotic, not parasitic, in their relationships.[63] In any event, if the concept of a parasitic discipline does have any conceptual purchase, there are some disciplines which are plainly parasitic and which have yet produced strong poets; literary criticism is an obvious example.

A second explanation that might be advanced for the absence of strong poets in university law schools could relate to the psychology of those drawn to the study of law. One should not assume that those studying and writing about law represent a cross-section of the intellectual community. Liam Hudson, in a study of students, suggested that law students exhibited special psychological features which marked them off from their fellows. In particular he suggested that they showed a tendency to have convergent, as opposed to divergent minds.[64] Convergent thinkers tend to concentrate 'upon the impersonal aspects of . . . culture'[65] and express their feelings with caution. They are, 'substantially better at the intelligence test than . . . at the open-ended tests [which seek to test flexibility of minds]'.[66] Divergent thinkers are better at open-ended tests than intelligence tests;[67] they 'move naturally towards the human aspects of . . . culture . . . and seem less prone to accept beliefs on trust'.[68] It might be argued that convergent thinkers are, by reason of their nature, less rigorous in their scholarship, less likely to make the leaps of imagination and language necessary to become strong poets.[69]

However, even if there is any validity in Hudson's observations, his study is now some twenty-five years old. The nature of law schools has changed; so might the nature of those working in them. Equally, even if matters remain as Hudson described them, this would only lead to the question, what is it about law schools which attracts this kind of mind,

---

61. See, for example, K. Popper, *The Logic of Scientific Discovery*, Hutchinson (1959) especially at 40–2.
62. See, for example, T. Kuhn, *The Structure of Scientific Revolutions*, University of Chicago Press (2nd edn, 1970).
63. Although their relationship may not always be an equal one.
64. L. Hudson, *Contrary Imaginations: A Psychological Study of the English Schoolboy*, Penguin (1967) 57.
65. Ibid., at 102.
66. Ibid., at 55.
67. Ibid.
68. Ibid., at 109.
69. Hudson himself would not accept this argument. See Hudson *supra*, n.64, Ch. 6 and particularly p.129.

if it is not something inherent in the discipline? And, even if Hudson's hypothesis is correct, is it the only explanation for the absence of strong poets in law schools?

One tension in any intellectual or artistic activity is between communication and creativity. On the one hand there is the desire to say things to others and thus to speak in a language they will understand. On the other hand there is the desire (exemplified in the strong poet) to say things anew. Communication can impede, delay or even prevent creativity.[70] Creativity can impede, delay or even prevent communication.[71] At the same time there is a second tension that Pierre Bourideu describes thus: 'On the side of what constitutes in Kant's terms "as it were the right wing of the parliament of knowledge" is authority; on the left is the freedom to examine and to object.'[72] Such tensions exist both in the social relationships within a discipline as well as in the psychology of individuals within the discipline.

From the previous sections of this chapter it may be argued that, in the past, British university law schools have vaunted communication at the expense of creativity, and authority at the expense of the freedom to examine and to object. If, as was argued in the last section, formal legal reasoning has been used merely to legitimate what has been done, and if what has been done has been eclectic and conceptually superficial, whether work has been judged good, or more accurately whether work has been judged acceptable, has been essentially a social matter. If there were no clear rules, fully analysed conceptual tools or precise ways of arguing, then judging a work necessarily becomes akin to judging a beauty contest.[73] In such a context, power, more than ratiocination, becomes an important feature in judging merit. If communication as a value is elevated over creativity, and communication is defined as the ability to communicate with the powerful, then authority subverts freedom.

The limited ambitions of university law schools, which still persist, also contribute to the lassitude in scholarship. The term 'lawyer', used as a description of those working in a law school, even when expanded to 'academic lawyer', suggests parameters to the permitted scope of inquiry which restricts the search for knowledge.[74] The term infers special skills particular to the academic lawyer and, more importantly, the (acceptable)

---

70. For an example of this, see any one of a thousand paperbacks produced for holiday reading on a Mediterranean beach.
71. For an arguable example of all three, see James Joyce's *Finnegans Wake*, Faber (1975).
72. P. Bourideu, *Homo Academicus*, Polity Press (1988) 62-3.
73. And one where the event was like something organized by Mr Morley rather than da Vinci's search for an accurate representation of the Golden Mean.
74. If the term 'academic lawyer' is used it is difficult to escape the nexus of 'legal research done by academic lawyers' and 'academic legal research is research done for lawyers'. 'Academic lawyer' connects with 'practising lawyer' more closely than it does with 'other academics'.

absence of certain skills to be found in other academics. Even to promote the desirability of writing for the 'full community of legal scholars'[75] suggests limits to writing that conflict with Husserl's remarks noted above. If one must write for the full community of legal scholars, one must write only that which they might understand. However, by identifying themselves as legal scholars (instead of scholars), that community has signified a limited language and limited range of interests that stops short of knowledge. To use the phrase 'legal scholars' is to accept that work done is conditional. It is to accept that at some point work done raises questions that a legal scholar, as opposed to some other form of scholar, cannot answer. It is thus to accept that this is a form of scholarship that is welded to belief rather than knowledge. So, finally, it is to accept that, in Bourideu's words, authority rather than freedom dominates the inquiry.

Considerations such as the above help explain the absence of strong poets in university law schools.[76] At the same time they suggest that any examination of flux in law made hitherto is unlikely to have been satisfactory. The absence of the strong poet is a symptom of the paucity of inquiry. Inquiry being limited, explanation is partial and, in the final analysis, partial explanation is a contradiction in terms.

Conclusion

The partial quality of doctrinal theory means that, even if it is used rigorously, reliance on it is not compatible with a search which is founded on a desire for apodictic certainty.[77] If legal scholarship has been weakened by, *inter alia*, a failure to think through the implications of connections between the concepts of change and law, will Critical Legal Studies be of assistance?

It is clear that the thinking in Critical Legal Studies, as with the case of any theorizing about law, is part of flux in law. The observer as well as the observed is part of the picture. Law is, at least in part, how it is seen. Does Critical Legal Studies add more than this?

There are strong arguments for the proposition that the rationalism of

---

75. D. Feldman, 'The Nature of Legal Scholarship' (1989) 52 MLR 498 at 505.
76. Which is not to say that they in any way justify the individual failings that they reflect. We should not blame others for our own actions or omissions:

> [B]y the sole fact that I am conscious of the causes which inspire my action, those causes are already transcendent objects for my consciousness; they are outside. In vain shall I seek to catch hold of them; I escape them by my very existence. I am condemned to exist forever beyond my essence, beyond the causes and motives of my act. I am condemned to be free. (Jean Paul Sartre, *Being and Nothingness: An Essay on Phenomenological Ontology* (Philosophical Library, New York) 439).

77. Even if the concern is with the somewhat different issue of the continued utility of particular linguistic forms used in discussing flux in law doctrinal theory would seem to be of scant assistance.

Husserl[78] and the nihilism of Critical Legal Studies admit of no connection;[79] that, whilst there are genuine insights within the Critical Legal Studies genre, the framework within which they have been put is unhelpful and, at a social level, replicates the authoritarian tendencies of previous legal scholarship.

Hutchinson and Monahan have argued that '[t]he ambition of Critical Legal Scholars is revolution, not reform',[80] and that '[t]he focus of attention must shift from the artifacts of the juristic stage to the reality of the citizen audience'.[81] Peter Gabel has advocated the benefits of trying to make a philosophy 'explicit among a group'.[82] Finally, Kennedy has written that '[w]e can achieve real freedom only collectively through *group* self-determination. We are simply too weak to realize ourselves in isolation'.[83] What all these comments[84] have in common is a belief in the priority of politics, a faith in the group and a distrust of the individual.[85] Raising public life over private life in this manner frustrates the quest suggested by Husserl. The search is for something that can be communicated and that can be usable. Scholarship is judged by reference to what it does for 'the movement'.[86]

If something that is said to have undermined the central tenets of legal thought can be seen to replicate so exactly the failings of previous legal scholarship, to have turned its face in much the same way against the search for knowledge, the question must be why?

Anthony Kronman has written that 'in his scholarly work, the academic lawyer serves himself: he takes the satisfaction of his own intellectual interests in the law as his paramount goal'.[87] To do this, and to do this in the manner suggested by Husserl, is to accept almost

---

78. On rationalism see John Cottingham, *Rationalism*, Paladin (1984), particularly Ch. III.
79. Although not all working within the Critical Legal Studies genre would accept the description of nihilism as appropriate for their work. See, for example, A. Freeman, 'Truth and Mystification in Legal Scholarship' (1981) 90 Yale LJ 1229 at 1230.
80. Hutchinson and Monahan *supra*, n.44 at 244.
81. Ibid., at 243.
82. P. Gabel and D. Kennedy, 'Roll Over Beethoven' (1984) 36 Stan. L Rev 1 at 5. In the same article he states, 'I think the value of philosophy depends on the developing inner reality of the group that's doing it' (p.12).
83. D. Kennedy, 'Form and Substance in Private Law Adjudication' (1976) 89 Harv. L Rev. 1685 at 1774.
84. And the many others that could be similarly cited.
85. Even where there is a belief that one should 'put the individual in the right frame of mind to achieve his or her own emancipation' (Hutchinson and Monahan *supra*, n.44 at 229).
86. See Gabel and Kennedy *supra*, n.82 at 26–8. Of course the definition of 'the movement' can change. Thus, for example, some forms of feminist analysis might be regarded as falling within the Critical Legal Studies genre, but in this case 'the movement' would be feminism generally. See A. Bottomley, S. Gibson and B. Meteyard, 'Dworkin; Which Dworkin? Taking Feminism Seriously' (1987) 10 J of Law and Society 47 at 47.
87. A. Kronman, 'Foreword: Legal Scholarship and Moral Education' (1981) 90 Yale L J 955 at 957.

certain risk of failure. Given such a task, it is not enough to provide answers others find useful (where others can share the blame if the questions were false or the answers trivial), it is not possible to contribute to some larger project (where no one can see who is responsible for notions put forward), and it is not even enough to fill 'a small shelf of books' (with the comfort of aesthetic satisfaction it suggests).[88] One seeks to understand, and if one does not understand, one fails and all that remains are some ramblings which are, by one's own account, of mere personal interest. And if one succeeds, for others, there is perhaps no more than there would have been if one had failed.

Philip Larkin has described this problem best,

And once you have walked the length of your mind, what
You command is clear as a lading-list.
Anything else must not, for you, be thought
    To exist.

And what's the profit? Only that, in time,
We half-identify the blind impress
All our behavings bear, may trace it home.
    But to confess.

On that green evening when our death begins,
Just what it was, is hardly satisfying,
Since it applied to one man once,
    And that man dying.[89]

The search for knowledge, about flux in law as with anything else, becomes a personal matter; with it comes the danger of self-indulgence, self-deceit and conceit.

To these fears, T.S. Elliot had already provided the answer:

For us, there is only the trying. The rest is not our business.[90]

---

88. Dom Moraes, 'Letter to My Mother' in *Collected Poems 1957–87*, Penguin (1987).
89. 'Continuing to Live' in P. Larkin, *Collected Poems*, Marvell Press, Faber and Faber (1988).
90. East Coker in T.S. Elliot, *Four Quartets*, Faber and Faber (1979).

Appendix 1

LEXIS searched and search units* (see note 37)

ratio and court (House of Lords or Privy Council) and date aft 1987 — 9 cases

obiter and court (House of Lords or Privy Council) and date aft 1987 — 17 cases

court (House of Lords or Privy Council) and date aft 1987 — 150 cases

ratio and court (Court of Appeal) and date aft 1987 — 103 cases

obiter and court (Court of Appeal) and date aft 1987 — 109 cases

court (Court of Appeal) and date aft 1987 — 1,992 cases

ratio and court (Queen's Bench Division) and date aft 1987 — 55 cases

obiter and court (Queen's Bench Division) and date aft 1987 — 94 cases

court (Queen's Bench Division) and date aft 1987 — 1,489 cases

ratio and court (Family Division) and date aft 1987 — 1 case

obiter and court (Family Division) and date aft 1987 — 1 case

court (Family Division) and date aft 1987 — 47 cases

ratio and court (Chancery Division) and date aft 1987 — 27 cases

obiter and court (Chancery Division) and date aft 1987 — 23 cases

court (Chancery Divisions) and date aft 1987 — 407 cases

At the time of these searches the database was said to be accurate up to August 1989

For a discussion of the general errors that may arise in using LEXIS as a mechanism for the empirical investigation of court practice, see A. Bradney 'The Judicial Activity of the Lord Chancellor 1946–1987: A

Pellet' (1989) 16 J of Law and Soc. 360 at 361. A particular error that may arise in connection with some of the searches above is that the word *ratio* has a common meaning other than that in the phrase *ratio decidendi*. Thus the searches may exaggerate judicial reference to that phrase. The possible impact of the combination of general errors and this particular one does not seem likely to be significant in the context of the point being argued.

14 Codification and criminal law reform

Edward Griew

The Draft Criminal Code Bill

Part I of the Law Commission's Draft Criminal Code Bill[1] (General Principles of Liability) is for the most part an attempt to restate the so-called 'general part' of the criminal law in a consistent modern language, with here and there the filling of a gap or the elimination of a perceived incoherence. But Part I is by no means pure restatement. First, effect is given to earlier Law Commission proposals[2] to stabilize the language of fault and to provide two interpretative presumptions: (1) that a newly created offence requires fault (at least recklessness, defined so as to require an awareness of risk[3] for its commission;[4] and (2) that a defence to a newly created offence applies if it would apply on the facts that the actor believes to exist.[5] Second, the Draft Bill adopts, with important modifications, the recommendations of the Butler Committee on Mentally Abnormal Offenders regarding the effect of mental disorder on criminal liability and the consequences of a finding of mental disorder, in place of the archaic *M'Naghten Rules* on 'insanity' and the present mandatory hospitalization after a special verdict.[6] Third, minor recommendations of the Criminal Law Revision Committee on intoxication[7]

---

1. *A Criminal Code for England and Wales*, Law Com. No. 177 (1989). Volume 1 contains the Commission's reasoned proposal for a Criminal Code, with a Draft Bill and other appendices. Volume 2 contains a commentary on the Bill. References hereafter to clauses or paragraphs are, unless otherwise indicated, references to clauses of the Bill or to paragraphs of the Report.
2. Law Com. No. 89 (1978), *The Mental Element in Crime.*
3. Clause 18(c).
4. Clause 20.
5. Clause 41. For comment on these presumptions, see text following n.64, below.
6. Clauses 34–40; Butler Committee, *Report* (1975), Cmnd 6244, Ch. 18.
7. Fourteenth Report: *Offences against the Person* (1980), Cmnd 7844, Part VI.

and of the Law Commission on duress[8] are implemented.[9] Fourth, the Law Commission permits itself a few other amendments or clarifications of the law of various kinds, some foreshadowed by earlier Working Paper consultations,[10] others proposed without prior notice. Most of these are likely to be uncontroversial;[11] but perhaps not all.[12]

Part II of the draft Bill provides a first major instalment of the larger body of 'Specific Offences' that this Part should in due course contain.[13] It consists of five chapters as follows: (1) offences against the person; and (2) sexual offences (these in large part give effect to recommendations of the Criminal Law Revision Committee (CLRC));[14] (3) theft, fraud and related offences; (4) other offences relating to property; and (5) offences against public peace and safety (all of which mainly re-enact, in Code style and with the most minor of modifications, existing statutory offences in these three areas).

Reform included in the Code

The Law Commission presents its draft Code as essentially a restatement of existing law.[15] However, the above summary makes clear that the

---

8. Law Com. No. 83, *Defences of General Application* (1977).
9. In clauses 22 and 24.
10. Clause 29(2) has the effect of abolishing the so-called 'delegation doctrine' in relation to offences created in the future (see Working Paper No. 43, pp.29–31). (This merely effects a transfer of function. At present it is the judges who, by heroic acts of construction, impose liability on (usually) licensees for the acts and guilty knowledge of their delegates. In future it must be Parliament by clear enactment.) Clause 30 incorporates minor amendments to the law on the criminal liability of corporations suggested in Working Paper No. 44.
11. Including the following: evidential burden on defence of intoxications having been involuntary (clause 22(7)); recklessness as to a circumstance to suffice for secondary liability, conspiracy or attempt, if it suffices under the definition of the (substantive) offence (clauses 27(1)(b), 48(2), 49(2)); incitement not to require fault in the person incited (clause 47(1), reversing *Curr* [1968] 2 QB 944); rationalization of the law on 'double inchoate offences' (clauses 47(5)(b), 48(7)(b), 49(6)(b)); conspiracy liability although agreement is only with one's spouse, a person under ten or the intended victim (Criminal Law Act 1977, s.2(2), not repeated in clause 48); incitement to commit the impossible to be possible (clause 50).
12. Possibly controversial: express exemption from secondary liability for one acting 'with the purpose of avoiding or limiting any harmful consequences of the offence and without the purpose of furthering its commission' (clause 28(6)(b), explained at paras 9.34, 9.35).
13. See paras 3.3–3.6 and Appendix C regarding the contents of a complete Part II. Offences omitted from Part II of the Code would, of course, be subject to the provisions of Part I (though see clause 2(3) for the non-application of a few, mainly interpretative, provisions to 'pre-Code offences' that survive enactment of the Code).
14. Fourteenth Report, *Offences against the Person* (1980), Cmnd 7844; Fifteenth Report, *Sexual Offences* (1984), Cmnd 9213; Sixteenth Report, *Prostitution in the Street* (1984), Cmnd 9329; Seventeenth Report, *Prostitution: Off-street Activities* (1985), Cmnd 9688.
15. Paras 3.28–3.30.

Code contains major law reform proposals in the areas of mental disorder, offences against the person and sexual offences. The Law Commission here adopts proposals of other bodies which, it should be noticed, do not have profound implications for the character or structure of English criminal law. Their subject-matters are relatively discrete departments of criminal law; and each has been surveyed by a committee conscious of the need to frame proposals that will fit into the existing pattern of criminal law conceptions and doctrines.

To replace the insanity defence, the Butler Committee contrived a regime significantly echoing the ancient defence in its essential two-limbed structure, in short:

1. absence of fault, or automatism, as a result of mental disorder would produce a qualified rather than an absolute acquittal, reserving social defence powers to the acquitting court (compare the effect, currently, of not knowing 'the nature and quality of the act' because of 'disease of the mind'); and
2. severe disorder (psychotic illness or severe mental handicap) would justify acquittal, but again in the qualified form, although the defendant knowingly did the act charged with the state of mind specified for the offence (compare, under the present Rules, a crazy failure to recognize that the act is 'wrong').

This is not the place to rehearse the Committee's arguments, or to praise the Committee's scheme or make the case for its adoption in the Code,[16] or to explain or justify the modifications of the scheme made by the Law Commission.[17] The present point is that the Commission's proposals are not so revolutionary as to compromise the status of the Code as a vehicle for the restatement of the law.

The same is even more plainly true of the incorporation in Part II of the Code of the CLRC's proposals on offences against the person and sexual offences. The former topic could hardly be omitted from the first instalment of a Code; if it was to be included, it would have been unthinkable to propose for re-enactment, even rewritten in Code style, the offences to be found in the Offences against the Person Act 1861; the revised scheme of offences proposed by the CLRC was available for adoption; and it was obviously useful to show how that scheme might look in statutory form and as part of the Code:[18] the incorporation of

---

16. See E.J. Griew, 'Mental Disorder and the Criminal Code' in Ronnie Mackay and Ken Russell (eds), *Psychiatric Disorders and the Criminal Process*, Leicester Polytechnic Law School Monographs, 1988.
17. See especially paras 11.16, 11.19, 11.26–11.28.
18. Even though a Select Committee of the House of Lords was considering 'the scope and definition of the crime of murder' by the time the draft of the chapter was finalized and the chapter's enactment without substantial modification was not to be expected.

the scheme is thus simply explained. A similar argument justifies the inclusion of sexual offences as proposed for revision by the CLRC. A simple rewriting of the existing law would have been relatively unhelpful, if not positively tactless. The Law Commission has gallantly undertaken to show how sexual offences, as apparently envisaged by the CLRC, would look in modern statutory form. The result is controversial (as any form of sexual offences law would be) and, it is made clear, distasteful in some respects to some members of the Commission.[19] Enactment of the Code as a whole does not depend upon inclusion of any particular chapter of Part II as an original component. One can well imagine Chapter II being omitted until an acceptable modern sexual offences law can be devised for presentation to Parliament by a courageous government. But however controversial the CLRC's work on this subject is, the revision of the law that it involves, like the proposed revision of offences against the person, would represent self-contained law reform of a non-radical kind. Neither chapter employs dramatic new conceptions of criminal liability; both chapters are drafted in harmony with a restated general part.

The making of the Code

Those who advocated codification just before the Law Commission was created assumed that reform of the law should precede its codification;[20] and the fact that the proposed Code is presented as essentially an exercise in restatement rather than reform will be a disappointment to some. The extent of the disappointment will depend on what is meant by 'reform' and I shall consider some possible varieties of reform below. But it will be helpful first to offer a realistic context for disappointment by reviewing very briefly the circumstances in which the Code was produced.

The codification project fell into two main phases. The first began in 1968 with the announcement of an intention to examine the criminal law with a view to its codification.[21] At this and all relevant times the Commission consisted of five Commissioners to cover all of its projects,[22] and had a tiny number of legal staff available for criminal

---

19. See, generally, para. 15.2; for specific reservations, paras 15.14, 15.20, 15.23, 15.29, 15.32, 15.34, 15.38, 15.39, 15.53, 15.69.
20. Gerald Gardiner and Andrew Martin (eds) (and as authors), *Law Reform NOW*, Gollancz (1963), p.12 (repeating Glanville Williams (ed.) *The Reform of the Law*, London, Gollancz (1951), p.19). The reference was to codification in general. Gardiner as Lord Gardiner LC promoted the Law Commissions Bill; Martin became one of the first Law Commissioners in 1965.
21. Law Com. No. 14, Item XVIII.
22. It had been created with the duty 'to take and keep under review all the law [of England and Wales] with a view to its systematic development and reform': Law Commissions Act 1965, s.3(1).

law. No Commissioner became a full-time codifier; no prospectus for the proposed Code was published; and the work was from the start ominously fragmented.

One kind of fragmentation was between the Commission and other bodies. A second was between general principles and specific offences. The Commission established a part-time Working Party to advise it on the general principles of the criminal law. This Working Party met 'each month for the next seven years'.[23] It published an early consultative document, *The Field of Enquiry*, containing 'provisional proposals as to the subjects which Part I [i.e. General Principles] should cover';[24] and it went on to produce Working Papers on a number of these subjects. Meanwhile it had been decided at the outset that work on specific offences should be divided between the Commission and the Home Secretary's Criminal Law Revision Committee. Whatever the reasons, political or financial, for this division of labour, the decision was a significant one for three reasons. First, the CLRC, like the Working Party, was a part-time body of prominent judges, practitioners, officials and academics, who had many other concerns. Second, it was committed by name and, it is thought, by departmental ethos, to revision rather than to reform.[25] Finally, despite the original announcement of collaboration with the Commission in the time of a Home Secretary who had championed codification,[26] references to the Committee have not referred to the project and Reports of the Committee have not tended to suggest a conscious involvement with it.

The Law Commission itself produced Reports on the mental element in crime, general defences and conspiracy[27] and attempt. It also studied and reported on large areas of the law of specific offences and some of these Reports led to legislation.[28] Given all else that the Commission was doing, the achievements were notable and too little appreciated. But there was no sign of a Grand Design in which the different classes of offences would be integrated with each other and with a 'general part' that would work equally well with them all. By the end of the 1970s the

---

23. Roy Beldam, 'Prospects for Codification', in I.H. Dennis (ed.) *Criminal Law and Justice*, London, Sweet & Maxwell (1987), at 3.
24. Law Commission Working Paper No. 17 (1968).
25. The creation of the Committee followed a call to the Lord Chancellor by the Society of Public Teachers of Law for the appointment of a Criminal Law *Reform* Committee: see (1958) 4 JSPTL (NS) 231 for the Society's Memorandum.
26. See the speech of Mr Roy Jenkins on Crime and Society on 1 July 1967, cited by the Law Commission in the Introduction to Law Com. No. 143, para. 7.
27. For a revealing account of the Commission's complicated involvement with conspiracy, and of the complex influence of contemporary events upon the law reform endeavour, see Derek Hodgson (now Hodgson LJ, formerly a Law Commissioner), 'Law Com. No. 76 — A Case Study in Criminal Law Reform' in P.R. Glazebrook (ed.) *Reshaping the Criminal Law*, London, Stevens (1978), 240.
28. Criminal Damage Act 1971; Criminal Law Act 1977, Parts I and II; Criminal Attempts Act 1981; Forgery and Counterfeiting Act 1981; Public Order Act 1986, Part I; Malicious Communications Act 1988.

Law Commission's Working Party had been disbanded and codification of any kind seemed to be a very distant prospect.

The second phase occupied the bulk of the 1980s, as a result of the Law Commission's invitation to a small team of academics to develop (in effect) a prospectus for a code and to formulate (in particular) 'the general principles which should govern liability under it [and] a standard terminology to be used in it'. It was significant that so long after 1968, the team was to consider '(a) the aims and objects of a criminal code . . .; (b) its nature and scope; (c) its contents, structure, layout and the interrelation of its parts; (d) the method and style of its drafting'. The implication is that the only firm conception by this time was that of 'a standard terminology'.

The academic team was yet another part-time group. It was to work independently of the Commission and in the interstices of its members' other duties. It is clear, therefore, that the codification project had drastically changed. The team was not in a position to make a law reform study of topics needing reform; it could not publish discussion papers or engage in wide consultation. It was the team, therefore, that interpreted its task as being one of restatement. It responded to its remit by preparing a Report to the Law Commission consisting in the main of a draft Criminal Code Bill with commentary.[29] There followed, after a period of public scrutiny, the present Draft Bill — a revised and extended version of the first draft, produced by the same team, this time in consultation with the Law Commission and under its policy direction.

Varieties of reform

In the circumstances thus briefly recalled, a systematization of existing law was possible, plus the implementation of extant law reform proposals. But other aspirations have been expressed.

A fundamentally rethought criminal law?

Critics of the Law Reform Commission of Canada have identified an 'ideological bias' in its work towards the recodification of the criminal law. They attribute this in part to a 'relative absence of a comprehensive and analytical discussion of what the criminal law should be trying to do'.[30] Such a discussion would involve 'an examination of the social and political contexts of [the underlying concepts of wrongfulness and justice which society allegedly holds]' and which the Code 'should

---

29. Law Com. No. 143 (1985).
30. Ross Hastings and R.P. Saunders, 'Ideology in the Work of the Law Reform Commission of Canada . . .' (1982–3) Can. B Rev. 206 at 209.

express in its General Part'.[31] A 'complete review and evaluation of the competing theories of criminal law' is said to be required; but the Commission substitutes for such a review 'an uncritical application of liberal pluralism',[32] In England and Wales, Celia Wells has suggested, codification will be 'a somewhat restricted exercise' if it does not follow 'an exploration of the role and function of the criminal law in modern society, and . . . an examination of its relationship with the systems of criminal punishment which bound it'.[33] She too might speak of 'ideological bias'; for she observes that a mere 'restatement, rationalization or systematization in itself involves a political choice' and that the failure of the Law Commission's academic team to 'measure its proposals against any explicitly stated principles' perpetuates 'the dual myths that there is a value consensus in society and that this consensus is reflected in the law . . . [T]he status quo is a political choice'.[34]

Such critics have not made clear, however, and it is hard to imagine, what practical process of 'review' or 'exploration' they contemplate; by whom it might be resourced or conducted; or what kind of enactable criminal law might emerge from the endeavour. As for 'ideological bias', what else is to be expected? Those undertaking the construction of a criminal code inevitably assume the maintenance in broad terms of the existing social and political order — on the basis of what other could they proceed? — and the appropriateness of a conventional conception of the functions of the criminal law in relation to that order. The making of a Code presumes the readiness of a contemplatable government to promote or support its enactment. The proposal to enact it, to be realistic, will also have to command the broad support, or at least not excite the active opposition, of a judiciary that is likely to be antipathetic to radically new conceptions. If the criminal law stated in the Code is not in its essentials the recognizable representative of the status quo ante, it might as well not be drafted except as a stimulant to thought.

My suggestion is that codification as an exercise is conservative by nature. A very important question is whether it is also conservative by tendency in the sense of tending to act as an inhibition to future desirable change that might otherwise take place. If it were, that would be a consideration to weigh in the balance when evaluating it as a legislative option.

A 'model penal code'?

A distinction is sometimes drawn between a mere restatement of the law and a 'model penal code'. Thus the Law Commission's academic team:

---

31. Ibid., at 212.
32. Ibid., at 216n.
33. 'Restatement or Reform' [1986] Crim. LR 314 at 322.
34. Ibid., at 315.

We were not asked to produce a 'model penal code' and we have not attempted to do so. The fundamental principles of the law are well settled and it would be neither politically feasible nor desirable to depart from them.[35]

The second sentence may be regarded as an expression of the broadly conservative point made just above. But if it is, it could be said to misrepresent the notion of a 'model penal code' as it is illustrated by the great Code with that title. It is true that Herbert Wechsler, principal architect of the American Law Institute's Model Penal Code, stated: '[W]e mean to act as if we were a legislative commission, charged with construction of an ideal penal code'[36] — a statement seeming to imply that 'model' means 'ideal'. But the Code's title is ambiguous. 'Model' is also a noun used adjectivally to express the Institute's purpose of developing a code as a recommended point of departure for individual States engaged in codifying or recodifying their own penal laws: the Code is a common model for local adaptation.[37] More importantly, it would be wrong to suppose that the Model Penal Code is offered as the ideal dispensation of a body writing on a clean slate after reconsideration of the very foundations of the criminal law. Rather, the 'General Provisions' of the Code, which alone might have influenced the Law Commission's team to any extent, are an ideal — a sophisticated and systematized — version of mainstream American, and indeed common law, doctrine. At the outset of the Model Penal Code project, it is true, Wechsler contemplated that the 'purposes and methods' of the criminal law ought to be subjected to the light of 'sustained and fundamental criticism emanating from without the legal group — especially the psychological and social sciences'. It is also true that he referred to the argument that the law 'employs unsound psychological premises such as "freedom of will" . . . [and] is drawn in terms of a psychology that is both superficial and outmoded, using concepts like "deliberation", "passion", "will", "insanity", "intent"'.[38] In the result, however, the published commentary on the General Provisions drew hardly at all on a non-legal literature — not at all, for instance, in relation to 'freedom of will' or 'intent'[39] The language of the law is modernized and stabilized, but (for all that appears) the 'concepts' that 'voluntary act', 'purpose', 'knowledge' and the rest are employed to express are unaffected by exposure to philosophical or scientific criticism.

---

35. Law Com. No. 143, para. 1.10. The Law Commission agreed: Law Com. No. 177, para. 3.30.
36. 'A Thoughtful Code of Substantive Law' (1955) 45 J Crim. L Criminol. & Pol. Sci. 524 at 525.
37. Cf. Herbert Wechsler himself, 'The Model Penal Code and the Codification of American Criminal Law' in Roger Hood (ed.), *Crime, Criminology and Public Policy*, London, Heinemann (1974), 419 at 422, in a passage citing that quoted in the text note 36.
38. Herbert Wechsler, 'The Challenge of a Model Penal Code' (1952) 65 Harv. L Rev. 1097 at 1102-3.
39. American Law Institute, *Model Penal Code: Tentative Draft No. 4* (1955).

The changes in the law proposed by the Model Penal Code do, it is true, go well beyond what the Law Commission has achieved. But the 'crowning achievement of the Code' lay, not in the richness of its more particular reforms, but in bringing 'unity and cogency to the chaos of the common law and its development',[40] and, in particular, in imposing structural, conceptual and linguistic order upon the subject as a whole. In this respect the Code has been a crucial influence upon scholars throughout the common law world, including those assisting the Law Commission. The assertion that the Law Commission's Code is 'not a model penal code' ought not to be allowed to conceal the significant extent to which the American model has affected its conception and method.

Abolition of common law offences?

It was for a long time assumed that the abolition, and replacement as necessary, of all common law offences was one reform that must precede codification.[41] Such offences are objectionable on a number of grounds:

- They lack the authority of Parliament;
- some are so vague and elastic as to constitute serious infringements of the principles of legality or fair warning;
- they tend to be antique in name and indeed in concept;
- most are triable only on indictment,[42] and on conviction on indictment are punishable by imprisonment theoretically without limit.[43]

But nothing in the end came of an early law reform exercise, sponsored by the Law Commission and undertaken by a subcommittee of the Criminal Law Revision Committee under Lord Justice Winn, directed to their abolition. The subcommittee, active in 1966–7, 'produced lengthy instructions to parliamentary counsel which covered the whole field of "common law misdemeanours"';[44] but draft clauses were never seen and the project was never revived.

Sir Derek Hodgson has asserted the impossibility, not at that time recognized, of 'dealing with all common law offences entirely out of the

---

40. Richard G. Singer, Foreword to *Symposium: The 25th Anniversary of the Model Penal Code* (1988) 19 Rutgers LJ 520.
41. See Derek Hodgson, n.27 above, at 245–6.
42. But not public nuisance or incitement to commit an offence triable either way (Magistrates' Courts Act 1980, Sched. 1), or common assault and battery (Criminal Justice Act 1988, s.39).
43. But not conspiracy to defraud (Criminal Justice Act 1987, s.12(3)) or common assault (Criminal Justice Act 1988, s.40(2)).
44. Derek Hodgson, n.27 above, at 246.

context of the branch of the criminal law in which each fell'.[45] This perception of an experienced law reformer ought to be heeded. Many common law offences have been abolished in the lifetime of the Law Commission with the enactment of modern criminal statutes;[46] other important offences (including murder, manslaughter, assault and incitement) would be replaced by the Code itself;[47] enactment of the Commission's draft Administration of Justice (Offences) Bill[48] would continue the process; and common law conspiracy to defraud may have been replaced by the time the Code is enacted.[49] However, the elimination of all common law offences is a long way off. It is not realistic to expect high priority to be given to reform of the more obscure or more politically sensitive branches of the criminal law. So either codification must be indefinitely postponed or for an indefinite time to come a strange assortment of offences must survive enactment of the Code (governed, of course, by most of its general provisions), including controversial offences concerned with public morals and the dangerous catch-all offence of public nuisance.[50] There is no doubt that the latter alternative must be suffered, however unthinkable it may have seemed twenty years ago.

By a brief provision of great symbolic importance, however, any judicial power to create new offences would be formally abolished.[51]

Reforms for future consideration

Mention was made in the first part of this chapter of important reforms incorporated in the Bill in implementation of extant recommendations. However, much law reform work has yet to be undertaken; indeed, of the work of law reform there is no end.

It must suffice to refer, by way of example, to some very varied matters which the Law Commission itself, in its codification Report, has mentioned as requiring investigation or as being the subject of calls for reform. There is a strong case for the recognition of a defence of excusable mistake as to the relevant criminal law; but the topic still awaits law reform study although the Law Commission's Working Party

---

45. Ibid.
46. Criminal Law Act 1967, ss.1 (effect of abolition of felony), 13(1)(a); Theft Act 1968, s.32(1)(a); Criminal Damage Act 1971, s.11(1); Criminal Law Act 1977, ss.5(1), 13(1); Forgery and Counterfeiting Act 1981, s.13; Criminal Attempts Act 1981, s.6(1); Public Order Act 1986, s.9(1).
47. Clause 4(1), Sched. 8.
48. Law Com. No. 96 (1979).
49. See Working Paper No. 104, *Conspiracy to Defraud* (1987).
50. On public nuisance, see J.R. Spencer, 'Public Nuisance — A Critical Examination' [1989] CLJ 55.
51. Clause 3.

listed it for examination as long ago as 1968.[52] A subject more recently identified is that of endangerment. A person may be guilty of an offence if he causes harm to person or property by unjustified risk-taking; but if he takes a risk of causing serious harm and no harm eventuates he will in generally be free of liability (save, perhaps, under legislation regulating a particular sphere of activity and not cast in terms of deliberate risk-taking). The Law Commission noted that a clause to penalize conduct endangering traffic, giving effect to a Criminal Law Revision Committee recommendation, had been criticized as improperly particularistic for a criminal code.[53] The subject deserves early study. So does the whole complex subject of the encouragement, assistance and attempted assistance ('facilitation') of crime. Although the draft Code gives statutory form to the familiar structure of the law of complicity and incitement. However, the Commission refers to 'searching criticism' to which this structure has been subject;[54] and it has made progress towards a consideration of the case for reform by setting out the arguments for and against the creation of an offence of facilitation in its Working Paper, *Conspiracy to Defraud*.[55] Fraud itself provides another example of a topic on which the Code provisions (faithful to existing law) are very far from perfect. The Commission's consideration of the provisions needed to replace common law conspiracy may perhaps lead to improvement in the law. Nevertheless, there is a case[56] for a further general revision of the law of theft and fraud; and that case would not be fundamentally affected if a new general fraud offence were enacted to fill the gap left by the abolition of the common law conspiracy offence.[57]

To the purist objection, applied to examples like these, that reform should precede codification the answer is short. Ideally, indeed, law reform would come first. However, the world of criminal law reform in this country has not been an ideal one. In relation to these and some other topics, codification must precede reform or never occur.

Codification as reform

The Law Commission makes the case for codification in its Report. It refers to the constitutional arguments and to the advantages to be gained in terms of 'accessibility and comprehensibility', 'consistency', and 'certainty';[58] and it considers certain 'arguments against codification'.[59]

---

52. *The Field of Enquiry*, p.15; and see Law Com. No. 177, para. 8.30.
53. Para. 14.58, referring to clause 86.
54. Para. 9.4 (see also para. 13.5).
55. Working Paper No. 104 (1987), Appendix C.
56. Referred to in para. 16.4.
57. See Working Paper No. 104, Part XII.
58. See paras 2.1–2.11.
59. Paras 2.14–2.16.

In the context of this essay the sum of the argument would be that codification in principle represents a general reform outweighing any law reform deficiencies of the particular Code. (This chapter has argued — what most will perhaps readily concede — that an attempt to effect all desirable reform as a platform for codification must delay that eventual structure indefinitely, while on the other hand the enactment of a Code will not preclude even quite major reforms thereafter.) I do not propose here to rehearse the whole of the Law Commission's argument. I wish rather to try to fortify it by suggesting that the particular style of codification proposed has a reforming merit of a kind that the Commission's passage may not clearly expose.

I refer in particular to the attempt that the Draft Bill makes to achieve intellectual and stylistic consistency in an integrated statement of English criminal law. This involves the imposition upon the law of a structural and conceptual discipline that it has lacked in its common law, or mixed common law and statutory, state. Some of the means employed are:

- the adoption of a relatively spare and, above all, a defined and therefore consistent language in place of the excessively rich and semantically unstable vocabulary hitherto in use;[60]
- the maintenance of as much consistency as possible in the analysis of criminal liability in terms of the elements of offences and of the distinction between offences (or their elements) and defences;[61]
- the formulating of specific offences in harmony with, and in the light of, the general principles that will govern them;
- an insistence, maintained in the style of drafting,[62] on the separation of substance (offences and their commission) from matters of proof and process; and
- the elimination of glaring inconsistencies in the law being restated — inconsistencies of a kind that both betoken and tend to perpetuate systemic indiscipline.

Two other aspects of the Draft Bill are relevant for present purposes. One is the relatively detailed nature of the statement of the law, partly by means of definition, more particularly by the elaboration of principles. The more detailed the Code, the less the need for established law

---

60. 'Knowledge', 'intention' and 'recklessness' are given consistent meanings for the purposes of the Code and of offences enacted in or after the Code 9 (cl.18); the dangerous terms 'voluntary' and 'involuntary' are eschewed, except in the traditional labelling of the varieties of manslaughter. The ambiguity of 'act' and its cognates is expressly exploited for the sake of economy of drafting (cll. 15, 16).
61. See para. 7.2. But the substantive consequences of the distinction are happily minimized, given the occasional difficulty of confidently characterizing an issue as one of offence or defence: see para. 7.3.
62. See para. 3.42.

to be rediscovered after enactment of the Code be resort to pre-Code case law or even by litigation. However, apart from its tendency to define and to state subrules, the Code, especially Part I, is detailed in another way, that is, in a certain analytical particularity, both within individual provisions and across the text as a whole. A commentator of the earlier Draft Bill diagnosed 'an obvious sacrifice of surface or immediate comprehensibility in the interests of certainty'.[63] It might be put another way: the Code insists on being very closely read as a way of ensuring that it is not misunderstood — as so much modern criminal legislation has so often been.

The other matter has already been mentioned:[64] the prescription of clear presumptive standards of liability — standards that will apply 'unless otherwise provided'. A 'subjectivist' interpretation of offences and defences is dictated wherever Parliament does not otherwise provide. It is possible to exaggerate the significance of this as a reflection of doctrinal bias in the codifier. The crucial policy is that of providing *a* presumptive standard. This favours order and clarity in the law, and economy and consistency in its application. And the effect is to place with the legislator (with whom it belongs) the burden of deciding, and if necessary prescribing, what the conditions of liability for a particular offence shall be. But how are government departments promoting penal legislation likely to behave? Would they be sufficiently ready to override a presumption in favour of negligence as the required fault, or of reasonable care as a mistake criterion, by expressly requiring recklessness for liability or granting a more generous mistake defence? Or would they be more ready, when it suits their policy, to take steps to provide clearly for strict liability or at most a concession in favour of due diligence, so as to displace recklessness as the Code-presumed fault requirement or a presumption that the actor is to have any defence that the facts he believes to exist would give him? Common sense so strongly suggests the latter as to compel preference for a 'subjectivist' presumption.[65]

The claim now to be made for a codification of the kind so described is admittedly speculative. It concerns the Code's capacity to influence future criminal law development, judicial application of the law and the quality of professional practice.

The Code should, first of all, serve both as stimulus and as firm basis for future reform. An attempt to state the criminal law as a disciplined whole tends to expose defects in a way which makes them harder to ignore or argue away. The future reformer has in the Code a structure to which he will deliberately adapt his proposals in both substance and

---

63. L.H.Leigh, 'Approaches to Codification', in I.H. Dennis (ed.) *Criminal Law and Justice*, London, Sweet & Maxwell (1987), p.28.
64. See above, text at notes 3 to 5.
65. And there must be a consistent standard for fault and for mistake as to 'exempting circumstances', for the reason hinted at in n.61 above.

form. If the reform needed is very radical, the Code should enable him to see clearly how the existing structure must be adapted to receive the new element. If, for example, a general offence of endangerment or of facilitation should be recommended, with whatever consequences for other offences or for the principles of accessoryship, careful drafting should be capable of integrating the necessary provisions with the enacted Code. The Code will be no more immune from amendment than any other major statute. It will be desirable, however, to effect major amendments at well-spaced intervals and under the supervision of a standing body responsible for safeguarding, as far as parliamentary processes permit, the structural, linguistic and conceptual integrity of the Code.[66]

Second, the drafting of criminal legislation must benefit from a number of features of the Code (including its established vocabulary and interpretative presumptions) and generally from the fact, known to the draftsman, that all such legislation will fall to be read as one with Part I of the Code, except where Parliament specially provides otherwise.

Third, it is probably fair to say that up to now the judges have not uniformly attributed a high value to consistency of principle or statement in this area of the law. The untidy state of the common law and the varied style of criminal statutes have not perhaps encouraged rigour. If there have been deficiencies, the Code ought to have a beneficial effect. The quality of the judicial response to the Code should reflect its status as basic statutory source of the criminal law and its style as partly described above.

Fourth, it is worth mentioning that there are many provisions in Part I of the Code in particular that it would not be reasonable or sensible to read or copy to a jury. The combination of analytical abstractness, relatively detailed statement and the interrelation of provisions will make it essential to 'process' the statutory text in the light of the factual issues in particular cases before questions requiring its application can be submitted to lay decision.[67] In this respect the Code may tend to sharpen the distinction between legal processing and fact finding. To the extent that it has this effect it will have worked further reform.

Finally, it is to be hoped that the status and style of the Code will raise practice standards, especially in the analysis of criminal law problems and the reading of this and other statutory texts. Practitioners may, with the advantage of appropriate training, be helped to take criminal law more seriously, as an organized body of principles demanding close attention, than is commonly the case. This could make a significant contribution to the quality of legal services and to the administration of justice. Before this comes about, however, criminal practice (including the magistrates' courts service and the Crown Prosecution Service) must surely become more attractive than it has recently been.

---

66. See in this connection paras 3.49–3.52.
67. On 'coping with complex provisions' and 'the judge . . . as mediator between the Code and the jury', see para. 3.43.

Index

Bar Council
  reform of the legal profession and 215, 218, 223, 225–227, 230
  role of, in law creation 11

City Code
  'capture' and 86–87
  characteristics of 73–74
  Financial Services Act 1986 and 82, 83, 84, 89
  flexibility of 74–78
  industry support for 80–82, 86–87
  public interest and 89–91
  sanctions under 82–85
  self-regulation and 72–93

City Panel on Takeovers and Mergers
  Appeal Committee of 74, 75, 80
  'capture' and 86–87
  composition of 73–74
  informality of proceedings before 78
  investigative powers of 85–86
  judicial review of decisions by 79–80, 88
  role of 74
  self-regulation and 72–93
  statutory regulatory bodies and 91–92

Competition law
  British 202–204
  EEC 202–205

Conflict of laws
  proper law of contract and jurisdiction agreements in 177–195

Criminal law
  Butler Committee report on 256–258
  codes and 262–264
  codification as reform of 266–269
  common law offences and 264–265

Criminal Law Revision Committee
  evidence law and 101, 106, 112, 113
  generally 15, 256–260, 264–266

European Communities
  Commission of 13, 205
  competition law of 202–204
  Council of 13
  Court of Justice of 13, 196, 197–202, 204, 205–212
  direct effect of law of 196, 205–212
  free movement of goods in 202, 203, 204–205, 208, 210
  references under Treaty Article 177, 196, 197–201, 202, 204, 206–208, 211–212
  role of, in change of law, generally 6–7

Evidence law
  Australian Law Reform
    Commission and 95, 99, 102,
    107, 108, 114, 115, 117
  burden of proof in 97-98
  child witnesses and 101-102,
    104-106, 114
  confessions in 107-109, 114
  corroboration in 100-101
  criminal proceedings in 107-113
  cross-examination in 99-100,
    112-113
  Devlin Committee and 109-110
  expert evidence in 113-115
  hearsay in 106-107
  identification evidence in
    109-110
  Law Commission and 101
  New Zealand Evidence Law
    Reform Committee and 108
  psychological research and 99,
    100, 101-102, 108, 114, 117
  rape complainants in 103-104
  relevance in 96-97
  similar fact evidence in 110-111
  vulnerable witnesses in 103-106
  witness demeanour in 98-99

Family law
  Law Commission and 57-66
  role of empirical work in 59-71

Intestacy
  rights on 63-64

Judiciary
  reform of the legal profession
    and 220-222, 232
  role in law determination of 14
Jurisdiction agreement
  court's discretion and 189-192
  effects of 185-192
  forum non conveniens and
    192-194
  interpretation of 181-183
  non-existence of contract
    containing 184-185
  scope of 183-184
  validity of 179-181

Land
  co-owners, disposition by, of
    53-55
  informal interests in 40-56
Law Commission
  conveyancing and 40, 48-49,
    54-55
  criminal law and 256-267
  empirical research and 59-66,
    71
  evidence law and 101
  family law and 57-66, 71
  role of 15-17
Law Society
  law creation and 11
  reform of the legal profession
    and 215, 228, 230, 233
Legal profession
  Benson Committee report on
    214, 215
  Green Paper on the work and
    organisation of 216-229, 232
  judiciary and reform of
    220-222
  Marre Committee report on
    215-216, 225-226
  reform of 213-234
  'Thatcherism' and 218-220
  White Paper on Legal Services
    and 227-232
Legal reasoning
  doctrinal approach to 243-245
  generally 235-255
  obiter dicta and 242-243,
    254-255
  ratio decidendi and 240-243,
    254-255
  stare decisis and 236, 237, 240,
    243
Legal scholarship
  critical legal studies and
    235-242, 244-245, 251-252
  generally 235-255
  role in changing law of 8

Lord Chancellor
reform of the legal profession and 216–217, 221, 230–231, 232–233
role in law reform of 17

Matrimonial home
co-ownership of 53–55, 63–64
deserted wife's equity in 44–46
generally 44–53
unregistered land and 47

National security
breach of confidence and 129–130, 133
case law definitions of 126–127, 128–130, 132–133
contempt and 128–129, 133
definitions of 120, 124–125, 126–127, 128–130, 132–133, 134–137
industrial tribunal and 124
interceptions of communications and 122–123, 131–132
justiciability of 120–124, 125–126, 127–128, 130–132, 133–134
justiciability under case law of 125–126, 127–128, 130–132
justiciability under statutory provisions of 121–124
legislative non-justiciability of 121–122
nuclear weapons and 127, 129, 135
official secrets and 128–129, 133, 135, 136
prosecution of war and 125–127, 135
protection of data and 121
race relations and 121–122, 150

security services and 129–130, 136
statutory definitions of 124–125
terrorism and 123
trade union membership and 130–131

Negligence
duty of care and 20–39
economic loss and 22–23, 26
expectation interest and 23
nervous shock and 22

Racial discrimination
citizenship, on grounds of 142
Commission for Racial Equality and 141, 147, 151–154, 155–156
indirect 141, 143–145
nationality, on grounds of 142
remedies for 151–154
reverse 146–147

Registered land
ownership of rights in, generally 42–43
registrable interests in 43–44

Social security law
Beveridge Report on 158–159, 161–162
incomprehensibility of 169–175
legislative text of 164–167, 169–175
poverty and 161–162
users of 163–164, 167–169

Tort
contract, relationship with 23, 24–25, 29–31, 34–35, 38
negligence in 20–39

Unregistered land
ownership of rights in, generally 41–42
registrable interests in 43, 48